WESTMAR COLLEGE LIBRARY

W9-BTH-505

MEMOIRS

OF

PRINCE METTERNICH

MEMOIRS

OF

PRINCE METTERNICH

1815–1829

EDITED BY

PRINCE RICHARD METTERNICH

THE PAPERS CLASSIFIED AND ARRANGED BY M. A. de KLINKOWSTRÖM

TRANSLATED BY MRS ALEXANDER NAPIER

VOLUME III.

NEW YORK

Howard Fertig

1970

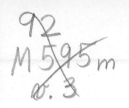

92
M595m
no. 3

DB
80.8
.M52
1970

First published in English in 1881
by Charles Scribner's Sons

HOWARD FERTIG, INC. EDITION 1970

All rights reserved.

Library of Congress Catalog Card Number: 68-9611

PRINTED IN THE UNITED STATES OF AMERICA
BY NOBLE OFFSET PRINTERS, INC.

79268

PREFATORY NOTE.

THE READER having now advanced well into the Memoirs of Prince Metternich, a few remarks as to their arrangement may not be without interest.

The two volumes already published contain a history of the Prince's career from 1773 to the peace of 1815, chiefly in the Memoirs he left behind him. These Memoirs do not extend, however, in their completed form beyond the period of the Congress of Vienna, with a brief exception during the closing years of the Prince's life.

The history of the important events contained in the present volumes is drawn, therefore, from the private correspondence of Prince Metternich, which is at this period very copious and interesting, and, being addressed to members of his family or to intimate friends, is less formal than the autobiography. We here meet also with the first impressions of the Prince on the events of the day, imparted freely in confidence, with no idea of their future publication, to some of the chief personages of the State.

The present volumes deal principally with the internal affairs of the Austrian Empire in the years 1816 and 1817 ; the period of the Congresses, 1818 to 1822 ; and the complications arising from the Russian advance upon Turkey, ending in 1829.

The succeeding volumes will embrace the period from the July Revolution of 1830 to the retirement of Prince Metternich in 1848, also the last eleven years of the Prince's life.

The reception which the earlier volumes of this work have met with from the public is a proof of the universal and lively interest taken in the life of the great Chancellor.

In the criticisms which have appeared, notwithstanding the diversities of national feeling and sentiment, the master-spirit of the great statesman, and the important *rôle* he played during the most brilliant period of Austria's power, are unanimously acknowledged.

A fresh generation has sprung up. These Memoirs will place before it a life-like portrait of Prince Metternich.

EDITOR.

CONTENTS

OF

THE THIRD VOLUME.

———◆◇◆———

FOURTH BOOK.

THE INTERNAL AFFAIRS OF THE EMPIRE IN THE YEARS 1816, 1817.

———————————

FIFTH BOOK.

LUSTRUM OF THE CONGRESS.

BOOK IV.

THE REGULATION OF THE INTERNAL AFFAIRS OF THE EMPIRE.

1816–1817.

1816.

_____ __ ___

IDEAS ON A CONCORDAT OF ALL THE STATES OF THE GERMAN CONFEDERATION WITH THE ROMAN COURT.

208. Metternich to the Emperor Francis, Verona, April 5, 1816.

208. During the negotiation of German affairs at the Vienna Congress, I made it my duty to direct the attention of the ambassadors there assembled to the advantages which must ensue to the whole German body politic, as well as to the Princes themselves, from a uniform treatment of the general affairs of the Church (now in a deplorable state) at the future Diet. I at that time maintained the closest intercourse with the vicars of Constance and Münster, who were at Vienna, and I believe that I prevented the acceptance of the views of a so-called deputation from the German Church then in Vienna, which consisted of some wild enthusiasts who, probably without intending it themselves, acted in the most exaggerated interests of the Roman Church. The principle that ecclesiastical affairs should be considered in council at Frankfurt met with general approval from the German Princes of the second and third class. The King of Wurtemberg alone, intent

upon his so-called rights of sovereignty, who had, in
consequence of those very principles, taken no direct
part in the last negotiations, endeavoured to isolate
himself from this ecclesiastical question also, and, without further ceremony, to enter into negotiations with
the Roman Court about a concordat of his own.

Cardinal Consalvi, whose general political conduct
cannot be sufficiently praised, remained faithful to the
promise I had obtained from him, that he would enter
into no separate negotiation with German Princes without my consent. He referred the matter to Rome.
The conclusion of the Congress, and the great military
and political events which followed it, brought these
intrigues to an end.

Since the meeting of the German Ambassadors at
Frankfurt I have given your Majesty's ministers instructions concerning this matter; and the efforts of the
King of Wurtemberg for a speedy and separate concordat with Rome smoothed the way quite naturally.
Up to this time I have succeeded in preventing this
concordat.

I agree with Councillor Lorenz* on the subject
of a common basis for the negotiation of the affairs
of the German Church, based on our ecclesiastical
principles; and I have only to point out the further
course of an affair which I consider one of the
most important that has to be decided at the future
Diet.

In this, as in every great negociation, very much
depends on the point of view from which it is taken
into consideration. In my opinion, Germany must be
induced to adopt an ecclesiastical constitution, and to

* He had given an official report concerning the future ecclesiastical
constitution, which was submitted to Metternich's attention.—ED.

accept our principles without our appearing too eager to obtrude those principles on Germany.

By a judicious course we shall, moreover, set a good example to the German Princes ; our principles will become popular in the very same measure as they seem to have sprung up in Germany ; our position with regard to the Roman Court itself remains correct and vigorous, and will even serve as a protection if we by our example bar the way to the exaggerated claims here and there put forth, as always happens in the course of human affairs. Urged by these various considerations, I should much prefer to make sure of the views of some excellent superintendent of a German church, and leave him undisturbed to take the initiative in the arrangement to be made. It seems to me certain that Baron von Wessenberg—who has meantime been appointed coadjutor at Constance, and has been confirmed in this office by the Pope—is most fit for our purpose : he enjoys the general confidence in Germany, and, I believe, also that of Councillor von Lorenz.

If your Majesty vouchsafes your approval, I propose to inform this minister of our ideas fully and without delay, and this can probably best be achieved by sending to him the vice-director of theological studies, Augustin Braig. Such an arrangement would ensure the most comprehensive application of our principles being made known to Baron von Wessenberg, who is already devoted to the political system of our Court, and to whom may be disclosed without reserve even the political and religious sentiments of the Imperial Court ; and the *Imperial Directorial-Embassy* in Frankfurt would be placed in a position entirely in accordance with my views—to support the wishes of the German Church, instead of taking the initiative in this matter.

For greater satisfaction I should not only approve but should think it desirable to send the above-mentioned Augustin Braig afterwards to consult with the Austrian embassy.

The nature of the negotiations about to commence at Frankfurt ensures there being sufficient time to carry out these measures.   But not till the Diet is constituted, which will certainly be three or four weeks after its opening, will it be possible for our embassy to broach the subject of ecclesiastical affairs, and urge the formation of a concordat of all the German States with the Roman Court.

Probably some of the greater German Courts, and certainly Wurtemberg, will attempt some protest. But such important principles are involved that their triumph would be certain if it were not for the petty spirit of the greater German Governments, which often conflicts even with their own State interests.   If, however, the idea of a general concordat should not be adopted, an opening is left for separate concordats based on the same principles, and the success of this opening can the less be doubted as these principles are equally suited to the authority and the financial interests of the Princes.   It will not, therefore, be difficult to show, that the dissentient Governments will lose, rather than gain by their contumacy; for whereas, separately, they will be weak against the Roman Curia, by union among themselves, and by union with the Austrian Church, they would gain in strength.   The principles of that body are a guarantee that the cogency of such arguments must be evident, and I do not know any example as yet of even the most absolute of German Princes, out of mere self-conceit, putting himself *deterioris conditionis* in a different position from the other German sovereigns

—a case which would inevitably occur if the King of Wurtemberg should conclude a concordat with the Roman See more advantageous to it than the concordats with the other German Courts.*

* The negotiations were begun in this sense, but were unsuccessful. In the course of the years 1817 to 1830 special concordats were concluded with separate States of the Bund: thus, in 1817 with Bavaria; in 1821 and 1827 with the States forming the Upper Rhenish Church Province; in 1824 with Hanover; in 1827 with Saxony; in 1830 with Gnesen and Posen, &c.; at last, in 1855, after Metternich's retirement, the well-known Concordat of the Apostolic See with Austria was concluded. The aged Chancellor welcomed the appearance of this document with the greatest satisfaction, and took pen in hand to narrate the history of the delay (of half a century) between his first idea of it in 1816 and its realisation in 1855. This paper, written with his own hand in August 1855, is given here to make the matter more plain. It is as follows:—

'The twenty-fifth anniversary of the birthday of the Emperor Francis Joseph (Aug. 18, 1855) has been celebrated in a manner as excellent as significant, by the signature of the Concordat with the Roman Chair.

'No one can be better informed than I of the circumstances which hindered the good work of withdrawing from the encroachments on the Church (called reforms) of which the Emperor Joseph II. had been guilty.

'Put together concisely and faithfully represented, the historical facts are as follows:—

'After the general peace was concluded in 1814–1815, I directed my attention to the painful consequences of Joseph's legislation in ecclesiastical affairs. While these weighed on the whole empire, their evil influence was particularly felt in Lombardy and Venetia, in the German States of the Bund, and in Hungary.

'The personal feelings of the Emperor Francis were, for political and religious reasons, inclined to the removal of certain conditions existing since the reign of Joseph II. It was otherwise with the officials; indeed, even among the clergy the Febronian doctrines had, with exceptions, taken deep root. In the upper departments of the Government I was alone on the side of truth in this important question. I did not allow myself to be discouraged by this position, and continued the solution of the problem on the principles I had laid down in my conferences with Cardinal Consalvi. To assist me in the great undertaking I had selected Propst von Justel, at that time Ecclesiastical Adviser to the State Council. In the year 1817 the marriage of the Archduchess Leopoldine with the heir to the Portuguese throne gave me an opportunity to continue the secret negotiations which I had begun with the Roman Chair. I caused Propst von Justel to be sent to Rome, and intended, if the prospect had been favourable of an agreement between the two Governments, to have gone thither myself, after the making over the Archduchess at Leghorn. This plan was not carried out, because I saw that the affair was not yet ripe for conclusion.

'In the year 1819 the Emperor went to Italy, and in the personal inter-course of his Majesty with Pope Pius VII., they came to an agreement, which was, however, frustrated by the difficulties which the Emperor found placed in the way by the authorities on his return to Vienna.

'Delays of every kind took place. One arose from the strong feeling of *Law* (the inviolability of the written law) which in the Emperor's mind amounted to scrupulosity. Another cause was the resistance of the lay and clerical canonists devoted to Febrionianism, against every agreement with the Roman Chair. The revolutionary outbreaks which, at the beginning of the third decade of the nineteenth century, disturbed the peace of Europe, and particularly of Italy, forced the questions between the Empire and Rome into the background : mutual concessions took place between the highest powers, when, I am convinced, an end ought to have been put to the founda-tion of the evil. But I stood alone at the centre of affairs, and therefore, in spite of my efforts, there remained nothing but empty negotiations.

'When, in the year 1835, the Emperor Francis, who morally quite agreed with me, was near his death, he ordered, in a testamentary document, that the controversy between Church and State should be terminated as quickly as possible, and appointed me and the Bishop of St. Polten (Wagner) executors of his will. The pressure which always follows a change of rulers prevented the immediate termination of the important task so dear to my heart ; soon afterwards the Bishop whom the Emperor had appointed died. I chose Abbot Rauscher to succeed him, and we took up our position against the officials, but did not succeed in bringing the affair to that issue for which at last a path was made by the Revolutions of 1848.

'The goal is reached! In this faithful narrative of events the key is given to the delay caused by erroneous ideas, false doctrines, and bureau-cratic influences—hindrances to the victory of truth, and even of common sense—to the best intentions of two Emperors and to my efforts.'

*THE TREATY OF MUNICH, CONCERNING THE
CESSION OF DETACHED PORTIONS OF THE
COUNTRY OF BAVARIA TO AUSTRIA.*

*Metternich to Von Wacquant, Austrian Plenipotentiary at
Munich, Milan, February 9, 1816.*

209. The time of the Prince Royal (at Milan) was
passed as much in direct *pourparlers* between him and
the Emperor as in my negotiations with the Prince
Royal and the Count de Rechberg. If it is difficult to
describe to you the persistence with which the former
pursued his favourite idea—that of the acquisition of the
greater part of the Palatinate—and the tedious conduct
of the latter, it is not so with regard to the result of
the negotiation. . . . The negotiation turned on three
points :—

1st. On the claim of Bavaria to an augmentation of
her share, to make up for the loss which she asserts that
she has sustained through our exchanges.

2nd. On her claim to contiguity of territory.

3rd. On her desire to see the negotiations of Munich
joined with those which we are reserving for Frankfurt.

The Prince Royal, and especially M. de Rechberg,
used every effort to sustain the first of these points. It
had been explained most positively to him that nothing
could alter his Majesty's conviction of the more than
sufficient importance of the indemnity offered to Bavaria,
and accepted by her, and that consequently we could

never admit or sustain a claim founded on a contrary principle.

In the first interview of the Emperor with the Prince Royal, the latter maintained with much heat a project for the acquisition of a line of communication which had been fully explained to us. The Emperor left no doubt on the Prince Royal's mind of his determination in the present negotiation not to maintain this project, which would certainly have met with insurmountable obstacles on the part of the Court of Baden. His Imperial Majesty merely promised his good offices for the cession of the circle of Main-and-Tauber. This proposal has been definitely accepted by the Prince Royal and by M. de Rechberg.

We met with very strong opposition on the part of the Bavarian negotiators, with the object of uniting the negotiation of Munich to that of Frankfurt, or, what was equivalent, of subordinating our direct negotiation to the one reserved for the latter city, and thus exposing it to new complications. The very decided declaration of the Emperor's determination not to lend himself to an arrangement which, if carried out, would prolong all the annoyances we have experienced in our negotiations with Bavaria for more than two years, has caused the bringing forward of a new Bavarian proposition. The Prince Royal asked, while consenting to the complete separation of the two negotiations, that the term of the surrender of Innviertel should be delayed until the end of the negotiation of Frankfurt, and his Imperial Majesty having declined this demand, the Count de Rechberg reduced it the next day to some districts of Innviertel, which should remain under the same clause, and as a pledge, in the hands of Bavaria.

The Emperor, seeing in the adoption of such a measure the very compromises he has decided to avoid, all
the more that the minds of our people, now united to
the Kingdom of Bavaria, and properly belonging to
it, are already too much excited ; and desiring, on the
other hand, to prove to the King of Bavaria that
he does not wish to prevent the conclusion of an important affair for considerations connected with mere
financial details, will endeavour to find a means of
attaining both these ends.   The simplest of all has presented itself to the mind of his Imperial Majesty.   M.
de Rechberg has sent to me a statistical and financial
valuation of the circle of Main-and-Tauber.   His Majesty
has decided to offer to the Prince Royal himself to
bear the loss sustained by Bavaria from the revenue
of this circle, counting from the day of the surrender
of the provinces which are to be restored to us, to the
day when Bavaria enters into possession of the indemnity claimed by her as compensation for her renunciation of the contiguity of her territories ancient and
modern. . . .

The Count de Rechberg having spoken to me of the
King's desire to possess the territory which crosses a
part of the road from Reichenhall to Berchtesgaden,
which has always been a part of Salzburg, the Emperor
sees no difficulty in granting this request.   He claims,
on his side, a free passage for his troops on the road
from Salzburg to Lofer by Reichenhall. . . .

. . . It only remains for me to tell you, Sir, of the
King's idea of the acquisition of the Palatinate.   The
Prince Royal, seeing the impossibility of engaging us
to support his wishes for the acquisition of the Pala-
tinate, and still less of imposing them on the Grand
Duke of Baden, has ended by requesting to be at least

assured of the intentions of our august master the Emperor in favour of an arrangement which Bavaria could be induced in time to propose to the Court of Baden—an arrangement which should be made amicably and according to the principles of a just compensation. His Majesty did not hesitate to assure the Prince Royal that such an arrangement would meet with no difficulty on his part; and that, on the contrary, he will be delighted to contribute, by an amicable intervention, to the reconciliation of the King's wishes with the interests of the Court of Baden.

You will find enclosed full powers for concluding and signing the treaty which you are to negotiate.

Metternich to Wacquant, Verona, April 8, 1816.

210. The present courier will give you the means of concluding and signing the final arrangement with Bavaria, and it will not be difficult for you to prove to the King and his minister that our august master the Emperor to the unexampled proofs of patience which he has given in the course of the negotiation has added the greatest condescension to the often unreasonable claims of the opposite party. . . .

The date of May 1 is fixed so rigorously that our generals have orders not to allow themselves to be stopped in the occupation of the places ceded to us by Bavaria by any protestation or opposition; therefore it will be necessary for your Excellency to insist in the strongest manner on this surrender, and, if need be, that you should throw on Count de Montgelas himself all the responsibility of any complications which may arise from defective instructions or from a want of good faith on the part of Bavaria. It will be easy for you to prove that the Emperor, determined as he is to admit of no delay or evasions in the recovery of his provinces, feels it impossible to modify any orders whatever given to his civil and military authorities, considering how distant the places to be exchanged are, both from each other and from the present abode of his Imperial Majesty.

I agree with you as to the possibility of the signature taking place on the 13th or 14th at latest.*

---

* The above mentioned treaty, dated April 14, was published in the usual way. In consequence of this, the places which had been abstracted in 1809 again came into the possession of Austria.—ED.

COUNT METTERNICH'S LEAVE OF ABSENCE.

211. Metternich to the Emperor Francis (Report), April 8, 1816; with the Royal Note attached, Padua, April 9, 1816.

211. I need not tell your Majesty how grieved I am that in a moment like the present I am unable to be of use to your Majesty. My feelings are so well known to your Majesty that they need no asseveration to confirm them. I send your Majesty through Count Mercy my first plan of the journey. I would have gone to Vicenza instead of Padua, but Scarpa warned me that the dampness of that town made it a very injurious residence in cases of rheumatic affections. This applies also to Stra and Venice. In any case, however, your Majesty may depend upon my earnest attention to the state of affairs in Treviso . . . *

METTERNICH.

I am convinced of your attachment to my person, and very sorry that you cannot be with me, but I wish you to stay as long as you can, and take care of yourself; and I shall only be glad to see you return when you can do so without injury to your health.

FRANCIS.

* A letter from Metternich to his mother gives the real reason of this short absence. It is written from Verona, dated April 13, 1816, and says: —'My eye is better; it has never been alarming, but inconvenient and tedious, like all affections of the eye. The cure which I have begun, and still continue, is doing me much good, in every respect. I have had three years of very great labour, and I prefer to take measures now, rather than wait for what might prove a very serious malady. The Emperor is exceedingly kind, and daily gives me proofs of confidence and attachment of which he perhaps hardly knew himself capable. I am more devoted than anyone else to him, and certainly in a more disinterested way than most of his servants.'— ED.

REGULATION OF MONEY.

212. A Memorandum by Metternich,* Vienna, October 12, 1816.
213. A summary view of the result of the gradual withdrawal of Paper Money. Autograph note by Metternich.

212. If the present conference is to have any useful end, it seems to me quite necessary to come to some decision as to general principles, or let it be clearly and distinctly explained why there can be no such agreement. In a matter like this, questions and answers, objections and counter-objections, may be repeated in endless multiplication, unless it is decided beforehand what we want to ask for, and in what order the questions shall be put.

The problem is, to introduce a fixed and regular monetary system to take the place of the present one, which is admitted to be in every respect defective, and to come to a decision upon the now discredited paper money in circulation, which (at least in its present quantity and quality) is the occasion of all these faults and incongruities.

Every possible measure concerning this paper-money runs on the lines of one of the following three systems :—

1. The retention of paper in a reduced nominal value. System of devaluation.

2. The abolition of paper money by law—with or

* Metternich was appointed, in 1816, President of the conference summoned to remove the financial pressure and restore the public credit.—ED.

without equivalent. System of legal or forcible withdrawal.

3. The abolition of paper money by a voluntary and therefore a gradual operation. System of gradual withdrawal.

The system of devaluation has the advantage of being simple in execution and rapid in its effects, and the Government remains in possession of its cash. There are, however, many objections to the adoption of this system, one of the greatest of which is that it is the second attempt of the kind, and would be as strongly opposed by public opinion as the finance operation of 1811, at a time of the greatest pressure, although the present attempt does not fall in a time of such pressure.

The system of enforced withdrawal from circulation is not capable of any great modification. A difference between a sudden and a periodical withdrawal of the paper money cannot, according to my conviction, exist; for any calling in of money by law, however it may be announced or declared, concerns the whole amount. Therefore, the only question here is, whether the possessors of the paper are or are not indemnified. No voice has been heard at present, among us at least, in favour of the abolition of paper money without an equivalent. Those who desire its abolition by a legal arrangement are ready to grant an indemnification to the holders of it, and since such compensation cannot be given in ready money, they are willing to give them interest-bearing national bonds. This second system may therefore be more briefly and more pertinently called the system of consolidation by law—that is, enforced consolidation.

The system of gradual withdrawal admits, indeed, of a far greater variety of combinations and operations.

But all are agreed that even with this system, as things are at present, the sum total, or at any rate the greater part, of the paper money must be withdrawn by national bonds that pay interest. Only these bonds should not be introduced compulsorily, like a system of consolidation by law, but by free operations as a compensation for the paper money. The system of gradual withdrawal, with the reservation of all the remedial measures applicable to it may therefore be called, in contradistinction to the others, the system of free consolidation.

Opinions are at present divided amongst us as to these two systems.

Both parties agree in the main point that the State must annually devote a considerable sum to pay the interest of the bonds replacing the paper money. If we estimate the paper money in circulation only at six hundred millions, this sum would amount with $2\frac{1}{2}$ per cent. to fifteen millions, with 2 per cent. to twelve millions.

The question therefore which must take precedence of all others is this. Can the State, besides the yearly interest due on the present interest - bearing debt, afford annually twelve to fifteen millions for interest on the new bonds?

This question is common to both systems. If it has to be answered in the negative, neither of the two systems can exist (least of all that of forced consolidation, which at once affects the whole mass of paper-money in circulation equally). If it be affirmed, this leads to the further inquiry whether it be better to expend those twelve or fifteen millions of yearly interest once and for all on the consolidation of the paper money, or to leave that sum to be disposed of by the Finance

Minister as a maximum for the introduction and per
formance of free operations of consolidation.

Second chief question :—Which of the two systems
of consolidation is the better and the more feasible?

1. Those who maintain the system of consolidation
by law must, I am convinced, show—

(*a*) That the compensation assigned by law to the
possessors of paper money will be real and not delu-
sive : in other words, that the value (namely, the market-
price) of the bonds in exchange for the paper money,
if not equal should be as nearly as possible equal to the
present real worth of this paper money, and should not
fall to $\frac{1}{5}$, $\frac{1}{6}$, or even perhaps $\frac{1}{10}$, $\frac{1}{20}$ of the nominal value
of the paper money.

(*b*) That, after an entire and sudden withdrawal of
paper money, other circulating media will be at once
or in a short time introduced, and that, in the absence
of this, the most ruinous stagnation in the circulation
would not be introduced into all trades great and small,
a result which would end in the general ruin of the
country.

(*c*) That after so rapid and extensive a revolution
the Government will be strong enough to raise (if even
by violent means) the money it requires for urgent
necessities, or rich enough to advance the money for an
indefinite time.

2. Can the system of free consolidation with the
same means as the system of enforced consolidation
(twelve to fifteen millions of annual interest) be applied
to compass the same ends?

It is incumbent on the Finance Minister to prove—

(*a*) That the gradual withdrawal of paper money
can be effected by the measures proposed or to be
proposed by him.

(*b*) That the operation will be uninterrupted and will not be prolonged beyond the shortest term possible.

(*c*) That, in case one of his proposed measures should fail by unforeseen hindrances, it would not be impossible to him to replace it quickly by some other and more effective one.

When these points are established, the two following, requiring the greatest attention, must be mentioned.

A. Without at the present moment deciding on either of the two systems of consolidation, I cannot conceal my conviction that, in setting forth the reasons for the forced system of consolidation, far more care and even severity must be used than in judging of the single measures which might be proposed for the execution of a free system of consolidation, for the danger is no doubt greater with the former than with the latter. Here (2), at the worst, it is but the further continuance of the present burdensome condition : there (1), the possible ruin of the country is at stake ; here (2), a principle already laid down is pursued : there (1), a system actually in force is abolished and replaced by one perfectly new. With a free consolidation, the Government remains from beginning to end master of its measures : in the consolidation by law, from the moment the law is proclaimed, every retrogression and even every essential modification is barred.

B. I should consider it an evil, the consequences of which would be incalculable, if the investigation of definite questions should check the Government in its progress along its regular path ; or if it should take measures not quite consistent with an impartial and prudent deliberation, or with the future application of the principles which must be established by it.*

Summary of the Results of the gradual Abolition of the Paper Money.

I. MAIN PROPOSITION.

213. 1. The paper in circulation shall be abolished.

2. This abolition shall not take place without a fair indemnification of its holders.

3. The rate of interest for the conversion of paper money into national interest-bearing bonds is $2\frac{1}{2}$ per cent.

4. The maximum of the charge on the State, arising from this conversion, is fifteen millions annual interest.

5. The national debt, hitherto paying an interest of about 15,000,000 W. W. must, at every change from the circulation of paper to that of a metallic currency, sooner or later be charged with 15,000,000 in C. M.

II. PRESENT STATE OF AFFAIRS.

1. The paper money in circulation amounts, the reserves of cash being deducted, to 600,000,000.

2. Of this about 40,000,000 is already abolished in virtue of the patents of June 1, and by the sale of 2,500 bank stock; the interest on the 40,000,000 amounts to about 400,000 florins C. M.

3. In the treasury are the war contributions and all other revenues, with the deduction of 10,000,000 C. M., employed in the operation in consequence of the patent of June 1.

---

* The patent of October 29, 1816, by which a free loan was opened for the withdrawal of paper money was the result of the conference to which the above memoir served as guide.—ED.

III. Proposed Operation.

A loan reckoned for the conversion of 120,000,000 to 150,000,000 withdraws in the first case from circulation the sum of 120,000,000 W. W., and costs the State for fresh interest 3,000,000 C. M.

IV. Further Course of the Operation.

	w. w.
I purposely separate from the sum total of	600,000,000
A sum of	200,000,000
Which I consider the minimum of paper that (in an altered form) must be kept in circulation, and for the abolition of which, if it ever takes place, quite different means must be employed. My examination, therefore, reaches only the sum of	400,000,000
Of these—	
1. Already abolished	40,000,000
2. Will be abolished by the minimum of the revenue from the next loan . .	120,000,000
3. I think it quite certain that in one way or other, beside the 2,500 already abolished in bank stock, 20,000 more (not altogether half the number prescribed in the patents) will have to be abolished, by which will be called in the further sum of	40,000,000
	200,000,000

Therefore, from the above 400,000,000 W. W. must still be withdrawn, by gradual free operations, 200,000,000 W. W.

As a beginning of these operations the State may apply—

1. Interest at $2\frac{1}{2}$ per cent. = 5,000,000.

2. Bonuses (by which the payment of higher interests than $2\frac{1}{2}$ per cent. would be avoided) from the store of ready cash, a sum of about 10,000,000.

V. RESULT OF THE WHOLE OPERATION. w. w.

1. Abolished already	40,000,000
2. Will be abolished :—	
(a) By the loan now proposed . .	120,000,000
(b) By bank stock	40,000,000
(c) By further operations by credit .	200,000,000
	400,000,000
3. One particular withdrawal without increase of the State's load of interest .	200,000,000
	600,000,000

In this way the interest to be paid by the State would be— w. w.

1. For the sum already withdrawn . .	400,000
2. For the proposed loan	3,000,000
3. For the 20,000 in bank stock . .	1,000,000
4. For further operations	5,000,000
	9,400,000

GENERAL REMARKS ON THE PRECEDING RESULT.

1. By this course the State remains in possession of all its stores of ready cash, with the exception of—

(a) The 10,000,000 already made use of under the patents of June 1, by which, however, the amount of paper money in circulation has been reduced to 40,000,000.

(*b*) The 10,000,000 to be used in case of necessity, to assist in the further credit operations.

2. By the present conversion of paper money the State has to bear, not only all the interest for the national debt (the paper money) at present paying no interest, but also the interest of the national debt hitherto paying interest in W. W., together with 15,000,000 C. M. ; an annual interest, therefore, of 30,000,000, immediate and without deduction. On the other hand, the interest of the new debt, when the operation is concluded, will not be more than 9,400,000 W. W., so that from the maximum, 15,000,000 W. W., will be saved 5,600,000 W. W., and, with regard to the present debt, the interest has not to be paid in C. M. till the whole operation is finished, so that the State gains for one or two years more the considerable difference between the amount of interest in W. W. and the same in C. M.

1817.

JOURNEY TO LEGHORN IN THE SUITE OF THE ARCHDUCHESS LEOPOLDINE, THE NEWLY-MARRIED CROWN PRINCESS OF PORTUGAL.

Extracts from Metternich's private Letters from June 10 to July 26, 1817.

214. Padua and Venice. 215. From Covigliajo—wretched accommodation —Cattajo—concert at the house of the Cardinal Legate—Abbé Mezzofanti. 216. Impression made by Florence—the Pitti Palace—the gallery. 217. Pisa—Campo Santo—the episode of Pernambuco. 218. The Catalani. 219. The Pope's illness — Fiesole—the Florentine dialect — the churches of Sta. Annunziata and Sta. Croce—Alfieri's monument by Canova —picture of the Last Judgment, by Bronzino. 220. The order of Elizabeth sent for Princess Metternich—Dr. Jaeger makes a sensation in Florence. 221. The portrait medallion presented for signing the marriage treaty—the expected arrival of the fleet. 222. The ladies in attendance on the Archduchess. 223. Plan of the journey. 224. To Leghorn—the island of Elba—the American admiral's ship—arrival at Lucca—return to Florence. 225. Preparations for giving over the Archduchess—anecdote of Zichy. 227. Arrival of the fleet—Metternich's journey to Lucca.

Metternich to his Wife, Padua, June 10, 1817.

214. I arrived here, as I intended, in the evening of the day before yesterday.

I have always fancied, and I am quite sure now, that summer is the proper season for Upper Italy. There is as little resemblance between the country, the towns, everything, in fact, in winter and summer, as between a garden in November, during the fogs and mud of that season, and that same garden in the month of June. No one can form any idea of the beauty of the country;

all the plantations, all the trees, which with us suffer
from cold, wind, and dust, are in full vegetation ; all the
fields covered with flowers, all those melancholy little
gardens of the Brenta full of roses and jasmines and
orange trees in flower ; all those houses, which then
looked so dilapidated, open and forming charming dwellings : in one word, everything is now beautiful. Venice
in June and Venice in December are two different cities ;
the heat there is moderated by the neighbourhood of
the sea ; every evening a breeze springs up which is
refreshing but not cold ; in the daytime it is as warm
as with us in those beautiful summer days when there
is no appearance of a storm. The Piazza in front of
St. Mark's is filled with large tents ; the people are
in the streets till daybreak ; the cafés close at five in
the morning ; the Giudecca and the Grand Canal are
covered with gondolas. I walked about Venice yesterday as if it were a city of the 'thousand and one
nights.' The women have no longer red hands ; blue
noses have disappeared, and the only ugly things I have
seen are those horrible old witches one meets everywhere, their grey hair streaming in the wind, and all
having bouquets of roses, or perhaps one great rose fastened to their horrid old wigs. I cannot help sending
you a sketch which is very much like one of these
nymphs of the lagunes, who was literally *coiffée* as you
see.

    215. *Covigliajo, June* 12.—I write to you, my dear,
from our last resting-place before Florence. This place
reminds me of the charms of our head-quarters in the
Vosges : there is here only one house, and that a very
bad one ; the Archduchess has one room ; I share one
with Floret : Madame de Khuenburg has a closet near
her mistress, without doors or windows ; the rest of

the suite sleep in the carriages. I do not know who chose the place, but certainly they could not have chosen a worse. We are in the midst of the Apennines, and no one would suspect we were in *la belle Italie* if it were not for the number of chesnut woods.

Yesterday morning we left Padua and slept at Ferrara, where we were received by three cardinals. The road from Padua as far as Rovigo is superb ; we stopped on the way to see a beautiful castle (Cattajo) belonging to the Duke of Modena. A wealthy gentleman named Obizzo took it into his head to bequeath it to the Duke, to show his claim to belong to the House of Este. The place is curious in itself, and for the beautiful and numerous collections of every kind gathered together by its last possessor. The road from Rovigo to Lagoscuro, where the Po is crossed, is detestable ; the only choice is between being drowned in the Po or smothered by the dust of a narrow causeway. Ferrara is superb, and if it had four times as many inhabitants it would be tolerably filled. We found there the Duke of Modena. The Cardinal Legate had arranged a concert for us in one of the great theatres, not being able to give us a play, which, for want of spectators, can only be managed once or twice a year. This theatre is finer than those in Vienna ; it holds 3,000 persons, and would do honour to a great capital. We left Ferrara this morning at five o'clock. The Cardinal Legate of Bologna gave us an elegant and very good breakfast at the University, a celebrated and magnificent place. The Librarian, Abbé Mezzofanti, is worthy of his position ; he speaks thirty languages, and as well as if he were a native of each of the thirty countries. I attacked him in German, and I defy anyone not to take him for a Saxon. He has never been away from Bologna, and never had a master. I asked how he got the right inflexions of the language. 'The inflexions,' replied he, ' all spring from the genius of language. I learnt in the grammar that each letter is pronounced in a certain manner ; I read and understood it in three months, I could speak it in six, and since then I have held conversations with Germans of different countries. I have done the same with all languages. Indian and Chinese are the only ones that have embarrassed me a little, for I have never had an opportunity of talking either with a mandarin or a brahmin, so that I am not sure if I have surmounted the vulgar pronunciation.' I made an inward sign of humility, and thought myself a perfect simpleton beside the Librarian of Bologna.

216. *Florence, June* 14.—We have been here since eleven yesterday morning. It would be difficult to explain to you the kind of impression which Florence must necessarily produce on everyone who loves what is beautiful and grand. All that I have seen up to this time far surpasses my expectations. Great God ! what men they were in past times.

Yesterday I went through the gallery of the Pitti Palace and Academy of Fine Arts, as well as the manufactory of *pietra dura*. To-day I have seen the great gallery. I shall return here every day that I am in Florence. I declare that I prefer it as it now is to the Museum as it was. It is difficult to form an idea of this immense treasury of all kinds of things ; the building is magnificent, and above all perfectly adapted to its object. The gallery of the Pitti Palace is a perfect quintessence of beauty, and the great gallery is as beautiful as that of the palace. The Venus de Medicis is infinitely better placed than she was at Paris. She is,

with four other magnificent statues, in the Tribune of
the Uffizi, which is lighted from above.   There are in
the same gallery seven or eight Raphaels, each more
beautiful than the other.   Among others there is one
which represents the painter's mistress, and it is beyond
conception.   I protest that the Grand Duke is the richest
man in the world.   All the monuments left here by
Leopold are worthy of the Medici : many even surpass
them.

The country is fine, more so, however, in my opinion, from culture than from its natural features.   The
town is on the Apennines, in a valley formed by the
Arno.   The soil is not very good ; nevertheless cultivation has made Tuscany one of the most productive
countries in the world.   It would be quite useless to
attempt to count the number of dwellings to be seen
from every eminence.   Besides hundreds of towns and
villages, from one window there may be seen, between Florence and Pistoia, more than four thousand
country houses and detached dwellings spread and
scattered on all sides.   The climate is divine ; there is
great heat from eleven till five, but the morning, the
evening, and the night are like what a day in Paradise will probably be.

217. *June* 18.—The day before yesterday I went to
Pisa, and returned yesterday.   Three or four very violent
storms during the day spoilt the illuminations a little,
but still they were magnificent.   Pisa in itself is very
curious.   There are three edifices close together, which
are as beautiful as possible—the Cathedral, the Tower
(*campanile*), and the Baptistry of St. John.   A fourth far
surpasses them.   The Crusaders, on their return, brought
vessels full of earth from Palestine.   They placed it in
a field, which they surrounded with a building, forming

a vast, simple corridor, in which are their tombs. Not being able to die in the Holy Land, they wished to be buried in its soil. This is called the *Campo Santo*. No one can be buried there without special permission from the Grand Duke, and there are many modern tombs. The corridors are used now as a museum. They collect there all that is dug up in the environs of Pisa, and the excavations are considerable.

The last news from Lisbon informs us that the Government has sent two vessels, intended to form part of the convoy of the Archduchess, to blockade Pernambuco, and they have done well. This will, however, cause a delay of two or three weeks. I shall therefore change my plans. In two or three days I expect the first news from Rome. I shall start (if I take this journey) as soon as they arrive, for that city, where I shall remain ten or twelve days, and then return to Florence. I accompany the Archduchess to Leghorn. If the fleet should be delayed beyond July 15, I shall make over the affair of the surrender of the Archduchess to M. d'Eltz, and shall be, as I told you when I left, at Vienna on the 22nd or 24th. I suppose this affair at Pernambuco will make a great noise at Vienna, and that our gossips are talking as if that town were between Purkersdorf and Sieghartskirchen. It appears that the rising has made no progress, and that the measures for repressing it were very well managed. It will have no effect on the departure of the Archduchess, except the necessity of hastily equipping two new ships to convey her, or rather to complete her escort. I beg you to mention these facts to the trumpeters of the good town of Vienna.

For the rest, my journey here is a great and inestimable benefit. I do not know how the great crisis brought about by this new complication would have passed over if I had not been on the spot.   If my good friends at Vienna cry out for or against my good fortune, I certainly have the conviction that I am doing what is just and right, and at the right moment; the only one in which great things can be done.   My presence in Italy has an incalculable influence on the progress of affairs.   If I could be vain of anything that Heaven has helped me to do in the last few years, it would be of the part I am playing at this interesting juncture in Europe.   The sovereign of all Italy could not be received as I am , all those who are on the right side—and they are very numerous—crowd round me ; they give me their entire confidence, and look for safety from me alone.   The Jacobins hide themselves, and they look upon me as a rod held over them.   If I have ever been inspired in any step I have taken, it was in deciding to come here ; and you are witness that I made up my mind in a quarter of an hour.

218. *June* 20.—Yesterday we passed a charming evening, a small party having been made at Madame Appony's to hear Catalani sing. The two Archduchesses came and all our suite.   She sang in such a way as to make all the company wild with delight.   She was in good voice, and you would have been as much enchanted as we all were.   Assuredly, if the Holy Virgin mingles her voice with the songs of the blessed, she must sing like this woman.

I shall not decide on my journey to Rome for two or three days.   The Holy Father is always so ill that he cannot attend to business ; and as it is to do business with him that I go there, I depend, thank God, on his faculties much more than on my own.

219. *June* 28.—Not only does my journey to Rome

become every day more problematical, but it is very probable that I shall not go at all. The Pope, although he is so far better that he has been taken from Castel Gandolfo to the Quirinal, seems unable to do anything; and as I was going to Rome entirely on business, I should give up my visit if I could not attain my object.

Yesterday I had a charming drive. About three miles from the town there is a mountain on which was built the ancient Etruscan town of Fesulæ, now Fiesole. There are some remains of antiquity: there are the walls of the old town, which date back to the time of Porsenna; and in the midst of a field of olives are the ruins of an amphitheatre, now almost entirely covered over by landslips. On a mound are the remains of a temple of Bacchus now transformed into a chapel. It would be difficult to find a more magnificent site; Florence with its innumerable villas is under your feet; you can trace the whole valley of the Arno, and the valleys which lead to Pistoia and to Volterra. It was here in this town that Catiline was defeated, and that this precursor of the ' *Nain jaune* ' * of our time ceased to threaten the existence even of the Republic. Many recollections, both ancient and modern, are connected with this place, and with every spot of earth on which one treads.

A remarkable thing in this country is the kind of culture which exists among the people. There is not a peasant who does not speak his own language with all the refinement and elegance of an academician of the Crusca. It is interesting to hold a conversation with these good people: their language is that of the drawing-room—no jargon, no shouting or raising of the voice,

* *Nain jaune* was an illustrated comic journal of the republican colour.— ED.

such as one hears in the rest of Italy.   A vine-dresser,
who looked like a half negro, acted as cicerone.   This
man related and explained everything to me like an
antiquary.   Among the things which have most struck
me are the details of the Church of the Annunziata, the
first which was used by the Order of Servites.   This
church is not very large, but beautiful, and exceedingly
rich in marbles.   It contains pictures of the first rank,
and there is, among other things, as in all the convents
of Italy, an interior court surrounded by an open corridor, and here all the arches between the columns are
painted in fresco by Andrea del Sarto.   There are about
forty paintings representing the foundation of the order,
all of inconceivable beauty of design and composition.
Here also is the superb painting of the Virgin with the
Infant Jesus and St. Mark, which is engraved in so many
ways.   One of the arches represents the triumph of the
Virgin; she is seated on a car drawn by a lion and a
sheep—charming in idea, so rich and withal so simple.
The car is surrounded by angels with ideal figures.
These paintings were paid for at the rate of twenty
crowns each.   The persons who had them painted took
care to have their coats-of-arms painted on them.   Their
descendants assuredly cannot regret the expense.   The
frescoes are in perfect preservation.   In this climate
nothing is injured, however it may be exposed to the
air.   Given a good painter and a roof, and the pictures
will be handed down to posterity.

In the Church of Sta. Croce are the monuments of
celebrated men.   Galileo has a fine tomb, and the
Countess of Albany has erected a superb monument to
Alfieri, executed by Canova.   A colossal female, perso-
nating Italy, is represented as weeping over his tomb.
The whole thing is more grandiose than beautiful.   I

know many things of Canova's much better conceived,
and which speak more to the soul.   There are magnificent paintings in this church, among others a 'Last
Judgment' by Bronzino, inconceivably fine as to execution.   Christ, seated on an eminence, holds His hand out
to the elect, who are issuing from a tomb at His feet.
The painter has taken care to place himself with his
wife and his daughter among them.   He seems to have
made sure of his own future state.   If all who enter
Paradise resemble the figures in this picture, it would
be a pity if there should be neither pencil nor palette
there.   I have seen, I do not remember where—at
Padua, I think—a small picture, the beautiful conception
of which made a great impression upon me.   Christ,
with an air simple though triumphant, holds up the
cross in the middle of a vast grotto.   It is the entrance
of Limbo.   On the right of the picture are the patriarchs
weeping with joy and love.   St. John the Baptist calls
to him a number of beings, who are coming from all
parts of the interior of the cave, and shows them the
cross.   There is an inspiration in this picture which is
quite magical.   It is no longer Christ suffering on the
cross, but Christ having triumphed over death, and
sharing His triumph with the just, who are entering
into His kingdom.   Expectation and happiness are
equally depicted on the faces ; Christ alone is calm,
and St. John more inspired than ever.   We hear him
cry from the abyss, ' The hour is come ! '
    I have told you of the paintings ; I will pass now to
the sculpture, and to something which, without producing *chefs-d'œuvre*, is not without merit.   It is curious to
see the manufactories of alabaster.   You order an enormous vase to-day, and they bring it you to-morrow.
You wish for your bust : a man takes a model of you

in clay in ten minutes, and in three or four days you have a bust in alabaster, a perfect likeness. Eltz was modelled to-day: a man took a lump of clay, and I declare to you that one could not think more quickly than he made the head, the nose, the mouth, &c. This sculptor, who is not a disciple of Gall, has proved to me— what we knew before, however—that the theory of the said doctor is true in every respect. Eltz was almost finished, but something was wanting; my man took a step forward, and with a firm hand he raised with his thumbs four or five bumps on the head and the sides of the jaws. From that moment the likeness was striking.

220. *June* 29.—I take advantage of the departure of the military courier to inform you, my dear, that M. de Maccalon has received news which leaves no doubt about the departure of the fleet. If the winds are favourable it will be at Leghorn about July 15. This same courier has brought with him three decorations of the Order of St. Elizabeth: one for the Archduchess, one for our Empress, and the third for you. The ribbon is rose-colour; but the sea-air has faded it so much that it is now a sort of straw-colour. It will be necessary to get new ribbon, and I will send you your decoration as soon as it has become rose-coloured again. As you love the pomps of this world, this news will make you very happy. I am sure that Leontine *****
will be more delighted than her mamma with the ribbon, and that she will have great pleasure in repeating to her nurse, *dass Mama hat schönes Band.* The order itself is superb; it is generally given only to queens or princesses of the blood.

I do not think I have ever told you about my eye.

---

* Metternich's daughter, afterwards Countess Sándor.—ED.

It makes more progress in one day here than it did in eight at Vienna. I am well satisfied, and so is my physician, who is becoming very famous at Florence. He saves every day four or five eyes; people are more backward here in that art than anyone can imagine. Almost all diseases of the eye, even when not serious at first, lead to blindness, not for want of good eyes, but for want of good doctors. Jaeger * has told me astonishing facts on this subject. Just imagine, here they do not know one of the instruments or curative methods which have been adopted by all the world for the last thirty or forty years. Another singular fact is that the poor people do all they can to make themselves blind, for here, as at Rome, it is the blind alone who can exercise the profession of mendicants. Jaeger offered to restore a man's sight to him; the man asked if he would also undertake his maintenance.

I have bought two pretty things: a charming copy of Canova's Venus and an enormous alabaster vase, at a ridiculous price. I shall not buy anything else unless I go to Rome, and, as I shall not go, I shall buy nothing.

221. *Poggio Imperiale, July* 1.—Here is your decoration from the other world, my dear Laura. You alone will have a new ribbon, for that which you will receive to-day has become hortensia instead of rose, which it should be, and certainly the rose need not be made more tender than nature has already made it. I send you your decree, with a translation into French, with which Mercy and I amused ourselves yesterday. The turn of the sentences is so original that we have tried to preserve it as much as possible. You must reply to the Queen. The decoration, from its form, seems

---

* Dr. Friedrich Jaeger, a celebrated physician in Vienna, who for many years was Metternich's private physician, and survived him.—ED.

to go back to the year 801—that is to say, till the time of Charlemagne.

The Marquis de Maccalon sent me yesterday, for the signature of the contract of marriage, a medallion with the portrait of the King surrounded by precious stones, but so shamefully painted that he would not let me keep it. The painter, who does not seem to be one at all, has aimed at making his Most Faithful Majesty smile. He has opened his mouth so wide that he was forced to show either his teeth or his tongue. The upper teeth show like a ball of ivory lying on a tongue, to say the least, as thick.

Everything convinces me that the fleet must arrive at Leghorn in eight or ten days. We go, therefore, without further delay to settle ourselves there till the moment of embarkation, and I will take my route by Modena and Parma to return to you, and prepare to be made a grandpapa.

Metternich to his daughter Marie, Florence, July 3.

222. Time goes on, my dear Marie, and I am expecting the arrival of this devil of a fleet as if it were the Messiah, in order to regain my liberty, or rather to win it again by handing over the key of the house to M. d'Eltz. It seems, however, that it will be here about the 10th of this month. We shall pass four or five days free at Leghorn, and then *vogue la galère.* It appears that the feminine part of the Portuguese Court is coming. This makes the ladies' journey to Brazil very doubtful. Of these ladies Madame de Khuenburg is estimable, and has most agreeable manners ; Madame de Lodrin is tall, and Madame de —— ugly. Both are very good. There you have their finished por-

traits. Old Edling is very well. His fall has bleached
him ; nothing is left of his olive-coloured Brazilian
cheeks but the cheek bones. His mind has recovered,
but he still wanders sometimes. For example, he asked
me yesterday (the subject was Marie Louise), 'Is she
not at Paris?' I said to him, 'Good God, no ; she is
at Parma.' 'True,' said Edling ; 'I had forgotten that
the Emperor Napoleon had bought Parma!' You may
be sure I said nothing more to him, for I do not like to
waste my words.

My health is very good. I have tested anew the
perfections of the Court *cuisine*.

I had a charming walk yesterday evening. All the
surrounding country is a succession of hills more or
less high. All offer the most delicious prospects, all are
planted, and too much planted for effect. The trees
are olives, figs, bignonias, catalpas, all in bloom ; the
gardens, even those of the peasants, are filled with
orange trees ; the hedges are composed principally of
jasmine, others of the flowering arbutus ; there are
clematis blossoms large as pompon roses, pomegranates
covered with flowers. The vines are not planted in the
same way as on the other side of the Po ; a vine is
planted by the side of a tree, and, being allowed to climb
up it, ends by covering more or less the whole of it, so
that the grapes appear to belong to the tree. All the
plants smell twice as sweet as they do with us ; and the
grass and the plants at the roadside are so aromatic that
by the evening one knows not what it is, but that all the
air is perfumed. What adds to the charm of the first
part of the night is the immense quantity of small
luminous flies, which they call here '*lucciole*.' They
fly in millions about all places covered with grass and
round the trees. Their light is at least as sparkling

and strong as the sparks from a steel. The whole
country seems on fire. The moon of Florence, which,
like that of Vienna, is near the full, is clear as she never is
with us. The air is calm at that hour, about fourteen
or fifteen degrees, light and clear. One can well understand how this beautiful climate has produced so many
painters and poets.

I intend to order at Rome two bas-reliefs from Thorwaldsen. I will have them placed in the two panels,
which I will make in stucco, at the end of the small
drawing-room at the villa. I assure you people will
come to see them.

Metternich to his Wife, Florence, July 10.

223. Here we are, my dear, at the 10th of the
month, and we do not yet know the exact day of the
arrival of the fleet. This is my plan of campaign. I
shall leave here on the 20th, whether the Archduchess
has been surrendered or not. I shall take eight days
from here to Vienna, for I shall stop one day at Modena,
and I only wish to travel from five in the evening to six
in the morning, so as to allow the hours of intense heat
to pass, during which I shall rest and dine. Consequently I shall be with you from the 27th to the 29th.
I shall spend three clear days at Vienna, and shall leave
again on the 4th for Carlsbad. If the fleet arrives here
on the 20th, I shall effect the transference before my
departure ; if not, I shall make over the affair to Eltz.
The day after to-morrow I shall probably pass four-and-
twenty hours at Leghorn, to inspect the place and
arrange everything proper for the ceremony. The
weather is so calm that the vessels cannot make much
way ; it is therefore necessary to reckon on three or
even four weeks' sailing, although with a fresh wind

the route from Lisbon to Leghorn takes fifteen or sixteen days at the most.

The Archduchess Marie Louise has been here since
the day before yesterday. We form quite a colony at
Poggio. After all, it would hold three times as many
people.

224. *Poggio, July* 17.—I set out for this place on the
14th, at six in the evening, with MM. d'Appony and de
Maccalon, the faithful Floret, the amiable Hudelist, and
Prince Jablonowsky, who had arrived from Naples.
We had five coaches. We arrived at three in the
morning at Leghorn. As we all had been clever enough
to sleep in the carriage, none of us cared to go to bed.
It was beautiful and fresh, and we had the prospect of
a very hot day before us. We therefore decided to go
at once to see the port and everything that would have
exposed us to the heat of the sun. We began by as-
cending the beautiful lighthouse which is at the end of
the new pier. There we beheld the first rays of the
sun gilding the rocks of the islands of Gorgona, Capraja,
Corsica, and Elba. About two miles seaward was the
American squadron, which had just left the roadstead
of Leghorn, and also two Neapolitan frigates and a brig
which the Dey of Algiers had bought at Leghorn, in
order to carry off Tuscan subjects in the open sea close
by. The whole view was magnificent. Gorgona is
about fifteen miles off; it is nothing but an immense
rock inhabited by fishermen and a small Tuscan garrison. Capraja and Corsica were so flooded with the
bright morning light that every valley could be distinguished; the island of Elba was very plain, but
Porto-Ferrajo is too near the level of the sea to be perceived at that distance. I could not see that island
without thinking of my forced march on March 5, 1815,

in consequence of the news of Napoleon's departure.
Having surveyed the whole neighbourhood of the port,
we returned, and then took some hours of repose ; at
midday we hurried through the shops, of which that of
Michelis is the most beautiful and certainly the only
one of its kind in the world.   There are sold the most
beautiful alabasters and magnificent marbles.   No one
could look at Pisani's who had examined those made at
Leghorn.   I bought several charming things at a ridiculous price, considering the workmanship.   I went
over the spot where the surrender of the Archduchess will
take place.   We dined at the principal hotel—which did
not deserve that title—and at six in the evening we embarked to pay a visit to the American Commodore.
To avoid the firing of guns I would not be announced,
and I remained on board till sunset, when they do not
salute. The flagship has eighty-four guns, and is one of the
most beautiful vessels I have ever seen. The Americans,
who have a great rivalry with the English, owed their
success in the last war to the new construction of their
ships of the line, some of which carry as many as ninety
guns.   They are constructed like frigates, but without
quarter-decks, and are fast sailers like frigates, and can
consequently overtake these vessels, which in England
never carry more than eighty guns.   They can also
avoid with the same facility vessels of the line of
greater tonnage.   The Commodore received us with
much distinction ; he immediately placed the whole
crew under arms, and showed me over every part of his
ship.   Its whole appearance and neatness are admirable.
I do not know if in these respects it does not even surpass the English ships ; on the other hand, the style of
the crew does not equal that of the latter.   The Commodore is a great amateur of the fine arts and fine

animals. He has pictures in his cabin, among others a
copy of the portrait of Pope Julius II., after Raphael, and
between decks and on the upper deck African gazelles
and a great Canadian bear. Between decks, where the
sailors dine, there is on each table a pyramid of very
clean vessels, which contain the drink for the sailors,
and a Bible distributed by the Bible Society of Boston.
The *maladie biblique* extends through both hemispheres.
After leaving the fleet, we had another look at the shops,
which the principal merchants had taken care to have
well illuminated. We retired at eleven, and at six we
started in the carriage for Lucca. Leghorn is a beautiful town, or rather it has one fine square, and one fine
street. There is great confusion in this street, and it is
like a very busy market. I saw the synagogue, the
most beautiful in Italy (there are twelve thousand Jews
at Leghorn, who enjoy great privileges). I wanted to
visit the Lazaretto for quarantine, but could not find a
moment.

I reached Lucca at mid-day. The town is old and
quite lovely ; the country is as charming as it is possible to see. Lucca is situated in a small plain, in the
midst of beautiful high mountains rich in vegetation.
They are clothed with olive trees to the very summit.
The country is not cut up as it is in other parts of
Italy, and the soil is excellent. At two o'clock I went
to Saltocchio, a villa belonging to M. Canamy, who
was Madame Elisa's *écuyer* and with good reason ; she
is charming. About two thousand steps from that is
Marlia, a quite divine place, which Madame Elisa has
had built and planted. The house recalls to my mind
the most comfortable French *châteaux*. The garden is
planted in the English style, and that marvellously ;
it is large and has a very uncommon appearance,

perhaps even unique of its kind, for I know of no other garden in the English style on this side of the Alps, planted with such a profusion of trees and exotic flowers; there are, for example, whole groves of magnolias. The climate of Lucca is a great deal milder than that of Florence; the heat is not so excessive during the summer, and the cold is never more than two or three degrees below zero during winter, so that the most delicate plants grow in the open air. After taking a turn in the gardens, we dined at Marlia, where I had invited the first people in Lucca. We started again at six in the evening and arrived at Florence at midnight. Two days could not possibly have been spent better or more agreeably.

225. *Florence, July* 12.—I shall go to-morrow to Leghorn, to prepare for the arrival of my Princess, and I shall leave here to-morrow at six in the evening. I shall be at Leghorn at one or two in the morning; I shall remain there the whole of the 14th, and leave Leghorn on the 15th at two in the morning; by daybreak I shall be at Pisa, which I have seen; I shall go to the stud of camels belonging to the Grand Duke, the only establishment of the kind in Europe; from there to the baths of Pisa, and dine at Lucca, where I shall pass the rest of the day. On the morning of the 15th I shall return to Poggio, so I shall have seen a great deal in a short time. The Portuguese fleet should, according to letters from Lisbon of June 10, have left that port on the 18th or 22nd, so it may be expected at Leghorn at any hour. I shall be delighted if it arrives there exactly on the 14th.

Here is a charming anecdote of Charles Zichy, the younger. He was at Parma last spring. The Archduchess invited him to dinner. A famous improvisatore,

Gricci, was to give a representation after dinner. Zichy took care to arrive first; after him the Cardinal Archbishop of Parma. These two gentlemen did not know one another. Zichy, however, guessed by the red stockings of the Cardinal that he must be some one of importance, and ended by breaking the ice, and presenting himself to the Cardinal, saying ' *Io sono Zichy.*' The Cardinal overwhelmed him with compliments, and would have embraced him : '*Signor Gricci, ah ! Signor Gricci; che piacere, che reputazione, che talento ! Avremmo il piacere di sentirla, d'ammirarla.*' Zichy, delighted to see that his name produced such an extraordinary effect, being pressed by the old Cardinal to give him a specimen of his *savoir faire* just to pass the time, hesitated, talked of his small merits, his services, of the Chamber, of all he had done for twenty years without advancement ! The arrival of Marie Louise alone put an end to the scene. She herself told me the story to-day.

226. *July* 23.—*L'homme propose, chère amie, et Dieu dispose !* This devil of a fleet is just eight days too late. A courier arrived here yesterday from Lisbon, having taken fourteen days, and he informed us that the fleet set sail on the 6th of this month. It may arrive to-morrow, the day after, or in a week or ten days, according to the wind. It is not likely that it will take more than three weeks coming, and in that case it will be at Leghorn from the 27th to the 29th. The embarkation of the Archduchess cannot take place for seven or eight days after it has anchored in the roads ; it must take from three to five days for re-victualling and embarking the luggage. I told you in my last, that if I had no news on the 22nd I should leave on the 25th. Now I cannot see that this will be

possible. The ceremonies would not detain me except for the sake of decency, but business will. I must see the Portuguese Commissioner, at least I can hardly help it, as he has business with me, and it will at least be very difficult, if not impossible, to avoid waiting till the moment of arrival.

227. *July* 26.—That blessed squadron has at last come to anchor at Leghorn. It was recognised and signalled yesterday at mid-day, at the distance of twenty miles. It entered the roads two hours and a half ago.

According to my calculations, it must take ten or twelve days to revictual. Consequently I leave to-day for the baths of Lucca, where I shall be at six this evening. I shall begin my cure to-morrow, and I shall only interrupt it during the two days which I shall spend at Leghorn, in order to complete my task. These days depend on the above-mentioned question of the revictualling of the Portuguese fleet.

AT THE BATHS OF LUCCA.

Extracts from the private Letters from Metternich to his Family, from July 28 to August 1817.

228. Description of Lucca. 229. Numerous guests. 230. Visit of the Archduchess to Leghorn—arrival of the English Admiral Penrose—description of the Portuguese ships. 231. The ceremony of surrendering the Archduchess—farewell. 232. The Archduchess's ship sets sail—Marie Louise. 233. Metternich's departure from Lucca.

Metternich to his Wife, Baths of Lucca, July 28, 1817.

228. I am here in the most charming spot in the world. The road from Lucca to the waters passes through the most picturesque valley that can be conceived. The mountains which border it are as high as the Styrian Alps (excepting of course the summits covered with perpetual snow). A majestic torrent rushes through it, and this most beautiful road brings us, at the distance of fifteen miles, to the baths and waters. I am living in the part called the Villa de' Bagni, a house which Elisa had built, or rather arranged, for herself; this will tell you that it is comfortable and well situated. I have a bath in the house itself, and the waters for drinking are close by. About a mile from this are the *bagni caldi*; they carry anyone who wishes to go there in a chair. It is a curious sight to see the quantity of open and covered chairs which cross a large wood of chestnuts and a very steep mountain. I can only compare the situation to that of Styria; add to that the vegetation of Italy, and you embellish the picture amaz-

ingly. The air is excellent, it is neither too hot nor too
cold ; the establishments for the baths are well conducted, and luxuriously carried out. Everything that
with us would be of wood is here of the most beautiful
Carrara marble.

The news which I receive from Leghorn do not
allow me to suppose that the embarkation can take
place before August 15. This proves to me that the
Portuguese are the slowest people in the world. The
ships require a number of things which the Government
at Lisbon had not time to procure, although they had
eight months in which to do it. The Admiral requires
ten days for revictualling ; I give him twenty, and that
brings us to August 15. If such is the case, I shall try
to finish my course of waters before quitting Leghorn,
and I shall leave that port straight for Vienna. If the
Admiral is, contrary to my expectation, more expeditious, I shall make an interval of two days in my cure.

229. *Baths of Lucca, August 2.*—My house is full
of visitors ; I have with me MM. de Maccalon, de Na-
varro, and de Mello ; Wallmoden and his brother, and
D'Aspre ; Louis Kaunitz and Golowkin ; the Abbè Justel
and two painters. I have, therefore, been obliged to
take another house to lodge those who cannot find room
in my palace. Everybody is enchanted with the place ;
they all declare that there cannot be anything more
beautiful, and I am of the same opinion. I think the
life of a Prince of Lucca is, without doubt, one of the
happiest and most to be envied. This little country has
everything and not too much ; it contains a town, a
country-house, a bath, a seaport, a lake, a river, &c.
You see the *embarras des richesses* is not excessive, while
that of choice does not present itself at all : in fact,
here ambition and enjoyment never being directed to

more than one object, the first must ever be limited, and the second become constant.

230. *Leghorn, August* 10.—I arrived here at eight in the evening. I found all the Courts and four thousand visitors. I have been to see my Princess, and I went with her to the theatre. The house is magnificent, not much smaller than La Scala, and has five rows of boxes. They gave us the ' Orazi,' by Cimarosa, a superb opera, but unhappily sung by those horrible Germans from the Pergola of Florence, against whom I have already expressed my wrath at the time of my arrival in this town. I find they have added to the troupe a second dancer from Milan.

I have just returned, and write to you immediately. The surrender will be effected the day after to-morrow, and the embarkation the day after that. The vessels will set sail the same day. I will tell you all about the ships when I have seen them. Admiral Penrose arrived here to-day in a seventy-four gun ship. We have, there-fore, a fleet of several different nations, who will add to the splendour of the *fête* by the number of their salutes. The Portuguese declare that they will deliver their Prin-cess to their Prince in forty or forty-five days, counting the passage of the strait.

August 11.—I have been on board the Portuguese vessels this morning. They are very fine. The 'Jean VI.' is pierced for ninety guns : it carries only thirty-six, for in every place where there should be one beyond that number they have made a cabin for one of the numerous ladies we are sending to Brazil. The Archduchess's apartment is as well cared for as possible ; it is spacious and furnished with much luxury. She has a fine grand dining-room, a bedroom, dressing-room, and bath. Be-sides all this, there is great tent on the deck, which

would easily hold three hundred people. The 'St. Se-
bastian' is of the same power, and Eltz will consequently
find himself lodged as if he were the ambassador of
Neptune himself. It is difficult to imagine all the
people that these vessels contain: besides the Austrian
ladies, there is the Portuguese Court—that is to say,
three officials of the Court. Each of these gentlemen
has his wife and children with him, and they all have
large families; the Grand-Master, Castel-Melhor, has five
children. The father, mother, and children have been ill
the whole way from Lisbon to this place. The number
of officers of every grade has been tripled. Above all,
remember that a considerable number of cows, calves,
pigs, sheep, four thousand fowls, some hundreds of ducks,
and from four to five hundred canaries, and large and
small birds from Brazil, and you must see that the ark
of old Noah was a child's toy in comparison with the
'Jean VI.' May God preserve this floating world from
shipwreck! The Admiral promises well: he engages
himself to arrive in thirty-five or forty days; you see,
therefore, that the Portuguese can sometimes be prompt.

231. *August* 12.—I have concluded my ceremony
to-day, and *con brio*, I flatter myself. The act of giving
up the Archduchess was very beautiful and very solemn.
Every one assembled at eleven, and a quarter of an
hour afterwards the ceremony commenced. It lasted a
good half hour, and M. de Castel-Melhor received his
royal Princess from my hand—unworthy from this moment to touch hers—as the Portuguese, both men and
women, in kissing it kneel on one knee. At two we had
a grand dinner, which, by the by, did not do honour
to the cook of his Imperial and Royal Apostolic Majesty.
At four we all paid a visit to Admiral Penrose, on the
'Albion,' a superb vessel of seventy-four guns. The

Admiral gave a grand collation to the Archduchesses
and the Grand Duke. The guns fired, and the show was
magnificent, with the immense number of pleasure-boats
that accompanied the Grand Duke, in which were the
princes and great personages. All the men-of-war gave
the royal salute, which is in my opinion one of the most
beautiful sights that the ingenuity of man has invented.
At six we conducted the Prince of Salerno and Mon-
seigneur the Archduke on board their frigate, and left
them there. They left that night with a fair wind for
Naples.

This same ' Albion' was a good deal knocked about
before Algiers. The vessel bears no marks, but there
are a number of men on board who have only one arm :
among others the Admiral's son-in-law, who commands
the ship.

August 13.—To-day at four I conducted the Archduchess on board. We embarked on that grand ship
the ' Jean VI.' As we passed through the port we were
saluted by all the batteries of the fortress, and by an
immense concourse of spectators. It took us half an
hour to reach the ship, which the Archduchess now
saw for the first time. She thought her apartment very
beautiful, and with reason : it would be difficult to make
it more elegant. All the ladies on board are well lodged :
other people as best they may. At six the Archduchess
Marie Louise came and joined us, upon which all the
guns began firing again. The sea was covered with
boats, and the most lovely weather favoured the *fête* ;
at night the two Portuguese vessels were illuminated.
Their outlines stood out marvellously on a sea calm and
smooth as ice. At ten, the wind becoming stronger and
the sea rising very much, we re-embarked on our frail
bark and re entered the port.

The sea having been smooth all the evening, no one of the Princess's suite was sick except one of her maids, who will most probably not accompany her. The wind is contrary, the immense quantities of luggage and different packages must be put in order, so that the squadron will not be able to set sail for four-and-twenty hours. I shall go on board again to-morrow, and at three I shall leave for my baths.

Before I start I will write you a line. The only person to be pitied on board is Madame de Lodron. She can only stand upright between the beams which form the ceiling of the cabin. Her bed is too short, so that it will be wonderful if she does not arrive at Brazil bent double by circumstances instead of age. You may guess what she will be like when she returns.

232. *Baths of Lucca, August* 16.—I have taken leave of my Archduchess. The squadron set sail yesterday morning at half-past five ; before ten it was lost to sight, and our poor ladies were left to their fate. Marie Louise left Leghorn yesterday, after the departure of her sister. She arrived here at mid-day ; dined with me and slept at Marlia, from whence she departed this morning by the Pontremoli road, which she wishes to see, because it will go through a great part of her duchy. A road which exists only on paper is not convenient for travellers ; so she will have to ride fifty miles on horseback. I shall go one of these days by Sarzana to the Gulf of Spezzia. It would take thirty hours for this excursion, which would be interesting to me partly from curiosity : it would be interesting to see the plan of this road, which is of very great importance to us ; and I should visit in passing the quarries of Carrara. I shall sleep at Massa, and the next day I shall return here. I shall choose for this expe-

dition one of the days of interruption ordered in every cure.

233. *At the Waters of Lucca, August* 29.—I shall leave here to-morrow morning and sleep at Massa, after having visited Carrara. The day after to-morrow (the 31st) I shall start early in the morning for Lerici, where I shall see the Gulf of Spezzia, then I shall return to dine at Massa and sleep at Pistoia. On the 1st I shall go to Modena. On the 2nd I shall sleep at Parma, where I shall remain on the 3rd. On the 4th I go as far as Verona, where I shall have a meeting on business with Saurau and Goëss. At Verona I shall decide according to the weather on the route by Bozen or by Ponteba; I shall then also be able to tell you the precise day of my arrival, which will not be before the 11th or later than the 12th September.

My visit here has had the best results for all the affairs which brought me to Italy, and for some which I had not expected, but which came before me during my visit. I regret nothing in my involuntary change of plan, happy as it is in its results. I am leaving a little country which is in every way very interesting, and from which I carry away a remembrance very dear to my heart. I have had the happiness of repairing many faults and follies, and I have prevented new ones being committed in a time more or less remote, which is very important for a country about to pass under another Government. I am more and more convinced that one only does well what one does oneself, and that one ought to be everywhere to do well.

My visitors have dispersed into all parts of Europe. Golowkin started this morning for his retreat in Switzerland. Wallmoden returned here from Leghorn yesterday. He will start to-morrow for Florence, with the intention of reviewing the troops which marched through that place from Naples. Kaunitz will accompany me to the Gulf, and we shall separate at Lucca the day after to-morrow.

Here you have an exact summary of all my doings and all my movements. I leave these places with real regret, but I look forward to seeing you again with infinitely more pleasure, so that the balance is altogether in my favour. One must see this country to know that such a country exists, and this knowledge is a great consolation.

CONCLUSION OF THE COURSE OF BATHS, ETC., IN LUCCA.

234. Metternich to the Emperor Francis, Lucca, August 29, 1817.

234. The course of waters and baths which have had so beneficial an effect on my health being now quite concluded, I shall to-morrow commence my journey back to Vienna.

My first business after my return will be to give your Majesty an account of my travels in Italy, to Rome, Naples, Florence, and Lucca (No. 245). I am glad to think that I have lost neither time nor opportunity of furthering your Majesty's service. It only remains for me to-day to offer your Majesty my most respectful thanks for so graciously permitting me to stay here and devote four whole weeks to my health, which has again given me strength to serve your Majesty with the same feelings of personal devotion your Majesty has long known me to possess.

METTERNICH.

I see with pleasure that the baths of Lucca have been of service to you, and take note of the other information.

FRANCIS.

Fogaras, September 12, 1817.

VISIT TO THE COURTS OF MODENA AND PARMA.

Metternich to his Wife, Modena, September 2.

235. I have arrived here, my dear, after the most charming journey possible. As I told you, I left the baths of Lucca on the morning of the 30th. I arrived at Massa the same day at two o'clock. After resting for half an hour, I went to Carrara, and I have returned to sleep at Massa.

The road from Lucca to Massa is charming. On reaching the summit of the high mountains which form the basin of Lucca, a magnificent plain opens to view of from three to four leagues in extent, and the immense reach of coast along the Mediterranean. The port of Viareggio lies at one's feet, and when it is clear Corsica can be seen directly opposite. The weather was superb. Massa is a small but very well built town; the *château* is large and very well arranged. From my bed I have a boundless prospect. The road from Massa to Carrara is newly made; it is lovely, and you leave the most beautiful country to find yourself plunged in a wild valley not less beautiful because the scenery is of a different kind. You arrive at Carrara, and if you did not know where you were, you would find it out from every stone of the pavement. The worst stone of the country is a beautiful marble. The poor people's houses are of grey or white veined marble. The inhabitants are, for the most part, comfortably off, for everyone can find employment in the numberless workshops connected with sculpture. There are at least thirty studios, large and small, in which may be seen everything that one can desire. The best Roman sculptors have their statues made at Carrara; they choose a block, put it in hand, and finish it afterwards in their studios at Rome. Others come themselves to live for several months at the fountain-head for marble. I found there Rauch and Tieck, two Prussians of great talent, who make the most beautiful things for the King. Among other things, Rauch is now making a copy of the Queen's mausoleum. After having seen everything, I returned to Massa. The next day, at six, I started for Lerici. The view, when you arrive at the top of the mountains, and perceive the Gulf of Spezzia quite under your feet, is of the greatest beauty. I embarked at Lerici, and crossed the Gulf as far as Porto-Venere; from thence I went round the Gulf itself, in order to see it thoroughly, and returned to Massa at four o'clock. I dined there and slept at Lucca. Yesterday I slept at a cursed place called Paulo, in the Apennines, where the Archduke had the kindness to send me a cook and attendants, which assuredly were not unnecessary. I arrived here this morning at eleven, and have spent the day in seeing the few curiosities Modena has to offer.

One thing which strikes me is the extreme difference of the climate of Tuscany from that on this side of the Apennines. I have often been told that Italy proper commences on the south of that chain of mountains, and this is quite true. I here find Lombardy and Venetia again, while Tuscany is quite a contrast. The plants peculiar to the south are not found here. The fact is most striking at Lucca, and above all at Massa. Lucca is farther south than Tuscany, and Massa is like Sicily. The coast being narrow and the mountains acting as reflectors, it never freezes, nor is there even snow at Massa. Oranges grow abundantly in the open fields, and all succulent plants can be acclimatised.

236. *Mantua, September* 5.—I arrived here this evening at nine, and I intend to leave again to-morrow at midday, and sleep at Verona, where the Governors of Milan and Venice are expecting me.

I stayed nearly two days at Parma—that is to say, I arrived there on the third at seven in the evening, and I left to-day at noon for Colorno, where the Archduchess gave me a dinner. Her establishment could not be more comfortable ; her Court is marvellously arranged, and there is neither too much nor too little of anything. Parma in itself contains a number of objects of interest. This town was the cradle of Correggio. The halls and walls are covered with his works ; he is for Parma what Giulio Romano is for Mantua. Nothing can be imagined more enchanting than what he has bequeathed to an age unhappy that it cannot imitate him, but happy to be able to admire him.

237. *Verona, September* 6, 10 *o'clock in the Evening.* — This morning I have seen all there is to see at Mantua, and much even that is not worth taking the trouble to see. I arrived here at three o'clock. At Verona I have been to see all that my unfortunate eye prevented me from seeing in 1816, and I shall leave in an hour with the

intention of staying to-morrow night at Bozen, which
is twelve posts from this.

I write by the present courier to Pepi * at Klagenfurt, where I shall be on the 10th. You will receive
news of me from that town by the courier who orders
my horses, and who will arrive at least fifteen or sixteen hours before me.

I hope I shall find you all in good health. I am
most anxious about the *pauvre petite*,† but I am far
from flattering myself that I shall find her convalescent.
May I but find her better!

Adieu! I have still to get rid of Saurau, Goëss,
and at least twenty people who are in my antechamber.
My travels have ceased to be a pleasure. I am always
tormented with honours, and consequently by annoyances of every description.

---

* Count Joseph Esterhazy, subsequently Metternich's son-in-law.
† Princess Hermine, Metternich's daughter, who still survives.

THE EXISTENCE OF SECTS IN CENTRAL EUROPE.

238. Metternich to Lebzeltern at Petersburg, Florence, June 28, 1817.

238. The progress of sects which are beginning to threaten the peace of many countries, especially in Central Europe, is an object worthy to occupy the attention of Cabinets.

The human mind generally revels in extremes. A period of irreligion, a period in which pretended philosophers and their false doctrines have tried to overturn all which human wisdom has recognised as intimately connected with the eternal principles of morality, has been necessarily followed by an epoch of moral and religious reaction. Now, every kind of reaction is false and unjust, and it is only given to wise and consequently strong men to be neither the dupes of false philosophers nor the sport of false religions. If any one doubted the intimate connection which exists between the moral and material world, proofs would be found in the march and progress of certain maladies of the mind, which present all the symptoms of true epidemics. For some time the Methodists have made great progress in England and America; and this sect, by following the track of all the others, is now beginning to extend its proselytism to other parts of Europe. There are at the present moment, principally in Upper Germany and Switzerland, hundreds of thousands of individuals morally affected by mysticism. The kingdom of Wurtemberg, the Grand Duchy of Baden, con-

tain an entire population, fanatical to the point of
abandoning all the comforts of this world to seek existence and happiness in the holy places which they
regard as the proper preparation for a future life.
There are in Swabia whole families who practise the
greatest self-denial, young men who will do nothing unless they are allowed to emigrate either to Palestine or
to some desert place, where, withdrawing from all
society, they can constitute among themselves a theocratic government more or less similar to that of the
Jews after their departure from Egypt. Some of these
sects have an exclusively moral and religious object.
Others betray decided tendencies towards a political
malady, and as Jacobinism, even extreme as it is, still
admits of further extremes, many of these sects wish
to found their new society on the principles of the
agrarian law.

You will have heard, Sir, of the extraordinary
errors into which the so-called *Poeschlianer* in Upper
Austria have fallen. A ramification of this same sect
has been discovered in the country of Wurzburg, and
young men, and especially young women, have given
themselves up to the most frightful torments, and even
to death, in order to render themselves worthy of Paradise. In Swabia there are a number of Independents,
a religious and political sect, who dream only of an
agrarian law, theocrats who wish for the law of Moses,
and many other associations, each one more fanatical
than the other.

You have doubtless seen in the Swiss newspapers,
and especially in that of Aarau, articles which the
Governments have been forced to publish against the
predications of Madame de Krüdener ; the tendency
of this woman is more dangerous than all the others,

because her predications are all intended to excite the
indigent classes against the proprietors. She invites
the poor to put themselves in the place of the rich,
and her fanaticism no doubt prevents her from perceiving that she thus establishes the most vicious circle
possible, as she would, in fact, thus give to people
formerly rich but now poor, the undoubted right of
ameliorating their condition in their turn, by putting
themselves again in the place of those who had dispos-
sessed them.

It is, doubtless, worthy of the wisdom of the great
Powers to take into consideration an evil which it is
possible, and perhaps even easy, to stifle in its beginning, but which can only gain in intensity in proportion as it spreads. The Courts must not forget that
there exist in Europe disturbers of the public repose,
who are deceived in all their calculations by a firm and
continued progress, and the just and liberal principles
of the great monarchs who have saved Europe. These
men, desperate, and forced from their last intrench-
ments, regard as their own property all questions of
disorder whatever, and it is perhaps reserved for us to
see the editors of the ' *Nain jaune* ' and the ' *Vrai Libéral* '
preach against the vanities of this world, and to see
Carnot and Barère make themselves the apostles of the
New Jerusalem. This subject deserves the most serious
attention ; it is connected with the well-being of society
and the tranquillity of States more closely than is
supposed, and the great Courts should not be slow to
take into consideration the means of checking the
designs of these fomenters of a new kind of revolution.

I beg you, Sir, to sound the Russian Cabinet on
this subject, and to inform us of its ideas. The Courts
will easily find means within their reach, whenever

they come to an understanding with each other about the matter, and it belongs doubtless to the first Powers of Europe to confine their views to measures beyond the reach of the Governments of small States, who can only expel a dangerous individual from so small a territory, and who, if they endeavour to save their own people from the contagion, can only pass it on to their neighbours.

THE BIBLE SOCIETIES AND THE EMPEROR
ALEXANDER.

239. Metternich to the Emperor Francis, Lucca, August 29, 1817.

239. I have to-day the honour to lay before your Majesty a matter perfectly new to diplomacy.

Some days ago a courier arrived from the Russian Cabinet, whom I at first supposed to have been entrusted with some important communications. The value of these communications your Majesty will see from the copy I enclose of Count Nesselrode's letter (No. 240); the second enclosure is my answer to the same (No. 241). Your Majesty has no doubt been long convinced that the Emperor Alexander can never keep to the ordinary ways of men. In 1815 he abandoned pure Jacobinism, but only to throw himself into mysticism; his tendencies being always revolutionary, so also are his religious feelings, and therefore he could not avoid assuming the protectorate of Bible Societies.

I pray your Majesty to regard my answer to Count Nesselrode as meant exclusively for the Emperor Alexander, and so to judge it. If I have entered into many special details, I did this to put an end, at the very commencement, to correspondence between the two Cabinets upon Biblical subjects and religious police measures. The Emperor Alexander will assuredly cease to love and care for such narrow-minded Christians, when I, as your Majesty's Minister, represent your Majesty's views.

I wish to leave no doubt in his mind that his notions of religious enlightenment are not those of your Majesty, and that consequently such questions do not admit so easily of amelioration. It is very hard to determine to what extent this madness will reach. In all the ideas of the Emperor Alexander, the design of proselytising stands first; with this object he wins over Jacobins in Italy and sects in Europe. Now 'the rights of man' give place to 'Bible reading.' It only remains for us quietly yet curiously to see what will be the next answer to my last despatch to Lebzeltern (No. 238), with respect to the dangers of mysticism and the common action of the Cabinets against its miserable results.

METTERNICH.

Nesselrode to Metternich, July, 1817.

240. Count de Stackelberg has informed us, my dear Prince, of your opinion with regard to the interview of the Sovereigns. His despatch crossed ours, and at this moment you doubtless know what we think on this point. You will have seen that we are agreed as to the utility and object of this interview. I may add to-day that we are not less so as to the locality of the conference, as well as to the indispensable necessity of inviting to it one of the most noted members of the French Ministry, and M. de Richelieu in preference to any other. The Emperor is entirely of your opinion, that no capital or even residence would be convenient or useful for the conduct of the affairs which must be treated of there, and this conviction applies even more to small than to great capitals. It seems to him, therefore, that Aix-la-Chapelle or Mannheim would answer every purpose, and his Imperial Majesty will go with pleasure in the course of next year to whichever of the two places is chosen. Before the meeting, but not till within a short time of it, the Emperor will propose an unimportant change. Instead of fixing on the month of June for the interview, he is anxious that it should not take place till some months later, for after the different arrangements his Majesty has made, and some necessary journeys into the interior of Russia, it would be scarcely possible for him to arrive in either of the places above mentioned before September 10 of our style. I do not think, Prince, that this delay can present the least inconvenience, considering that even on November 14, when the third year of occupation expires, we shall still have two months to discuss and decide this important business.

The uniformity which has characterised the opinions put forth by our Cabinets on the subject of France promises happily for the discussions which will take place on this subject. That being decided, the other questions which may be mooted at this meeting of Sovereigns and Ministers would not seem to be of a nature to present insurmountable difficulties. All leads one to hope that it will essentially contribute still further to consolidate the happy agreement which subsists between the principal Powers of Europe. The Emperor is so convinced of the beneficial effect of this grand harmony of principles among the four Courts who have laid down the bases of the general association, that he feels it a matter of regret when, even in questions which are not of general interest, he sees that particular circumstances have provoked, in the States of one of the four sovereigns, measures which do not entirely correspond to the views of the others. Thus, his Majesty has been grieved that you have not allowed the

Bible Society to exist among you, although it is formed
by Protestants, and notwithstanding certain considerations, which his Majesty respects as much as he regrets,
have obliged you to abolish so beneficial an institution,
and above all one so agreeable to the tolerant principles of your august master. I need not tell you, my
dear Prince, how much his Majesty looks forward to
the time he will pass with the Emperor Francis, and if
the interview is of real utility as far as business is concerned, it will be not the less agreeable to the Emperor
to enjoy the consolations of the most cordial and unalterable friendship.

From what Count de Stackelberg tells us, I conclude
you are still in Italy, and I have charged the courier to
join you there. I hope this journey will bring you all
the pleasure you hoped from it. You have my best
wishes. Allow me, Prince, to join, &c. &c.

Metternich to Nesselrode, Lucca, August 20, 1817.

(Supplement to No. 239.)

241. Your courier, my dear Count, joined me here
on August 18, in a corner altogether out of the world,
where I am taking care of my health, of which for some
years it has had much need. I am sure now that I
have done right to take the Lucca waters, as I cannot
take those of Carlsbad. I am very well, and I regret
not having more than ten or twelve days longer to remain in a charming retreat which unites all that can be
desired in the way of health and repose. Imagine to
yourself the most beautiful parts of Switzerland and
Styria under the best Italian climate ; perfect waters,
not so strong, but very much resembling those of

Carlsbad; good and pleasant society, a charming residence, which Madame Elisa Bacciochi certainly did not prepare for me, and you may conceive how I shall soon be regretting the pleasures of the past.

The despatch which I have addressed to Lebzeltern will have proved to you, my dear Count, that our views coincide with those of your august master concerning the interview of 1818. In reply, I may say that the Emperor Francis will repair to Aix-la-Chapelle, or to Mannheim, whichever is most convenient to the Emperor Alexander. The result of the conference will be like all those which have preceded it, the Sovereigns and the Cabinets will part once more with perfect harmony of views and wishes.

I am pleased, my dear Count, to rectify an error which I find in your letter. We have never abolished a Bible Society among us, for one never existed. I believe, however, that I am in a position to assure you that the Emperor will never allow the establishment of one, and the confidence you have in me induces me to acquaint you with his Majesty's reasons.

I begin by referring to our position with regard to the Holy See—that is to say, by assuring you that no Catholic Power is more independent than we are of all direct submission to the Court of Rome. The heir of so many Emperors of Germany, and the nephew of Joseph II., knows what is due to God and his crown. Our ecclesiastical departments perhaps even push their dogmas on the rights of the Crown too far, but if so, the excess is assuredly not in favour of the Court of Rome.

The Catholic Church does not encourage the universal reading of the Bible, and it acts in this respect like a father, placed above the passions and consequently

the storms of life. The Church not only allows but
recommends the reading of the Sacred Books to men
who are enlightened, calm, capable of judging the question. She does not encourage the reading of mystical
books, or of passages full of crimes and obscenities
which the Book of Books contains only too often in histories simple like the first ages, and like all that is true.
For myself, I think the Church is right, and I judge by
the effect which the reading of the Bible has on me at
the age of forty, so different from that which the same
reading produced on me at the age of fifteen and twenty.
I can only compare this difference with that of the impressions produced at different periods of life by the
reading of the classics, the contemplation of the beauties
of nature, or the monuments of art.

I read every day one or two chapters of the Bible:
I discover new beauties daily, and I prostrate myself
before this admirable book; while at the age of twenty
I found it difficult not to think the family of Lot unworthy to be saved; Noah unworthy to have lived;
Saul a great criminal, and David a terrible man. At
twenty, I tried to understand the Apocalypse; now I
am sure that I never shall understand it. At the age
of twenty a deep and long-continued research in the
Holy Books made me an Atheist after the fashion of
Alembert and Lalande, or a Christian after that of
Chateaubriand; now I believe, and do not criticise. I
have read too much, and seen too much, not to know
that reading is not necessarily understanding: that it
would be too bold in me to condemn what through
ignorance, or insufficiency of knowledge, I comprehend
so imperfectly. In a word, I believe, and dispute no
longer. Accustomed to occupy myself with great moral
questions, what have I not accomplished or allowed to

be wrought out by the simple course of nature, before arriving at the point where the Pope and my Curé beg me to accept from them the most portable edition of the Bible? Is it bold in me to take for certain that, of a thousand individuals chosen from the millions of men of which the people are composed, there will be found, owing to their intellectual faculties, their education, or their age, very few who have arrived at the point where I find myself?

Now, my dear Count, in this very simple reasoning, which is also the Emperor's, we find the motive of his Majesty's constant opposition to the introduction of Bible Societies, and in this matter his ideas coincide with those of the Holy Father.

There is another consideration which bears upon this at the present moment, and which seems no less strong than the reasons above set forth. The world just now is sick of a peculiar malady, which will pass away like all other epidemics; this malady is called mysticism. I have recently addressed to Lebzeltern a long despatch on this subject (No. 238), which he has probably shown to you. I assure you that at the present day it would be easier to renew successfully the sermons of Peter the Hermit, than to make individuals attacked with this malady understand that God desires to be served otherwise than by the spilling of blood, and that men are not to be judges of their neighbour's conscience. See what is passing in Germany; see the success of the preaching of Madame de Krüdener, whom you have very wisely sent back to Russia, and of so many other unfortunates who understand the Sacred Books in their own fashion, which, be sure, is not that of God and the Saviour.

It is commonly believed that the Pope does not wish

Catholics to read the Bible, with the view of preventin, their being enlightened. It is possible, and I admit that Gregory VII. and Alexander VI. may have taken this into account; but that was not the reason of the ancient practice of the Church and the moral precepts of the Councils. A Pope may sometimes fear the light, but it is permitted even to the wisdom of the Church to fear the fire: if a Pope does not wish the faithful enlightened, the Church does not wish them to be dazzled. The Pope is wrong, but the Church is right, and the Emperor Francis takes in this matter the side of the Church, while at the same time he despises and rejects all prejudice.

You see, my dear Count, that I am writing to you from a retired place, where I have plenty of leisure to write, and also to forget that you will have scarcely time to read my letter. Throwing myself at the feet of the Emperor, I beg you to rectify the mistake he has made when he supposed that any Bible Society whatever has been suppressed among us.

For the rest, no transaction in the kingdom is more free than the reading of the Bible according to all the different rites. You may find thousands of copies in all the libraries: it is bought, and extracts carefully chosen are distributed in the schools. The Protestants in Austria read it, as everywhere else, in their own language and according to their own version. For myself, I read only Luther's translation, the best which has ever been made in any country, and in a living language.

Adieu! I need not tell you how happy I am to think that there is no longer any such thing as distance in Europe, thanks to the resolution taken by the sovereigns of meeting in person at places where they think they can act together for the common good. This great and noble brotherhood is of far more value than all the treaties, and will ensure for a considerable time what the good Abbé de St. Pierre wished to establish for ever.   Receive, &c.

P.S.—I believe I said in my last despatch to Lebzeltern on the subject of the interview of 1818, that the Emperor my august master would arrange the meeting to suit the convenience of his Majesty the Emperor Alexander.   If I have not said it, I do so now, and I hasten to inform his Imperial Majesty of the project of September 10.

INTENTIONS OF NAPLES WITH REGARD TO THE PRINCIPALITIES OF BENEVENTO AND PONTE-CORVO.

242. Metternich to the Emperor Francis, Lucca, August 17, 1817.

242. The Court of Naples seems to intend to improve the occasion of the death of the Holy Father to lay violent hands on Benevento and Pontecorvo, and it appears that this was one of the principal reasons for the removal of your Majesty's army corps from the kingdom. The Neapolitan Ministry has, in consequence of this idea, engaged in an intrigue in Petersburg, and even ventured to make a similar attempt in England. The first I discovered in a secret manner; the other was told in confidence by Herr Aroust to our ambassador. I undertake to say that these designs shall not succeed.

The very first notion, the groundwork of modern politics is and must be peace, and the fundamental idea of peace is the security of property. If the first Powers of Europe depart from this principle, States which are small and scarcely independent must follow them, willingly or unwillingly.

Whether Benevento and Pontecorvo shall belong to the King of Naples or to the Roman See is immaterial; but that Naples, either by intrigue or force, should in 1817 give the first example of an alteration of possessions settled by the act of Congress—this is a most important question.

I will myself give your Majesty an account of the whole position of affairs, and the explanations of the Cabinets, so soon as they are given. It is not possible to wait for your Majesty's commands, therefore I proceed exactly in the strictest sense of the principles above set forth, because I know they are those of your Majesty.

The Neapolitan intrigue gives me a good opportunity of making all the Courts aware of your Majesty's principles, and the nature of the Imperial politics. If heaven has, in the last few years, richly blessed the efforts of Austria, the world has to thank for this happiness the upright and invariable character of her policy. All that may be attempted by others against it will be shipwrecked. I beg your Majesty to accept this consolation from my hand at the moment of parting, while the consciousness that I have never misled your Imperial Majesty is the highest reward I can receive.

One new and fortunate turn in great political affairs is the vigilance, almost amounting to tension, of England against the views of the Russian Emperor. The conduct of the latter, and his interference in the internal affairs of Spain have brought about this advantage. England, France, and Prussia draw closer to us, and we have beaten Russia and Spain out of the field by the Parmesan victory. I will very shortly despatch a courier to your Majesty with information on these matters. Your Majesty is at the present time the only preserver of peace in Europe ; and not peace merely, but all forms of it lie in your Majesty's hands.

MATTERNICH.

God grant that I may be able to secure peace in

Europe during my own life and, if possible, to my successors. Your greatest pride and consolation must surely be to have conducted me to the position in which things now are.

FRANCIS.

ORGANISATION OF THE CENTRAL ADMINISTRATION IN AUSTRIA.

243. Metternich to the Emperor Francis, October 27, 1817.
244. Report.

243. May it please your Majesty! For some time your Majesty has been pleased favourably to regard my views on certain points in the internal administration, and to-day I consider it my duty to touch upon the first steps in the execution of this very important matter.

In the enclosure (No. 244) your Majesty will find the plan worked out, which, as a first draft, is slight, but still contains, I believe, all that is really important.

Your Majesty knows from long experience that all desire for unnecessary alteration and dangerous disturbance is far from me. In my Report there is nothing glaring, nothing revolutionary, not a single dangerous principle. I uphold order, because, from an administration internally too complicated, disorder must ensue. In a kingdom like Austria, where so much has been prepared by the glorious government of a Maria Theresa, and the theoretical experiments of your Majesty's predecessor—in a kingdom in which every occasion proves that true public spirit animates the majority of the nation ; lastly, in a kingdom where your Majesty comes forward in your own august person as the most successful lawgiver for the welfare of the people—it requires no extraordinary efforts to act for the general good. The cause of the existing evil (and where is there none?) must be sought and found, and the result of this attempt must be set forth in simple phrases. This work I have undertaken as soon as I felt myself sufficiently enlightened and strong enough for the task.

Everything that I now bring before your Majesty I bring as the result of a conviction which—standing the test of a long self-imposed probation—has grown in my mind from the strongest evidence. Your Majesty will find in my work nothing new to your Majesty. All the points now shown in a connected form I have brought before your Majesty separately in many confidential conversations; the defect in the administration and the means of remedy have long been evident to me, but I hesitated to express without consideration and proof what must have such important consequences.

With every day my mind has gradually limited itself to rendering the propositions more simple. I have looked into everything and considered everything, and the result of what I venture to call my *certainly true propositions* is, without any doubt, extremely gratifying.

No time is less suited than the present to bring forward in any State reforms in a wide sense of the word. But, happily, the machine of State is constructed on such good principles that, in a wide sense, there is really nothing in the machine itself to be altered. Everything that I have proposed concerns the first principles of the whole. And here I do not venture on one reform tending to the overthrow of normal forms, but merely a regulation of the parts, and those, indeed, the already existing organic parts of the central authority of the State.

In my plan I am intentionally silent on the future condition of Hungary. This subject, one of the most important which can occupy the attention of the State, is of so complicated a nature that it cannot be handled in a fragmentary manner. Your Majesty has heard the proposal for the subversion of the Hungarian Government often and boldly expressed. Even in the year 1811, at a period in which such an undertaking would inevitably have caused the overthrow of the monarchy—and in 1813, when, if not so dangerous, even then every energetic expression of it would have been impossible— this question was brought forward as if it were a mere matter for peremptory decision. If I at that time expressed myself against the idea, I did not at all mean to deny that, with time and opportunity, with cooler reflection and more undisturbed repose, the great work of the *civilisation* of Hungary—for this must first of all be the question—should be brought forward with due effect. The few remarks which I have made on the connection of my ideas on the central government of the whole monarchy with the position of Hungary are indisputable. In proportion as the action of the supreme power is strengthened will the obstacles disappear which even now are so powerful against a more reasonable and, for Hungary itself, invaluable alteration in her administration and constitution.

That by the carrying out of my proposals every evil will be avoided in the future, I am far from expecting. But that a reliable Government, resting on enlightened principles, set forth in the clear words which are the necessary consequence of clear ideas, smooths the way for all good, while, on the contrary, a confusion of ideas in the Government stands in the way, is not to be denied. Besides, there is no human institution which, if it rests on clear fundamental principles, does not improve as it progresses ; while a tendency to still greater inability and confusion is the inevitable result of a contrary position.

And in this truth, confirmed as it is unmistakably by the experience of all ages, lies one of the chief reasons which must incline your Majesty to enter upon a firm organisation of the very foundation of the administration.

The Government, as it is at present, rests in its daily working too entirely on the principle of centralisation. The machine of government goes on, because its springs are well put together and well guided, and because there is at the head of the administration a monarch capable of ruling. How little this would be the case on the occurrence of that sad catastrophe which in the course of nature must befall the monarchy is known to your Majesty ; for your Majesty is as man and as father what your Majesty is as monarch—clear and unprejudiced in opinion and judgment ! Your Majesty is called to look forward and provide for that time, and to this end there is but one road which promises success.

Under your Majesty's eyes, under your Majesty's fostering hand, the chief Government must be organised in such a manner, as may best preserve it from going astray, or at least not make it easy to do so. Let your Majesty only think what would be the present progress of affairs without your Majesty's presence, without the influence on which that progress is almost exclusively founded. But the strength and durability of a great Government rests not alone on the establishment of principles; at first, (and for States, years are often no more than moments) not only the chief leader, but all the instruments must grow accustomed to the new sphere of action. Your Majesty has done nothing for posterity even if during the latter period of life your Majesty should pass some great administrative measure intended for the future; for the only possible guarantee for the duration of a moral work lies, not merely in principles, but in the choice of means for the execution and maintenance of the new system. A feeble successor to your Majesty would then find it as difficult to overthrow a sound and well-established Government as it would be impossible for him to produce or inaugurate one.

Your Majesty will be pleased to accept this my humble Report with the same gracious favour of which I have already received so many proofs. It expresses my deepest conviction shortly and simply, as alone is worthy of my aims, and of your Majesty's comprehensive insight.

Report.

244. The daily observation of the course of public affairs in the monarchy, affords proof that, with a number of good laws and administrative rules, the Government still does not possess that degree of strength which constitutes the true idea of a monarchy. The cause of this want of strength is, I believe, confined to the organisation of the supreme administration. To discover without prejudice how this evil became possible and in what it consists we must above all consider the principles of the formation of the collective monarchy into its present whole. This idea clearly and truly set forth will make evident the means of improvement.

In political and administrative respects, the Austrian Empire, from its numerous constituent parts, forms a federal State under one common monarch.

The greater portions of the monarchy—Hungary, Bohemia, the two Austrias, Transylvania, Croatia, &c.— have old and peculiar constitutions, which are more or less in force, but still always exist. New additions, such as Tyrol, Vorarlberg, Galicia, the two Italian kingdoms, &c., even those which were ancient possessions of the Archducal house, have had permanent constitutions granted by their monarchs, with due regard to their former circumstances and present needs. These countries, so different in climate, speech, manners and customs, had their own crowns, which were all borne by the Austrian Emperor, and three separate coronations took place on his accession to the Government.

These circumstances are undoubtedly worthy of the deepest consideration of the Government, for in them are seen the separate nationalities of the different parts of the Imperial State. In this as well as in many other respects the position of the Austrian monarch is like that of no other.

In its political and geographical aspects the Austrian State forms an open country in the midst of the European continent. Surrounded on all sides by greater or smaller neighbours, it lacks, from the highest point of view, a connected military frontier. The monarchy must consequently seek in itself, in the common feeling of its peoples, in their political, military, and financial administration, its greatest strength.

Convinced of this truth, I am none the less sure that, if Austria requires a greater expenditure of strength for her self-preservation than any other European State

(Prussia excepted), with us, as ever, true and independent strength is only found as the result of an intelligent, definite, and well-arranged system of government.

In following out this idea, there are for Austria but two positions worthy of consideration :—

Either the entire merging of all the separate parts of the monarchy in one single form of government ;

Or, the careful regulation of the reasonable long-existing differences sanctioned by speech, climate, manners, and customs in the various districts of the monarchy, under a strong, well-organised Central Government.

The idea of thorough incorporation was the foundation of the Emperor Joseph's system of government. During his time the boldest theories were launched. He made an attempt at fusion, and a few years sufficed to see it repealed.

Although the unity of all the executive means which an administration has at command may be the most active and convenient form of power for a Government, certainly the thorough amalgamation of such heterogeneous parts can only be the result of a mighty revolution ; or at best, a Government can, under such circumstances, only escape the dangers of a revolution by the greatest consistency and energy. This truth is undeniably proved by the events of the three last decades.   How difficult a real system of fusion must be in a kingdom which contains so many different languages and races of people, whose provinces were mostly brought together by conquest, follows from the nature of things. The miscarriage of the attempt, and especially its entire repeal by the Emperor Joseph, renders the case still more difficult, so that I am quite convinced that a forcible system of fusion is an empty and dangerous hypothesis, and since something of the kind is now necessary, I desire to bring forward the *Idea of a Central Representation of the nation.*

Only the investigation of the question remains—In the Austrian kingdom how can the greatest possible increase of strength be attained—

(*a*) In respect to the nationalities of the populations and their existing constitutions;

(*b*) With the least possible modification of the present forms of government.

I lay it down as an undeniable position that a Government in order to be strong needs more than good laws. Besides sound principles, its mode of action must be in harmony with its position, and this is not the case in Austria. The monarchy consists, as we have said, of the most heterogeneous elements. This heterogeneous character, however, is regarded unequally, sometimes insufficiently, sometimes too decidedly, even on the very steps of the throne itself. Hungary and its annexed States enjoy privileges which even tend to impair the action of the great machine of State, while other provinces divided from each other both by name and constitution, lose their distinctive features only too entirely in the existing central administration.

Hence for Hungary there arose a privilege which nearly amounted to the idea of independence, while the nationality of the other Austrian States was lost by friction between the Government and the provinces. By its present organisation the supreme German power withstood the undeniable tendency to fusion, while the machine of State itself—as I have shown above—rested and must rest on an entirely opposite principle, in accordance with its best interests. This tendency, arising as it did from the organisation of the chief authorities, became powerless by continued friction; under its influence the healthful object of the centralisation of administrative power degenerated into a mania for details, which would destroy the spirit of the highest administration. This evil can be checked by a word of the monarch, by one single measure; and the disappearance of most of the present difficulties will give the Government that degree of strength and activity which it requires for the good of the monarchy. As I do not believe that a true and enlightened centralisation is possible in the ways hitherto attempted, it is the object of my endeavours to attain this end, and that, too, by a much easier path.

From a certain stage downwards the monarchy is very well and wisely organised. The arrangement of its provinces, its organisation in *circles*, &c., could certainly not be replaced by any other with greater respect for the nationalities of its subjects, or greater care and regard for justice and mercy in its administration. But in the very highest stage of all is the Government itself, the centre of all power, and of this only we here speak.

Good must follow from an explanation of the official positions in the Government, grounded on fundamental principles clearly put forth and practically employed.

The supreme power in every great monarchy is subdivided in the branches of the administration, which are separate offices, yet all united for one end. These spheres of action are, in modern times, in which the public feeling busies itself principally with political and administrative subjects, certainly better understood and explained than they are in most States, and perhaps than they ever were before.

The different branches or departments of business in every great State may be properly divided as follows :—

1. Foreign affairs.
2. Internal administration (home affairs)
3. Finance.
4. Military affairs.
5. The administration of justice.
6. The police.
7. The Board of Trade (*Rechnungs-Controle*).

It is hardly possible to think of any business which does not fall under one or other of these heads.

The business in each of these separate departments may be divided into two parts :—

a. Affairs as seen from the highest—that is, the moral—point of view.

b. The executive, or technical part.

In every well-ordered body these two parts must be separately considered, and the technical part, as containing the means of execution, is ever closely connected with the moral part, though always subordinate to it.

In this sense the appointment of a Finance Minister, who already supplies the place of the President of the Chamber of Commerce, is an arrangement which answers extremely well. The immediate and natural sphere of the Finance Minister cannot be questioned.

A similar arrangement—the inevitable consequence of every improved organisation—should now take place in the administration of home affairs. To express my ideas plainly on this reform, I can only ground them on the above-mentioned principles.

I begin with the axiom that the system of fusion, requiring as a first measure the renaming of the kingdoms and provinces (as happened in France at the beginning of the Revolution), is excluded from all consideration. On this hypothesis the following arrangements seem to be the most suitable :—

1. The head of the department of Home Affairs shall receive the title of High Chancellor and Home Minister.

2. Under him four Chancellors, forming with him the Ministry of Home Affairs. Their sphere is marked out by the nationalities of the provinces and the relations arising from local considerations.

To these may be nominated :—

a. A Chancellor for Bohemia, Moravia, and Galicia, under whose care these countries should be placed.

b. An Austrian Chancellor, under whom should be the Austrian provinces above and below the Ems, Styria, the Innviertel, Salzburg, and Tyrol.

c. An Illyrian Chancellor, over Illyria and Dalmatia.

d. An Italian Chancellor, over Lombardy and Venice.

In this organisation the Home Minister is the guardian and representative of the unity of the Government.

Each Chancellor in the Ministry represents the immediate affairs of the provinces under him. He represents in those provinces the idea of the unity of Government and maintains its principles as much as possible under the given circumstances.

Every Chancery (*Kanzellariat*) must have the necessary number of officers of different grades.

All the fundamental and higher points of administration will be brought before the Home Minister in conference. The immediate arrangement of the administration belongs to each Chancellor in his own sphere.

It is evident that by this organisation the Hungarian

and Transylvanian Chancery will be reduced from the high position they take at present to a share in the general administration.

In this course I see the first step to a gradual reformation in both these countries. But since in the present work I do not wish to confuse the real and immediate improvements easy of accomplishment with the far more extensive and difficult reforms required in Hungary and Transylvania, I will enter no further into this matter.

As in the Chamber of Commerce so in the administration of home affairs the evil exists that matters, which, though of the most different forms, yet belong to one and the same branch of the administration, are, for want of centralisation, the business of inferior officers or managed still more injuriously by means of Reports from the different countries (*Länder-Referate*). It is necessary for the general good that these matters should be brought under proper direction. . . .

It is not, however, at all my intention to carry out every possible improvement without preparation, as it were at one blow, and—as is unhappily the case at present—without a strong administrative Government. My Report is to-day confined to the following measures:—

1. That your Majesty will vouchsafe to decree the formation of Ministries, and first of all, in addition to the existing Ministries for Foreign Affairs and Finance, a Home Minister and a Minister of Justice. Neither the Police nor the Board of Trade seem to me at all suitable to be raised to Ministries, and they may retain the title of Presidents without injury.

2. The organisation of the Home Ministry under a Minister and four Chancellors.

The natural and inevitable consequence of the first measure will be the organisation of this Ministry in all its different departments.*

METTERNICH.

* It is known that in consequence of this Report a single high office was established under the name of the ' United Chancery ' (*vereinigte Hofkanzlei*), which added to the Bohemian, Galician, and Austrian, the Illyrian-Italian provinces, hitherto under the *Central-Hofcommission*, and brought them all under one common head.

The Royal Patent referred to described this measure, declaring that ' This Supreme Central Home Ministry shall, in accordance with our system of unity, lead all countries and peoples to the same individual and general welfare, bring the public obligations into equal proportions, spread culture and education on just and uniform principles, and at the same time observe and foster, with the greatest tenderness, the various peculiarities and differences in speech, manners and customs, climates and hereditary distinctions.

' As a result of these principles, we are led to the formation of one great Chancery, and to appoint and nominate, under our Home Minister—

' A Bohemian-Moravian Silesian,
' An Austrian-Illyrian,
' A Lombard-Venetian, and
' A Galician Chancellor.'

Count Saurau was at the same time appointed Home Minister and High Chancellor; Count Lazansky was made Chancellor for Bohemia, Moravia, and Silesia; Freiherr von Geiszlern was Austrian-Illyrian Chancellor; and Count Mellerio the Lombardo-Venetian Chancellor.

In the same year Prince Metternich wished to proceed with the reform of the central administration. It was part of his plan to reorganise the provincial Diets (*Provinzial stände*) and to form from these bodies a central representation of Austria—a *Reichsrath*. In the above Report mention is made of a ' central representation,' and if it is not placed in the most favourable light, yet the connection of such an institution with the greater centralisation of the administration is pointed out. The attentive reader will not fail to observe the prudent care with which the minister evidently strives to preserve his proposals for reform from any appearance of novelty. But that Metternich's ideas of reform were not limited to the creation of a Home Ministry is proved, beyond doubt, by evidence in the Chancellor's own hand of a subsequent period. The passage alluded to was apparently written for the unhappily imperfect ' Autobiography,' and is as follows:—

' While I declared [it was in the year 1817] as a fact defying all scrutiny, that the Austrian Empire possesses peculiar and exceptional conditions of existence and prosperity, and that it could only be a question of using, not removing, those conditions, the problem was, as far as I was concerned, limited to the discovery of the forms to be used and the means of carrying them out. The first is expressed in the idea of the strengthening of the Central Government; the other led me to the point whether this increase of strength was to be found in centralisation according to the French idea, or by a consideration of the separate parts of the kingdom in relation to the Imperial power. My answer could not be doubtful. The question was of the preservation, not of the disintegration, of the Empire, and I took my stand on the principle of the legislative regulation of the parts and the simultaneous strengthening of the Central Government in its legislative and executive departments.

'In those parts there exist representative Diets which must be formed into one central body. The task was then, in spite of the difficulties inseparable from such a form, easier to define than the present state of things. I propose, therefore, a revision of the Diets in order to form a Reichsrath, which would extend from the centre outwards—from the Emperor to the landed proprietors selected—to be completed by delegates from the different Diets. To this new central point the scrutiny of the budget and every law will be submitted which concerns the community.

'The Emperor Francis saw the importance of the thing, but put off its examination from year to year and, after his recovery from a severe illness which he had in the year 1827, declared his firm determination to take my Report into consideration. At the end of the year 1834 the Emperor told me that he reproached himself for not having carried out the matter, but that before the end of the year 1835 the declaration should be made. Two months afterwards he was no more!'

We must confine ourselves to these extracts, for we have not succeeded in finding the Report to the Emperor Francis here alluded to, which is hardly to be wondered at, considering the dilatory conduct to which the matter was exposed for eighteen years.—ED.

THE INTERNAL CONDITION OF ITALY, AND MET-TERNICH'S DESIRE FOR A NATIONAL GOVERN-MENT OF THE LOMBARDO-VENETIAN KINGDOM.

245. A memorandum by Metternich to the Emperor Francis.
246. Metternich to the Emperor Francis (Report), Grätz, November 3, 1817.

245. Your Majesty will vouchsafe to remember that in October of last year I took occasion to lay before your Majesty the necessity of becoming acquainted with the action of the Government and the particular causes of the general dissatisfaction of the Italian States.

My principal object was, first, if necessary, to be able to act beneficially on the Government; secondly, from the data collected, to gain a firmer footing for administrative principles in our own Italian provinces.

At the same time I took the liberty of getting well-informed men to go to Florence, Modena, Parma, and Rome, and bring reports to your Majesty for this purpose. Your Majesty vouchsafed to look favourably on my views, and allowed me to accept from Counts Diego Guicciardi and Tito Manzi the offer I had invited them to make.

These gentlemen have now returned from their travels. Tito Manzi cannot but confess that everything which he saw and heard during his mission in Italy convinced him of the great and general dissatisfaction there prevailing. He divides the evils weighing upon Italy into two classes, namely :—

General trouble, from which no State in the peninsula is free; and

Particular grievances of each of these States.

Manzi ascribes the first of these to two principal causes : one resting, according to him, on nature itself, which has for three years been very severe on this country ; the second he ascribes to the results of the conquest, which, by overthrowing political order, has shattered the foundations of the public welfare.

On closer enquiry into the particular grievances, Manzi described the attitude of the separate States given back to Italy—rulers being set against the people, as well as the latter against their Governments. He began with Naples and Sicily, then came to Rome, and from thence to Tuscany, Lucca, Modena, and Parma, concluding with Piedmont.

Your Majesty will permit me to follow the same course.

Naples and Sicily.

Manzi regrets that Austria did not support the party which strove to raise Prince Leopold to the throne of Naples, and had not made the division of the two crowns conditional on the union of that Prince with the Archduchess Clementine. The prejudice of the ex-minister of an illegal Government for these revolutionary ideas ought not to cause surprise, and it is quite natural that he should look at Austria's advantage in this matter after the fashion of Napoleon, Murat, &c. But what would have been useful and serviceable for them would be prejudicial to a legitimate Government, whose policy must rest on the indestructible foundations of justice and integrity.

Your Majesty will vouchsafe to remember that in the course of the winter of 1815, the attempt was made by the ambassador, Prince Jablonowski to find out the point of view from which his Court regarded these ideas ; being ordered, however, to reject immediately any such communication, as so contrary to the principles of your Majesty that our ambassador dare not venture to bring it to your Majesty's knowledge.

It is not surprising that Tito Manzi, who knows nothing of the negotiations which accompanied the Act of Union of the two kingdoms, dwells on the unpleasant impression which this measure has produced on the Sicilian nobles, who had wished to be released from the constitution of Lord Bentinck, on condition of a complete reinstatement in their rights and privileges. The Neapolitan Government, on the other hand, intended the overthrow of Bentinck's constitution, because it was not in itself adequate to the end proposed, and because it tied their hands. For the same reasons also they could not wish to restore the old, and this the less because Sicily, instead of contributing in just proportion to the burdens of the State, was financially, under both constitutions, itself a considerable burden. By the union of the two kingdoms, however, the Government secured the great financial advantage of a gradual introduction of the Neapolitan administration into Sicily.

Your Majesty will remember that the happy conclusion of these negotiations was a great cause of satisfaction to King Ferdinand IV. He owes it also unquestionably to the interposition of your Majesty with the English Government. It was no easy task to induce the British ministry to surrender a constitution drawn up by Lord Bentinck, and introduced into Sicily under English influence—a question which, as it was a Parliamentary question, was exposed to twofold difficulties. But it suited our interest to enter into the designs of the Neapolitan Court, and thus prevent Sicily from serving as an example to the kingdom of Naples subsequently, and also to prevent the numerous constitutionalists of this kingdom (supported by this example) from seeking to induce the ministry to give them also a representative form of government. The union of the two kingdoms was, moreover, the surest means of rendering impotent the awkward reports which were current with regard to Austria's design of placing Prince Leopold on the throne of Naples, and made the separation of the two crowns impossible for the future.

These were the grounds which moved your Majesty to support the present negotiation. To your Majesty King Ferdinand owes its happy termination, but he and his ministry attributed the greatest importance to the carrying out of this change, and to the declaration of Austria and England that it would not be opposed by these two Powers. It would, then, be false and ungrateful of the King to wish it to be believed that he was constrained or forced to these measures by your Majesty. Such an assertion could be believed by no one, and if it were really made would redound only to the disadvantage of the King himself.

Rome.

It is certainly remarkable that a former minister of Murat's should do such full justice to Cardinal Consalvi and his views as is done by this Tito Manzi. Whether he speaks of him well or ill, both are with foundation ; and although one may regret that the Cardinal-Secretary supported his own work so feebly and was himself the cause of the *motu proprio* failing so entirely, nevertheless the great service cannot be denied him of having had the courage to inaugurate in the States of the Church a form of government and principles well suited to prevent (at least during the course of his ministry) a violent reaction which would have been dangerous to all the Italian States.

If the course of the business of the administration was often interrupted by the disorder existing in the bureaux, yet it cannot be denied that the action of Cardinal Consalvi and the strength of his policy were successful in securing the peace of the capital, getting rid of the brigands or holding them in check, and by means of a very small armed power (a body of from 15,000 to 17,000 well-clothed and well-disciplined men) making the Government respected.

The Cardinal's political principles are known to your Majesty, and Manzi does him injustice, I think, when he doubts the sincerity of his feeling for Austria. Cardinal Consalvi is certainly as much devoted to us as the head of the Papal Ministry from his office can be, and certainly no less sincerely desirous to remove the hindrances which arose in consequence of Prince Kaunitz's negotiations (No. 249) with the Papal See, for he shared our feeling of the necessity (for the maintenance of peace in Italy, and the support even of the Papal Government) of a thorough agreement between the Roman and Austrian Courts.

Monsignor Pacca, Governor of Rome, and Head of the Police, is, according to Cardinal Consalvi, of all the Government officials, the most important. He seems to be a man of great resources, strong character, and much activity, but perhaps somewhat too severe. He would, if he were not restrained, be inclined to take energetic measures against the dissidents (*Sectirer*), and especially against the adherents of the last Government. Happily we succeeded in bringing him into confidential relations with us, and we made use of them to persuade him to a similar course with ours in police business.

As Manzi remarked, there can be no doubt that in the Legations, and especially in Bologna, there existed a so-called Austrian party, which cherished the hope that your Majesty would on the death of the Holy Father take this province under your protection. During my residence in Tuscany an attempt was even made to gain me over to this. I, however, rejected this idea as contrary to your Majesty's principles and opposed to the late transactions. And, in fact, in spite of all the advantages that a union of the Legations with the Lombardo-Venetian kingdom seemed to offer, I was far from being convinced that this union would be a real gain for the monarchy. I believe rather that Bologna, from the day when it belonged to Austria, would have become the centre of the opposition party against the Government in Italy, and that the same unquiet spirit which now led to the desire to join us would be turned against us as soon as Bologna came into our possession.

Tuscany.

Unpleasant as is the picture drawn by Manzi of the present state of Tuscany, of the weakness of the ministry, of the individuals composing the Archducal ministry, and of the sadly altered feeling in this country, I cannot but feel that it is quite a true one. The data which I was able to collect during my stay in Florence, the results of my own observations, my conversations with the Grand Duke and his ministers, convinced me that no State in the world is more easy to govern and make happy than Tuscany. It would likewise depend on your Imperial Highness, even while materially lightening the burdens of the people, to become the richest monarch in Europe. Manzi calculates the revenues of these States alone at twenty million livres. I reserve to myself to show your Majesty in a separate Report that the revenue amounts to nearly double that sum. With such comparatively important resources, one cannot but be astonished that the Archduke's treasury is always empty, that the loans to the fiscal board make twelve per cent., that many useful public institutions lie idle, that all classes of the population are more or less discontented ; and, lastly, that a land so highly favoured by nature should have lost even the hope of a happier existence.

I will report verbally to your Majesty on this matter, and on the little I was able to effect during my residence in this interesting country, as well as give an account of my efforts to prepare the way for more confidential relations between the two Courts.

Lucca.

Some months ago (May 1817), I was able to lay before your Majesty, through Lieutenant Werklein, Manzi's views on the causes of the discontent in this country, as well as on its government. The provisional Governor may have allowed himself to be urged by his subordinates to many false measures ; but yet he is a worthy man, who by his zeal, activity, and integrity, has a claim on your Majesty's favour.

At my departure I had the opportunity of observing that all classes of the population, although they desired the termination of the provisional (Austrian) Government, did full justice to our principles—indeed, that they even reckoned on our support if their future ruler tried to govern them at all in imitation of the Madrid Court.

Modena.

The short time (twenty-four hours) that I stayed in Modena did not suffice to show me whether and how far Manzi's assertion of the dissatisfaction reigning there among all classes was well founded, and whether it was true that the Archduke does not enjoy the affection of his subjects. I should be more inclined, however, to suppose that there is some exaggeration in Manzi's opinion of the administration and the ruler of this country. If the country is really badly governed, which I am far from positively asserting, certainly the fault must be with the Archduke, for he alone administers the government. To judge from some conversations with him, I should, however, suppose that he carries on this administration more like a wealthy and prudent landowner than as a sovereign.

What Manzi observes of the general discontent may arise from some cause easy of explanation. This little country furnished the greater number of the distinguished servants of the State in the late Kingdom of Italy, and many of them had reached the highest places in that Government. Deprived of their offices, without prospect for the future, they regret their former influence, their emoluments—in fact, they have lost all that nourishes and flatters human ambition. The latter circumstance made it necessary to return to their fatherland, where they were but coldly received by their sovereign, and apparently subjected to a strict observation; hence they naturally formed in Modena a centre of opposition to the present Government. Now, however, the Duke begins, in spite of his prejudice against the whole class, to give some of them civil and military appointments.

It is certain that between the Duke of Modena and the Roman Court, or, more properly, between that Prince and the Cardinals, close relations exist, and that this powerful party in Rome exercises in Modena a real influence detrimental to our interests in Italy. There is also no doubt that the Courts of Modena and Turin are in daily confidential agreement, which, far from being favourable to us, is intended to undermine our influence in Italy. Lastly, it is not to be denied that the Duke of Modena takes a part in complete opposition to our interests, which are, indeed, difficult to be comprehended by any Prince not of the House of Austria. But your Majesty knows him, and that he holds obstinately to his opinions; hence I believe that to attack these too sharply would risk the danger of alienating him from us permanently. These considerations led me, during my very short stay in Modena, not to touch on so delicate a question, but to confine myself to laying the foundations of the happiest relations.

Parma.

If my residence of two days in Parma was too short to learn the course of the Government there, its defects and its advantages, as well as those of the persons entrusted with its direction, and to gain a right idea of the grounds of the dissatisfaction and its influence on public feeling, yet this short stay was sufficient to convince me that Manzi's deplorable picture is in many respects too strongly drawn. Since the removal of Count Magaroli, her Excellency the Archduchess devotes herself eagerly and anxiously to business. She presides over the ministerial councils, and the final decision rests with her.

Parma is not a fertile district; its commercial resources are unimportant. It has suffered much of late
years from the passage of troops, from the want so
prevalent in Italy, and, lastly, from an epidemic resulting
from this distress. It is therefore possible that the
public burdens are not connected with the present position of affairs; moreover, the finances do not seem to be
so badly managed as Manzi describes, since I have found
a balance in your Majesty's coffers, in spite of the expenses of a too costly army, an expensive Court, and
large assistance to the public institutions.

Piedmont.

Of all the Italian Governments the Piedmontese is
indisputably the one which calls for the most anxious
attention. This country unites in itself all the different
elements of discontent, and from this point of view I
find Manzi's representation correct.

His remarks on the anxiety which the arming of
this Power must create are not so just. The King of
Sardinia, indeed, constantly occupies himself since his
restoration with the formation of his army, and chiefly
with the preparation of the means of bringing it quickly
to a strength out of all proportion to the population and
finances of his States. However, the results have not
so far corresponded with his efforts or his expectations.

I observe, too, that notwithstanding the widespread
and well-founded grounds for dissatisfaction in the Sardinian States, and even in Genoa, which bears the yoke
of this Power with great impatience, and does not conceal its annoyance, a revolutionary movement is not to
be feared in this country.

Consequently, it is the intriguing policy of the Turin
Cabinet alone which requires our careful observation.

Your Majesty will have seen on many occasions that my attention has been directed to it, and that I have given this Cabinet itself distinctly to understand that none of its intrigues are unknown to us, and that we shall find means to prevent their success.

There is no doubt that the Turin Cabinet entertains ambitious views which can only be gratified at the expense of Austria. I had lately the opportunity of giving the Cabinet of St. James's a convincing proof of this, and urged them to join us in keeping watch on the proceedings of the Turin Cabinet. To this our efforts must, in my opinion, for the moment be limited. The Sardinian Court is, especially since its union with Genoa, too much bound to maintain its relations with England to venture on a political course contrary to that Power. This powerful motive must therefore weaken the ambitious designs entertained against us by the Sardinian Court long enough for us to ally ourselves closely with Great Britain, and we shall always have this counterpoise also to oppose to its intrigues at the Russian Court. In addition to which the king's present Ministry neither appreciates nor enjoys the confidence of the other branches of the Government; it is divided in its views and intentions.

Under such circumstances, the present position of things in Sardinia affords us the means by constant observation of its movements, and a continuance in our own straightforward and proper course, of rendering innocuous the feeling entertained against us by that Government.

The Affairs of the Dissidents in Italy.

I have for some time been certain of the existence in Italy of several secret fraternities, which, under different names, foster a spirit of excitement, discontent, and opposition. The designs and resources of these, their leaders and relations to each other and to foreign nations, are all points needful for us to discover in order to form an estimate of the dangers which may grow out of them for the peace of Italy. Two years of active and unbroken observation convinced me that the actual existence of these different sects ·cannot be denied, and if their tendency is mischievous and in opposition to the principles of the Government, on the other hand they fail to enlist leaders of name and character, and lack central guidance and all other necessary means of or ganising revolutionary action. In design and principle divided among themselves, these sects change every day and on the morrow may be ready to fight against one another. Manzi is here, I believe, quite right when he observes that the surest method of preventing any one of them from becoming too powerful is to leave these sects to themselves.

If these explanations are for the moment less disquieting, yet we must not look with indifference on such a mass of individuals, who, more or less adversaries of the existing order of things, may easily be led to disturb the public peace, especially if it is ever united by the alluring pretext of Italian independence.

England has for the moment relinquished these chimeras, and since she gave her consent to the union of Genoa with Piedmont and the withdrawal of the Bentinck constitution in Sicily, she has almost entirely lost the confidence of the Independents.

If we can accept Manzi's idea, the Roman Court secretly protects the sect of Guelphs, and makes use of the assistance of Modena to counterbalance the influence of Austria in Italy and extend its own. He thinks,

79268

too, that this Court constantly trembles lest disturbances should break out in these States caused by the Independents and numerous adherents of the late Kingdom of Italy. The present Papal Ministry is too enlightened not to see that no Italian State has more reason to guard against a revival of the agitation than the States of the Church, and that their greatest strength lies in close relations with Austria, and I cannot believe they will attempt to use against neighbours so dangerous a weapon, which may be turned against themselves.

France, whose policy has always consisted in upholding a party in Italy to paralyse the influence of Austria, has under her present Government too great an interest in holding in check the revolutionary elements which are obstructive to her own government, to encourage and support similar elements in foreign countries.

Spain, not hitherto of much political importance, will at first confine herself to gaining some adherents in Lucca and Parma who certainly do not belong to the class of Liberals.

Our anxiety regarding foreign influence can, therefore, only reasonably fall on either Prussia or Russia.

Prussia is too seriously engaged with the moral position of her own provinces to turn her attention outwards. The influence of Austria in Germany is necessary to her, and our relations with the Prussian Court exempt us from any anxiety lest, under present circumstances, she should encourage complications in Italy.

As to Russia, though I do not permit myself to entertain any suspicion against the feelings and views of the Emperor Alexander, which I believe to be sincere and pure, I am yet very far from being easy as to the spirit and the principles revealed by his ministers and innumerable agents in Italy. It is unknown to me whether the latter are or are not provided with instructions from their Court in this respect. In either supposition it is clear that they are actively employed in a way quite contrary to the interests of Austria, and furnish their Court, if ever a war breaks out between Russia and Austria, with the means of preparing very perplexing complications for us on the side of Italy. It has long been my endeavour to obtain such undeniable proofs of this as will enable me to appeal to the rectitude of the Emperor Alexander, and call upon him to stop a scandal so opposed to the feelings which he expresses to your Majesty.

If the Russian Cabinet is carrying on this game without the knowledge of its sovereign, he will know how to put a stop to it. If this is being done by his command, the Emperor Alexander will never be able to stand by a proceeding so different from the just principles he has proclaimed ; and since it must be a matter of interest to him not to place himself in a false light before the eyes of Europe, or to compromise himself prematurely, the certainty that none of the intrigues of his agents are unknown to us will induce him to restrain their dangerous activity, at any rate for a time.

If these views be correct, I may flatter myself with the hope that, even if we admit the supposition of foreign influence, the sects in Italy will, for the present, occasion no real danger, if without active interference we continue to watch them.

Résumé.

The consideration and review of these data on the moral condition of all the Italian Governments (with the exception of the Lombardo-Venetian kingdom) furnish the following results :—

That the discontent is universal ; that if this discontent was a natural consequence of the sufferings engendered by the last unfavourable years, and of the political changes which have taken place since 1814 and 1815, it must also be ascribed to the bad administration of the Governments ; that in Italy, especially in its southern regions, and in Bologna and Genoa, there is undoubtedly a great ferment in the minds of the populations supported by the different sects, the tendency of which is without doubt dangerous, while the sects themselves, from the want of known leaders and of concerted action among themselves, are not nearly so dangerous as we might fear ; that, notwithstanding the existence of this explosive matter, a revolutionary movement in Italy is not to be feared so long as it is not set on fire and maintained by some foreign Power ; lastly, that at the present moment no Power can in this respect occasion real alarm.

If this picture is very far from being satisfactory, it yet gives us some ground to moderate our fears, and at the same time some advantages by which we may profit to make the Austrian Government popular in Italy, and to gain reputation and win the alliance of neighbouring nations, none of whom are content with their present lot or with their Governments.

Lombardo-Venetian Kingdom.

Even the most zealous adherents of the last Government admit that the administration of the Lombardo-Venetian kingdom had many essential advantages in comparison with the other States of Italy. They allow that all classes of the population were equally subject to the laws in Lombardy and the Venetian provinces; that the nobles and the rich did not maintain the upper hand; that the clergy were kept in subjection; that the changes made in property and sanctioned by law were respected, and that a veil of oblivion had been drawn over the past—that is to say, that no one was exposed either to public or private persecution. Apart from the justice done in this respect to the principles of the Austrian administration, it would, however, be a mistake to infer from this that general dissatisfaction was not prevalent in the provinces subject to your Majesty. Your Majesty has been informed of this state of things by the governors of the provinces and by the presidents of the police courts, and it cannot be unknown to your Majesty that the tedious progress of business; the design attributed to your Majesty of wishing to give an entirely German character to the Italian provinces; the composition of the courts, where the Italians daily see with sorrow German magistrates appointed to offices; and the prolongation of the controversies between the Vienna Court and the Papal See, are the main causes to which this discontent is ascribed. Since these causes appear to me to be all more or less of a kind capable of removal, and since the paternal views of your Majesty have in this respect long been known to me, I think it my duty to repeat again, with the greatest respect, how important it would be, from a political point of view, to remove as soon as possible these defects and shortcomings of the administration in this most interesting part of the monarchy, to quicken and advance the progress of business, to conciliate the national spirit and self-love of the nation by giving to these provinces a form of constitution which might prove to the Italians that we have no desire to deal with them exactly as with the German provinces of the monarchy, or, so to speak, to weld them with those provinces; that we should there appoint, and especially in the magisterial offices, able natives of the country, and that, above all, an endeavour should be made to unite more closely with ourselves the clergy and the class of writers who have most influence on public opinion. I do not doubt that it is possible to attain this most desirable and beneficial end without encountering great difficulties, and even without being exposed to the necessity of departing from those general principles upon which the administration of the other parts of the monarchy are based—principles which unquestionably must be preserved in the interests of the common weal, though their application may admit of many modifications. I cherish, lastly, the hope that whenever your Majesty is induced to set in motion the salutary designs long contemplated, and to establish the well-being of these provinces on an enduring basis, public opinion will declare itself for Austria, discontent will disappear with its causes, and the Italians will at last regard Austria as the only Government which can afford a sure support to public tranquillity. If ever this day should come, then the influence of foreigners will cease to be feared, and we shall gain one far more essential with our neighbours— the influence given by opinion.

Metternich to the Emperor Francis, Grätz, November 3, 1817.

246. I have the honour to submit to your Majesty in the accompanying documents the results of the labours which I undertook in Italy, and of the observations which I there made. That my chief work, which I enclose with this (No. 245), is drawn up with perfect truth, and contains a faithful picture of the present state of things in Italy—for this I vouch. The result of my observation, which has grown to be absolute conviction, is that the Austrian Government has only to observe a steady course in order to play in Italy a part to which your Majesty is in every respect called. A great work has been done by the new relations in which your Majesty has placed the Government of the Lombardo-Venetian kingdom. In consequence of this constitution public opinion will pronounce entirely in favour of your Majesty, and in these measures lies all the good which we are entitled to require of administrative measures ; they fulfil naturally the just wishes of a nation, and they are of a nature to strengthen the power of a Government. This purpose can always be attained in the ways now indicated.

In our Italian provinces there prevails at this moment the greatest dissatisfaction with the measure—in itself very natural, and supported by solid grounds—for the extension of the general custom-house laws to these countries. This extension has been made with a view to local demands and local relations ; against which nothing can be said. Wherein, then, do the difficulties (among which I include some natural and easily obviated grievances) consist? A casual conversation with the President of the Chamber of Commerce has given me information on this point.

In the Lombardo-Venetian province there is little taste for manufactures : most of the articles in daily use Italy imports from foreign countries. France and England have made the greatest advances in manufactures. These two States, with an industry peculiar to them, supply all the markets of Italy. In Austria, too, the manufacturing spirit is in a torpid condition, Our manufacturers care but little to make themselves known in foreign countries, and the Italian provinces were and are in this respect for Bohemia and Austria still foreign countries. Now we have made such decrees for protection and prohibition that none of our manufactures are known in Italy. The merchant beyond the Alps, therefore, naturally thinks himself abandoned and neglected. Impressed with a feeling of this great disadvantage, the Board of Trade now makes arrangements to send samples and patterns to Italy.

The sending of samples, the renewal of correspondence between the retail dealers of Milan and the manufacturers of Bohemia, ought to have been the first measure. The Government ought to have taken care that on the day of the prohibition the Italian merchants had had before their eyes the equally good and equally cheap, if not cheaper, wares. The second measure would then have been quite naturally the prohibition of foreign wares, and this would have silenced the outcry, or reduced it to an empty groundless criticism of a few ill-affected persons.

I will venture to touch on another circumstance which deeply affects the minds of your Majesty's Italian subjects.

Your Majesty is too well acquainted with the state of

things in Italy not to be aware that, in nearly the whole of the peninsula, it is the custom in all the most cultivated classes to send the sons who are destined for literary or commercial professions to Tuscany for instruction in the language. If your Majesty will authorise the provincial guilds in Tuscany to grant permission for the study of the *Humaniora* to young people from ten to twelve years old on the representation of their parents, without further interrogation, this would produce an excellent impression on the cultivated part of the community, and it would be a great object to the Government to retain business men who are masters of the Italian language. This remark is the more important as the educational arrangements in the monarchy are not only such as to interfere with or prevent the journeys of young people, but even those of foreigners and strangers.

ANNALS OF LITERATURE.

247. Metternich to Professor Matthäus von Collin, December 10, 1817.
248. Metternich to Carl Böttiger, December 27, 1817.

247. His Majesty the Emperor has commissioned me to take the new literary journal under my immediate though unacknowledged direction.

The notice I herewith enclose may therefore, with the slight alterations I have made, immediately appear.*

The contract is concluded with the Messrs. Gerold, the publishers.

I appoint you, sir, to be chief editor.

As second editor I appoint M. Pilat. It will be his business to be entirely at your disposal, and to act as middleman whenever it happens that you are prevented from direct intercourse with me. The conduct of the business, however, rests, sir, entirely with you.

The criticism of the journal may be divided into

---

* The object of the *Jahrbücher* may be inferred from this notice : 'Everything properly considered as belonging to the duty of a literary journal will also be the object of this *Jahrbücher*. It will endeavour to include reviews of the most important writings by contemporaries in the whole sphere of knowledge ; impartial criticism will be its first law and the groundwork of our best efforts.

'The *Jahrbücher* will devote especial attention to the encouragement of knowledge in the Austrian States, where great industry is already shown by the learned men of the Fatherland in many branches of knowledge, and there is a great increase in the peculiarly Italian literature ; it will also strive to bring before its readers those works in every literature by which science or art can be advanced. The object of this institution is especially this : to give a satisfactory survey of the most important of the great and noble works of contemporaries who, however divided by national peculiarities, are all led by one and the same aspiration for the advancement of knowledge.' — ED.

two parts. To the political part I will myself attend. The literary and scientific part will be entrusted to one who was well known when President of the Chief Court of Police. The necessary introduction I will forward without delay.

In carrying out this matter and in all measures necessary for the conduct of the business, I shall, sir, always await your reports and suggestions.

Metternich to Carl Böttiger, Vienna, December 27, 1817.

248. I have received your esteemed letter and first literary report, and read them with great pleasure. I beg of you to continue the same and to rest assured of my gratitude.

In the enclosure you will find an invitation to take part in an undertaking long proposed and always desired by yourself. The new journal rejoices in the protection of the Government. The first expenses of an institution which can only be maintained by its success will be granted on the part of the State. His Majesty the Emperor, from a feeling of the utility of the more than ever laborious work of which the truly learned men of the present day are capable, will furnish the necessary funds for the undertakings of our most eminent men in particular departments of science and literature. This is the only kind of interference suitable for the Government. The character of the learned men who have been invited to join in the editorship will ensure that the criticisms in the *Jahrbücher der Literatur* shall always be of a thoroughly learned and truly cosmopolitan character. I should, however, not have thought it proper, sir, to send you this invitation myself if I had not been encouraged to do so by my former personal acquaintance. Receive, &c.

RESULTS OF THE NEGOTIATION WITH ROME ON ECCLESIASTICAL AFFAIRS.

249. Metternich to the Emperor Francis, Vienna, December 1817.

249. When I left Vienna for Florence last June the chief subjects of negotiation with the Holy See with which I was charged by your Majesty were the following :—

(*a*) His Holiness to renounce the right he has hitherto held of nominating archbishops, bishops, and other dignitaries in the former Republics of Venice and Ragusa.

(*b*) The practice to be given up of requiring the newly appointed Italian bishops to go to Rome to have their appointments confirmed by the Pope.

(*c*) The proceedings against the preconisation of the newly appointed Bishop of Brünn to be given up, and the misunderstanding removed with regard to the Bishop of Munkatsch.

(*d*) The differences to be arranged which had arisen on the part of the Pope, as to the oath to be taken by the Austrian bishops at their installation, and the ceremonies to be observed thereat.

(*e*) The reservations to be made for the preservation of our rights on the cession of the clerical jurisdiction hitherto practised on Piedmontese territory by the Archbishop of Milan and Bishop of Pavia.

(*f*) The Papal confirmation to be obtained for the

new dioceses arranged by your Majesty in the States of Lombardy and Venice, in Tyrol and Vorarlberg.

Your Majesty knows the reasons why I thought it best not to make use of your Majesty's kind permission to go to Rome, which reasons restricted me to a confidential correspondence with the Cardinal Secretary of State, Consalvi, and this at a most unfavourable time* in consequence of the illness of the Pope and the unusual compliance just then shown by France towards the Holy See in the formation of a concordat. I am, however, happy to be able to inform your Majesty that all these points have been arranged according to your Majesty's wishes, except concerning the journey of the newly appointed Italian bishops to Rome ; and with regard to this latter point, such modifications have been arranged that (by putting aside the *quæstio juris* to be decided at a more favourable opportunity) there is every hope of attaining the aim *de facto*.

With regard to this, the following explanations will give further details :—

(*a*) His Holiness the Pope has not only agreed to the renunciation in question but has issued a bull, by virtue of which the sovereign right of your Majesty and your successors is acknowledged for ever—the right, that is, to nominate the Patriarch of Venice and all archbishops and bishops in the whole territory of the former Republics of Venice and Ragusa, as far as they are incorporated in the Austrian kingdom.

(*b*) Unsuccessful attempts have been made to induce

* Metternich reported to the Emperor Francis from Florence, July 19, 1817 :—' The Pope's health is always in the same very uncertain condition. The state of things in Rome, however, is such that we shall gradually gain all reasonable objects without an actual negotiation. My non-appearance in Rome causes much surprise, and I make use of this feeling in the way which seems to me most useful.'—ED.

the Roman Court to declare that the newly appointed bishops in Lombardy and Venetia are exempt from the obligation that binds all other Italian bishops to go to Rome to have their appointments confirmed, but we have been given to understand, confidentially, that his Holiness may probably be willing to grant dispensations in single cases, where the newly appointed bishop, from age, weakness, or want of means, is unable to take the journey to Rome.

(*c*) The Bishops of Brünn and Munkatsch nominated by your Majesty have, in consequence of the negotiations, already received the Pope's confirmation with the bulls referring to it, and consequently have taken their episcopal seats.

(*d*) The Roman Court makes no further objection to the explanation as to the oath of the bishops and the ceremonies observed at their installation, and has tacitly acknowledged the practice by giving the apostolic confirmation to the above-named Bishops of Brünn and Munkatsch without insisting upon an alteration of the usual oaths and ceremonies.

(*e*) In order to be secured against the disadvantages which might have arisen from giving up the clerical jurisdiction hitherto practised by the Bishops of Milan and Pavia, an official declaration has been obtained from the Court of Turin that this renunciation shall have no effect whatever on the temporalities and corporations, seminaries and religious institutions, which have had property, personal or otherwise, or drawn their revenues from Piedmontese territory, but that they shall continue in their undisturbed possession and enjoyment.

(*f*) His Holiness has declared his willingness to sanction the new division into dioceses as arranged by your Majesty, and to send the bulls concerning it as soon as the documents still wanting have arrived in Rome. These documents I shall therefore despatch immediately.*

* Besides the measures mentioned in this paragraph, referring to the regulation of the home affairs of the Empire, Metternich had a great influence on many other arrangements of importance for the Empire, although documentary evidence of the same is not forthcoming. Thus Tyrol got back its old constitution of States; Dalmatia was divided into five districts; the kingdom of Illyria was formed of Carinthia, Carniola, and parts of the maritime States; all the provinces of Austria in Germany were declared parts of the German Confederation, &c. All these arrangements were brought about by the co-operation of Metternich during the first years of peace, 1816 and 1817.

A statesman of Prince Metternich's character, who enjoyed the full confidence of his monarch, and possessed a great amount of experience gained in difficult times, as a matter of course extended his care to the internal development of the Empire, because of the close connection of the internal condition with the foreign affairs with which he was entrusted. But the nature of a well-arranged official organisation accounts for the fact that only on rare and very important occasions are any documents to be found by the head of a department on subjects foreign to his sphere of action. For the personal intercourse with the monarch the proceedings at the green table of the conference, where the interchange of ideas takes place verbally, leave, as a rule, no written traces—at least none of a kind to be accessible to future inquiry. Besides, it is to be remembered that during Francis's reign, nobody more strictly enforced the legal limits of competence in his officials than the Emperor Francis himself, while during Ferdinand's reign the power of the Chancellor of State in the home administration (much over-estimated by contemporaries) was baffled by many paralysing influences. The want of autobiographical memoirs for this and the next period, explains our being induced by the title of the book which here closes to make these short remarks (illustrating the subject and partly forestalling its history) on Metternich's proceedings in the department of home policy.—ED

BOOK V.

LUSTRUM OF THE CONGRESS.
PAPERS AND DOCUMENTS.

1818—1822.

LUSTRUM OF THE CONGRESS.

1818.

THE WATER-CURE AT CARLSBAD.

Extracts from Metternich's private Letters to his Family, from July 8 to August 26, 1818.

250. Arrival at Carlsbad. 251. Begins the waters. 252. Arrangement of the day. 253. Madame Catalani—Valabrègue and Goethe. 254. From Königswart—Strassenbau—the Abbot of Tepl. 255. Anxiety about Metternich's father. 256. His death. 257. Departure from Königswart.

Metternich to his Wife, Carlsbad, July 8, 1818.

250. Here I am, my dear, in this place of charms and delights. It will deserve that name from me the day I am thoroughly re-established in health. I came at a deuce of a pace from Vienna here; I took only forty hours on the journey; they could not do more in England or Italy. I left Collin at five in the morning yesterday, passed three hours at Prague, and reached Carlsbad at midnight precisely. The town is overflowing with strangers.

251. *July 11.*—I am still expecting Staudenheim,* naturally enough, for he could only arrive to-day if he did not leave Vienna till Wednesday. I do not trust his talent as a courier; I have never seen a little man like him post quickly, and I give him eighty hours

---

* I r. Staudenheim was Count Metternich's private physician.—ED.

to make the same journey as I did in forty. If he does not arrive during this day, I shall begin to-morrow to drink the Neubrunn. It is the best known and the safest spring, although the least powerful. After that I shall go wherever Staudenheim wishes to take me ; you know that I always follow blindly the advice of my medical man. For the rest, I shall begin my cure under very good auspices. My health is improved by the journey, and were it not for a cursed lumbago which seized me yesterday when stooping to wash my face, I should be very well. Yesterday I could hardly walk ten steps during the day. To-day I am better, though still suffering very much. I do not know how it is that I have the talent of getting ill on every occasion.

I have arranged my manner of life according to the customs of the place. I am in bed every night at half-past ten, and I rise at six. Everybody is at the waters at half-past six ; they breakfast at ten, dine at three, and eat no supper.

252. *July* 13.—I wish Baden was situated like Carlsbad, which is really charming. I have never staid here long enough to know all the surroundings ; the roads are all good : during the last twelve years they have been made on all sides. One can now get to Eger in three hours, and consequently to Königswart * in six. We have the most beautiful weather : it is very hot, and you know how I appreciate heat at this season. I live entirely by rule. From six to eight in the morning I rush about with seven or eight hundred persons like so many fools. We meet at nine for breakfast, and this is very pleasant ; the tables are laid before the different houses, and those who like join together ; so I made them take mine to the door of the house where

---

* A property belonging to Count Metternich.

Schwarzenberg lives, for it is better situated than mine ; we recommence our walking after breakfast till mid-day. I dine alternately at home and with Charles or Joseph Schwarzenberg. We take every day, at five o'clock, a walk of two or three miles. I go to the Salle at eight, or I have a whist-party at home ; and all Carls-bad is in bed at ten. This way of life would suit you very well.

253. *July* 30.—Madame Catalani arrived here yes-terday, having been expected with much impatience. She will give a concert on the 1st. I shall therefore not leave till the morning of the 2nd, though I finish my course of waters to-morrow. Staudenheim, who never trifles, forbids me to drink them on the 1st, for he says they have made me well and that too much of them would be luxury. On the other hand, he wishes Madame Catalani to take them with great assiduity for thirty days, for she appears to him an excellent subject for Carlsbad. For the concert the day after to-morrow the orchestra will be composed in the following manner : —*Leader of the orchestra* : an old organist of the chapel, who has been trying to cure a liver complaint for three years and not succeeded ; *clavichord* : a Prince de Biron, who always lies, except when he says he plays this instrument well ; *first violin* : a Saxon Colonel ; *second violin* : a Prussian Captain ; *violoncello* : the Prussian General Count de Hacke. We are still in search of other instruments ; the trumpeters only are hired. They are the keepers of the great court, who announce the arrival of visitors with the sound of the trumpet. If this concert creates a *furore*, it will be fortunate !

At the first rehearsal of the concert, which took place at my house, Goethe arrived. I introduced him to Madame Catalani, saying he was a man of whom Germany was proud. Valabrègue * asked me, ' Who is Goethe?' I told him that he was the author of ' Werther.' The unhappy man did not forget this ; for lo and behold! some days afterwards he went up to him and said : 'My dear Goethe, what a pity it is you could not see Potier in the part of " Werther! " It would have made you burst with laughing.'

254. *Königswart, August* 3.—I came here yesterday, and I shall remain until the 5th. Besides, Franzensbrunn is so near that I hope often to return here, in order that I may see that the most is made of the new establishment at Marienbad, which is a real godsend for this property. Within the last three years I have added more than four thousand *toises* (six feet) of roads. Now, one is able to go from Eger to where the road branches off from the Sandau and Altwasser road to the *château* on one of the finest roads possible, and I am going to have it planted with trees. The peasants, who formerly destroyed all the trees, are now beginning to preserve them. We must next make a road from Grossichdichfür to Marienbad, and this road will be costly, on account of a steep hill in the Walderl which it must avoid. I shall finish it, however, in less than a year. The Abbot of Tepl, who is coming to dine with me to-day, ought to contribute towards it. This Abbot is terribly afraid of me ; I do not know how the absurd story has been spread through the country, that the Abbey is to be secularised, and that the Emperor wishes to make me a present of it. I contradict it in vain, the noble convent trembles none the less, and I can obtain from it all which is just and reasonable, in consequence of its dread that the Emperor may be unjust and myself unreasonable. The Königswart property is at any rate

* Catalani's husband.

much improved by the neighbourhood of these new waters.

Metternich to his Mother, Franzensbad, August 13.

255. It is with a broken heart, my dear mother, that I write to you in the most painful moment of my life and yours. A letter which I received to-day from my wife does not allow me to hope for my father's restoration to health. From all I hear I feel sure that he is dying the death which nature has reserved for advanced age—a gentle death, free from the suffering which accompanies acute disease. If I consulted only my own feelings, I should start immediately for Vienna, but everything is against my doing so. Staudenheim actually forbids me interrupting the cure which has begun, and which promises the most satisfactory results. He declares that the waters here must not be interrupted in their course, and that by interrupting them I should undergo all the inconveniences he is anxious to avoid. And should I find my father, even if I set off immediately? Everything is arranged for my journey and arrival on the Rhine before the end of the month. I shall find there all the men whom I ought to meet before the meeting at Aix-la-Chapelle, and the delay which attends this meeting, far from being inconvenient, may be of incalculable advantage in its results. In conclusion, should I be performing a duty which would benefit my poor father? Would not my sudden arrival do more harm than good? This is the consideration which has most weight with me, but the sad event which we are now expecting could not have happened at a moment more painful to me. If my father should live, and expresses a desire to see me, were it only for one moment, I would put aside all these considerations and come to you. A moment's happiness in this world would not encroach on the eternal joy which awaits him.

You see, my good mother, it is for you to direct and decide what I ought to do. There are times in which it is scarcely possible oneself to know how to act for the best.

If the sad event takes place, apply to Bartenstein for everything. I have given him full directions. My brother has written to me (for which I beg you to thank him) to assure me that he will do all he possibly can. I believe I thought of everything in my last letter to Bartenstein.

I would strongly advise you to go and join my family at Baden. You will be better there than at Salzburg; you will avoid the trouble of a long journey, and will feel at home.

. . . . In conclusion, my dear mother, take care of yourself, and remember that, if you can do no more for him, you owe it to us to think of yourself.

My poor father in leaving this world will at least have the consolation that I have never given him a moment of unhappiness, and this is the sweetest feeling of my life. He cannot refuse me his blessing, and I shall know how to deserve it.

Adieu, my dear good mother. I embrace you, and implore you not so much to think of yourself as of all of us.

256. *Franzensbrunn, August* 14.—I wrote yesterday, my dear mother, in all the anxiety of a painful uncertainty; to-day, when I have received the news of the loss we have sustained, I can only repeat what I said to you yesterday. Although the blow was expected, it is not the less dreadful. The courier arrived yesterday just as I was going to bed. It consoles me for my

absence to think that my poor father was unconscious.
He died without perceiving that he was treading the
valley of the shadow of death, and he felt none of its
horrors—a happy death, not reserved for everyone!

. . . I have ordered here everything necessary for
depositing the remains of my father, as far as arranging
a more suitable place of repose than the tomb which
now exists in the parish of Königswart. I intend to
make a place of sepulture which will one day contain
us all. Those who ought not to be separated in this
world should not be isolated in their last resting-place.
I have ordered obsequies in all the parishes, here as
well as at Ochsenhausen and in Moravia. If my father
needed prayers to assist him to his place in the other
world, those of his own people will not be wanting.*

Adieu, my dear mother. May God preserve you for
many years, and give you in this heavy trial that
strength of mind which should never abandon us, even
in the most trying moments. I charge all my family,
who are no less yours, with those duties which I should
have desired to fulfil myself.

Metternich to his Wife, Königswart, August 26.

257. I write to you, my dear Laura, a few hours
before my departure. I am feeling very sad. Everything which separates us is painful to me, and I feel
more and more every day the pain of being separated
from my dear little family. I should like to have you
always with me, or never to leave Vienna. Few lives
are so fatiguing as those which are spent in the highest
walks of life, and in the midst of important and intricate affairs. Formerly these affairs could be carried on
quietly. How many difficulties there are in my career,

* See on the same subject No. 283.—ED.

and how different are they from those of all former ministers, and perhaps even from those to come!

I shall be at Frankfurt on the 29th, and spend two busy days there. I shall have the entire Diet on my hands. I know already that most of the ministers there are trembling at my appearance; of my forty-eight hours I shall take at least from twelve to fifteen to lecture the well-intentioned and to do justice to those who are not. My two days at Frankfurt will, however, be worth at least a hundred as far as business is concerned.

On the 1st I shall go to see the Duke of Nassau, and from there go on to Johannisberg. The Duke has paid me many attentions, and deserves at least a visit from me in return. They write to me from Frankfurt that he has a hundred men at work making a road as far as the *château* from the point where one leaves the main road. The monks of Fulda had taken care to leave this road impracticable, for fear of attracting too many visitors. My cellars being empty, I do not run the same risk, and I prefer some *toises* of a good road to many bottles of wine. He has, moreover, ordered his keepers to furnish me with game, and his gardeners with the fruits of his forests and gardens. As I shall probably only remain there a short time, I shall make no great ravages in either the one or the other.

I am also informed that, since the inhabitants on the banks of the Rhine have learnt that the Emperor is coming down the river, they have been making immense preparations along the whole route. It is no doubt the part of Europe where the Emperor is most loved, more even than in our own country. The whole scene will be admirable. The Emperor will have a real fleet. There is not one more yacht or boat to be hired on the river; all are taken by the people living on the banks, and the whole population will be on the river side. I foresaw this, and I believe it will be a success. These demonstrations prove better than the Jena news-papers what is the opinion of the people. We shall have a splendid article for the 'Observer.'

I wish you were all with me, my dear ones!

JOURNEY TO THE RHINE.

Metternich to his Wife, Frankfurt, August 31, 1818.

258. I arrived here comfortably, my dear, the day before yesterday, in the evening, and alighted as usual at Mülhens' house, where I am lodged as I should like to be all my life. One cannot understand how a little re-tired grocer has had the taste to build and furnish a house like this, nor how a man so avaricious could spend six hundred thousand florins to be well housed.

Yesterday I spent the most agreeable morning in the world. From ten till four, I received all the Confede-ration, deputations from the magistrates, *corps diplo-matique*, &c. To increase the pleasure, I had caught on the way, from the intense cold and infernal damp, one of my nice colds in the head, and as the Diet *in corpore* is not made to heal anything, I was obliged to go to bed in the evening and try to get into a perspiration. Staudenheim, who never trifles, told me this morning that I had better remain in bed all day, and I, a gentle in-valid, submit.

I shall stay here to-morrow and the day after, and go to Johannisberg on the 3rd. One has no idea of the difference of the climate of this country from our own. I was ready to die of cold in Bohemia, and here we have not had one single cool day. It has rained for eight days, and been warm all the time, which is very promising for the wine. I have had extravagant offers for the vineyards of Johannisberg, but I have refused them all. One was an offer of fifty thousand florins to be paid immediately, the wine to be sealed and laid down for six years at Johannisberg, then sold for our common benefit— that is to say, that I should divide the profits besides the fifty thousand florins. But I do not wish to divide, and I hold, moreover, that it is better to establish the reputation of the cellar.

259. *September* 4.—. . . . You can have no idea of the effect produced by my appearance at the Diet. An affair which perhaps would never have ended has been concluded in three or four days. I am more and more convinced that affairs of importance can only be properly conducted by oneself. Everything done second hand is vexatious and troublesome, and makes no progress. I have become a species of moral power in Germany, and perhaps even in Europe—a power which will leave a void when it disappears : and nevertheless it will disappear; like all belonging to poor frail human nature. I hope Heaven will yet give me time to do some good ; that is my dearest wish.

260. *September* 11.—At last, my dear, I am ready to start. I shall sleep to-morrow at Johannisberg, and go on the following morning. I shall dine at Coblentz, and spend the 14th and 15th there, and on the 16th I shall return to Johannisberg and remain there till the 22nd.

I derive real pleasure from these different journeys ; I go to revisit the scenes of my youth, and I expect to find them changed, as I am changed myself. The walls remain intact, but the men have nearly all disappeared. I am convinced that I shall not find five persons of my acquaintance at Coblentz ; I will give you all the details, and though they cannot interest you, they will my mother. I shall go and visit all the spots she knows, and where she passed the best years of her life. She was beautiful and beloved there, and what more is necessary to make a place pleasant and its remembrance dear ? This is the good side of women. We men need more to make us carry away agreeable recollections of our sojourns. I count my recollections only by public affairs, negotiations, and treaties—happy if the latter do not ruin me altogether.

My visit here has been crowned with great success. I arrived at Frankfurt like the Messiah to save sinners. The Diet wears a new aspect since I have taken a part in it, and everything which seemed so impossible is concluded. I do not believe that twelve days ever bore more fruit at an equally important period. All that the intriguers were aiming to take to Aix-la-Chapelle, to interrupt the progress of affairs, is no longer in their power. In a word, I have a conviction that I have served the cause better at this moment, which does not appear to offer immense advantages, than on twenty other more brilliant occasions. This will, however, be none the less useful.

I shall see Johannisberg for the first time to-morrow, and it must be very beautiful, for all who have seen it rave about it. I have seen it in imagination twenty times : now I am going to see it in reality, and I hope I shall not be disappointed. I often think of my poor

father : he would have taken a thousand times more
pleasure in the place than I do ; and it would have been
worth more, because he would have been the proprietor.
Neither had he the happiness of seeing a good arrangement for the *médiatisés* which will shortly appear. I
promised it to him during my stay at Frankfurt,
and felt that I was fulfilling a duty towards him in
keeping my word, and I declare to you I have more
satisfaction in that feeling than in the thing itself.
What a happy time he would have passed in my place
this morning ! Perhaps he envies me from the other
world—if envy can be felt there—the hour I have had
the misfortune to pass with an infernal M. de Schmitz,
the man of business to the house of Linange, and
all the *médiatisés* whom he adored when here on earth.
I do not know if at the age of seventy I shall like
tiresome people and pedants : I certainly cannot stand
them now.

I was present yesterday at a conference which Staudenheim had with the hereditary Prince of Hesse-Homburg. The latter consulted him about a malady which
Staudenheim declares to be flying gout, but which with
the Prince takes the appearance of everything—that is to
say, it resembles insanity. I was sorry I had not a shorthand writer with me ; he would have furnished an excellent chapter for a comic romance. The point on
which the negotiation between the doctor and the
sick man was broken off was that of the sick man's
breakfast. The Prince did not wish to be deprived of
half a yard of sausage with which he was accustomed
to begin the labours of the day. Staudenheim got into
a rage, the Prince began to swear, and they seemed to
have the sausage by the two ends, and to be struggling
who should wrench it from his adversary. Stauden-

heim ended by carrying off the sausage, and the cure is about to commence under the auspices of the Princess Elizabeth of England.

261. *Johannisberg, September* 12.—I have been here, my dear Laura, since five o'clock this evening. I arrived early enough to see from my balcony twenty leagues of the course of the Rhine, eight or ten towns, a hundred villages, and vineyards which this year will yield twenty millions of wine, intersected by meadows and fields like gardens, beautiful oak woods, and an immense plain covered with trees which bend beneath the weight of delicious fruit. Thus much without. As for within, I find a large and good house, of which in time a fine *château* may be made : but we are still far from having that. I have spent nearly ten thousand florins in the last two months to make it what may fairly be called passable. My friend Handel has chosen the paper-hangings and furniture. The papers he has put on the walls are inconceivable : above all it is inconceivable where he could have found what he has chosen. The evil is, however, confined to three rooms ; the rest of the apartments are painted in one colour.

First of all, I ran through the *château*, the stables, and places for making the wine. I have not visited the cellars, because there is no wine in them, and because I am just recovering from rheumatic fever. I have made the acquaintance of Father Arndt, the famous manager of the place, and the best of *employés* for an estate of this kind. Picture to yourself an old abbé of about sixty, virtuous from position, and I believe by conviction, who has not even the first and commonest defect of old monks. This good man has such a horror of wine that he has not drunk one bottle since he has been at Johannisberg ; yet he is the best *connoisseur* of wine in the canton, but he judges of it by his nose. It is sufficient for him to smell a bottle of wine to decide its quality, its growth, and its year; he can even distintinguish mixtures, and has never been known to make a mistake. Heaven made him for this business, as he was not born a pointer. He reckons on forty-six casks this year, *at least*: when he adds this phrase, it is understood in the country that forty-six means fifty-two.

I am here with Floret, who only regrets that the year 1817 was so bad, and that he cannot find a small remnant from the preceding years; Swoboda, who does not believe that beyond the frontiers of our beautiful kingdom there can be a tolerable country; and M. de Handel, proud as Artabanus of the choice he has made of the furniture. He has particularly drawn my attention to a cupid, which unfortunately has all its limbs dislocated, and which is conspicuous above one of the doors from its excited attitude. He seems to have drunk all that Father Arndt has not drunk. Handel boasts, too, of his choice of a great round table, the top of which weighs a hundred pounds, and which rests on a crane's foot so small that Gentz will never enter the room in which it stands for fear of being maimed.

I hope to start to-morrow at ten in the morning, so as to arrive at Coblentz at six in the evening.

Metternich to his Mother, Coblentz, September 15.

262. I must write to you, my dear mother, were it only that you may have a letter from your son, written at this place.

I arrived here the day before yesterday, just as night was closing in. It would be difficult to imagine anything more beautiful than the road from Bingen.

I believe it is even preferable to the descent by the river. One rolls along an excellent road, which in another two years will leave nothing to be desired ; at present, the railings by its side are in many places only too necessary.

The environs of Coblentz are greatly improved by the fine roads which meet there from every direction One is astonished to find oneself in the avenues in front of the *château* without having been jolted at the foot of the Chartreuse and across the gardens where old Kintelius used to fancy he was practising gardening. The trees that we saw planted in front of the *château* are very large; it is like being in the midst of a forest. This is a sad sight for those who saw them when they were mere sticks. The *château* itself has the look of a deserted house : doors, windows, all are broken. It is at present used as a military establishment. The King wishes to rebuild it, but its destination is not absolutely decided. The town itself is where we left it. The interior of this old town is improved—not that the houses are changed, but the streets are better paved, and the terrible signboards which obstructed the view have given place to boards like those in Paris. It is evident that the town has passed some years under French domination ; its influence is visible in many things— notably in the shops. Among other things, the foun- tains in the squares are well constructed. In front of the church of St. Castor there is a fountain with the following inscription :—' *Erigée par le préfet l'an* 1812, *mémorable par la campagne de Russie* ; ' and below, ' *Vu et approuvé par nous, Commandant russe à Coblentz, le* 1*er Janvier*, 1814.'

They are making fine strong fortifications on the three points which command the town—at Ehrenbreitstein, on the mountain of St. Peter (*das ehemalige Brun-nenstübchen*), and behind the Chartreuse. The environs of Coblentz are certainly among the most remarkable on the Rhine. Our garden near the Moselle is now a field. I have been to see the house, the entrance to which is as it must have been always, but the riding-school, the coach-house, the old door, the walls be-tween the two courts—all have disappeared. There is a little wall, with two doors with pillars form-ing the entrance to the court, and a small public square has replaced the houses which obstructed the entrance. The house is in the most pitiable state, and very dirty ; there are no traces of what it once was. The Court of Appeal occupies the greater part, and the small house is inhabited by a general, who, I suppose, finds himself pinched for room. I went through the garden ; the English part is replaced by a score of large trees, planted without order where the old thickets were ; the hermitage has disappeared : the hillock on which it stood still marks the spot. The meadow remains ; the *espalier* is converted into great trees such as grow in the fields ; on the terrace the lime-trees are immense, and partly obscure the view. The frescoes alone have resisted the ravages of time ; the stable wall is covered with them, and they struck me as being exceedingly bad.

Of our old acquaintances there only remain here the old Count d'Eltz (who is dying), and Count Remus, who lives in the Burresheims' house for some months in every year. The two ladies, his aunts, are alive, and intend to marry when they can find husbands. The rest of the gentry have disappeared, they and tleir little fortunes. Faithful to the customs of the country, all these gentlemen have ruined themselves more than the Revolution has ruined them. Count de Boos is the last to leave; he is now at Sayn, where he is dying in consequence of a visit he made to Paris, where he destroyed his health and lost all his fortune at play. Kerpen's house displays the name of a linendraper's shop. Leyen's house, which is in very good condition, is occupied by the military governor. The castle of Kesselstadt is transformed into an iron manufactory. Bassenheim's house will, one of these days, fall on the head of a general who is living in it. The Laacher-Hof bears beneath its ancient name an innkeeper's signboard. I lodge at the Hôtel de Trèves, which is one of the worst inns in Europe—the best is at Thal.

There are no traces of the old *château* below Ehrenbreitstein: it is replaced by a battery of twenty-four guns.

This rough sketch will give you an idea of the town, which is, indeed, in its old place, but is not at all the old town itself. Since I have been here I have not met two people I know. It is quite sufficient to come here, as I have done, to see that five-and-twenty years will swallow up a whole generation. The streets are full of the children of the children of our time, and they look upon me as upon a being from another world.

I spent yesterday morning in receiving the civil and military authorities and those of the town; I took a walk with Chancellor Hardenberg—whom I found, to my great satisfaction, in the best of health—and I dined with the Governor. To-day I go to Engers; dine with minister Ingersleben, do some business, and to-morrow return to Johannisberg. This is all I have to tell you; nevertheless, I suppose, my dear mother, that you will read my letter with the interest one always feels in old memories.

Metternich to his Wife, Johannisberg, September 18.

263. I am here, not as if in the country, but as if at a Congress. Yesterday I had Chancellor Hardenberg, Count de Goltz and General Wolzogen, Count de Buol, Steigentesch, Wessenberg, Caraman, Maccalon, the Counts Münster, Rechberg, and Wintzingerode. I have with me Mercy, Spiegel, Langenau, and Gentz. The Chancellor left yesterday for Kreutznach ; Bethmann and half a dozen Frankfurtese arrive to-day. To lodge all these people I have hired two houses at the foot of the hill.

What a view ! What a rich country ! What indescribable beauties for a man who does not know the Rheingau ! Everyone who arrives stands amazed on the balcony, and yet the view is nothing in comparison with that from the drawing-room, which forms the eastern corner of the *château*. When the air is clear you can follow the course of the Rhine in a direct line for more than nine leagues ; when it is hazy, the river, which is immense, touches the horizon and looks like the sea. It is continually covered with two-masted vessels in full sail, and its banks are like those of a little stream, the grass reaching to the water's edge. I have just had plans made of the *château* and the neighbourhood. I have sent for an excellent architect from Frankfurt to arrange the plan according to my directions ; it will be only necessary to make a very few changes to turn the *château* into a very comfortable habitation, able to accommodate a numerous family and a dozen visitors. Near the *château* is a place which is cultivated as an English garden, and which is suited for nothing else. In it, facing the Rhine, there is a hillock on which I intend to erect a monument, probably an obelisk, in remembrance of the events of 1813 and 1814. I shall thus raise on the most classic ground of Germany, and at very little expense, a truly national monument. Freestone costs nothing, and a few blocks would make a beautiful thing, which above all should be simple. M. de Handel has been ordered to send you a work which contains a very good description of the course of the Rhine. I intend it for Marie, so that she may know what she will see one day. Have it sent to her, but read the chapters from Mayence to Coblentz, and especially the one at the end of the book, which is called *Volks-sagen*. You will read there the most charming histories, which will recur to you on taking this journey at every step. There is not one picturesque site which does not contain a ruin, and each ruin has its history ; each story is full of gallant and chivalrous sentiments ; the subjects might inspire the most beautiful pictures in the world to adorn a beautiful edition of this work. Read particularly the history of the Emperor Frederick of Adolphseck and *Ritter Brömser von Rudesheim*. This family is merged in ours ; we were its heirs ; the scene of the events belonged to us, and I was obliged to sell it to satisfy some usurers. The ruin, the most beautiful on the banks of the Rhine, has been bought by Count Ingelheim, who occupies himself in transforming it into a dwelling-house, and that in the best possible taste. He manages the exterior very well, and hollows out, in the walls, which are from twenty-five to thirty feet thick, commodious apartments in a most suitable style. This old *château* could only have been a Roman castle, and this is proved by the discovery lately made of a vault in which were a number of funeral urns very well preserved, and beside each urn a sabre, a lance, the top of a helmet, and

many Roman weapons. Not wishing to disturb anything, they cleared the entrance to the vault, and closed
it with a glass door.

. . . I have received a splendid decree from
the King of Naples, giving me the title of Duke of
Portella, the first place in the kingdom where the
Imperial troops halted in the campaign of 1815.
There is a compliment in the choice of the name, and
it is a good remembrance to perpetuate in the family.

264. *Mayence, September* 23.—I left Johannisberg
with great regret yesterday and I took a tender leave of
it. When you see it—and that will be a happy day for
me—you will understand my regret. I found my quarters here prepared in the old house on the *Bleiche* which
my father occupied, and which I left in 1788 to go to
Strasburg. That is thirty years ago ; I have grown
old ; the house has renewed its youth without having
improved ; it has lost the appearance of a mansion to
take that of a middle-class house.

The Emperor arrived here at seven o'clock. You
will see from what Hudelist tells you what he has done
to-day. I spent the day in work, then in walking in
the streets, dining with the Emperor, and paying visits
to the Princess of Hesse-Homburg and the Princess of
Denmark, who is very pretty. I passed three hours in
the evening with the Emperor, who is glad to see me
again, and then went to see the last scenes of ' Titus,'
which was very tiresome this evening. There is no worse
theatre than that of Mayence, unless it is that of Baden.

We shall prolong our visit here until to-morrow, so
as not to meet the King of Prussia at Coblentz. The
Emperor will embark on the 25th, and dine at Johannisberg ; we shall be a large and pleasant party, including
nearly all the princes who are here.

We shall sleep on the 25th at Bingen, on the 26th at Coblentz, on the 27th at Cologne, and on the 28th at Aix-la-Chapelle. The Emperor Alexander does not go to Italy. I need not tell you that delights me.

265. *Bingen, September* 24.—I arrived here in such good time, my dear, after a charming day, that I am able to take this opportunity of sending to Frankfurt, and write to you by the military courier.

You will read in the paper an article containing the details of our day, but neither papers nor letters can convey to you the truly ravishing scene we have enjoyed. I do not believe that the voyage of Cleopatra, that beautiful queen, with all her nymphs and adorers surrounding her, could have been more picturesque than ours. The skies were extremely favourable ; the most beautiful day, the best wind, the best people and the most *amoureux* : this is the only word which expresses the sentiment all feel here towards the Emperor ; hundreds of boats, thousands of cannon and petards firing, about twenty bands, besides the music of the Austrian regiment and garrison at Mayence ; a burning sun, a cool wind, and thousands of smiling faces ; all this on the Rhine and on its banks. These are the elements which composed the *fête*, which nevertheless was only a simple journey.

The Emperor was struck with the view of Johannisberg, and the Prince of Denmark declares that in Denmark and even in Norway there is not a more charming situation under the softest sky. I gave him a very good dinner, and I found that I had enough Johannisberg of my own without having to borrow. I am, moreover, convinced that it never attained more celebrity than during the last fifteen days. But, I am far from desirous that it should preserve that character ; I should very much prefer to pass some weeks there with you and the children, with neither sovereigns nor ministers. The book I have placed there to receive the names of visitors looks to-day like a protocol of Congress. May God spare me from seeing it filled thus !

We shall leave to-morrow at eight in the morning, and shall be at Mayence between one and two. The Emperor, who much likes to see attachment shown to him, is enchanted with the country.

We have superb weather, and Father Arndt announced to me to-day with an air truly Bacchic that he will answer for the year. I said my *fiat* with much benignity.

RESIDENCE IN AIX, AND RETURN JOURNEY TO VIENNA.

Extracts from Metternich's private Letters, from October 1 to December 25, 1818.

Metternich to his Wife, Aix-la-Chapelle,
October 1, 1818.

266. Here I am at last, my dear, in this town, at the end of my journey, but far from the end of my wishes.

I wrote to you last from Bingen. I coasted the Rhine as far as Coblentz, where the Emperor arrived by water some hours after me. We slept there, and I pursued my route next day as far as Cologne. I dined at Bonn, and walked about the town for about two hours. Nothing is so charming as the situation of Bonn; the beautiful mountains which terminate the valley of the river seem to embellish the scene so as to make you leave it with still more regret. These mountains, known by the name of the Siebengebirge, have a magical effect. On one side are the ruins of Roland-seck, and on the other, those of Drachenfels. In case they did not send you from Frankfurt the description of the Rhine by Schreiber, I enclose a copy now. You will find in the article ' *Volks- agen* ' the history of these two castles. Further on begins the immense plain which loses itself in the Ocean and the North Sea—a luxuriant plain, covered with towns, villages, fertile fields and superb forests.

I arrived at Cologne about seven o'clock. An immense crowd had assembled to meet the Emperor. My six horses and the carriages of my suite made them take me for him. In vain I stopped every five minutes to assure the people that I was unworthy of so much honour—it was no use ; on arriving at the gate they began again in fine style. The bells, the shouts, the excitement of a population of sixty thousand souls who crowded against my carriage, drowned my voice as well as Gentz's, whom by chance I had met at Bonn and induced to come with me. It was as much as I could do to prevent them taking the horses out of the carriage. I was furious, and Gentz trembled in every limb. I only heard one sensible voice in the crowd : a man to whom I declared that it was I, myself, said to me : ' Well, we love our Emperor enough to shout twice, if you are not he.'

I arrived at last at the house of the old patrician Geyger. Monsieur, Madame, and Mesdemoiselles, his daughters, whom I had never seen, took possession of me as I alighted from the carriage. I was covered with old and young kisses ; the whole household wept, shouted and swore. They wept with joy at embracing me—me the Austrian Minister ; they shouted *Vive l'Empereur !* and they swore at the fate which had overthrown the ancient order of things. Surrounded by all the authorities of the place, I dragged the family into a room, and implored them to be reasonable. They replied by a spontaneous and positive assurance that they believed they were so, and they could and would not act otherwise. I began to see that my attempts were futile against such a determination, and delivered myself up to their kisses with heroic abandonment. Restored to liberty myself, I saw that Giroux * had been seized by the servants; they seemed not to perceive that he had neglected his beard for a week.

At last the Emperor arrived at his house, two doors from mine, and the crowd and the kisses moved twenty steps farther on.

Certainly if anyone imagines that the happiness of having been French and being now Prussian has at Cologne and on the banks of the Rhine obliterated the remembrance of ten centuries, he is much deceived. The Press nevertheless groans under this lie!

The voyage on the Rhine has been one continual triumph for the Emperor, and has ended by becoming quite embarrassing to him. The whole thing recommenced on his arrival at Aix-la-Chapelle. Everything breathes of the Empire in the natal city so beloved by Charlemagne. The people see in the Emperor only his successor; they are silent when any of the other Sovereigns passes, and never cease shouting wherever the Emperor appears: *Es lebe unser Kaiser!*

The situation of Aix, of which I had only a confused remembrance of twenty-six years' length, is very picturesque. It is very undulated, and well cultivated. The weather is magnificent and tempts one to walk. We are very well lodged, and the measures which have

---

* For many years a faithful valet of Count Metternich's.

been taken to prevent a crowd of diplomatists from arriving leave us very much at liberty.

After dinner this evening, we went with the Emperor to visit the Cathedral. The King of Prussia came too, for he had not seen the relics, which date from the time of Charlemagne, and which are only shown to the public every seven years, or when a Catholic crowned head comes to visit them. We were shown :—

1. A small coat of Jesus Christ, which we call in Vienna *ein Kinder-Röckerl.*

2. A dress of the Holy Virgin.

3. The girdle which Jesus Christ wore on the cross.

4. The linen in which Herodias carried the head of St. John the Baptist.

One can hardly believe that these objects are correctly named, but it is none the less true that when they were given to the church by Charlemagne a thousand years ago, that prince would not have acquired them had they not shown proofs of the highest antiquity. Their preservation can only be accounted for by the extreme care that is taken of them. They also show the skull of this Emperor and many of his bones, which show how tall he was. A *prie-Dieu* had been placed on his tomb, and the Emperor knelt on it and prayed. The people, who had forced the doors to see the Emperor, all fell on their knees instantly, and I thought the King seemed very uncomfortable, standing in the midst of his people. In his place, I would not have come.

The Emperor Alexander arrived here the same day, in the evening. I spent three hours with him, and we were just on the same terms as in 1813.

Our conferences began to-day under the most favourable auspices, and I have every reason to hope

that in three, or at the most four, weeks we shall finish
our labours.

The results will be generally satisfactory. The Emperor Alexander will go from here to Vienna. No more
is said about his journey to Italy and I do not think he
will stay more than a fortnight at Vienna; consequently,
by December 1 all will be restored to order.

267. *October* 5.—It is horribly cold to-day: it
hails, and it freezes. The Emperor, who suffered much
inconvenience yesterday, remained in bed; to-day he
feels better, and has risen. As for me, I had a bad cold
yesterday, and I am very little better to-day. The result of this happy coincidence was that neither the
Emperor nor I were present yesterday at a dinner
given by the King of Prussia in honour of St. Francis,
nor at a grand ball given by the town. It is perhaps
for the first time in my life that I felt really glad that
my health prevented me from going out. I will wager
that the whole town thinks that the Emperor and I have
sacrificed their *fête* to some profound political calculation. We must let them believe this, and, to keep up
the delusion, I shall acquit myself perfectly to-day.

Our business is progressing quite marvellously: this
means that it will soon be finished. I have never seen
a prettier little Congress; this one will produce no bad
blood in me, I promise you. You will excuse me from
telling you about our protocols, and they are what occupy
us most. I make one of a party of whist every evening
with the Prince de Hatzfeld, Zichy, Baring, Labouchere,
Parish—that is to say, with men who do not find themselves distressed, or even incommoded, by the loss of a
good round thousand or so. We met at first at Lady
Castlereagh's, but there is an inconceivable atmosphere
of *ennui* connected with that house. By common con-

sent we renounced the charms of my lady, and fixed upon my drawing-room, which is somewhat smaller than your little room hung with nankeen.

268. *October* 10.—We signed yesterday with France the treaty of evacuation. We have lost no time, having in eleven days settled the diplomatic affairs, made a payment of two hundred and sixty-five millions, and arranged everything relating to the march of the troops. The effect which this has produced in France is already known, for we receive our letters from Paris in forty hours ; all goes well and will continue to do so.

Our affairs here will be concluded by the end of the month. I shall be at Vienna most probably on November 15, or soon after.

I informed you lately of our plans for the journey to Italy. The Emperor intends to leave Vienna between February 10 and 15. He will pass the last days of the Carnival at Venice ; the four first weeks of Lent at Naples ; the last two weeks and Easter week at Rome ; three weeks in Tuscany ; three in Lombardy; this will bring him back to Vienna towards the middle of July.

269. *October* 18.—Our affairs here are advancing rapidly. I will give them no margin beyond the 4th or 5th of November.

As for amusements, there are none. We are overwhelmed with youthful talent: every day there are concerts of virtuosos aged four and nine years. The last arrival is a little boy of four years and a half, who plays the double-bass. You can easily judge of the perfection of the execution.

There are not even any remarkable shops, and the trash they offer costs just double what the best of its kind does in Paris and London. If the shopkeepers have speculated on our purses, they have reckoned without their host. I do not know anyone who buys more than what is strictly necessary.

Our ladies here are Lady Castlereagh, three or four English more or less old—that is to say, they are between fifty and sixty (quite youthful for London)—the Princess de la Tour, Madame de Nesselrode, and three Russian ladies. It is with the ladies as with the shopkeepers : there is a total want of admirers.

270. *October* 27.—The courier bringing the sad news of the death of poor Hudelist arrived here this morning, and I need not tell you how much I regret him. He possessed the most essential qualities, and merits which I shall scarcely be able to replace. My labour will be doubled, and perhaps even trebled, for some time ; I have been so accustomed to depend upon him for all details, that I shall always regret what I can no longer have done by him, and certainly not so quickly by any other *employé*.

I am writing to Madame Hudelist, and I beg you to send the letter to her yourself, telling her that I have chosen this way, because I am convinced that it will make its reception less painful to her. I hope the Emperor will do something for her, the more so as I am sure her husband left very little money.

. . . The day before yesterday I went to Spa with M. and Madame de Nesselrode, the Count and Countess de Lieven, Steigentesch, Zichy, Lebzeltern, the Prince of Hesse, and Floret. We passed the night there ; and yesterday morning went through the environs of Spa ; dined there, and returned here at eight in the evening. The weather was superb, and our trip well arranged. Spa is empty : we were the only strangers there, therefore we excited much interest. The road from here to Spa is charming : nothing is so beautiful as the country about Limbourg, with its meadows and innumerable houses.

271. *November* 3.—Our affairs here are in their decline. I do not believe that they can go on beyond the 15th of this month, the day fixed for their conclusion. If this is the case, I shall be at Vienna by the end of November or the beginning of December, and certainly I shall be glad enough to find myself there.

Lawrence, the greatest painter in the world, is here by command of the Prince Regent, to take portraits of the sovereigns and ministers. That of the Emperor is almost finished, and mine also. I suppose you will see these two, for Lawrence is going to Vienna to paint Prince Schwarzenberg. I do not believe that there could be a better picture than that of the Emperor. My portrait, I believe, will be excellent. I shall try to get Lawrence to paint Clementine.*

Our life goes on much as usual: we confer, we walk, we dine. I have my party in the evening, and I go to bed. All the strangers have left us; there are none remaining.

272. *November* 11.—I may now tell you, my dear, that we are very near the end. The last conference will take place—unless anything unforeseen occurs, which is not likely—on the 16th or 17th. The Emperor will leave the same day. He will be at Vienna on December 2, after stopping five days at Munich.

I expect to leave on the 18th for Brussels; I shall remain there until the 23rd or 24th, and I shall be at Vienna on the 7th or 8th or 9th.

I shall certainly not go to Paris. I could only stay there four or five days, which would be entirely taken up by Princes and ministers, and I see no good reason

---

* Princess Clementine, the Prince's daughter.—Ed.

why I should wantonly expose myself to such drudgery, I shall therefore part from the children at Brussels.

Marie is wonderfully well. She has had all the success possible here ; and as it does not amount to much altogether, I think I may boast of it. She has been to see the Emperor, who—to please her, I believe—put on a Chasseur's uniform. She spent yesterday evening in dancing polonaises with the Emperor Alexander and the King of Prussia, and at this moment she is at the theatre, to see a man named Wurm, an excellent comic actor from Berlin, with whom she is enchanted.

You will read in all the newspapers, among other things, that I have had a frightful fall from a carriage, and that I remained unconscious during, I believe, five or six hours. The fact is that I have had no fall, and consequently have had neither accident nor fainting fit. About a fortnight ago in starting from the Emperor's house in one of the excellent Court equipages, the axletree broke, the carriage leaned on one side, my servant opened the door, I got out of the carriage, and went on foot to a *soirée* at Madame Catalani's. The coachman fell off, and has been made famous. All the English papers have correspondents here : they must write something, and, having nothing to say about the progress of affairs, they amuse themselves with killing the ministers.

Our portraits by Lawrence are really *chefs-d'œuvre*. Mine, which is almost finished, is one of the best.* He will take it to Vienna, where I shall make him copy it, as I shall never be painted again.

I am sure Marie will tell you her ideas about it. You will laugh when you see it.

* The portrait of Prince Metternich engraved by Professor Unger for this work is the one mentioned here.—ED.

273. *November* 16.—Our business is concluded. The Emperor Alexander left this morning for Brussels. Our Emperor starts to-morrow for Vienna. I leave the day after to-morrow, early in the morning, for Brussels, where important business awaits me. I shall be detained there four days, between that and the infernal etiquette which naturally accompanies it.

I spend my days in work, and all I can tell you is that I am marvellously well, and not yet quite driven out of my mind. A courier leaves this evening for Vienna. I shall return here on the 22nd or the 23rd, and remain two or three days, because the Conference is in abeyance until my return. I shall be at Vienna from the 8th to the 10th December, and the Emperor will be there on the 2nd. The Emperor Alexander will follow me closely; he will arrive at Vienna on the 12th.

274. *November* 21.—I wished to leave to-morrow, but the impossibility of carrying out my intention was shown at the Conference this morning. We do not know how to avoid having one to-morrow morning, and probably another in the evening, which will be the last. I send on my carriages in advance to-morrow evening, and I shall leave with the Duke of Wellington. We shall be at Brussels in fourteen or fifteen days. You know my plans as far as Vienna. I do not foresee that they can undergo any important change.

On November 23, Brussels; the 24th, 25th, and 26th, I stay there; the 27th, Antwerp; the 28th, Aix-la-Chapelle; the 29th, Cologne; the 30th, Coblentz.

December 1, Johannisberg; the 2nd, Frankfurt; the 3rd, 4th, and 5th, the journey to Munich; the 6th and 7th, I stay there; the 8th, Alt-Œttingen; the 9th,

Wels; the 10th, Kemmelbach or Amstetten; the 11th, Vienna.

You see that I shall be only one day in advance of the Emperor Alexander, which is certainly not too much. His visit to Vienna not being on business, the mere fact of his presence will not trouble me, for we have become the most intimate friends. Marie, when she saw us the first time, was quite astonished—she had never seen us except on bad terms with each other. She danced several polonaises with him, and also with our Emperor, at the ball given by the town to the sovereigns on Sunday last. The Emperor was as charmed to see her as if he had known her all his life. '*Sie ist eine der Meinigen,*' said he to me twenty times; '*Die habe ich lieber als alle die Anderen.*'

Our business is over, and our conference of to-morrow is nothing more than a winding up; everything is well arranged, and I believe that we shall gain honour in Europe. I have never seen more perfect agreement between the Cabinets; our affairs—the rough as well as the smooth—ran as if they went of themselves. The result is what I foresaw and above all desired.

I do not know what I would give now to have got over the rest of the journey between this and Vienna. I shall take this journey with the feeling of a postillion who returns empty to his starting-point, and who twenty times curses the length of the road he still has to traverse before he can get to his bed.

275. *Donauwörth, December 6.*—. . . . I found Prince Hardenberg at Aix-la-Chapelle, and worked with him all one day. I passed a night and a morning at Johannisberg, where I saw forty grand casks arranged in the finest cellar in the world. The wine will be excellent, and twelve thousand ducats' worth might be sold to-morrow. It will be worth twenty thousand in five years. I shall have neither rest nor respite till you have seen this place, which is really a glorious possession. Nothing resembles it in beauty, and the house only requires a little care to become very beautiful. If one had only a cottage there, one would seem to possess the world.

I shall stop at Munich on the 8th, and I shall be at Vienna on the 11th, in the evening, or, more probably, on the morning of the 12th. You will be forewarned of my arrival by one of my carriages, which I shall send on from the last place I sleep at, which will be either Wels or Enns.

. . . . Good God! everybody seems to be dead amongst us! I learnt all these catastrophes in a way which would have been pleasant if it had been on any other subject. I saw Count d'Eltz at Coblentz. He had just returned from Brazil, and is there on business connected with the property of his father, who is dying a frightful death. . . . I offered my sympathy, and asked him for news from Vienna. I had not heard for more than a week, as my letters were waiting for me at Frankfurt. 'They have cut off Jean Palffy's leg,' said he; ' but his brother is still more to be pitied, for he lost one part of his body after another in his journey to Italy.' 'That is dreadful,' said I. 'Yes, two days before the death of Count de Wallis.' 'What! is he dead?' 'The Count de Kuefstein is buried.' 'What! he also!' 'The sacrament has been administered to Marshal Colloredo ; and his brother, Marshal Wenzel, is dying.' I implored him to leave off, for he did not seem to have half finished.

Metternich to his daughter Marie, Vienna, December 17.

276. Here I am, my dear Marie, at home; but you are not there, and I assure you that you are much wanted. We think much more of you than of ourselves. We follow all your steps, and I think I can guess most of them.

On my arrival I found Mamma and the children in the best of health. Victor is as tall as a full-grown man. Clementine is improved. I do not think Leontine has grown much. Herminie is really as well as possible. Mamma has told you of the funny mistake I made when I arrived, in taking Leontine for Herminie. I enquired about her leg, and she thought I was mad. She was sleeping in her new room, instead of her sister. I thought she had grown very much ; but never mind. Thoughts make a slip sometimes, like the tongue, and one cannot extricate one's self.

We are here, not amongst *fêtes*, for the Emperor Alexander does not wish it, but in the sweet and quiet little pleasures of the Court. The Emperor Alexander has at length made the acquaintance of his aunt.* He passes whole days in kissing her hand, and calling her 'my dear aunt.' The presentation took place before dinner by the Empress. At the very moment the Emperor kissed the hand of his dear aunt I thought of Herminie, and I agree with her that Aunt Pauline is everybody's aunt.

Good bye, my dear Marie. The journey to Italy is decided upon, but there is an alteration in it, which is in your favour. The Emperor will leave on February 13, and in the beginning of March he will be at Florence instead of Naples—that is to say, he will

* Duchess Pauline von Wurtemberg, sister to Prince Metternich.—ED.

begin by spending nearly three weeks of the month of March in Tuscany ; from there he will go to Rome for Holy Week, and after that, about April 17 or 18, to Naples.

277. *December* 25.—I was sure that Paris would suit Pepi very well. He has taste, and is accessible to good impressions. Paris is the city for society, as London is for commerce. The one cannot be compared to the other, for they are perfectly different. Vienna is like other populous cities; she may count more streets than some perhaps, but cannot boast of being greater. The human mind needs continual friction to enable it to rise above the common level. It is natural that an assembly of more than five hundred thousand individuals in one place, under a beautiful sky, in a fertile country, must offer facilities to a development, to an industrial and commercial activity, very different from that of other less populous centres. This is the secret of the perfection of Paris and London, which both resemble ancient Rome, ancient Heliopolis, and still more ancient Babylon. The same causes always produce the same effects, and the latter are only modified by the progress of knowledge, science, and art. Now, a very slight elevation of mind or refinement of taste leads people to prefer the very best to the tolerably good. Be sure that as often as this preference does not take place, it is from the lack of these qualities, or the result of the presumption inseparable from ignorance. This is not, however, at all connected with happiness. Happiness may depend on a single object or a single taste, and consequently on a single necessity ; it is sufficient for happiness to find some small corner in which this individual taste may be satisfied. This explains why you are happy at Lanschütz, I in my garden, and Mamma in

Herminie's room. Nevertheless, everybody is not equally exclusive or equally moderate in his tastes; so, though you and I are happy at Lanschütz and at Rennweg, we are equally happy on the Boulevards, at the Museum, and even in the Catacombs; while Mamma is only happy in that one room at the *Chancellerie.*

METTERNICH'S CORRESPONDENCE WITH THE EMPEROR FRANCIS ON THE JOURNEY TO AIX.

Twenty-one Reports from Prince Metternich to the Emperor Francis, with his Majesty's notes, from July 8 to November 17, 1818.

278. *Carlsbad, July* 8, 1818.—I hasten with much respect to inform your Majesty of my arrival here yesterday. Carlsbad is very full of strangers, among whom are diplomatists from all countries, who are here, some only to confer with me, some to observe my meeting with Count Capo d'Istria, who is expected here on the 10th.

As I passed through Prague yesterday, the chief burgomaster came and asked me whether a meeting of the monarchs would take place at Prague. I asserted the contrary. He then told me that a few days before, he had received an official order to repair the second storey of Schloss-Hradschin at his own cost. I assured him there was some extraordinary mistake, and advised him to wait your Majesty's commands before he incurred any expense. I therefore beseech your Majesty to make your commands known ; it is possible that some reparation was intended, but this did not appear in the instructions, and evidently some great mistake must have been made. In any case, I consider it my duty to inform your Majesty of an error of this kind, which must cause a great outlay, the object of which I cannot see.

I consider Prince Schwarzenberg is in much better health. He is in good spirits, and the cure is so far quite successful.

METTERNICH.

Received this Report, and I have already given the necessary orders for the case to be inquired into as to the repairs to be carried out at the Castle at Prague.*

FRANCIS.

Baden, July 15, 1818.

279. *Carlsbad, July* 9.—Letters from Copenhagen announce the sudden death of the widowed Queen of Sweden. She had been with the King in the evening, and died at five o'clock in the morning.

The King, who was going to Norway, has put off his journey till after the funeral of the Queen.

As a political event, this is of no importance.

METTERNICH.

Received this Report.

FRANCIS.

Baden, July 14, 1818.

* This note, as well as all those on the following letters, is written by the Emperor Francis himself.—ED.

280. *Carlsbad, July* 14.—May it please your Majesty to observe enclosed, a very interesting letter from Lebzeltern, in London.   The English Cabinet is most favourably disposed, and the opinions of Lebzeltern in every respect well founded.

Your Majesty will also find enclosed a private letter from Marquis de Caraman, which contains information of a so-called Ultra-Royalist conspiracy.   I say so-called, because it does not appear to me to be of that nature. A few days will suffice to prove the truth of this.   I believe myself that the whole thing is an intrigue of the Ultras on some party grounds.   From Paris I have very little news of the matter.

May it please your Majesty to notice that the French Ministry, or, more properly speaking, Count Richelieu, hopes, since the late retreat, that my intervention between the Ministerial party and Monsieur the King's brother may bring about some approximation.   Monsieur himself has come to me with the same end in view. In a few days I shall be in a position to lay before your Majesty the steps I have taken in this important matter.   No moment is more proper than the eve of a meeting of the monarchs to be crowned with a result of this kind, hitherto certainly unattainable.   I intend to use these last hours, so full of tension, with all my might to guide both parties to straightforward and thoroughly confidential ways.   It is a great satisfaction to me that equal confidence is placed in me by both parties.

According to private letters received from Berlin to-day, the King will arrive with the Emperor Alexander towards the end of this month.   A military encampment which the city had intended to prepare for the diversion of the sovereigns has been countermanded, and the Emperor Alexander will employ the interval between his arrival in Prussia and the meeting in visiting his sister. Whether this will include a visit to Stuttgart I know not, but I rather doubt it.

In any case no good can come of the Emperor's moving about in this way before the interview takes place ; but I cannot confirm the truth of the intelligence I submit to you until the next official news from Berlin, which I am hourly expecting.

METTERNICH.

This Report received and enclosures returned.

FRANCIS.

Baden, July 21, 1818.

281. *Carlsbad, July* 22.—May it please your Majesty to receive a statement of Count Thurn's, by which your Majesty will see that the Emperor Alexander continues to treat the Prince of Hesse with the greatest attention.

The Emperor now begins to occupy himself with the condition of the peasantry in the Russo-Polish provinces. That there is plenty of good material is undeniable ; but, on the other hand, the Emperor runs some risk of kindling a conflagration in the interior of his kingdom. The Russians are in general very well under control ; what would be the result of further progress is very difficult to determine.

Count Capo d'Istria comes here about the 26th or 27th of this month, to await his master's arrival from St. Petersburg, which will not be before the 15th of next month.

In the meantime I am looked upon by the chief people here as bearing an accredited mission from your Majesty, and to me there is no difference between

Vienna and Carlsbad, except the change of place. I endeavour to get as much time for distraction as possible, and can heartily praise the waters here. On the 31st of this month I leave Carlsbad, and as there will be three or four days' interval between the two courses of the water-cure, I shall give myself till about August 4. On the 5th I shall begin the waters at Franzens-brunn. The difference in the condition of Field-Marshal Prince Schwarzenberg is most astonishing. His internal complaint gets better every day ; the Carlsbad waters do not, however, act directly on his other complaints, and he is, therefore, ordered to try some baths, from which his physician hopes the best possible result. His weakness has already been so far conquered that he can walk for some hours.

METTERNICH.

Received this Report, and I hope that the waters and baths may have the same happy results for you as for Prince Schwarzenberg.

FRANCIS.

282. May it please your Majesty. The news that the Emperor Alexander will arrive on September 27 instead of the 15th, and that the opening of the Conference must be delayed for fourteen days, will create a very bad impression in France. Matters are not really altered, but the delay and uncertainty are trying, and must be equally unpleasant to the Government and the nation.

This gain or loss of time leads me to consider whether I could not make good use of those twelve free days by going from the Rhine to Paris.

The following considerations are in favour of this:

1. I should see for myself clearly what at a distance is often obscure.

2. It would give me an entirely different position at the Conference at Aix among the other Cabinet ministers, who have not, like me, been on the spot.

3. If there is any chance of Monsieur's agreement with the Government, to bring about which I am urged by both parties, I would not willingly lose any opportunity of helping forward so desirable an object. The situation requires great management. I have sent the Marquis de Caraman from Carlsbad to Paris with a mission on this subject, and have sent back with him an individual whom Monsieur sent to me about eight days ago. In the success of this affair lies a considerable guarantee for the future, while from the continuance of this unhappy disunion there is every chance of the most distressing consequences. The moment before the interview of the monarchs is urgent, and requires urgent means to be used to act on both parties.

4. I should, lastly, find a very strong inducement for the journey to Paris in the fact of Lord Castlereagh's journey through that city, which seems possible.

If your Majesty is pleased to entertain these opinions, I will proceed to Paris, and act according to circumstances under your Majesty's full authority. These circumstances being every day liable to change, I must make the best use I can of them at the time.

I therefore beseech your Majesty to keep this mission a deep secret. If I am to carry out the affair I must receive a command, the day when the meeting of the monarchs is put off, to make use of the delay to ascertain the state of things on the spot. If I do not take this journey, the public must know nothing of the matter.

In any case I shall go up the Rhine at the end of this month, and the Chancellor Prince Hardenberg,

Count Münster in the name of the English Cabinet. and several others, intend either to meet me. or to come to me at Johannisberg, so that we may talk over the affairs of the Conference.

Should your Majesty be pleased to entertain my idea of a sudden journey to Paris, I should in any case not go before September 7, and return on the 23rd to your Majesty at Mayence.

I humbly beseech your Majesty to give your gracious commands as soon as possible concerning this secret commission.

METTERNICH.

Franzensbrunn, August 7, 1818.

I allow you to go to Paris, if you find it will be useful, and I shall expect you in any case on September 23, at Mayence.

FRANCIS.

Baden, August 11, 1818.

283. May it please your Majesty. The sad event which has befallen me and my house makes it my duty to express to your Majesty my deepest gratitude for the favour your Majesty has continually vouchsafed to my lamented father during his long career. In his earliest youth he was attracted to the service of your Majesty by the example of his ancestors, and still more by his own feeling. His only wish and all his efforts had but one end—the honour and advantage of the Imperial House and of the State. Your Majesty has lost a servant, weakened, it is true, by age, but still a faithful and attached servant. His constant desire was to see me fulfil the duties which his age and circumstances no longer permitted him to undertake, and his greatest consolation was the feeling of the success of my exertions during the troubles of a most anxious time. When he was asked by my family, a few days before his end, whether he did not wish to see me in Vienna, he said, ' My son is doing his duty. I can give him my blessing as well at a distance, and to-day belongs to him and his business.'

These words console me for not having seen him, and having been unable to fulfil the duties of a son.

I now implore your Majesty's favour for the house of which I am now the head. For myself, your Majesty has so long treated me as a father that gratitude alone is becoming in me. If the subversion of things of late years has placed my family merely in the relation of all other vassals and subjects of the Imperial House, my only wish is that my successors may do from a feeling of duty what they would in all probability have done of their own free will.

METTERNICH.

Franzensbad, August 19, 1818.

I feel deep sympathy for the loss of your father, and count as surely on your attachment to my person as that you will influence your family and successors to follow in your footsteps, and become able and faithful servants, like yourself.

FRANCIS.

Vienna, August 19, 1818.

284. *Franzensbrunn, August* 18.—May it please your Majesty. I went yesterday to Carlsbad, to have some conversation with Count Capo d'Istria, who had been there for some days.

The result of this conversation was, in my opinion, important and satisfactory. I can indicate the principal points in it to your Majesty, who always desires to be informed of the course of great political affairs.

These are as follows :—

1. The Emperor of Russia, though hesitating between many conflicting moral motives, does not abandon the fundamental principle of the maintenance of peace. To this he is impelled both by his distance from all that is influenced by the playing with soldiers, and by his religious principles ever growing more vigorous.

2. The Emperor and his Cabinet give themselves up more and more every day to moral and political proselytising. Hence the many intrigues, great and small, so irritating to us and most other Governments, and hence the deluge of emissaries and apostles.

In this active movement the intention is, however, not to be mistaken (it lies, obscurely or plainly, in the Emperor's mind)—of trusting to time and the course of things to favour the extension of Russian influence. But an influence of this kind does not even grow to be a power.

3. Count Capo d'Istria is extremely against the form of the next meeting.

First, he does not wish the monarchs to appear personally at the same, and he regrets that his master should be the special and almost only cause of this. With this opinion I quite agreed.

Secondly, he desired either no meeting of the monarchs and the Cabinets, or that it should be universal.

His reasons are as follows :—

He believes that so great a measure will only excite the jealousy of the Powers not admitted, strain the public mind excessively, and injure both monarchs and Cabinets by the want of results.

Here I differed entirely from him. My reasons are the following, and I explained them to the Count so far as possible, considering the difference between the plans and actions of our two Governments.

The five Courts which are assembled at Aix are not only invited there, but by the treaty of November 20, 1815, they are bound to come. All the European Courts have by their consent acknowledged and confirmed this treaty and all its stipulations.

The fulfilling of a right, and still more of a duty, cannot excite the jealousy of those who are beyond that right and duty. No Government fears the question which is referred to Aix being decided by the five Courts, for they are summoned for that purpose; but all Governments fear lest the four or five Courts should venture to bring forward more than that one business. Therefore, the four Courts must carry out this one business only at Aix, and therefore have we insisted that the four Courts long before the meeting should solemnly make this engagement. Our care must now be that it is maintained and fulfilled.

The feeling of the revolutionists only is excited, not at all that of well-disposed persons. Since this is undeniably and certainly the case, the beneficial result of the interview will be that nothing will be altered in the existing order of things. This result will be for your Majesty and the Cabinet—which since 1815 has taken a decided course—the highest triumph.

But for the Court which pays homage to the so-called spirit of the times on every occasion, and revives by its expressions the hopes of innovators and sectaries of every kind—for this Court the result will be, at so important an epoch as that of Aix-la-Chapelle, in the highest degree injurious even in the eyes of these innovators themselves.

In these short sentences lies the important difference between the Austrian and the Russian calculations. Ours have, up to this time, been triumphant, and I doubt not that this will be again the case at Aix. That the Russian Minister does not like the coming conference in the shape it has already taken is quite natural. That we, on the contrary, are agreeable to the said form is no less so. Much here depended on the first word, and we spoke it at the right moment, and thereby avoided a number of difficulties in a sense totally different from Count Capo d'Istria's fears.

I have, moreover, already gained so much ground in the English and Prussian Cabinets that in the conferences I foresee no possible digression from the course appointed.*

285. *Franzensbrunn, August* 20. May it please your Majesty. As I am aware of your Majesty's gracious feeling for Field-Marshal Prince von Schwarzenberg, I consider it a duty respectfully to inform your Majesty of an opportunity of doing him a great kindness with very little trouble. His eldest son, Friedrich, has been for more than a year a cadet in his father's regiment of uhlans. By strenuous efforts he has distinguished himself to the satisfaction of his father, and it is his wish that he should be promoted to be sub-lieutenant. If your Majesty would deign to do this as of your Majesty's own thought, so great a mark

---

* On the document of which this is a copy is written a note in the Chancellor's handwriting, but of a much later date: 'This Report is important because it shows the grounds of the difference in the views and course of the two Imperial Cabinets. Count Capo d'Istria was the representative of a trifling political school; personally he had in his eye only the Hellenic cause, which was in the year 1818 in preparation. The alliance system between the great Powers was detested by him for this reason, and for its opposition to the Liberalism which found a zealous representative in the minister who was more Greek than Russian.'—ED.

of favour to the Field-Marshal would excite his deepest gratitude.

If your Majesty vouchsafe to grant this request —which I make without his knowledge—I suggest most respectfully that your Majesty should write to this effect to the Field-Marshal, and that as soon as possible, since otherwise he may come forward with a direct request.

I am the more inclined to take the present step, as the King of Prussia has, since the arrival of Field-Marshal Blücher at Carlsbad, sent an adjutant to him almost weekly to enquire after his health, which is much declining.

METTERNICH.

I will immediately act upon your suggestion.

FRANCIS.

Baden, August 25, 1818.

286. *Franzensbrunn, August* 20.—Enclosed in this your Majesty will deign to receive a Report from Prince Kaunitz, which shows how the cause is progressing in Rome.* If the Roman Court follows the course hinted at, it is hardly possible to foresee what complications it may bring about in Germany. It is our duty to make this clear, and to give our support at once to the reasonable party among the Cardinals.

Your Majesty has deigned to approve my last instructions to the ambassador, Prince Kaunitz. I will immediately write to him urgently in the same sense.

---

* This Report, of July 10, expresses the fear that in Rome a party of *Zelanti* among the Cardinals were striving against the conciliatory attitude of Consalvi, and urging the Pope to vigorous measures against the Courts of Bavaria and Baden—the former, because it stultified by new laws the Concordat just concluded ; the latter, because it took under its protection the Vicar-Capitular Wessenberg, at Constance, who was threatened with an interdict.—ED.

I respectfully beg your Majesty to have the present Report, with its enclosures, handed to Councillor von Hudelist.

METTERNICH.

Noticed, and the Report given to Von Hudelist. Our endeavour must be to act in such a way that the Catholic religion may not be needlessly injured by hasty measures or an excess of zeal.

FRANCIS.

Baden, August 25, 1818.

287. *Königswart, August* 26.—Your Majesty will be pleased to receive, in two enclosures, the instructions I have issued on the 23rd instant to Freiherr von Vincent, in the extremely important affair of the reconciliation of Monsieur with his brother the King of France.

Your Majesty will deign to remember that in the spring your ambassador was instructed by Monsieur to express his wish for a possible reconciliation. Baron Vincent at once informed the Duke of Wellington of the circumstance, and of his conversation with the Prince; he also informed the Duke of Richelieu of the matter.

I at once answered Freiherr von Vincent, begging him to make known to the King's brother the readiness of your Majesty to co-operate in the good work of reconciliation, but expressing my personal conviction that, first of all, Monsieur himself should make all possible efforts to attain this end.

I took this course—

1. Because, from the steps taken by His Royal Highness in consequence of my reply, his own standpoint will be made clear.

2. Because I wished to ascertain whether Monsieur

had taken the resolution from motives of his own, or whether he had been impelled to do so by the Ultra-Royalist party, or one of its numerous subdivisions.

3. Because your Majesty's intervention in a domestic matter can only safely be permitted if the intervention of a third person is desired by both the parties at variance.

My expectations in this respect were fulfilled : several attempts at reconciliation were begun, partly by Monsieur, partly by the ministers. They were all without any result.

Nearly at the same time, in the course of June, steps were taken on the part of the Ultras and the Duke of Richelieu, to invite me to take part in the business. I informed the Duke that I should certainly be empowered to act in this matter by your Majesty, but that the moment did not seem to have arrived when the intervention would be really successful, and then I must have to do, not with one or other of the Ultra-Royalist parties, but with Monsieur himself.

I had this information also conveyed to Monsieur.

Upon this, Monsieur actually sent to me at Carlsbad a confidential person, who had no direct contact with the party, and negotiated as the immediate organ of the Prince himself. This individual was sent back to Paris to inform Monsieur—

1. That the matter was now placed on a proper footing.

2. That Freiherr von Vincent would be commissioned to act personally as mediator.

I informed the Duke of Richelieu of the state of things through the Marquis of Caraman, whom I sent to Paris, showing him also that, in order to gain time, I would push on the negotiation as near as possible to the interview at Aix-la-Chapelle, feeling convinced that success could only be secured by the greatest despatch. Monsieur is weak ; he must himself make the approaches to reconciliation, and if time is given for him to confer with the party all will be lost.

The Duke of Richelieu agreed with my views.

When all these things were discussed I sent the above-mentioned instructions to Freiherr von Vincent, the purport of which will itself explain to your Majesty the standpoint in the business which I must think to be the best.

Despatch No. 1 is to be shown to both parties.

Despatch No. 2 contains the instructions for Vincent alone.

Not till we reach the Rhine shall I be able to tell your Majesty the result of the steps your Majesty's ambassadors have taken.

I received yesterday, just as I was starting for Franzensbrunn, a letter from the Duke of Richelieu, in which he urgently entreated me to come to Paris, to conduct the business in person. I shall not come to a decision till I know the result of the first steps. These, at any rate, must be taken by some other person: if I find they go well I will take the journey; if not, I will make my excursion to Paris depend on the circumstance of Lord Castlereagh's presence in Paris. If he does not choose that road, and there is no certain prospect of the success of the mediation, I shall not take the journey.

I flatter myself that your Majesty will vouchsafe to approve of the conduct of the business so far. I consider it the most important affair of the moment, but I am far from being confident of success. The parties stand so aloof from each other that very great impartiality will be necessary on both sides in order to bring about an approximation. Although the success of the affair does not depend on the mediator alone, it is none the less honourable for your Majesty and your Majesty's Cabinet to be chosen by both sides to carry out so excellent an object, and nothing, perhaps, shows so well the position of your Majesty in the political affairs of Europe as this very thing.

METTERNICH.

Acted upon, and the enclosures returned. Only one thought strikes me—namely, whether Monsieur, if he is weak and thoughtless, may not perhaps bring about some mischance or mistake from his knowledge of our views with regard to Russia and the conduct of the Emperor Alexander.

FRANCIS.

Baden, August 30, 1818.

288. *Königswart, August* 26.—Your Majesty will please to receive in the enclosed Report from Herr von Handel information as to the reception your Majesty may expect on the Rhine.

I know the feeling of the people in those districts, and have advised your Majesty's journey up that river because I was convinced that it would have the character of a triumphal procession.

Besides, the party of the disaffected will receive a serious blow from the demonstrations made by the Rhinelanders. The open and spontaneous expression of a hundred thousand people is better and more convincing than all the declamations of Jena Professors and students.

The great difference will also be seen between the journey of your Majesty and those of the Emperor

Alexander and the King of Prussia, and this will certainly be for the advantage of Germany.

METTERNICH.

Noticed with pleasure.

FRANCIS.

Baden, August 30, 1818.

289. *Frankfurt, August* 30.—May it please your Majesty. At the moment of my arrival here I received the enclosed letter from the Prince of Hesse, which a courier brought me from Berlin.

I think it would be well for your Majesty to send the necessary orders to Prague, in order to show every possible attention to the Dowager Empress.* Everything had been arranged for her reception at Schloss-Hradschin; the cooks she will of course bring with her. That your Majesty should send part of the household depends entirely upon your Majesty's wishes. Four gentlemen in attendance seem to me necessary, and an individual who can act as Master of the Household. For this purpose one of the Princes of Prague—perhaps Prince Lobkowitz—would be suitable.

Your Majesty will find in your impending journey a reason for not visiting the Empress in person. In any case I have the honour to enclose the draft of a letter which, when your Majesty has received the news of her arrival, can be sent to Prague.

The inferences which might be drawn from the Prince of Hesse's letter are entirely contradicted by what Count Capo d'Istria told me, that the Emperor Alexander had unfortunately not given up the plan of travelling—at least in Upper Italy—till the end of the meeting at Aix.

Which of them is here mistaken, Count Capo d'Istria

* Empress of Russia.—ED.

or the Prince of Hesse, seems to me only too certain.
I have, however, in any case written to the former
fixing the arrangements in Carlsbad, so that his answer
to me may reach your Majesty with the desired information without delay.

What the Emperor Alexander intends to do in
Switzerland in November, and why he chooses to make
the passage of the Simplon at this time, is, indeed, by no
reasoning to be discovered.

The Emperor's resolution will, however, no doubt
decide your Majesty to go to Milan, but no preparations
can be made until the truth is known with regard to the
travelling plans of the Emperor Alexander.

METTERNICH.

290. *Frankfurt, August* 31.—Your Majesty has requested me through the Lord High Chamberlain to
propose certain gentlemen to attend your Majesty to
Aix, besides the two in permanent attendance.

In my opinion, these should be chosen from reliable
young men of good address, who may be of service for
any mission that is required.

I propose therefore :—

1. Count Ladislaus Wrbna.
2. Count Bellegarde.
3. Count Felix Woyna.

Count Wrbna wishes very much that his nephew,
Major Pozzo, might be chosen for this honour; I find
nothing to object to in his person, but, in the present
case, very much against his name. Since he is a lord-
in-waiting (which he ought not to be, for the Pozzo
family was never one of the Corsican nobility), he would
be suitable, like any other lord-in-waiting, for attendance

on your Majesty; but just at this meeting at Aix, a kind of attention might be anticipated which would be in no way beneficial.

If your Majesty wishes for four instead of three lords-in-waiting, Count Schönfeld or any other good-looking young man might be chosen.

I much regret that not one Italian seems to be at the disposal of your Majesty.

METTERNICH.

Noticed; and, as Count Felix Woyna is with his regiment in Hungary, I have chosen Counts Wrbna, Bellegarde, and Schönfeld to accompany me to Aix-la-Chapelle.

FRANCIS.

Baden, September 9, 1818.

291. *Frankfurt, September 4.*—May it please your Majesty. My residence in this place, which was not at all intentional, but arose from a slight attack of rheumatic fever (the consequence of exposure to some extremely bad weather during my journey from Bohemia), has, however, had the most happy results. Since my appearance in Frankfurt a thorough moral revolution has taken place; the different parties had, as was expected, made some attempts at reconciliation, and what has never happened before has been accomplished under my immediate direction.

I can now answer for it that the Report of the Bundestag on the military organisation of the Bund will be returned by the assembly in the course of this month. This Report is the very work itself, for it is the result of the unanimous deliberation of the first and most influential Courts with the co-operation of the military representatives of the whole of the German Govern-

ments.   As soon as the Report is returned the assembly
will adjourn for two months and take holidays.   This
time coincides with that of the conferences at Aix.   In
this way, all political difficulty is obviated, and by the
conclusion of the business all Russian interference will
be prevented.

During the journey your Majesty will see some of
the German Princes.   At the right moment I will send
your Majesty a short sketch of the sentiments which it
is much to be wished should emanate from your Majesty.   Every word spoken by your Majesty at this time
will produce the greatest effect.   One must be in the
midst of Germany to understand on what a moral height
your Majesty's Court now stands.   In this respect so
much ground is gained that it can only be lessened by
its own fault.

I shall be at Johannisberg by the 7th inst., and on
the 13th I shall go to Chancellor Hardenberg, with whom
I shall go Coblentz on the 14th and 15th.   On the
16th I shall return to the Rheingau, where Count
Münster and several other diplomatists will be waiting
for me.   On the 22nd I shall pay my respects to your
Majesty at Mayence.

METTERNICH.

Noticed ; and I shall expect the sketch of what you
wish me to say in Germany.

FRANCIS.

Baden, September 9, 1818.

292. Please your Majesty.   From the news which
arrived yesterday by the Princess of Hesse-Homburg, of
the health of her mother, the Queen of England, it seems
that she is already given up by the physicians.   They
do not think that she can live more than a week longer.

The death of the Queen will hasten the meeting of Parliament within six weeks' time, in order that new measures may be taken for the care of the King. Lord Castlereagh, who had foreseen this, has already prepared the necessary measures, so as not to interrupt his stay in Aix.

METTERNICH.

Noticed.

FRANCIS.

Persenbeug, September 17, 1818.

293. *Schloss-Johannisberg, September* 18.—May it please your Majesty. There is a mistake in the arrangements made out for your Majesty's journey which I can alter from this place without any delay. They have stationed your Majesty's horses at Darmstadt: in the list the station of Langfeld is mentioned, which has long ago ceased to exist. The station is now removed to Dieburg; the road from Darmstadt to Mayence by Groszherau is disused and, in every sense of the word, impracticable, because bridges and roads have been built in a quite different direction. At Kostheim, your Majesty and the whole suite must from this old road cross the ferry over the Main, which would take more than half a day. There is certainly some error here, which has probably arisen from the use of an old post-book by the person who prepared the list.

The Elector of Hesse, too, is already in Hanau, or rather at Wilhelmsbad, close by, in consequence of the hope which was held out to him that your Majesty would alight there. At Frankfurt, your Majesty is expected by the whole population with indescribable joy. According to the list made out, your Majesty would avoid Hanau and Frankfurt and stop at Darmstadt, whose Court has taken such a miserable course in German affairs, and in no way deserves this distinction.

I have told Herr von Handel how the road now runs *de facto*, and that he must follow it, and station the horses on it, *de facto*.

Since your Majesty thinks the first day from Mayence too short, I will make preparations for your Majesty to stay the night at St. Goar. This is a good day's journey on the Rhine—that is, if your Majesty does not desire to travel after dark, which presents more difficulty, especially on the river. Your Majesty's retinue will travel by land along the banks of the Rhine, where there is a new high road. If the weather should be bad, your Majesty may choose this mode of travelling instead of going on the river.

As your Majesty will see by the enclosure, the Emperor Alexander will not come to Aix till the 28th. The King of Prussia hopes that your Majesty will not arrive till that day, in order to give him the advantage of himself receiving your Majesty. It will thus be possible for your Majesty to pass a day at Coblentz, where the new fortifications are well worthy of your Majesty's attention ; I should the more wish that your Majesty should inspect these works with Duka (Ordnance-Master) as they are made on a new principle which with the greatest security unites a saving of expense of certainly two-thirds.

The works are very far advanced and conducted by Saxon engineers, who are distinguished by real talent. It is almost incredible that what is already finished has cost no more than 800,000 thalers. By the end of this year Coblentz will afford room for 60,000 men.

I send to meet your Majesty at Esselbach Herr von Handel, to receive your Majesty's orders for the journey from that place to Aix, and carry out all the arrangements, allowing for the proposed delay of one day.

METTERNICH.

Received and noticed. The enclosed Reports are herewith returned.

FRANCIS.

Aix-la-Chapelle, September 29, 1818.

294. *Johannisberg, Sept.* 19.—In passing through Hanau, your Majesty will see the Elector. Annexed to this your Majesty will find a Report of General Wacquant concerning the Elector's very great wish to attain the Royal dignity.

My feeling is entirely against the thing. In relation to the Bund, nothing now ought to be altered, even in name; the dignity of the Crown certainly requires that the domain of a king should consist of more than one circle.

The Elector seems conscious of this, and suggests the most futile expedient of a collective Royal dignity, which must deprive that dignity of all value.

I propose, therefore, with all respect, that your Majesty should declare with regard to this matter that it is of a nature which your Majesty cannot alone decide.

If the Elector should ask your Majesty's advice, whether he should make any advances towards the other monarchs (he has already approached Prussia on the subject), your Majesty should advise him not to do so, and promise to talk over the matter confidentially at Aix.

With respect to the German Bund, your Majesty might say to the Elector—

' That your Majesty observes with sorrow the course that the Elector has lately taken at variance with his distinct promise to your Majesty's Cabinet.

' That your Majesty would make the proposal of a division of the combined contingents into three corps, which, however, would by no means allow Hesse to be with Wurtemberg. Each one of the confederation must keep to his own geographical position. The crossing of the regular line of halting-places must be avoided. The corps would have to be as equal in strength to one another as possible. Too strong corps would form armies, and too weak corps, divisions, which give a great opening to the passion for incorporation.

' How the three corps should be composed will have to be immediately arranged by your Majesty's minister ; but that Hesse can never be with Wurtemberg results from the geographical position of the two States. That it could not be agreeable to the Elector to abandon his own country, and withdraw from it to an artificial line—a line on which the whole Bavarian army would be drawn up between Hesse and the corps to which Hesse's army wished to be attached : a line, too, which must be crossed by way of Saxony.'

If your Majesty should wish for more details on this question, Herr von Handel, whom I send to Esselbach to receive your Majesty's orders, is quite able to give your Majesty every information.

I have, besides, conferred with the ambassadors assembled here, in order to bring the military question to a conclusion in the first place here in Frankfurt— before Aix-la-Chapelle. I flatter myself that in this respect the last three weeks which I have spent here have effected more than anything which has been done, and have certainly led to the happy result of withdrawing every complication from Aix-la-Chapelle.

I shall have the honour to expect your Majesty in Mayence on the 22nd.

If your Majesty should give a regiment to the Elector, this could only be done in consequence of good conduct on his part as to the affairs of the Diet. I cannot express any desire for such a favour to the Electoral Prince. Neither his personal attitude nor the value of his services entitle him to receive it.

METTERNICH.

The Elector has spoken to me of his desire for the Royal dignity in a way that showed how much he is bent on attaining it. I gathered from what he said about the German contingents that he had given up his idea of joining his troops in one corps with those of Wurtemberg. No mention was made of the subject of the regiment. I return the documents that were enclosed, and take notice of the other contents of your Report.

FRANCIS.

Aix-la-Chapelle, September 27, 1818.

295. *Aix-la-Chapelle, October* 7.—Annexed I have the honour to lay before your Majesty a preliminary survey of the military negotiation at Frankfurt.

A slight glance will convince your Majesty that the work touches on all the chief questions of a vigorous military organisation. Your Majesty will deign to observe that it is worked out in detail with the same cogency as the Report to the Bund, which I expect in two or three days.

This affair is certainly one of the most important of the present time, and, if I do not regret the great and continuous labour it has cost me for more than a year, it is only from the feeling of having rendered a true service to your Majesty and afforded substantial support to society in Europe. The most difficult matter was the bringing to an agreement at the right moment so many opinions or feelings, often separated by the most paltry and unworthy considerations. Nothing, too, could be more judicious than to show that, at the very moment of the evacuation of France, Germany is able to bear arms, and to render impossible any interference from Aix-la-Chapelle with purely Federal affairs.

In this respect I consider my last stay in Frankfurt as a moment favoured by fortune beyond all calculation.

The Bund will adjourn from the 12th instant till January.

METTERNICH.

Received and noticed. You will lay before me as soon as possible the details of the military organisation of the German Confederation, for what you enclose is only a summary of the subjects which this organisation concerns.

FRANCIS.

Aix-la-Chapelle, October 8, 1818.

296. *Aix-la-Chapelle, October* 25.—Your Majesty. The painter Lawrence has received the necessary materials which he was expecting, and will wait upon your Majesty to begin the sittings. He has made his arrangements in the Town Hall.*

METTERNICH.

Received and noticed.

FRANCIS.

Aix-la-Chapelle, October 26, 1818.

* The portrait of the Emperor Francis taken by Lawrence is in the Waterloo Chamber at Windsor.—ED.

297. *Aix-la-Chapelle, October* 28.—Your Majesty. I hasten to lay before your Majesty a Report that has just arrived here from Rio Janeiro, as it contains the news of what we may hope is the happy prospect of the pregnancy of the Archduchess Leopoldine.

METTERNICH.

Received and noticed. The Report enclosed is returned herewith.

FRANCIS.

Aix-la-Chapelle, October 29, 1818.

298. *Aix-la-Chapelle, November* 17.—Your Majesty. In the Conference to-day the Duke of Richelieu made a proposal as to the affairs of Spain with regard to her colonies, which will be followed by so important a discussion that I was obliged to submit to the unanimous wish of my colleagues that I should assist at the debate. In any case I must be back here next Saturday, the day when the Duke of Wellington will take part in the Conference.

I have therefore determined to leave for the Conference at Brussels on Saturday, the 21st instant, instead of to-morrow, the 18th. Most of the ambassadors will then leave Aix-la-Chapelle also on the 22nd.

This delay will not affect my whole journey, but I have thought it proper to inform your Majesty of it.

The King of Prussia is still so suffering that he probably will not be able to go to Brussels at all.

METTERNICH.

Received and noticed.

FRANCIS.

Aix-la-Chapelle, November 17, 1818.

THE CONGRESS OF AIX-LA-CHAPELLE.

Autograph (pencil) memoranda by Metternich on loose sheets.

Act of Guarantee.

A.

299. The Emperor Alexander proposes a reciprocal Act of Guarantee concerning the present possessions of each of the contracting parties.

It appears that the Emperor Alexander even aims at establishing the *casus fœderis* on a common basis, against any extension whatever, by any of the parties, of his present possessions. He explicitly confines the act and the guarantee to possessions in Europe.

B.

Not only is there no difficulty about the Courts of Austria and Prussia taking part in such an act, but they will find it a great security. It is not so with the British Government, who will find it impossible to take a direct and obligatory part in so extensive an act of guarantee.

C.

Ought the Continental Courts to reject the proposition of the Emperor Alexander because England cannot be one of the contracting parties?

Ought they to conclude the treaty with the exclusion of England?

These are the most important questions of the moment.

Is there any form which would offer all the advantages resulting from such a treaty?—namely

1. The feeling of security which would follow such a transaction;

2. The moral impossibility for the Emperor Alexander to attempt any extension of his frontiers;

3. The strength which the civil party in the Prussian Government would acquire over the military party, who aim only at disturbing the possessions of their neighbours;

4. The effect which such an act would produce on the minds of people and parties, especially the latter, who would no longer see any chance of success for their criminal hopes, except in political movement.

Considering the principle of harmony and moral solidarity which ought to exist between all the Powers, and especially between those of the Continent and England, what could be the form which, without making the material question of the guarantee bear upon England, would shew the moral concurrence of that Power?

The Coalition and the Quadruple Alliance.

300. The Coalition was a general alliance. The Quadruple Alliance is not that, and never has been.

It is formed on a peculiar element in the Coalition.

It is to last twenty years, for its moral aim is applicable to all times and all circumstances, while the Coalition had, and could have but one aim, and consequently must have a definite termination.

The Coalition dates from the alliance of the two Powers which were first united against France; it was strengthened at Kalisch, at Teplitz, at Frankfurt, at Basle. It was completed in 1814 by the passage of the Rhine; it came to an end at the signature of the Peace of Paris.

After the opening of the Congress of Vienna no trace was left of the Coalition. France was at the Congress placed on the same level as the other Powers.

The Quadruple Alliance, however, remains strong and intact in its moral and general dispositions. This it was which on March 15 served as a nucleus for the new Coalition, which came to an end, like the first, by the signature of the Treaty of Paris on November 20.

The Quadruple Alliance, therefore, is not to be, and cannot be, confounded with the general alliance, which was nothing more than the Coalition.

The Coalition was, and could only be, an element of war.

The Quadruple Alliance is, and has always been, a principle of peace.

Now, it would be almost as impossible to merge the Quadruple Alliance in a general alliance as it would be to merge the elements of peace and war together.

And to this principle of peace, which forms the first and essential basis of the Quadruple Alliance, France chiefly owes it that she was not subdivided in 1815, and that the ill-feelings which the reception of Bonaparte in France necessarily provoked among the Courts and the peoples of Europe were mitigated and controlled.

Abridged Summary of the Situation on November 1, 1818.

I. PRINCIPLES.

1.

301. One alliance exists, the Quadruple Alliance.

The *casus fœderis* of this alliance is specially suitable to its form.

The safety of the four contracting Courts requires that it be explicitly maintained.

The interest of France requires it also.

Consequently, prudence indicates one law for the five Courts :—

1st. The maintenance of the Quadruple Alliance.

2nd. In this maintenance, any appearance of menace to France—tranquil, governed by her legitimate King and under constitutional forms—must be avoided.

The means of attaining this double end should be sought in the choice of forms and expressions in the political transactions to be settled during the meeting at Aix-la-Chapelle.

2.

France, however, does not find herself placed in a situation analogous to that of the other Powers.

She is just issuing from the revolutionary movement ; she is a prey to many parties ; her territory has been set free ; the Quadruple Alliance exists, and this fact alone makes possible coercive action against France, if the latter should be again thrown into a revolutionary crisis. France should not be, either in her own interest or in that of the four Courts and of Europe, abandoned thus to herself. It is therefore necessary to unite her to these Courts by a political combination.

This end cannot be attained by means of a treaty of alliance—

1st. Because it is not in the interest of a system of peace to create new alliances ;

2nd. Because a treaty of alliance demands a *casus fœderis*.

There is no possibility of establishing a *casus fœderis* between the five Courts, and the endeavour to establish one on the maintenance of peace among States not admitted to the alliance would be absurd.

The means of attaining the end desired by the four Courts, and which ought to be desired by the King of France, may be found—

1st. In the terms of Article VI. of the Treaty of Alliance of November 20, 1815 ;

2nd. In the form of a diplomatic agreement (other than a treaty) between the five Courts, having for its one definite end the maintenance of the general peace.

3.

The diplomatic agreement bearing only on the five Courts, it would be necessary to deprive it of any tendency to disturb the other Courts of Europe. The means will be found—

1st. By its being drawn up in an exceedingly clear and precise manner suited to establish the agreement between the five Courts on the principle of the preservation of peace and the maintenance of the best relations among themselves ;

2nd. In a definite engagement between the five Courts not to attempt to extend the action of their agreements to interests peculiar to other Courts ;

3rd. In the enunciation of these facts to the Courts which have acceded to the transactions of the last few

years, and in the positive assurance of the determination
of the five Courts—

(*a*) That they do not wish to arrogate to themselves
the right of discussing or deciding a question which is
beyond their direct interests ;

(*b*) That they are decided, and engage themselves,
never to touch upon a question connected with the interest of a third party without the direct intervention
of that third party.

II. FORMS.

1.

The sanction of the Quadruple Alliance must take
place between the four Courts.

Confidential communication of the act which contains
this sanction should be made to the King of France.

2.

The establishment of the diplomatic agreement between the five Courts.

3.

The communication to Europe of the fact of this
concert.

Ad 1st. The sanction of the Quadruple Alliance
should be recorded in a secret protocol.

Ad 2nd. The concert to be established between the
five Courts demands—

An invitation to France ;

A protocol which will regulate the agreement
between the five Courts.

Ad 3rd. A communication to the other Courts
should take place, either under the form of a declaration of the five Courts, or that of a uniform and circular

despatch of the five Cabinets to their accredited ministers at the Courts of Europe.

Right Principles.

302. The treaty of Chaumont forms the basis of the Quadruple Alliance.

This treaty contains some permanent stipulations, and others which are temporary.

The treaties between the four allies, subsequent to that of Chaumont, contain the same differences.

It is now necessary to maintain : 1st, the permanent clauses of the Quadruple Alliance ; 2nd, the *casus fœderis* against France ; 3rd, to fix the meetings on the principle—

(*a*) Of periodical meetings, with six months' notice if there is no necessity to hold one ;

(*b*) Of extraordinary meetings, to be called for on special occasions.

THE RESULTS OF THE CONGRESS AT AIX-LA-CHAPELLE.

MEMOIR, BY FRIEDRICH GENTZ, AIX-LA-CHAPELLE, NOVEMBER 1818.*

303. It is neither by the number of its decisions, nor by their direct importance, that the Congress of Aix-la-Chapelle stands forth in the political transactions of our time. It had in reality only one question to decide,† and it honourably acquitted itself. The moderation, the kindliness, the delicacy with which everything was treated in these conferences that related to the evacuation of French territory, and to a number of points connected with it, might serve as a model to

---

* This memoir was sent by Gentz to Metternich with the following lines :—
' I have drawn up, for my new correspondent (Prince Souzo), a sketch of the most important negotiations at Aix, as an introduction to my future communications. Of this the accompanying *Observations générales* form the conclusion. It is very possible that your Excellency may find their point of view somewhat too elevated ; I feel it myself, to a certain degree ; but it is difficult to tone oneself down in handling so great a subject. In any case, I believe, your Excellency will find these remarks not quite unworthy of your approbation, and if I am not deceived in this hope I shall be sufficiently rewarded.' These concluding remarks have been published (Prokesch, *Dépêches inédites,* 1876, vol. i. p. 396).—ED.

† An article in the Treaty of Paris, of November 20, 1815, contained the declaration that after the space of three years the Allied Powers, in concert with the King of France, were to decide whether the condition of France was such that the foreign troops could be withdrawn, or whether the occupation must continue for five years. It was to decide this question that the Congress of Aix-la-Chapelle was summoned. Beside the three allied monarchs, there were there assembled the Austrian diplomatists, Metternich, Vincent, and Gentz ; the Russians, Capo d'Istria, Nesselrode, Lieven ; the Prussians, Hardenberg, Humboldt, Bernstorff ; the English, Wellington, Castlereagh, Canning ; the French, Richelieu, Rayneval, and Mounier.—ED.

future negotiations, and if France herself has not done sufficient justice to these proceedings, they will not the less be a matter of history.

Considerations of the greatest weight prevented the sovereigns and ministers there met together from approaching, without urgent necessity, other subjects of discussion—especially from approaching them in regular and official forms. But all those which were the subject of their confidential deliberations were treated in a spirit of peace, justice, and wisdom, and not a resolution was taken, not a protocol signed, which did not tend to consolidate public order, or to devise remedies for complications which might endanger it.

Nevertheless, it is not by its positive and material results alone that we must judge of the Congress of Aix-la-Chapelle ; we must look at it in its general effect, in the whole of the political and federal relations which it has established or materially strengthened, and in the influence which the mind which directed it may exercise on the present and future destinies of Europe. From this elevated point of view the Congress of Aix-la-Chapelle is an event of the highest importance, of which the superficial observer takes in perhaps only a few separate features, and which a statesman alone—looking into the hidden causes and meanings of things—can appreciate.

Not being able to include here all that belongs to so vast a subject, I shall confine myself to some observations on the political and moral tendency of the conferences of Aix-la-Chapelle, under three heads, which seem to me to deserve particular attention.

I. Concerning the General Political System.

The whole of the European Powers have since 1813 been united, not by an alliance properly so called, but by a system of cohesion founded on generally recognised principles, and on treaties in which every State, great or small, has found its proper place. One might deny that this state of things is what, according to the old political ideas, characterised a federative or well-balanced system. But it is not the less certain that, in the present circumstances of Europe—circumstances which she will not quickly get rid of—this system is the one most suited to her needs, and that the destruction of that system would be a dreadful calamity ; for, as not one of the States comprehended in it could remain isolated, all of them would enter into new political combinations, and adopt new measures for their safety ; consequently new alliances, changes, juxtapositions, intrigues, indescribable complications, by a thousand different chances, all equally fatal, would bring us to a general war—that is to say (for the two terms are almost synonymous), to the entire overthrow of all social order in Europe.

We must remember that during the year 1817, and up to the summer of 1818, some of these terrible dangers occupied, not only the idle conjectures of the public, but the thoughts of statesmen, filling them with great uneasiness and the most sinister presentiments. At that time a change of policy in Russia was particularly dreaded : different symptoms, perhaps misunderstood at the time, had given rise to the suspicion that the Emperor Alexander aimed at a close alliance with the House of Bourbon in France, Spain, and Italy. Such a combination would have put all the

intermediary States in the most critical position. It
would have certainly provoked a counter combination
between Austria, Prussia, and England. The Powers
of the second and third rank would have been divided
between the two standards. Germany, the central
point of Europe, now united, would have run the risk
of again being torn in pieces, in more senses in one. The
jealousies, fears, disputes, provocations—inseparable
from such a state of things—would have soon placed
these two opposite political bodies in a thoroughly
hostile attitude, and the first serious contest would have
caused an explosion.

It is true that these suspicions and disquietudes had
in a great measure disappeared some months before the
meeting at Aix-la-Chapelle ; but that meeting has
brought about two inestimable advantages. First,
that of having entirely cleared the ground, removed all
doubts, and fully re-established the confidence of each
of the Cabinets in the proceedings and principles of the
other, and in the stability of the general harmony.
Secondly, that of having by confidential interviews,
earnest discussions, and the contact of intelligent minds,
imbued the sovereigns and their ministers with the
necessity of maintaining intact a system which, whatever its theoretical merits or defects, is at present the
only one practicable, the only one which conduces to
the real interests of all the Powers—the anchor of
salvation for Europe.

II. Concerning the Position of the Powers with regard to France.

The confirmation of the Quadruple Alliance, in case of
new catastrophes occurring in the interior of France,
and menacing the repose of her neighbours, is one of

the most solid benefits which we owe to the Congress of
Aix-la-Chapelle. It was not easy to draw the line
between an imperious attitude, which, instead of subduing a storm, might perhaps have raised and accelerated it, and a contingent measure of precaution, merely
sufficiently imposing to carry weight ; but competent
judges will acknowledge that it has been done with
much prudence and discretion. It is allowable to
consider the danger against which this measure was
aimed as more or less probable, as more or less imminent ; but it is impossible not to admit the reality of
its existence, and that, in the present state of things,
France is the country least disposed to respect the
general tranquillity, the best placed and best organised
to disturb it, and the one which some years hence
will be able to attack it most successfully. So long as
the Quadruple Alliance exists, strengthened as it is at
present by the whole military weight of Germany, the
most audacious head of a party, or even a King of France
carried away by popular excitement, would not lightly
give the signal for fresh conflicts. Thus at least one
of the clouds which threaten our dark horizon will be
held in check by a proper union of strength ; and, had
we only given this one security—enclosed, so to speak,
in the general association which makes the basis of the
state of peace—the Congress would have deserved well
of mankind.

III. Concerning the Moral and Political State of Europe.

All European countries, without exception, are
tormented by a burning fever, the companion or fore-
runner of the most violent convulsions which the civilised
world has seen since the fall of the Roman Empire.
It is a struggle, it is war to the death between old and

new principles, and between the old and a new social order. By a fatality, so to speak inevitable, the re-action of 1813, which has suspended but not terminated the revolutionary movement in France, has aroused it in the other States. All the elements are in fermentation ; the equilibrium of authority is threatened; the most solid institutions are shaken to their foundations, like the buildings in a city trembling from the first shocks of an earthquake which in a few instants will destroy it. If in this dreadful crisis the principal sovereigns of Europe were disunited in principles and intentions ; if one approved what the others condemned ; if but one amongst them looked on the embarrassments of his neighbours as a means of advancing his own interests, or if he regarded the whole prospect with blind or criminal indifference ; if, in short, the eyes of all were not open to the revolutions which are preparing, and the means which remain to them for preventing or retarding the explosion, we should be all carried away in a very few years. But, happily, such are not the dispositions of the princes who are protectors and preservers of public order ; their intimate union, ' *calme et constante dans son action*,' is the counterpoise to the disorder which turbulent spirits try to bring into human affairs ; the nucleus of organised strength which this union presents is the barrier which Provi-dence itself appears to have raised to preserve the old order of society, or at least to moderate and soften the changes which are indispensable. Now, this truly sacred union, of which the Holy Alliance is but an imperfect symbol, was never manifested in a more re-assuring manner than at the time of the conferences at Aix-la-Chapelle. Not that they approached any of these dangerous questions, which would have been pre-

texts for general agitation; they discussed neither the
form of governments, nor the representative system,
nor the maintenance or modification of the privileges
of the nobility, nor the liberty of the press, nor anything touching the interests of religion. They carefully
avoided giving opportunities for malevolence or indiscretion by putting into the formal documents wishes
or declarations of which each carried the principle in
his mind, but the enunciation of which would have
provoked vexatious and hostile criticism. They did
better than that. Sovereigns and ministers understood
what the common good required. They felt keenly
the need of mutual confidence and more direct agreement than that which treaties could establish; they
sacrificed secondary interests, which under less serious
circumstances, might have divided them, to the para-
mount interest of uniting to defend the trust which
Providence had confided to them, and put aside every
other consideration, to preserve authority in the shipwreck by saving the people from their own follies.
Without entering into unnecessary engagements, they
have all agreed on the course to be followed amid the
tempest, and the only title which they have solemnly
brought forward to justify and authorise this course is
the declaration that justice, moderation, and concord
shall ever preside in their councils.

Thus it is that the Congress of Aix-la-Chapelle has
fulfilled its high mission. The general impression it
has made in Europe is its best witness. While maintaining a silence suited to its position and dignity,
only interrupted by a small number of publications, it
has everywhere encouraged the friends of order and
peace, and terrified innovators and the factious. A
Congress of diplomatists cannot, as such, change the

destinies of the world ; but it can guide them, it can moderate them, it can prevent many evils which would aggravate them ; and if the effects which may reasonably be expected from the last meeting of the sovereigns should be stultified by events above human calculations, it will still have the glory of having been the support and the consolation of right-thinking men.

METTERNICH'S PROJECTS FOR DIFFERENT
REFORMS IN PRUSSIA.

304. Metternich to Prince Wittgenstein, Prussian Minister of State, Aix,
November 14, 1818 (with two enclosures).
305. On the condition of the Prussian States (Enclosure No. 1).
306. On educational affairs—Gymnasium and the Freedom of the Press
in Prussia and Germany (Enclosure No. 2).

304. I have the honour to send you, my dear
Prince, the two sketches enclosed, confident as I have
long been of your patriotism.

I do not come unbidden to plead for a cause
strange to me. I have in these sketches laid down
plainly my creed as the head of the Austrian Cabinet.
Our intention is pure, like our views ; we do not
separate our fate from the State which in every respect
is nearest to us. The moment is urgent. What to-day
may yet be possible will not be so to-morrow, and
assistance is only possible as long as free power is in
the hands of the King.

I beg you, my dear Prince, carefully to consider
both these documents. I have divided them because
they belong to different branches of the administration.

The first (No. 305) is my view of the next form of
administration suitable for Prussia, and rests on one
single proposition :—

The central representation by representatives of
the people is the disintegration of the Prussian States.

It is so because such a reform takes place in no

great State without leading to a revolution or following
upon a revolution ; because in the Prussian State, from
its geographical position and its composition, a central
representation is not possible ; because this State
requires before everything a free and sound military
strength, and this does not and cannot consist with a
purely representative system.

According to my firm conviction, the King ought to
go no further than the formation of provincial Diets in
a very carefully considered, circumscribed form. If
the idea of a central representative body, chosen from
the different Diets, is referred to by me, this is because
a similar idea already exists in the Royal declaration,
which is known to the public and is the . only one
possible. Beyond this all is pure revolution. Will
these very limited ideas not also lead to revolution ?
This question the King should ponder deeply before he
decides.

The second paper (No. 306) is no less important in
its object, and is as urgent as the first in its application.
It needs no comment, for fact speaks daily for my
proposition.

I have, under the seal of secrecy, imparted these
two projects to the Chancellor of State, Prince Hardenberg. I put the present copies into your hands, my
dear Prince, and I leave it to your judgment whether
you will submit them to his Majesty. In the first
audience granted me by his Majesty some propositions
were received with such free and outspoken conviction that his Majesty made me wish to write them
down. I believe, too, that I fulfill a duty to my own
Fatherland in offering our true and impartial opinion
on the position and the dangers of our closest allies.
Receive, my dear Prince, this proof of confidence, &c. &c

On the Position of the Prussian States.

305. It would be superfluous to enter upon a consideration of the importance of the existence of Prussia for the whole of the European State-system. This springs from the nature of things ; it is founded on the present condition of Europe, and this universal admission is manifested by the late negotiations.

But for Austria the existence of Prussia has a special and peculiar value.

In a similar position with respect to neighbouring States ; the chief members of a Bund which has the right to reckon on their support, and the duty of rendering the same support to them in return, the two States can never separate their interests without danger and difficulty to both. They must together prosper or together suffer ; the peace, the strength, or the weakness of the one will always react for good or evil on the other.

The strength of States rests on two fundamental conditions—their political and their administrative conformation.

The first is at the present time more than ever beyond the calculation, as beyond the will, of Governments. The limits of States are of late years firmly and inviolably fixed by diplomatic negotiations. What might be improved in them lies consequently beyond the sphere of discussion. Political repose rests on fraternisation between monarchs, and on the principle of maintaining that which is. To oppose these fundamental principles would be to shake the edifice to its very foundations ; the consequences of such an undertaking must certainly be to any State more productive of danger than utility.

But the form of administration remains in the hands of the Government wherever the power has not been given away. The efforts of parties are constantly directed to lead Governments astray from this truth. The revolutionists always calculate on the paternal feeling of the reigning princes; wisdom, however, bids the monarch, above all, to maintain the right, to protect his people from theoretical projects, and to prove and consider everything, and make choice of the best.

Wherever the limit has not yet been overstepped—that is to say, wherever the monarch can still act independently—the carrying out of this last principle is quite possible, and this holds good for Prussia. The course now chosen by the King will decide much more than the fate of his own kingdom. What an incalculable influence the next internal organisation of the Prussian States must have on Germany and Austria is self-evident. This is felt by the unelected representatives of the so-called voice of the people. The party has so far remained true and consistent in its course. It has sought in Prussia the support for its lever, and perhaps has found it only too readily. The moment has arrived for the King to give his verdict. His decision may be the certain triumph of the revolution over the whole of Europe, or may save and maintain the peace of Prussia and the world.

What will the King do? This question may, perhaps, be answered in a few sentences.

The main condition of every form, its utility or its worthlessness, will be determined by a true knowledge of the body to which it is to be applied.

The Prussian States, although united under one sceptre, consist of many different portions, separated by geographical position, climate, race, or language. It has in this respect much similarity with the Austrian, although the position of the latter is in every way more advantageous. The separate parts of the Austrian monarchy are more solid ; their geographical position is better ; they all form a well-rounded whole. Of the two kingdoms Austria would herself be more suited for a pure representative system than Prussia, if the differences of her populations in language and habits were not too important. How can that which is impossible to be carried out in Austria succeed in Prussia ?

Under existing circumstances in the two monarchies the certain result of the attempt would be that in the desire for a really representative central system, the kingdom would fall into separate parts—parts which have not then to be made, but which are already there as parts, and show more substantial differences than even Holland or the Netherlands.

The success of the central representation in this kingdom does not need consideration ; the introduction of it has given to all Europe a great and decisive proof of the uselessness of such a scheme in a whole formed of such essentially different parts, and in this way it may have done some good.

In another respect the kingdom of the Netherlands offers a second experience which is not to be despised. This kingdom requires above all for its maintenance a strong military power, and this very important condition of its existence as well as that of Prussia is enfeebled by its constitution, as would be the case in Prussia if a central representation were introduced. This has been felt by the civil party in Prussia, which has long ago raised its voice against the army, and proposed a senseless system of a mere arming of the people in the place of the standing army. The Prussian State would ap-

proach its internal dissolution if ever the King of
Prussia should appear, not at the head of an army,
but as the leader of seven or eight separate masses
of men.

Promises, however, have been made on the part of
the Government; they must be redeemed. The pressure
of the people is to obtain some guarantee against despotism, especially on the part of the Germans, from a
remembrance of former times, and from the dreadful
abuse of power of which the German princes, in their
arrogance, have been guilty since the year 1806. This
pressure was originally for the restoration of government
by Diet, until, overpowered by the voices of the revolutionists, it made its appearance in the form of a desire
for a central representative system. It is easy to imagine
from the obscure ideas of the majority as to the real
nature of popular representation to what delusion
this gives rise; and if the national mind has really
changed, it becomes all the more incumbent on the
monarchs to examine everything, and to resolve only
upon what is truly good.

The King has promised a purely representative system. He will accordingly give to his people the guarantees which alone are suitable to his kingdom.

The Prussian monarchy may be divided naturally
into several divisions :—

1. The Marks of Brandenburg ;
2. The Kingdom of Prussia ;
3. The Grand Duchy of Posen ;
4. The Duchy of Silesia ;
5. The Duchy of Saxony ;
6. The Duchy of Westphalia ;
7. The Grand Duchy of the Lower Rhine.

It is still to be considered to what divisions Pome-

rania, Lower Saxony, and Berg will be joined. They
are at any rate not fitted to form single States, and it is
probable that Pomerania will be united to the Marks,
Lower Saxony to the Duchy of Saxony, and Berg to
Westphalia.

Each of these provinces is entitled to take part in a
representative system by Diet, but these Diets are by no
means to be cast in exactly the same forms without
regard to their local concerns, which are, for instance,
in the Grand Duchy of the Lower Rhine very different from others, as Silesia, the Marks, &c. &c. By
an enlightened regard for local concerns, the surest
foundation will be laid for the happiness of each State
in itself and the welfare of all the States as a whole.

Such Diets should be formed before anything else is
done.

If ever the Budget question or legislation in the
highest sense should make a central representation advantageous to the State, or if the solution of this question should be hereafter unavoidable, an expedient
might be found by choosing not less than three members to be sent from each Diet, expressly called together
for that purpose.

This central body would at least be more easy to
guide aright than a combination of deputies strange or
even hostile to each other, who would never be brought
to agree in one political aim.

The following main points will suffice to show briefly
our views :—

1. The Prussian State shall continue to exist in the
form of separate provinces.

The executive power to reside in the King. He will
have ministers at the head of the different departments,
and a Council of State.

Each province to have an Upper and a Lower administrative board.

2. Each province to be represented in a way suitable to its local relations.

The presidents of the Diets to be named by the King.

The principal features of the action of the Diets will be as follows :—

In their assemblies, legally summoned, they shall have the right to transmit to the Government all requests and remonstrances on matters concerning the welfare of the province, the Diet, or single individuals.

It will rest with them to distribute the taxes according to legal principles, to watch over the just division of the public burdens in the provinces and prevent all abuse and injustice in this respect.

3. The King will introduce this system of representation and reserve to himself the subsequent decision as to the co-operation of the provincial Diets by means of a central representation composed from them for the passing of the Budget and higher legislation.

The Government must be careful, before the introduction of Diets, to arrange the provinces in their different parts and regulate their administration, and a central representation can only be the result of such arrangements.

4. It is no doubt a question worthy of consideration, what connection there might be between a Council of State in the extensive form of the Prussian Council and the central representation as chosen from the different Diets, and whether some members of the Council of State, as such, might become members of the central representation.

On Education, Gymnastic Establishments, and Liberty of the Press.

(Supplement to No. 304.)

306. As important perhaps for the decision of the Prussian Government are the questions arising from the intrigues of the various peace-disturbing parties in Prussia as well as Germany.

The means of checking the growing evil are two-fold. The first and principal the King will find in his own will; the second, in the closest agreement with Austria. The first refers to the Prussian State itself; the second to a common course to be followed at the Diet. These last might gain in safety by an agreement between the two chief German States, and confidential conferences with the chief Courts before they can with advantage be brought before the Diet.

The subjects which we think necessary to point out here are :—

I. The question of Education.
II. The establishments for Gymnastics.
III. The Liberty of the Press.

I. EDUCATION.

No impartial observer can now doubt that the innovators in Germany—and most of them are found among the learned caste—have relinquished the hope of actively influencing the present generation with their revolutionary spirit, and still more of moving them to action. The characteristic features of the Germans will always hinder the success of such an attempt. The German is cold, prudent, and faithful. He speculates more than he acts, especially when the action involves a rending of the civil and domestic ties. The patriotism of the Germans has various aims ; there are in the common fatherland separate voices of the people ; provincial patriotism is the nearest to the German citizen : he grasps it from the cradle, and thirty generations have shown no reason why it should not be honoured as the deepest and most natural feeling, for the Branderburger and the Austrian, the Bavarian and the Hessian, are all alike Germans. The political formation of States often operates on the mind of the people for centuries longer than the institutions themselves exist ; the remembrance of the German Empire, too, is still fresh and vivid, particularly in the lower classes. Even if there is no more an Empire, there is still a Germany, and the nucleus of ancient provinces under ancient Princes.

Conscious of the futility of the undertaking, the plan of the innovators—for they act on a settled plan—has taken quite a different character, a character which suits itself to the feeling and personal relations of the leaders : that which the present generation cannot perform is reserved for the next, and in order that the next generation may not follow the footsteps of its predecessors, the youth must be seized as he leaves boyhood, and he must undergo a revolutionary training.

Where the revolution in its coarsest form cannot pervert and incite to insurrection the already educated, a people shall be educated for revolution.

This plan is followed at some of the German universities, and if we have not the necessary information to enable us to judge exactly how far many professors at the Prussian universities join in it, we believe we are not wrong in considering it more than probable that they do so.

The Royal Prussian Government is well aware of the signification of the German *Burschenschaft*, and that the mischief cannot be too soon checked is beyond a doubt. But that this can only be accomplished by the united action of the German Governments is just as certain.

II. Gymnastic Establishments.

The mischief here is closely connected with life at the universities : the inventors, the invention, and the execution belong to Prussia.

The gymnastic establishment is a real preparatory school of university disorders. There the boy is formed into the youth, as in the higher school—the university—the youth is formed into the man.

We here declare our firm conviction that it has become a duty of State for the King thoroughly and entirely to destroy this evil. Palliative measures are no longer sufficient. The whole institution in every shape must be closed and done away with, offenders being made liable to legal censure.

As the institution was founded and still exists in Berlin itself, and as the branch institutions seem all to depend on and spring from the mother institution, the evil must there be uprooted. If offshoots continue to exist, this will be a fit subject for consultation with those German Governments which may not be clearsighted enough, and may further encourage the evil.

III. Liberty of the Press.

This point, the most difficult of all, can only be regulated by a close agreement between Austria and Prussia, and by this means with the other German Governments—if, indeed, it possibly can be regulated.

Every measure must be grounded on the following principles :—

1. The broadest views as to real substantial works ;

2. The most decided difference between such works and pamphlets and journals ;

3. Respect for the independence of the single States forming the Bund, and the certainty that no State may remain in the Bund which does not possess some efficient law on this subject, whether it be preventive or repressive.

ON THE QUESTION OF THE JEWS.*

307. The Edict of the Emperor Joseph is in full force in all the German States of Austria. The Hungarian Constitution is opposed to one part of its execution, but this fact is independent of the wishes of the King.

Schools for Jewish girls exist everywhere. Where the community is not large, the children of both sexes frequent the Christian schools; every Jew is at liberty to educate his children in Christian educational establishments.

Jews can, under certain restrictions, and in countries where the constitutions do not directly oppose it, become landed proprietors.

They are subject to the military conscription, like the Christians. All grades of the service are open to them: there are staff-officers at this day who are Jews.

Distinctions of every kind—except those which require the formula of a Christian oath, such as the orders of knighthood—are given to them. Men remarkable for their civil virtues and honourable estate have acquired titles of nobility, which place them in the same rank as Christian noblemen.

---

* The occasion of this judgment seems to have been the appearance of a ' *Mémoire sur l'état des Israélites,* par un Ministre du Saint Evangile,' which was dedicated and presented to the monarchs assembled at the Congress of Aix-la-Chapelle. Besides which, the representatives of the Jews in Vienna presented a petition to their Majesties, imploring an inquiry to be made into the state of the law in respect to the civic rights of members of the Israelitish faith.—ED.

They may adopt any profession they like ; if there are very few in the Civil Service, it is because they do not choose that career, or, rather, that those who do aspire to it enter the bosom of the Church.

Nevertheless, in many places it has been necessary to take measures of precaution in carrying out the edict of the Emperor Joseph, even after it has been in force many years, because of the abuse by Jews of the concessions granted them. Devoted to business, from father to son, assisting each other with large capitals, they prefer to gain by either lawful or unlawful trade what would cost both care and trouble to attain by other means.

The laws of the Emperor Joseph have, however, been of real benefit; the most satisfactory example that could be cited in support of this truth is the difference between the Jews of Galicia and those of ancient Poland.

One of the great difficulties in devising any measure relating to the position of the Jews arises from their number. Any hasty reform bears heavily on an immense mass of men whom nothing can persuade to renounce old customs or adopt new ones.

1819.

ROME, NAPLES, AND PERUGIA.

Extracts from Metternich's private Letters, from March 5 to
June 22, 1819.

Metternich to his Wife, Vienna, March 5, 1819.

308. Very much against my will, my dear, I have
been obliged to put off my journey till the 8th. I have
yielded to Staudenheim's orders, and he has found a
powerful ally in the worst weather that heaven ever
sent to any part of this lower world. The thermometer
is constantly at one, two, or three degrees above zero.
It rains, there is a thick fog; sometimes a few flakes
of snow come to enliven us; the men cough, the women
sniff, the children squall. Here in three sentences, I
give you a picture of society in Vienna, and its
charms.

This is the plan for my journey. I intend to sleep

on the 8th, at Schottwien; the 9th, at Leoben; the
10th, at Klagenfurt; the 11th, at Ponteba; the 12th,
at Conegliano; the 13th, at Verona; the 14th, at
Modena; the 15th, at Scarica l'Asino; the 16th, at
Florence.

309. *Friesach, March* 10.—Thanks to the despair-
ing anticipations of Floret, who always thinks it is impossible to reach any place, I have arrived here in such
good time, my dear, that I am able to write to you.   I
shall send my letter by post to Klagenfurt, so as to
ensure your getting it safely.   I left Kraupach at seven
this morning, the most wretched hole on earth; I dined
at Unzmarkt, and here I am at Friesach at seven in the
evening.   I found a good deal of snow between Kraupach and Neumarkt, where the level is high, but it
disappeared as we descended towards Carinthia.   I
shall find it again in the Julian Alps.   To-morrow I
shall sleep at Tarvis.

You see, my dear, that the journey is going on very
well.   Everybody is in good health, and Kaunitz is just
the same as in 1799.   He does not speak of his grievances: it seems as if he had none; he eats, sings,
whistles, laughs, and sleeps, like everybody else, and
carries it so far that I believe he is only restive, like
some horses, which are very gentle and quiet for
months together, and begin to rear and kick at certain
times and in certain places.

In the course of my travels I have made a discovery
in natural history.   The magistrate of Judenburg was
waiting at the door to compliment me.   All magistrates everywhere are constantly complaining; he of
Judenburg had no complaint to make of men, so he fell
back on *mice*.   The burgomaster having assured me
that the mice had ravaged the fields, I asked him if this

plague had existed for a long time. " My God, yes—
ever since the French came ! " " What ! did the French
bring mice in their train ? " " No, but those devils of
men encamped near the town ; they eat so much bread
that they filled the fields with crumbs, and we have had
all the mice of Styria since." Hate is blind !

310. *Florence, March* 18.—I write to you at last,
my dear, after having waited from hour to hour for the
possibility of sending this off. I have had the quickest
and the best journey possible. Once on Italian soil, it
was so much accelerated that I was obliged to increase
the number of my stations. I slept at Tarvis on the
11th, at Conegliano on the 12th, at Verona on the 13th,
at Bologna on the 14th, and arrived here on the 15th,
in nine hours, a thing without example. The Emperor
made the journey in ten hours, and it was said to be a
miracle ; I made it in one hour less, and the miracle
was one no longer. Where ordinary travellers ascend
the high mountains of the Apennines in carriages drawn
by oxen, I went at a quick trot with eight horses. The
animals in this country must have lungs made differently from those of our ultramontane cattle. I have
had nothing to complain of on the way, except an excess
of attention. At Bologna, the Cardinal-Legate waited
upon me with invitations from two societies, and to two
suppers—one at his own house, and the other at Mare-
scalchi's, where I lodged. In my difficulty of choice I
went to bed, and left the two parties to arrange the
suppers as they liked, after having fraternised with his
Eminence for nearly two hours ' *in camera caritatis.*'

. . . . We are here in the midst of flowers ; the
houses are still cold, but there are good chimneys, and
even stoves in all the rooms.

The Emperor has been received with real enthusiasm

by the Tuscans. He is marvellously well. Venice gave him a cold in the head; I was right enough to avoid that charming resting-place.

Florence is still full of English; they are beginning to move towards Rome. The Emperor leaves on the 29th of this month. I intend to start with Marie on the 26th. We shall go that day to Leghorn, on the 27th to Pisa, the 28th to Sienna, the 29th to Radicofani, the 30th to Viterbo, and we shall be at Rome on the 31st.

I am lodging here at the Palace Dragomanni. The mistress of the house is a widow, and is that wild dancer of the *Furlana* whom you have seen at Madame Elisa's balls in 1810 at Paris. She is nine years older, and dances no longer, but my virtue is as safe as if she still danced with her old impetuosity. I have never liked paroxysms or hurricanes. The windows of my bedroom look on a garden where everything is in flower. Just beneath me there are orange-trees in the open air, covered with fruit, and the flowers just peeping out. I am astonished, for, after all, the heat is not great; the sun is everything here, and the sun of Tuscany is quite a different thing from the sun beyond the Alps.

311. *March* 22.—The town gave a *fête* to the Emperor yesterday. The *fête* was beautiful, simply owing to the locality; it was held in front of the Palazzo Vecchio. The people assembled in the old palace inhabited by the Medici before they acquired the Pitti Palace. Everything there breathes of their presence, though it is three hundred years since they left it. The Uffizii galleries were illuminated. There was a coloured fire, which did not add much to the beauty of the illumination. What I liked best of all was to see the beautiful statues of Michel Angelo, Benvenuto Cellini, &c., the *chefs-d'œuvres* of architecture of that epoch, brilliantly illuminated, which, in fact, enables me to say that I have seen it all as the creators themselves saw it. Caraman raves about Florence ; he declares that to be there is like being in an enchanted palace ; and he is not far wrong. Nothing that one sees there is like anything one sees elsewhere.

I shall leave on the 26th, and will follow strictly the route I indicated in my last letter.

312. *Rome, April* 2.—Here we are, my dear. I shall not undertake to tell you what we find in Rome ; I leave that to Marie. Do not think, however, that she is exaggerating, for that is simply impossible. Imagination attains to what has been presented by the senses— in vain we delude ourselves : that circle is never left. Rome must be seen to be believed in. All that the most beautiful cities in the world can show of magnificence in detail is gathered together here, and certainly surpassed.

Rome has been to me like a person I tried to imagine without having seen ; such calculations are always deceptive. I have found everything different from what I supposed ; I expected Rome would be old and sombre—it is antique and superb, brilliant and new. I do not know what I would give to take you for a single instant to the window of my drawing-room ; and this window is nothing compared to one in a dressing-room which is prepared for the Empress ! Picture to yourself the most splendid view, so rich that one would accuse of excessive exaggeration the painter of such a scene. Opposite and beneath me I have St. Peter's, the Castle of St. Angelo, the Column of Antoninus, innumerable obelisks and palaces, each one more magnificent than the other; fountains throwing up an enormous volume of water ; to the left, the Coliseum, St. John Lateran ; opposite, the Vatican, &c., &c. These, indeed, are a number of names, but they give no idea of the objects. St. Peter's and the Vatican together are as large as the city of Turin, which contains sixty thousand souls. The square of St. Peter's alone would contain two hundred thousand. The only thing which could give any idea of these spaces are the Tuileries, the Square of Louis XV., and the Champs Elysées. The *garde-meubles* are, taken separately, only miserable hovels compared to twenty private houses which count for nothing in Rome. The Farnese Palace is one of the largest and most lofty—well, the high-altar of St. Peter's is six feet higher than the palace, and it is in bronze.

We arrived here the day before yesterday, before nightfall. The cupola of St. Peter's may be discerned a little this side of the last posting-stage. The country is nothing but a desert. The soil, the best in the world, requires only hands to cultivate it. At last, after the most disagreeable journey, one arrives among ruins, with numbers of posts here and there, on which hang the bodies, old and new, of brigands who have committed murder on this very spot. It is more like the gates of Tartarus than those of the Holy City. But, once free from all this, the grandeur of Rome becomes overwhelming.

Arrived at the Consulta, where I live, and where Cardinal Consalvi waited upon me with a crowd of men whom he had provided for my establishment, I was literally terrified at first at the sight of my apartments. They consist of twenty-five magnificent rooms. Marie has at least half that number for herself. I began yester-

day by going to see the Pope, whom I found in very
good health, much better than I had expected. He is
infirm, but with an infirmity quite natural to such an
advanced age as his. He let me know, through the
Cardinal, that he will see me whenever I like.

I sallied forth, therefore, first of all to pay my
respects to him. He received me as he would an old
friend ; he spoke to me of our correspondence while he
was a prisoner at Savona. He came forward to meet
me, had a stool placed beside him for me, and we con-
versed for an hour. Pepi and my gentlemen were waiting in the antechamber. I begged for permission to
present them to him ; he walked to the other end of the
room to ring for them to be shown in. I presented
them ; he said a few words to them, and ended by conducting me, on leaving, as far as the first room. I defy
even those who are too attentive to do more. He con-
verses very well, with great facility and much liveliness.
During an hour of conversation, on everything in the
world, he laughed for a good quarter of an hour. Certainly no interview between Pope and minister, meeting
for the first time, could have been more kindly. He
likes to speak of his troubles under Bonaparte, and he
reminded me of more than twenty anecdotes of my
conversations with the latter on his account. He told
me to come and see him, how and when I like.

The apartments destined for his Majesty are of ravishing beauty. Besides the magnificence of the locality,
the greater part of the furniture was made under Napoleon, who had intended the Quirinal for his own palace.
The Pope has had everything finished, so that in these
apartments may be found all that is beautiful in ancient
and modern art. When the Louvre is finished it will
not bear comparison with the Quirinal. The first ante-

chamber—a room as large as the Redoute at Vienna—
is common to the Pope and the Emperor. It is used as
a peristyle to the chapel, which is prepared for some of
the functions of Holy Week. This chapel holds five
hundred ; three thousand have applied for admission.
There are more than forty thousand foreigners in Rome,
counting both masters and valets.

The apartments of the Pope contrast singularly with
the magnificence which surrounds them ; they are more
than simple.

From the Quirinal we went to St. Peter's ; from St.
Peter's to the Vatican. What say you to this life?

It is a fact that St. Peter's seems small, in consequence of the harmony of all its parts. It is only when
one examines, when one measures, that one begins to
doubt the evidence of the eyes. The marble angels
which support the basins for holy water are placed
on the two first pilasters beyond the entrance. You
think them quite near ; they seem to be about the
height of Leontine: as you approach them they increase till they become colossal. The four pillars on
which the cupola rests, which is six feet more in
diameter than the Pantheon, seem merely of ordinary
dimensions. Well, the thickness on the narrow side is
thirty-two paces. Picture to yourself this church,
which has twenty chapels, each of which would make
an enormous church, and each of which has a cupola
higher and larger than that of St. Charles Borromeo,
all inlaid with marble, all the ceilings in mosaic,
representing magnificent pictures. There is not an
ornament which is not either in marble, porphyry,
antique alabaster, or gilt bronze ; not a corner which
is not as completely finished as a snuff-box ; gigantic
monuments everywhere, executed by the first masters

of all times ; such magnificence of every kind was never gathered together in ancient times.

St. Peter's as a church is the chapel of the Vatican. You remember the gallery of the Louvre. Put twenty like that one after another, and you would hardly have the space which is filled with statues, marbles, monuments of every kind ! Nevertheless, in November next they will open a new wing with halls and galleries, which they will fill with statues that are now in warehouses. Besides all these halls and galleries, there are also eleven thousand rooms and closets, all habitable, in this same house.

What galleries are those painted in fresco by Raphael ! This marvellous man painted one—perhaps the most beautiful—at the age of eighteen.

We walked straight on, we did not stop at all— looked about us very little, and yet we walked for five hours.

Our days are arranged. We shall go out every day from eight till mid-day, and from four to six. It is too hot between mid-day and four o'clock. To-day it has been warmer than it generally is with us in the month of June.

April 3.—Yesterday morning we went to see the Forum of Trajan, a magnificent ancient ruin.

Then we visited the studios of Canova and Thorwaldsen, two very remarkable artists. What Canova has done already, and what he is at present doing, is inconceivable. This man reminds one of the best days of Greece.

The Emperor arrived at half-past four. We waited upon him in his own apartment. On arriving he went first to see his Holiness, who came to meet him as far as his own legs would carry him. The Emperor has been received with much pomp and great enthusiasm by the people. The whole population of Rome turned out to meet him.

April 4.—I close my letter just as I am starting for the Quirinal, for the Feast of Palms. The ceremony will last three hours : I shall be consequently too late to write to you on my return, as the courier must start so as to arrive in Munich in time to meet the one who goes from Vienna to Paris.

Marie has doubtless told you of our walks yesterday morning. We passed four hours in the Rome of the Cæsars, in the midst of the most magnificent ruins of edifices the most sublime and the most gigantic that human genius ever created. The *Forum Romanum* is a town of temples and monuments. The excavations made by the French and continued by the Pope allow one to walk once more on the pavement of the *Via Sacra*, along which all the triumphal processions wended their way.

A mass—partly upright, partly lying confusedly on the earth—of trunks of gigantic columns of porphyry, and the most beautiful marbles and granites from the East, of capitals and other *débris*, shows what this place must have been. Imagination alone cannot realise it. The Pope, who does an immense deal for art (or rather Consalvi does it in his name), intends to excavate the whole of the Forum. It is a great undertaking, for the old pavement is covered by from fifteen to twenty feet of earth and ruins, and the great difficulty is to know where to throw the earth from the excavations.

The Coliseum cannot be described. Its ruins do not resemble those of a building : they look more like those of a mountain. According to the most moderate calculations, eighty thousand spectators could have been seated there with ease. Each place still bears its number, like the stalls in the Court Theatre at Vienna, which, however, has only this one resemblance to that of the Rome of the Cæsars.

313. *Rome, April* 10.—We live in the midst of Pagan temples and in Christian basilicas; the last three days we have alternated between the Sixtine Chapel, the Museums of the Vatican, and the Church of St. Peter's. The last of the grand religious ceremonies will take place to-morrow; the place alone would make it very beautiful, for it is to be at St. Peter's. The functions on Holy Thursday and Good Friday were beneath my expectations. For one thing, the Holy Father did not officiate, so the High Mass was reduced to the ordinary service; besides, there is no doubt that what I have seen at the Sixtine Chapel was not equal to the ceremonies which formerly took place at the Electoral ecclesiastical Courts; and the washing of feet and the repast of the Apostles are infinitely more imposing at Vienna. The ceremonies here take place in halls and chapels much too small, although in the largest palace in the world. These places are encumbered with strangers: for one Catholic you see eight or ten Protestants, for the most part English. The guards are obliged to use their halberds: the Pope, the Apostles, the sovereigns—all is confusion. On Holy Thursday they pass from the Sixtine Chapel to the Pauline Chapel: from thence to the hall where the Apostles dine. There is a fight at each door, and generally blood flows. Yesterday, for example, an English lady, fancying herself stronger than a guard, had her cheek pierced by a halberd. One hears nothing but cries of ' My shoe!' ' My veil!' ' You are

crushing me!' 'Your sword is running into my leg!'
'Give way, please!' and then 'knocks and blows' in
abundance. The noise ceases, and the ceremony is
over. Last year an Englishman, determined to pass
between two guards who were in line, forming a
passage for the Pope, had his nose taken off between
the shoulders of the two guards (they wear cuirasses on
Holy Thursday). You may imagine that the holiness
of the place and the unction of the service gain nothing
by these occurrences.

In my opinion the effect of the illuminated cross in
St. Peter's surpasses all description. This immense
basilica, enveloped in darkness, is lighted from a single
focus ; the cross, about fifty feet in height, so suspended
as to have the appearance of sustaining itself, is wonderfully beautiful.

The effects of light in the side chapels are marvellous ; the tombs seem to be reanimated. On one of
the pillars Pope Gregory XIII. seems to be coming out
of his niche. The magnificent lion on the tomb of
Clement XIV., by Canova, has the appearance of
springing to defend the approach to the tomb. Seen
from the end of the church, the cross is framed by the
four columns of the high altar ; each step presents a
new and magical effect. Picture to yourself all this
space illumined by a single ray of light, this light losing
itself in the vast space, and only reflected by the
ceilings in gilding and mosaic ; this is the time to judge
of the immensity of the edifice. The door is opened in
the middle of the church, and thus the cross is seen
from the other side of the Piazza of St. Peter's. At that
distance it seems about the size of a bishop's cross.
The Piazza is dark, and the cross is the only light
visible.

The Pope's benediction has also a striking effect. The moment when the Holy Father, carried in a chair, appears at the window in the front of the church, and rises to bless the people, all the people falling on their knees, is most solemn. But it seems as if bad luck attended all the religious ceremonies at Rome. After the benediction the Holy Father sits down ; he remains at the window ; a cardinal advances and throws to the people indulgences written on sheets of paper. All the ragamuffins assemble, struggling and fighting to get one of these papers. There are shouts and laughter, as when one throws money in the street ; the victors make off as fast as they can, and use—I know not how—their indulgences.

I acknowledge that I cannot understand how a Protestant can turn Catholic at Rome. Rome is like a most magnificent theatre with very bad actors. Keep what I say to yourself, for it will run through all Vienna, and I love religion and its triumph too much to wish to cast a slur upon it in any manner whatever. In all this it is evident that Italian taste has much influence in the ceremonies ; what pleases and excites laughter on this side of the Alps causes weeping on the other, and *vice versâ*. One ought never to forget to make this allowance—looking on and keeping silence, but above all taking good care not to betray it.

I can imagine Gentz's fears, which, however, are certainly more reasonable than many others which he has had within the last few years. The assassination of Kotzebue is more than an isolated fact. This will be seen by-and-by, and I shall not be the last to take advantage of it, notwithstanding the blows which I do not fear, however much I may be exposed to them. I do not allow myself to be put out ; I go my own way, and if all the ministers did the same, things would not be as they are. I assure you that the world was in perfect health in 1789 in comparison with what it is now.

Marie will tell you more than I can of what we are doing; she can only tell you what is good, except of two dinners which we had yesterday at the Vatican—oily dinners, without butter or eggs: infernal, and worse than all the doctors' stuff. We took the only sensible course—that is to say, we ate nothing.

314. *April* 13.— . . . Here we are safely through our feasts and fasts, which is indeed a happy circumstance. Marie will tell you of the pomp of Easter Day, which surpasses all that one can imagine of splendour and magnificence. Even what is not in good taste is fine; I mention specially the decoration of St. Peter's, which is much more magnificent when the pillars are simply of marble and porphyry than when they are draped in crimson damask. But these thousands of yards of damask, lace, and festoons silence the criticisms of the enlightened amateur; they overwhelm him, and he can criticise no longer under so immense a weight. The religious ceremony in this vast building, where strong barriers arrest the impetuous strangers; the crowd of cardinals, bishops, priests, guards; the immense space which is given up to worship alone, a space in which men seem to dwindle in the same proportion as the mind expands —all is magnificent.

The illumination of the cupola is equally so. On this occasion it was not confined to the cupola, the whole front and colonnade were on fire. The first illumination was designed by Michel Angelo. The second, which in less than two seconds encircled this immense edifice as the clock strikes a certain hour (eight at night), was simply beyond description. After looking

at this for some time, one wished the first to return,
which shone at intervals between the torrents of light
from thousands of jets of fire.

The fireworks at the Castle of St. Angelo were the
most beautiful I have ever seen, and I suppose the most
beautiful that possibly can be seen.

You doubtless remember the *girandole* let off in the
Place Louis XV. in 1810. Well, this was the same
number of rockets fired from a separate plateau, and
thrown to a height of a hundred and fifty or two
hundred feet, giving to the whole the appearance of
Vesuvius in eruption. The rest of the fireworks represented the ancient edifice, with its hundreds of
columns, its immense fountain, &c. The whole thing
ended with three clusters of rockets, of which one was
let off from the top of the building ; the two others were
on a lower level and extended on each side. To complete the effect, guns were fired from the batteries of
the castle. The sight was worthy of the best days of
Rome.

I beg you to show this letter to Pilat : it will save
me having to send him a description, and will furnish
him with a good article for his ' Observer.' I hope
it will arrive before he is assassinated by some Jena
Liberal.

Good-bye, my dear ; we are all as well as could be
wished. I hope that you are well too. We walk, we
see all there is to be seen ; I work, I dine, and l sleep.
This is my way of life at Rome, and Staudenheim may
be easy, for my health was never better. The weather
is just like the end of June with us. The trees are all
green, the lilacs are in blossom, the roses have been out
some time.

Good-bye. My love to you all !

315. *Naples, April* 30.—We have been at the foot of Vesuvius, my dear, for four days.

The situation of Naples is more beautiful, and at the same time more grand, than I had imagined. Everything there is on an immense scale. The mountains are high and rugged like the Alps. Vesuvius is a prodigious mass, certainly larger than the Schneeberg. It is seen from everywhere, except the house in which I live. It forms part of the inner frame of the great basin of Naples. The Pompeian side is charming, although exposed to continual risks. This terrible neighbour will fall in some day; it will die out as twenty other volcanoes have done in the chain of the Apennines; but it may still cause many disasters before it disappears. Since April 13 it has been unceasingly active; a large column of smoke is rising from the three craters, and a stream of lava rolls down its side. It is sometimes so bright as to be seen by day. At night it resembles a stream of molten iron.

The cultivation and charm of the country have far surpassed my expectations. The country between Terracina and Naples is very like Upper Styria, especially the environs of Cilli and Laybach; add to this valleys the size of those on the Rhine, vegetation quite inconceivable for richness and intensity, Vesuvius always in sight, at every instant new vistas over the sea and over the most picturesque islands in the world, and you have an idea of travelling in this country. I have seen many things in this world, but nothing more beautiful, nor more satisfying both to mind and body.

Marie will tell you all I have left unsaid. She has so much my way of seeing and judging of things that I can trust perfectly to her letter. The bad weather is in our favour. Marie will be able to write you a volume.

The difference of age,. sex, and tastes is, however, evident in her letters and mine. She does not hesitate, for example, between Naples and Rome. I should have great difficulty in giving the preference to Naples over Rome, and I should wish for both cities, to be able to enjoy alternately the marvels of nature, and those created by the grandest human intelligence.

The Emperor will remain here until May 25. I shall leave one day before him.

316. *May* 3.—Marie, in her last letter, gave you a description of what we have seen. I have made one more excursion than she has, for I took advantage of an hour of beautiful sunshine a few days ago to pay a visit to the magnificent Bay of Pozzuoli and Baiæ. Marie, meantime, was in attendance at the Court, and she revenged herself to day, while I was engaged at a grand dinner with the King, by going to Pozzuoli itself. All these places are so near each other that it only takes one or two hours to go from one to the other. Heaven has been pleased to create the most beautiful sites in the world, and men have had the good sense to make use of them.

There is no greater proof of the good taste of the ancients than the choice which they made of Herculaneum, Pompeii, Baiæ, &c., in which to pass the most beautiful months of the year. All these places were to the Romans what Hietzing, Hütteldorf, and Baden are to the Viennese.

This is a fair comparison, even from the point of view of the moral grandeur of the men who live no longer and of the men of to-day who live too much.

The weather being in a state of convalescence, we

intend to-morrow to take a trip to Pompeii. This can be done in one morning.

We were present yesterday at the procession of St. Januarius, who worked his miracle at eight o'clock in the evening in the church of St. Clare. This procession, which we saw leave the cathedral, is most curious. Thirty-six busts of saints and *saintesses* in good solid silver, carried by *lazzaroni* clothed in a sort of mountebank livery or dressing-gowns, more dirty even than those who wear them, and that is saying a good deal— these *lazzaroni* have their heads covered with ragged caps ; priests and monks, who are not more occupied with their holy functions than the spectators ; all running, shouting, dashing against each other, and crowding pell-mell. This is what I saw. As the miracle is performed during a whole week, I shall be present at it one of these days. It is necessary to see the people here to form any idea of them, and it is a fact that they are a hundred times cleaner and more civilised than they were twenty years ago. The Government has done much, and does more every day.

St. Carlo will not be opened till next Sunday, at the end of the double *neuvaine*. In the meantime, I was present yesterday at a rehearsal of 'Zoraïde,' Rossini's opera, and I saw the house thoroughly. It is unquestionably the most beautiful in Europe. Like St. Peter's, it seems smaller than it is, owing to its perfect proportions and rich decorations. It has a hundred and eighty boxes, all very large, and it accommodates six thousand spectators. Nevertheless, we can hear perfectly in every part of the house. We shall have eight of Rossini's operas, and the last of his compositions are perhaps the most beautiful. I spend my evenings in listening to the singing of Davide and the principal artistes of Italy.

All our servants spent last night on Vesuvius. I could not help laughing when I heard some one say to the King this morning that the *coup d'œil* which he had seen last night of Vesuvius covered with flambeaux was superb. I doubt whether Giroux will go to see Vesuvius ; he still denies that the mountain as he sees it is a volcano. He says that, as it only spits fire and vomits smoke, it cannot be a volcano ; and that he is not fool enough not to know that a volcano is just like the fireworks which he saw at Rome.

This Vesuvius, my dear, is a most imposing and splendid spectacle. Unhappily, I cannot see it from my window, but from everywhere else—that is to say, a hundred steps from my house. It can be seen as soon as it is dark, like an immense beacon. A great eruption, such as that of 1814, must indeed be a wonderful sight. The mountain is so near the city, the slope to it is so direct, that a new crater—and a new one is being formed with each eruption—will one day place it in great danger. The Neapolitans, however, never think of this ; they are like sailors, who forget that there is only a plank between them and the deep, and one is tempted to forget, in the perfect enjoyment of a nature so beautiful and smiling, that danger may be so close at hand.

317. *Naples, May* 4.—This morning I went to see Pompeii. Nothing is more curious than this relic, seventeen centuries old. Fate seems to have buried it to give future generations a complete idea of Roman customs. Scarcely a twentieth part of Pompeii is uncovered. One can walk in the amphitheatre, the forum, the basilica, in two theatres—one for tragedy and the other for comedy—in four temples, in the midst of the tombs, through three streets on the original pavement; one can enter more than a hundred shops and houses, on the doors of which the name of the proprietor is written : and all these places are just as they were the day they were engulphed. The altars of the temples and the tombs are as fresh as if they were in a sculptor's studio; the town is large enough to have contained from thirty to forty thousand inhabitants; the temples, the forum, and the theatres are as beautiful as they could be in a Roman capital, and as they ought to be in a Christian one. We have all very bad taste in 1819.

318. *May* 7.—I meant to have despatched a courier to you eight days ago. We lead such a busy life here that days pass like hours; it will leave us, however, a very agreeable recollection. I suppose Marie has given you an account of what we have done lately. Our trip to Baiæ was certainly one of the most beautiful that could be imagined; that district is as classic as it is beautiful, and that is saying a great deal.

I do not know if you have a translation of Virgil's Æneid; at any rate, try to get one, and read the beginning of the sixth canto. He describes all the places where we have been, and really it is difficult to express what one feels on setting one's foot on the Champs-Elysées, approaching the banks of Acheron, and the ferry where Charon crossed and recrossed with his boat. You find yourself on the very spot where Æneas embarked, you enter the grotto of the Sibyl of Cumæ; in a word, you do all that seems to belong only to the domain of fancy. It is natural that a religion entirely sensual should find its paradise in a land of delights:

the Christian religion, entirely intellectual, looks beyond the clouds, to a country vast and* vague as thought itself.

Marie will tell you that we drank your health on the highest rising ground in the Champs Elysées. No description could do justice to the beauty of this situation. Twenty different points of view, immense rocks, islands as picturesque as possible, unparalleled richness of vegetation, a soft and gentle air; in the distance Vesuvius throwing an immense column of smoke high in the air; the ground covered with ruins of palaces and temples—I can only give you a very feeble picture of what is indeed far beyond imagination.

The Gulf of Baiæ bears the palm even over that of Naples, and the Romans had some of their principal establishments there also. Pozzuoli, Baiæ, Cumæ were three large towns, and, to judge by what remains, the country must have been for miles covered with houses. The sea has, besides, gained on the coast in consequence of earthquakes and volcanic eruptions. The shore is always strewed with fragments of mosaic and remains of architecture deposited by the waves.

We are going to-day to make the ascent of Vesuvius. Have no uneasiness on our account. We shall dine at home at one o'clock; we shall be on the summit about six o'clock, and from it we shall see sunset. We shall want a little darkness to judge of the effects of the lava, and we shall be at home by ten or eleven o'clock. Vesuvius is paying us great attention. Without being in complete eruption, it has been active for nearly a month. Last night, for example, it was furrowed by five streams of lava. In this state it has the effect of an immense charcoal fire, suspended some thousand feet in the air; every five or ten minutes there rises from the

crater an immense jet, like the bouquet in fireworks.
The column of fire is of different colours; in this respect,
again, it resembles fireworks. Nature works here in a
manner at once very patent and very mysterious. One
sees but cannot understand it.

319. *May* 12.—I begin my letter to-day, my dear,
with Vesuvius. I told you in my last that we were going
there, and I promised you that we should return safe
and sound. We have kept our word.

On May 7 there met at my house Tini Grassalkowich,
Thérèse, her pupil; Schönburg, Kaunitz, d'Aspre, Paar,
and all my gentlemen except Mercy; we dined at one
o'clock, and we arrived at the hermitage, which is
about a third of the distance, at four o'clock. We let
our horses rest for half an hour, and went on again for
half a league, to the foot of the great cone which forms
the modern Vesuvius, since it separated from Mount
Somma to engulf Herculaneum and Pompeii. Between
the hermitage and the cone there are immense torrents
of old lava, a veritable chaos, worthy of the lower
regions. Up to this time it is tolerably easy, but here
begins a fatigue one may call supernatural, for God
never made Vesuvius to be climbed by men. Picture
to yourself a slope, not like the roof of a house, but
something like the bell in St. Michael's tower, many
hundred feet high, covered with rolling stones large
and small, rocks, hardened lava, the scoriæ of lava,
not a plant, not a place to rest.

We had prepared four seats. These seats were
placed on two litters, which four men carried on their
shoulders, two others drawing them with ropes. These
men had to be relieved every five minutes. Those who
walked were dragged by two men, who had belts round
the waist for that purpose.

Tini, Marie, Kaunitz, and I occupied these seats. I left mine when we had got about a third of the way, for I would rather have broken my leg than be carried any further. Of the four porters, there was always one at least on the ground. What completes the charm of this journey is that, once undertaken, there is no going back. No one can descend by the same way he came, and the descent, which I will describe to you by-and-by, only begins at the summit of the mountain.

After going up for an hour and a half of this climbing, we arrived at the fresh lava, where everyone is obliged to walk. They choose for a path the streams of three or four days old, for they are hard on the surface and less rugged. Imagine a canal covered with flagstones of all shapes, badly joined, and instead of water a mass of iron red-hot just beneath the surface, and you will have some idea of this path. At this point Marie would go no further. You know what a coward she is, and I cannot understand how she allowed herself to be carried so far up. But when she felt her feet scorching, when the first puffs of sulphurous vapour reached her, she began to cry, and I had her taken down by the help of Pepi and four men. There only remained about fifty feet more to climb, and our task was accomplished.

Once arrived at the summit, we saw craters on all sides, and quite close to us, for the present plateau is not much larger than two-thirds of the Place de la Cour at Vienna. It is in the form of a funnel in the middle, and on each side rise two veritable chimneys made of sulphur and calcareous substances, about six feet high, and of which one has an opening of perhaps fifteen feet in diameter, and the other of four feet at the most. It is from these chimneys that the flames and fire issue, for the lava makes its appearance nearly a hundred feet below the summit on the side of the mountain.

The smoke and flames rise unceasingly from Vesuvius in its present state; the form and appearance change every instant; the chimneys alone remain the same. Every five or ten minutes an eruption is announced by a subterranean noise, and a slight trembling of the mountain. The noise resembles a discharge of twenty large guns in the interior of a vault. Then an immense jet of fire rises above the craters, like the bouquet in fireworks; burning scoriæ shoot up to the height of eighty or a hundred feet, and fall back into the funnel and on the sides of the mountain. There is no danger if one stands out of the wind.

The flames, the smoke, the burning substances hurled into the air, the noise of the explosions, are as different from the most splendid fireworks as are generally the grand spectacles of nature from those of human device.

I could scarcely tear myself away from a spectacle full of beauties beyond description, and at the same time full of awe impossible to describe.

The view from the summit of the mountain is simply magical; it takes in all the islands, bays, and coasts; the whole country lies before one as on a map. We watched the sun sink down into the waves of the sea, and then sought for a safer place to wait the approach of night; we found it about fifty or sixty feet lower down, out of the way of the eruptions, and above the flow of lava, which at night takes quite a new aspect. Rivers of lava, reaching as far as one can see, there issue forth. The course of lava is very slow; I do not think it advances more than two feet a minute. About half past nine, we began our descent, by the light of the volcano, the lava, the beautiful Naples moon—that moon which Caracciolo compared to the London sun—and twenty torches.

This descent, which is made on the opposite side to the ascent, is at once more convenient and more inconvenient, more serious and more ridiculous. Sinking to the knees first in cinders, then in sand, one allows oneself to slide down perpendicularly, and in ten minutes you are at the foot of the cone, like an avalanche, and with a real avalanche. There is no danger, no fatigue, and it is like nothing that one has ever done before in one's life.

Marie came to meet us at the spot where we fell— for it was a fall most literally. She was in raptures at seeing me again, and we had an excellent supper, which Jablonowsky prepared for us at the hermitage.

All that I have told you is a very faint sketch of a most extraordinary picture. Well, in the midst of so many perils, no misfortune ever happens to any obedient pilgrims. There are sometimes amateurs who pretend to know much more than their guides, and some accident may happen then ; while if you are docile you get off with little fatigue and no risk. Our principal guide generally goes three or four times between Portici and the summit of the mountain in twice twenty-four hours. None of our guides, porters, guardian angels—call them what you will—allows a single day to pass without taking this journey, for a sum of barely six francs. The path from Portici to the crater is constantly—day and night—like a great thoroughfare : all foreigners wish to have seen Vesuvius ; the Neapolitans themselves are the only persons who never go up ; just as I have never been to the top of the Kahlenberg.

I am delighted to have seen what I shall never see again. No one has any idea of the thing without having been there, and an eruption of the volcano would no longer astonish me. The road by which we went up to the summit a few days ago exists no longer. The stream of lava is much larger, and it is necessary to take a different direction.

I suppose Marie has told you of the Villa Gallo, a veritable *chef-d'œuvre* of nature, and one of the rare examples where the proprietor has had the good sense to embellish it by beautiful plantations. A summer passed in this place must be enchanting. Yesterday the king gave a ball at his Palace of Capo di Monte. It was a beautiful *fête*, and any *fête* illuminated by the lava of Vesuvius is always most striking to strangers. The Neapolitans alone do not trouble themselves about it.

320. *May* 19.—I can only write a few words, my dear, for I write between our return from Pæstum and the departure of the courier, whom the Emperor has delayed only to await my arrival.

We left Naples the day before yesterday, and slept the same night at Salerno. We stopped on the way to see a temple, or rather a church, built near Nocera by Guiscard, the Norman king, with *débris* taken from Pæstum; and the Abbey of Cava, a charming place, celebrated for its scientific collections. Yesterday we passed the whole day at Pæstum, and returned to Salerno at eleven o'clock at night. This morning we visited Vietri, and came back to Naples two hours ago.

Pæstum is worthy of the highest admiration. The three temples, still standing—and which may, from their great solidity, stand for many centuries more—date back to fabulous times. They certainly belong to a time anterior to the foundation of Rome. Their style of architecture resembles the Doric, but it is not so refined as that which has borne this name in later periods. Placed originally in a city renowned for its delightful environs, and for the quantity of roses its gardens contained, they stand now, in the midst of a plain given up to buffaloes and aquatic birds. The situation is magnificent, for it stands on the Gulf of Salerno; but the country ceases to be habitable towards the middle of June. The malaria arrives in this country as soon as it is depopulated. This place is interesting to me, among other things, because it is the most southerly that I have ever visited. The distance from Naples in a straight line is nearly sixty miles. The weather was very favourable for us; it is now settled fine, and " fine" here is a very different thing from what it is with us. Marie complains of the heat—I think, without cause, for though the sun is certainly scorching between eleven and four o'clock in the afternoon, there is always a breeze from the sea; the air is cool, the heat is slight, and I am in my element. Also, I never remember to have felt better in health.

The departure of the Emperor is fixed for the 31st of this month. He did not wish to refuse a pressing invitation from the King to remain here for his *fête*-day, the 30th. I intend to start on the 28th, on account of the arrangements for the horses; the King will perhaps not like it, but I shall do all I can to get a few days more at Rome, where there are still many things for me to see.

Metternich to his Mother.

321. *Naples, May* 21.—The Emperor's journey has been in all respects a success, and my only regret is that what we now see in passing is not what I shall have to see all the rest of my life. Our tastes are so much alike that I am convinced you would be the happiest person in the world in this country. All that nature has ever made most beautiful, most majestic, and most charming she has thrown here in a perfect flood on all that one sees, feels, and touches. You love mountains : well, this is like Switzerland ; you love a clear bright sky : you have it here with a constancy unknown among us. This country is all that one could wish ; it contains all that one finds wanting in other countries, and if the people were but in harmony with nature nothing would be left to be desired.

. . . The Emperor was on Vesuvius last night. He saw the sun rise, a superb sight from such an elevated spot, which looks over countries equally magnificent.

. . . I intend to leave for Rome on the 28th of this month. I shall leave the Emperor at Milan in the beginning of July, and I shall be at Carlsbad on the 15th, or soon after. I go there simply because Staudenheim wishes it, for my health is very good Hot climates are made for me—or rather, which is more modest, I am made for them. I sleep better, I have a better appetite, and, in a word, I am a different being than when seated behind a stove. I have the same nature as the palm-tree, which will not grow where it is cold, and which dies in a hot-house. Here they grow sixty feet, and without asserting that I shall reach the same height, I can boast of flourishing like them under the influence of the same sky.

Metternich to his Wife.

322. *Rome, June 6.*— . . . The Emperor, who intended to leave to-morrow has put off his journey till the day after the feast of Corpus Christi; not because he wished to see the religious ceremony at Rome, but because the little Archduchess Caroline is slightly indisposed, and Stifft has advised the Emperor to let her stay here a few days longer. Instead of leaving on Friday the 11th, I shall start on Saturday the 12th.

. . . You are mistaken in thinking that I shall not be at Carlsbad in time. I shall be there for certain between the 15th and the 20th of July, and I beg you to tell Staudenheim that I shall be delighted to see him there.

. . . Besides, a great deal of business awaits me there, for while I go to establish my own health, I cannot forget that Europe, and especially Germany, is in a far worse case than all the drinkers of water whom I shall meet at Carlsbad. I shall return to Vienna in the beginning of September, and I should be very glad if I could have been there sooner.

The Emperor, however, cannot arrive till about the same time; if, therefore, I had continued to travel with him all the time, I should not be much more advanced.

. . . Two days ago we took a trip to Tivoli. Everything in this country is gigantic. Tivoli far surpassed my expectation with respect to its situation, the magnificence of its falls and of its vegetation. The word *cascatelle* sounds so small that one does not expect to find twenty cascades, containing an immense volume of water, precipitated from a height of four or five hundred feet, dashing over rocks of a form and structure altogether extraordinary, for they are themselves only the product of the waters. I cannot understand why there is not a single exact picture either of Rome or its environs: only portions of the city or the neighbourhood are represented. I suppose it is the extent of the undertaking which frightens the artists. I will bring you a view taken from one of the windows of my drawing-room, which was drawn for me by a French artist of great merit. This view is exact, and you will tell me if ever you have seen, at any theatre whatever, a drop-scene which could be compared to it. The decorations of the *Triomphe de Trajan* are the merest trifles compared to what is seen here from every window, provided always it does not look on a blind alley.

Lawrence has taken up his abode at the Quirinal, and all Rome goes to see him. His reputation is made as thoroughly as that of the Coliseum. Cammuccini says he is the Titian of the nineteenth century. My portrait meets with great approbation; Clementine's is charming, and I am sure that if ever she comes to Rome she will be obliged to wear a veil, in order not to lose too much in the eyes of the many curious people who are anxious to see her because of her portrait. He has begun the portrait of the Pope, and is next going to take Cardinal Consalvi.

323. *June* 10.—This morning we had a grand ceremony, one of the most beautiful in Rome—the procession of Corpus Christi. It may well be superb, for the procession passes through all the colonnades of the Piazza of St. Peter's. The ceremony is so thoroughly religious, that it seems to me nothing could be added or taken away without injury. I do not care for ceremonies in general: they leave a void in the heart, and do not even satisfy the senses: but I must do justice to

that of this day.   It would be impossible to adore the
majesty of God with more submission or with more
dignity.

324. *Perugia, June* 17.—What is most annoying to
me in the matter* is that probably I shall be obliged to
leave the Emperor at Florence, and consequently shall
not go to Milan.   I shall console myself no doubt for
not going to Lombardy, but I believe I should have
been able to be of service to the Emperor there, and I
therefore regret that I cannot accompany him.

You see that in any case I am determined not to
arrive later than the middle of July at Carlsbad.   In
this I am not yielding to Staudenheim's pedantry, for it
may be as hot, and even hotter, towards the end of
August than in the middle of July at Carlsbad, as it is
everywhere else ; but such important business requires
me at a certain time that I choose the opportunity of
being most useful, and sacrifice the chance of being less
so.   Besides, I reckon on the most beautiful weather
coming at the end of the summer, for the spring, and
even the month of June, have been so cold that warmth
must surely have its turn.

. . . . Marie has sent you a most beautiful rosary
which the Pope gave me.   I make you a present of it,
but it must remain in the family as a *souvenir.*   The
Pope has been good and kind to everybody.   I passed
two hours with him the last day I was there, and I am
convinced there never was a man in his position so
plain and simple, and at the same time so enlightened.
He had tears in his eyes when he spoke to me of his
regret at the Emperor's departure, and he told me why.
He had from the first been more than pleased with the

* The illness of the Archduchess Caroline.

Emperor, who always improves on acquaintance, and he said he should again feel so lonely! The Quirinal has really become once more a cloister. In this immense palace there only now remain the Pope—whose Court is not larger than that of a ' *Hofrath* '—Cardinal Consalvi, and Lawrence. The annual expenses of the Pope amount to three thousand crowns.

The portrait which Lawrence is painting is a real *chef-d'œuvre* ; he has taken the Pope full-face, seated in the grand chair in which he is carried during the solemn ceremonies. The Pope's countenance is good and *spirituelle* ; he is somewhat worn, but his eyes are those of a young man, and he has not a single grey hair. You know how clever Lawrence is at eyes and hair ; so he is here on his own ground. Lawrence spent all his time with me at Rome, and he cried like a child when I left. I asked him the price of Clementine's portrait ; he said to Floret, whom I sent to ask him, that he should have looked upon the very question as an insult, only he knew me so well. ' I painted Clementine,' said he, ' for the love I bear her father, her mother, all her family, and for self-love too ! '

. . . . Thorwaldsen has finished my bust. It will be perfect. This artist will see you very soon ; he will spend a fortnight at Vienna on his way to Warsaw, where he is going to erect a monument to Poniatowski. I have given him a letter for you ; you will be well pleased with him, for he is as modest as he is clever. These qualities always go together.

325. *June* 19.—I am waiting to leave here till the Emperor goes, or rather I wait for the chance of meeting Capo d'Istria at Bologna. In this case I shall go from here to that city by the Forli route, to join the Emperor at Florence afterwards. I shall leave Italy on

July 20 at the latest. You shall, however, have the exact itinerary. You see I shall not accompany the Emperor to Milan.

. . . . I am at this moment passing through one of the most magnificent and picturesque countries in the world. I have never seen a situation like that of Perugia. Every side is alike grand. The town is situated, like most of the towns in the Apennines, on a high elevation, and looks over more than a hundred leagues of country. The land below is hilly, and covered with fields, beautiful as gardens. The mountains in the distance are as high as the Alps. Every inch of the ground is famous. To the right, near the Lake of Thrasimene, Hannibal defeated the Romans. Before me is Assisi, famous as the birthplace of St. Francis, and for a Temple of Minerva, built by Augustus, and one of the best preserved I have seen ; Spoleto, the ancient residence of Astolphe and Desiderius, kings of Lombardy ; thousands of olive-trees, green oaks, a magnificent vegetation. The orange-trees have ceased since Rome.

At Spoleto I was shown as a curiosity an *espalier* of lemons, which were only covered during the three months of winter. I felt rather melancholy when they told me that ; I had just come from a country where they are always in flower ! I have often told you my nature is the same as that of the orange-trees. Their climate is necessary for me to bear good fruit. The air here is as cold as on our mountains ; it is very healthy, and the best proof of this is furnished by a visit which Jaeger paid to the hospital to-day. He says it is an immense place—everything is large in Italy—and he only found there ten or twelve old invalids. The doctors told him they could not make a living here, the hospital being always the most deserted place in the town, which has nevertheless a population of seventeen thousand souls.

By comparing the country towns of Italy with those of any other country one is able to form an idea of the intrinsic value of these places. Perugia is what Iglau is with us—a country town about fifty leagues from the capital. Here there are ten palaces, each of them larger than the old Liechtenstein palace. I occupy one which is certainly more than twice the size. These palaces are full of old but beautiful furniture. There are also splendid pictures, and a great number of marbles. The palace which the Emperor occupies would be the most beautiful house in Vienna. The proprietor is a young man who has married a sister of Prince Odescalchi, and he refurnished it three years ago, at the time of his marriage.

There are two theatres at Perugia going on at the same time; an opera house as large as that of the Kärntnerthor, and one for comedy as large as the Wieden; three large churches, magnificent, of which two are painted entirely in fresco by the best masters, among others Pietro Perugino, Raphael's master; a university in a magnificent situation, and an academy of fine arts better appointed than that of Vienna.

In all these places, which are full of idlers, there are singers who would give great pleasure at Vienna, bad comedians playing detestable pieces, a crowd of mendicants too lazy to gather the fruits which fall into their mouths and the vegetables on which they walk. After all, out of a hundred of these sluggards, eighty of them are clever, and often not one who would be unbearably tiresome. There is not one who has not all the appearance of poverty, yet nevertheless has his purse well furnished.

I do not believe that any two countries can be less alike than Germany and Italy, and yet our wiseacres at Vienna wish, cost what it may, to make Italians of the Germans. Their plan will succeed marvellously!

Metternich to his daughter Marie, Perugia, June 22.

326. So you are at Trieste, my dear Marie!— and I am at Perugia—just as you left me.

. . . . We had the Cardinal here for two days. He shed tears on hearing you were gone. The last battle I had with him was about an armchair, which he never liked to sit upon, because at my writing-table I had only a common chair. Now, there were at first none but grand yellow armchairs in my room, and, as they are too high, I had had an old chair brought from the antechamber for my writing-table. The dispute was settled by the Cardinal marching off to the antechamber to find a similar chair for himself, but he did not allow me to accompany him.

When he left he again embraced Giroux, who gave me an account of this second embrace with tears in his eyes. 'That Abbé is a very good man,' said Giroux to me; 'but I do not know why he loves me so much. He patted me on the back, and then embracing me said, " Good bye, old man ; if ever you need anything write to me, or to our mutual friend, my old valet." He is a good man, is that Abbé.' I remarked that his friend was not an Abbé, but a Cardinal. 'Well! how the devil should I know? Abbé or Cardinal! the first are black, and the second are red ; what does it matter to me?'

HOMEWARD JOURNEY FROM ITALY TO
CARLSBAD.

Extracts from Metternich's private Letters to his Family, from July 4 to September 1, 1819.

327. Plan of the journey. 328. Postponement of the journey of the Emperor Francis to Milan. 329. From Verona—difference of climate. 330. From Innspruck. 331. From Carlsbad. 332. From Teplitz—reminiscences of the year 1813. 333. Walks with Adam Müller. 334. End of the Carlsbad Conferences.

Metternich to his Wife, Florence, July 4, 1819.

327. I have made my plan to-day, my dear.

I intend to leave here next Saturday, July 10. I shall be at Bologna on the 11th, at Verona on the 12th, at Trente on the 13th, at Brixen on the 14th, at Innspruck on the 15th, at Munich on the 16th, at Ratisbonne on the 17th, between Ratisbonne and Carlsbad on the 18th.

The Emperor will arrive here on the 7th. It is possible that my departure may be delayed for one or two days; you see that, even in this case, I shall be at Carlsbad on the 20th or 21st, at the latest.

328. *July* 9.— . . . The Emperor is right to postpone his journey to Milan. The season is over for a tour in Italy, and instead of being grilled for fifteen days in Lombardy,* he will return there one day to

* In a communication from Metternich to the Emperor Francis, from Verona, dated July 14, 1819, Metternich writes, after a consultation with Bubna, in these terms:—' Bubna agrees with me as to the resolution your Majesty has taken to postpone your visit to Milan. Better no visit at all than one of only a fortnight.'—ED.

spend two or three months in a manner more useful, and also more cool. I declare that Carlsbad is a real sacrifice for me, as the Emperor is going to Vienna. Nevertheless, I ought to go, for so many people are expecting me there that it would be doing a very bad turn to these poor travellers to leave them all in the lurch. The affairs which I have to arrange there are, besides, so important that I suppress my regrets by the feeling of duty. I declare, however, frankly, that Carlsbad is insupportable to me.

329. *Verona, July* 14.—I arrived here yesterday about eleven o'clock in the morning, my dear, after having suffered tolerably from the heat.

I left Florence on the 11th, at nine o'clock in the evening. I went as far as Bologna in one stage, where, of course, a cardinal met me with all sorts of music, a grand dinner, &c. I went to bed in the midst of the *fanfares*, and slept six hours as if it were night. I left Bologna at seven o'clock in the evening, and made my triumphal entry into Verona yesterday, the 13th, at ten o'clock in the morning. When I get back to Austria there will be a truce to trumpets and cymbals. I shall leave this evening, and go in one stage as far as Brixen, where I shall sleep to-morrow, and on the 16th I shall be at Innspruck.

The difference of climate is very striking from Salerno to the foot of the Alps. Tuscany is the hottest without being the most southerly for vegetation. Different plants mark the different regions : aloes and cacti are found as far as Terracina, myrtles and orange-trees as far as Narni, olives and pomegranates as far as the highest chain of the Apennines, which separates Tuscany from the Legations. From the northern declivity of these mountains the climate is much the same as with us. The mulberries alone show a difference of climate, although they do very well with us. The sky loses its brightness ; the Alps are covered with thick clouds ; and the atmosphere is slightly foggy.

330. *Innspruck, July* 16.—I wish to let you know, my dear, that I am in Germany. I made a good and rapid journey from Verona here, but my *cara patria* has received me badly. I arrived at Innspruck twenty-four hours after the snow. The cold here makes one shiver, especially a man who comes from the Cape of Policastro. I hope Carlsbad will treat me better; I shall at any rate find hot water there. I, who, scarcely six days ago, drank a large glass of iced orangeade every night before going to bed, will this evening drink hot punch to prevent myself freezing. No more orange-trees, but firs ; no more magnolias in blossom, but elders ; no more grapes, but strawberries beginning to redden. I saw the harvest at Naples two months ago, and I have just passed through fifty leagues of country where, in the best cantons the fields are just beginning to turn yellow, and where, in the colder places, the summer crops are still in blade. I come from the Cenerentola, and have just left Hanns Dachel. High mountains are most beautiful, but I like to see them ; we shall be on the level at Innspruck, but that will make no difference to the view, there is so much fog.

331. *Carlsbad, July* 26.—I did not write to you by the first courier whom I sent from here, for I could not find a moment to do so.

I leave to-morrow for Teplitz, where I shall spend three whole days. The present moment is one of life or death. It appears that Teplitz is a place destined for my great operations.* By the help of God, I hope to defeat the German Revolution, even as I have vanquished the conqueror of the world. The German revolutionists thought me far away, because I was a hundred leagues off. They have deceived themselves; I am in the midst of them, and I will now deal out my blows. You will observe a singular coincidence between the discoveries and arrests in Prussia and Germany and my passage of the Alps. I suppose this will be seen at last when it is known that all Germany is assembled round me. Count Münster is here; Rechberg, Wintzingerode, Berstett, Baron de Marschall (acting minister of Nassau), and Bernstorff (the Prussian), will be here before August 1. We shall do a great work. Will it be a good one? God will decide. It will be great, for on it will depend the welfare or the definite destruction of social order. This is between ourselves.

332. *Teplitz, July* 27.—My dear, I am writing to you in the same room, and on the same table, where I signed the Quadruple Alliance six years ago. It is just about the same time of year. Everything has changed since then, except myself.

I have not revisited this place since 1813. It has been a long road to get here again. What events have happened since the day of my arrival here in that year of grace! Seated at the same desk, thinking over all which then occupied my mind, bringing before my mind's eye what existed then, and what exists no longer, I cannot resist a slight sensation of vanity, and an immense feeling of contentment and satisfaction. But if I think over what is, if I compare it with what ought to

---

* See Metternich's interview with King Frederick William III. in Teplitz, No. 351.

be, and with that which so easily might have been, I deplore the fate of the world, ever given up to the gravest errors, and to great faults committed in consequence of petty calculations and great illusions. My mind conceives nothing narrow or limited ; I always go, on every side, far beyond all that occupies the greater number of men of business ; I cover ground infinitely larger than they can see or wish to see. I cannot help saying to myself twenty times a day : ' Good God, how right I am, and how wrong they are ! And how easy this reason is to see—it is so clear, so simple, and so natural ! ' I shall repeat this till my last breath, and the world will go on in its own miserable way none the less.

Reason and justice can only be departed from by paths covered with blood and tears. To hear people talk one would think they were giants; follow them, and you soon perceive that you have only to do with phantoms. The one giant produced by the eighteenth century is no longer of this world ; all that moves that world at present, is of a miserable character. It is very difficult to play well with bad or indifferent actors.

333. *Carlsbad, August* 22.—I have brought here, for my own private pleasure, a man of more mind and knowledge than almost anyone in the world. A certain Adam Müller—not the prophet, but the Austrian Consul-General at Leipzig. When my head is worried with business, I make him come ; he accompanies me to the Posthof, and beyond, and I talk with him without rhyme or reason. This morning he proved to me that he is the most learned man in the world about clouds. He thinks that he knows as much as I know little about them He says there are two kinds of clouds, male and female : that separated, they produce nothing, absolutely nothing, like a monastery of Capuchins separated from a convent of nuns. These clouds end by meeting : they are excited, they marry, and behold rain, thunder, and all the noise in the world.

At the first rain, say to your neighbour that two loving clouds have just been made happy ; you will seem to have said something foolish, but this is true physics, and even philosophy.

334. *September* 1.—Here I am, thank God, delivered of my great work.* The labour passed off happily, and the child has come into this world. I have every reason to be satisfied with the result, and I ought to be, for all I wished has come to pass. Heaven will protect an enterprise so great and so worthy of its support, for it concerns the safety of the world. What thirty years of revolution could not produce has been brought about by our three weeks' labour at Carlsbad. It is the first time that a number of measures have appeared together so anti-revolutionary, so just, and so peremptory. What I have wished for since 1813, but what that terrible Emperor Alexander has always prevented, I have accomplished, because he was not there. I have at last been able to follow out my own thoughts, and publicly declare all my principles, sustained as I am by thirty millions of men—or rather fifty, if we count all the Austrians not Germans. Now the great thing is to carry them out well, and I believe they will be well carried out.

My colleagues have addressed such thanks to me as I believe no Minister has ever received.† Victor was so touched that he carried away the letter to copy for

---

* See Results of the Carlsbad Conference, No. 353.—Ed.

† See Letters of Thanks in No. 355.—Ed.

you, and he tells me he sent it to you yesterday. Make no use of it, however, except to read it.

One thing is certain, that there never was seen more exemplary agreement and submission than in our conferences. If the Emperor doubts his being Emperor of Germany, he deceives himself greatly.

A curious fact is that the worst German Jacobins have not dared to attack me. That which they have not done they will soon not be able to do. I have shown, moreover, that the best means of attacking an evil is to attack it in front. This is true of political blows as well as those of a cudgel. The dead shout no longer, and among the living I shall have many to shout in favour of my theories. It will yet take fifteen days, however, before the shell explodes at Frankfurt.

I shall leave to-morrow for Königswart, where I shall remain five or six days. From thence I shall go direct to Vienna. I intend to arrive there from the 10th to the 12th. You will be informed of my arrival at least twenty-four hours beforehand.

THE ASSASSINATION OF KOTZEBUE AND ITS CONSEQUENCES.

Correspondence between Metternich and Gentz, April 1 to July 1, 1819.

Gentz to Metternich, Vienna, April 1, 1819.

335. Your Excellency will, in all probability, have heard from Mannheim the dreadful occurrence which has taken place there more quickly than by letters from this place. We learnt the news early yesterday through the ' Allgemeine Zeitung ' and by despatches from Carlsruhe addressed to Tettenborn, of which I enclose copies * (Nos. 336–337).

The thing is dreadful enough in itself, but its origin and evident connection with the great maladies and dangers of the time elevate it in the eyes of those accustomed to take a large and comprehensive view of things to a still higher degree of horror and terror. When we lifted the first warning voice against the excesses at the Wartburg our mouths were stopped with allusions to ' the innocent, virtuous efforts of German youth ' and their ' meritorious teachers ; ' and this is what they have come to !

Your Excellency will have already followed up the whole history of this widespread malady with such assiduous attention, and appreciated it with so much intelligence and wisdom, that it would be quite super-

---

* ' I looked these through yesterday in haste : I now remark that only one of the papers deserves the name of a despatch, the other is a letter from Varnhagen, which I send with it.'—Note by Gentz.

fluous here to attempt to follow out the past, which no longer belongs to us. Empty lamentations lead to nothing, and all personal considerations must be silenced when such important concerns are in question. The greatest catastrophes in the moral as in the physical world may be, not, indeed, for those who fall under them, but for others, useful and even beneficial, if results are brought about and measures accelerated which would have been much longer in coming into operation, or would, perhaps, never have done so.

The practical reflections which this last outrage have produced in me are roughly as follows :—

1. The hatred of the revolutionary rabble against Kotzebue was of long standing, had many causes, and was fostered with a devilish art. But I am quite convinced that the attempt on his life was caused principally—indeed, exclusively—by the delusion that he excited the Emperor Alexander against popular writers and the universities, and made him averse to liberal ideas. It is well known how much the whole party had formerly reckoned on the support of that monarch ; and that his apostacy was a frightful blow to them was sufficiently evident. The consequence of the senseless challenge to Stourdza, which seemed to make an end of all uncertainty, had brought the party quite to despair. Actuated in turn by rage and by fear, it sank into a state of frenzy, from which sprang this crime. Then, too, Kotzebue was murdered because these madmen in their delusion believed that he had caused the desertion of a protector from whom they had the greatest expectations. This view will hardly escape the Emperor of Russia. He is personally insulted by this crime against a Russian Staatsrath, as well as by former proceedings against another. His

attitude at the time of the Wartburg excesses, his utterances on every opportunity since that time, the principles and dispositions which he displayed at Aix-la-Chapelle, all lead us to expect that he will take this matter in the most serious light. I do not wish the explosion to be too violent or too loud, because it might be embarrassing to us in many ways. But I should consider it a happy thing if he took this opportunity to declare without reserve his own way of thinking, seeing, and feeling, and then endeavoured to act upon Prussia, Bavaria, and Germany with prudence and moderation, but yet in a very determined manner— a manner calculated to put an end to all indecision and uncertainty.

2. I hope that through this dreadful occurrence and the consequences which must inevitably follow it, we shall for some years escape the debates on the freedom of the press in Germany. For I can hardly believe that any State of the Bund would be shameless enough now to expect the carrying out of the freedom of the press by those Governments who have not hitherto sanctioned it. And it is my firm conviction that Austria must seize the first occasion when such a word is uttered in the Bundestag to declare emphatically that she considers the article of the Bund (an article never to be pardoned) that speaks or dreams of uniform arrangements in this matter—which concerns the duties and rights of supremacy and sovereignty—once and for all impracticable and abolished, and will take no part in any discussion regarding it.

3. The necessity of taking some steps with regard to the condition of the German universities will now be more evident than ever. We are, indeed—this I feel only too strongly—still not one step nearer the solution

of this difficult problem ; but yet we have gained so much that no one can now stigmatise discussions on this point as high-treason against Germany. But it is my most earnest desire that on this important matter nothing may be brought before the Bundestag, nothing publicly said or written by authority (the lampooners may write what they like), before the first German Courts (I mean only Austria, Bavaria, Saxony, and Hanover, to the exclusion of all others) have arrived at a decided and mutually binding understanding on the measures to be adopted. This will cost much time and trouble, but the effect of the last blow will not pass away in six months, and Kotzebue's blood will cry for vengeance somewhat longer than to-day and to-morrow. The result is no slight matter, and it is not to be arrived at in one or two conferences. But the greatest evil of all would be hasty, undigested, feeble measures, which must inevitably lead to mischief. It is a misfortune that, for reasons known to your Excellency, we cannot in this matter claim the first and leading part ; but this cannot prevent us from being active and useful.

The murder has created no very great sensation here. The only man, to my knowledge, who has spoken out well and strongly about it, is Count Sedlnizky, who understands somewhat better than most people what we have to expect.

Some matters have very much vexed and oppressed me. Among the latter I do not count the rude and unseemly speeches of Baron d'Aspre, because I have never expected anything better from him, but they annoy me because you bestow on this man favour which is envied by many who are more modest. I am very sorry that he is going to Italy; for he will talk very foolishly about matters there too, and unless your

Excellency keeps a strong hand over him he will compromise you frightfully.

This letter will probably go by Cæsar. Lawrence,
who wished to leave three days ago, still remains, and
therefore cannot now be in Rome by Easter. The trees
begin to come out, but a green Easter it cannot possibly
be.

*Freiherr von Berstett, Minister from Baden, to Freiherr
von Tettenborn, Ambassador from Baden to Vienna.*

(Enclosed in No. 335.)

336. Your Excellency will be no less dismayed
than we all are at the following very sad news.

(Extract from the Directorial Report of the Neckar Circle,
March 23, 1819.)

'Yesterday evening at five o'clock the Russian
Staatsrath von Kotzebue was mortally wounded in his
own house. Stabbed in several places with a poniard, he
died of his wounds after giving his evidence. The
assassin — a man to all appearance about four-and-
twenty years of age—hurried out of the house after
acomplishing the deed, and in the street, in front of the
house door, he stabbed himself in the breast. At the
present moment he is still alive, but whether he is still
conscious is not known with certainty. From papers found
in his coat pocket it appears that he is a student in the
university, named Carl Friedrich Sand, and was
studiosus theologiæ. At the tavern, where, according to
the landlord's account, he had arrived that morning
alone, he had given the name of Heinrichs, a student
from Erlangen. From some documents found upon
him it is evident that he had long premeditated this
crime, and devoted himself to death. He seems to

have bound himself to this, which makes the crime the more horrible. We expect in the morning still more exact circumstantial evidence, which we shall not fail to forward as soon as possible.'

The paper found on the murderer was also sent, and was a proclamation to the Germans, of extraordinary form, calling upon everyone to arm, and containing a number of extravagant and enthusiastic ideas which betokened revolutionary frenzy. The Grand Duke has given orders that the strictest investigation should be made, to find out all traces connected with it, in order that these dangerous and fantastic disorders may be checked by some comprehensive measures. Your Excellency is implored to use every effort to bring forward all matters connected with this insane conspiracy of heated fantasies, which thinks to find Germany's welfare in criminal acts ; and, above all, to endeavour to bring about that people should seriously consider and comprehend the general measures the necessity for which this frightful event only too loudly proclaims. His Royal Highness is much grieved that this horrible deed—although an isolated act, as it certainly seems, and performed by a student from a foreign university—has taken place in your country. I earnestly beg of you to let me know as quickly as possible all that you hear on this matter.

Varnhagen von Ense to Tettenborn, Carlsruhe,
March 24, 1819.

(Enclosed in No. 335.)

337. I hasten to give your Excellency the full particulars of the dreadful occurrence in Mannheim, which has this day filled everyone here with horror and

dismay! A young man, who had called yesterday
morning to speak to Herr von Kotzebue, was told to
return in the afternoon about five o'clock. Kotzebue received him in a sitting-room and talked with him some
time, but the man, approaching to give him a paper,
pulled out a dagger, and almost in a moment the unfortunate man fell, and in a few minutes breathed his
last. The noise summoned a servant, who found his
master on the floor and the murderer brandishing the
dagger and crying 'Does anyone else here wish to
die?' Threatening in this way, he accomplished his
exit, ran frantically up the steps, and fell on his knees
at the house door; and while he joyfully thanked God
for the success of his great work, he stabbed himself
twice, making himself unconscious, which, however, did
not last, and although he still lives he is very weak, for
he wounded himself most seriously. This deed, said a
paper found by his side, he had done for (pretended)
love of Fatherland and freedom, with full consciousness
and after long premeditation : he called upon the hu-
miliated German people to a courageous rising, to the
slaying of all the evil-disposed, to the perfecting of the
Reformation, to the union of Church and State, he
wished his example to be followed, &c. &c.—all in a
fantastic, ranting style, foolish enough, but not mad.
Another paper found near him contained the words:
'Sentence of death against August von Kotzebue, executed March 23, at half-past five in the afternoon,
according to the decree of the University of . . .' This
statement leads to the supposition that there is some
conspiracy and fraternity, which fills all hearts with
horror and fear. What can be done against a man who
kills himself? Shall the Order of the Assassins be re-
produced in the West? With us, in Germany, the

thing will make a frightful impression! The murderer is a *studiosus theologiæ* from Erlangen, about four-and-twenty years old, named Carl Friedrich Sand; no one knows his birthplace, but he is supposed to be from Courland or Anspach.

The Grand Duke is very much shocked by this event: he will have it dealt with carefully as a matter of interest to all Governments. But I fear that all investigation will be fruitless.

The Russian Emperor will be beside himself; but what can he do, with all his power? To whom will he turn? All ministers and councillors will believe themselves threatened. I would not be Herr von Stourdza just now, nor, indeed, many others! I am so affected that I could eat nothing this morning, and poor Rachel is beside herself with tears and hysterics. Certainly it is a dreadful affair. With great respect, I am, your Excellency, &c., &c.,

VARNHAGEN VON ENSE.

Metternich to Gentz, Rome, April 9, 1819.

338. I have received the news of Kotzebue's assassination, with all the preliminary details. It remains to be seen whether the Grand Duke of Baden has strength enough to follow up the investigation, and, if he has this, whether he has people in his courts of justice who will conduct them fairly. Things are at the present time so that no definite idea can be formed beforehand about anything.

I have, for my part, no doubt that the murderer did not act simply from motives of his own, but in consequence of a secret league. Here we find great evil and some good, for poor Kotzebue now appears as an *argumentum ad hominem* which even the liberal Duke

of Weimar cannot defend. It will be my care to draw
from the affair the best possible results, and in this endeavour I shall not be found lukewarm.

It appears to be quite certain that the assassin was
an emissary of Behme of Jena. The university which
was to carry out the plan may have been chosen by
lot, and which of the fraternity was to follow up the
deed by the sacrifice of his own life may also have been
chosen by lot ; and there is no doubt that it was followed out. Many data go to establish this view.

We shall now very soon see what the Emperor of
Russia will say to the loving treatment of his *Staatsräth*
in Germany.

While in Germany Russian agents *propter obscura-
tionem* are murdered, in Italy the Russian agents preside over the clubs of the Carbonari. This abomination
will soon be checked.

Our residence here has already had very happy
results. The Emperor will, as it seems, be loaded by
the Holy Father with honours and all marks of respect.
His attitude and manner are excellent : the public, who
received the Emperor with true delight, begin to adore
him personally. All the foolish reports spread abroad
by the many who like activity of that sort before our
arrival have disappeared, and people begin to see that
here, as at Aix-la-Chapelle, we alone have not lied with
respect to the object of the journey.

I beg of you to mention these assertions, which rest
on simple fact, in Vienna, and to contradict all rumours
to the contrary. Especially you may assure people
that the Emperor will not bring one single Jesuit back
to Vienna—which will not much delight the Penkler
Society.*

* Of the ' Penkler Society' were several men who were intimate with

Rome is very different from the picture I had made for myself of the place. I thought Rome would be ruinous and sombre. Instead of this it is splendid and cheerful. Everything which shows the grandeur of antiquity is here united with the grandeur of the middle ages. The new has two sides. The two last Popes—*i. e.* Pius VI. and Pius VII.—have done more for art than all their predecessors in the way of discovery of the old. Consequently it is impossible to imagine the splendour of the galleries of the Vatican. Think of twenty galleries like the one *Musée du Louvre*, and you will still be far from the truth as to the situation and collections of the Vatican of the present day. This wealth of treasure far exceeds the idea I had formed. The Papal residence, the Papal Court, is the most gorgeous that worldly power can produce. The spiritual grandeur I have hardly yet discovered. This remark applies even to St. Peter's. To my mind it is the most magnificent of churches for splendour and size, but the least spiritual in the world. Me, at least, it can never invite to pray.

What impression it makes on Schlegel I do not know, for he finds the Papal cook so excellent that he has hardly any time left to see anything.

The remains of antiquity are also far beyond every imagination. All other buildings in the world, in extent, massiveness, and perfection, are nothing compared with

the writer of this letter, as well as the person to whom it was addressed—such as Adam Müller, Friedrich von Schlegel, Zacharia Werner, Josef Anton Pilat, and Friedrich von Klinkowström. Besides these there were also Zängerle and Ziegler (afterwards bishops), Professor Ackerman, Domherr Schmidt, Stift, Dr. Johann Emmanuel Veith, and others. Affinity of sentiments, and similar aims in a strong Catholic direction, united all these men in a circle, the centre of which was P. Clemens Maria Hofbauer. The hospitable house of Herr von Penkler was open for their social meetings: hence the name of the society.—ED.

the remains of ancient Rome. The Palace of the
Cæsars, which covered the whole Monte Palatino (the
whole of the original city of Rome), a palace as large
as the city of Vienna within its walls ; the Coliseum,
in which 80,000 men could be comfortably seated ;
the Baths of Caracalla, in which 3,000 could bathe in
separate rooms, where there are only marble baths, each
as large as the ladies' baths at Baden ; the remains
of all these places, in separate fragments each as large
as ever a new palace, are mostly covered with luxuriant vegetation. This all makes a sight of which one
can form not the least idea, let one have seen what one
may all the world over. Rome remains to-day among
the cities of the old and the new world like Chimborazo
among the mountains.

And all this splendour lies in a plain of the most
glorious soil in the world ! In the neighbourhood of
Rome—the so-called *Campagna di Roma*—is contained
the hardest problem to be solved in the present day.
How can this, under any supposition whatever, be once
more brought under cultivation ?

Canals must be dug, trees planted, fields ploughed,
and houses built. About five years ago a cardinal,
born in the Legations, attempted to settle a colony of
300 families in the healthiest part of it, and had them
well supplied with all necessaries. In two years the
malaria had reduced the colony to twenty persons. In
the city three quarters are no longer habitable ; so
that at present the finest palaces, such as the Villa
Borghese, the Villa Albani, &c., &c., stand empty, for
to spend one night in them is most dangerous. And
yet close by one of these pest-houses may be one in
which the air is fine and wholesome. The water is
excellent.

Cæsar arrived to-day, and your letter of April 1 tells me that you regard the affair of Kotzebue as I do. Your remarks on the immediate motives for it appear to me quite correct. But just because they are so they show that this horrible crime is not the affair of a *studiosus theologiæ*. Sand was a young student distinguished at the University of Erlangen for quiet, good behaviour. In the year 1817 he left Jena, and distinguished himself at the Wartburg. In the year 1818 he went back to Erlangen, and lectured for the *Burschenschaft*. He was ravished with the glorious *Leben der Freien* of Jena and lectured boldly, and then went back to Jena.

I beg of you earnestly to entreat Tettenborn to urge his Government to go thoroughly into the investigation, and not to allow it to be cut short.

At the same time I beg of you yourself to revise the article which Pilat will have inserted from Rome in the 'Observer,' so that there may not escape in it any *capucinades*. My constant efforts are directed against ultras of all kinds, till at last I, too, shall be stabbed by the dagger of some fool. But, if the rascal does not come behind me, he will get such a box on the ear as he will long remember, even if he hits me.

Till then farewell, and pray continue to write to me.

Gentz to Metternich, Vienna, April 14, 1819.

339. Enclosed you will find the copy of a letter I have last week received from Adam Muller.* I hear that he has written directly to your Excellency, but since I have no knowledge of anything which goes through the Chancery, I do not know whether and how

---

* Adam Müller was then Austrian Consul-General at Leipsic.

far the letter to me contains facts which are not perhaps included in the Report to your Excellency. The circumstance of the news of the murder having arrived earlier in Leipsic seems, on further explanations, not to be anything remarkable, for it is a fact that immediately after the murder a courier was sent from Mannheim to the Academic Senate at Jena, and returned there on the 26th.

I should bewail it as a real calamity if Sand does not die of his wounds. His preservation can do no good, and may do much harm. I do not believe, as I have already said, that any further statement of his will be of the least value. A conspiracy properly so called certainly will not come out, and the men whom it would be of the greatest importance to convict would not be caught. We should be in no way benefited by the misfortune which the complicity of other young men would have brought upon this, and perhaps many other honest families. On the contrary, it is hardly possible to imagine what may happen if Sand lives. If the stern course of the law is stopped, or it is delayed in the course of its processes (as I have many reasons for thinking possible, and, indeed, quite certainly foresee), all the good effect which might be produced by so sad an event will be lost. If the matter is taken up in earnest, and the criminal punished with the whole force of the criminal law, it cannot but be, with the present general feeling, that thousands and thousands, excited by a romantic enthusiasm for him, will fancy him a hero, a martyr to the good cause, a victim of obscurantism, and become ten times more violent and culpable than they already are. For these reasons I shall thank God very heartily if His hand cuts the knot.

For the rest, all German papers watch like bloodhounds for the first word of the 'Observer,' on this unhappy history. But my conviction is decided and immovable that the 'Observer' must keep silence. No one can doubt our feeling on the matter. We spoke when everyone else was silent. Our articles on the excesses at the Wartburg, which are not forgotten, contain everything which can be said on the late event, which is a natural consequence of what before happened. Just because it would be so easy for us at present to swagger with our warnings and wise sayings, it is more noble and dignified to relinquish this easy business, which has already been partly assumed for us by others. Besides, our silence will be more imposing to these miscreants than the most persuasive article. They will undoubtedly believe that there is some secret behind—that we will not speak because we are determined to act. And this—I will answer for it to your Excellency with life and limb—will terrify them much more than the most threatening words.

Now as to the action required : I do not see any necessity for your Excellency's return to Germany. The condition of the German universities is an illness which calls for a particular consultation of the physicians, to conduct which, time and a conjunction or concurrence of favourable circumstances is required. As soon as I am made in some measure acquainted with your Excellency's views on this important and critical affair, I will endeavour to explain to you my ideas on the form of the negotiation itself. I see plainly that the Bundestag must join in it; but if the Bundestag is left to take the initiative and conduct the business, without a firm, systematic course being agreed upon beforehand, I am quite certain that no good result will be attained.

Müller to Gentz, Leipsic, April 3, 1819.

(Enclosed in No. 339.)

340. . . . With regard to the Kotzebue history, I beg you not to be led by the Berlin newspapers to believe that Varnhagen is the author of that despatch.

In order to see that the *coup* comes from Jena, I beg you to remark the following circumstances :—

The murder took place on the evening of the 23rd and was known in Frankfurt on the 25th. The news would, in the ordinary way, only have reached Leipsic by the first Frankfurt post on the 29th. Instead of this, it had already arrived on the 27th, through two Jena students, and that by the roundabout way by Jena. On Saturday the 28th, the President of Police and the Rector of the University betook themselves to these two students to learn the details, for no courier or other news had arrived. It is also not to be denied that the murderer was known as a fanatical adherent of Professor Luden in Jena, and there studied anatomy for his purpose for a fortnight ; also, that immediately after the reception of the news of the success of the attempt, the Burschenschaft evidently broke up and constituted themselves into several fictitious associations of Allemanns, Markomanns, Suavians, Vandals, and so on : while on March 23 a portrait of Kotzebue, with a dead bat fastened beneath it, was to be seen on the black board at Jena.

Further, do not imagine that this is to be considered merely as one dreadful specimen of the kind, and that the murderous band will allow themselves to be intimidated by a few measures, and those half-measures such as the present Government can take. The confusion of ideas, and the firmness in an evil direction, are far greater than you can imagine.

Here, in this quiet place, you may hear Sand publicly called a Scævola. The only satisfaction is that the Grand Duke of Weimar, Krug, and such like people, are greatly embarrassed. . . .

Gentz to Metternich, Vienna, April 23, 1819.

(Answer to No. 338.)

341. Your Excellency's kind letter of the 9th inst. has delighted and relieved me, and I thank you heartily that, surrounded as you are by so many interesting objects, which certainly claim all your time, you were able to send me so much interesting information.

The reasons which your Excellency points out for attributing the assassination of Kotzebue to a regular, perhaps wide-spread, plot, have certainly some weight, and I wish that nothing may be omitted which can serve to clear up this point. But still I do not give up my opinion about it. The most important points on which it depends we have long discovered and known. That our academic youth have arrived at this degree of criminal madness is known to us, and we need no further explanation about it. We must act on the root of the evil; the ramifications are unimportant affairs, and can at most lighten the labour of the arm which must lay the axe to the wild stem itself—its true strength must be in itself.

Your Excellency will notice what trouble the newspaper writers are taking to describe Sand as a highly-interesting youth. They may be right for what I know. I myself do not believe that Sand was a mere miscreant; but all the worse for those who could push on a spirit

good and noble in itself, to go beyond the worst of criminals ! The real culprits are, and will ever be, Fries,
Luden, Oken, Kieser, and others of the same kind, of
whom the universities must be purified at any price
before any reformatory measures can have the slightest
effect.

Metternich to Gentz, Rome, April 23, 1819.

342. I have now given the necessary instructions
to Count Buol with regard to the regulation of the
affairs of the German universities. The last proposal of
the Duke of Weimar appeared to me a good ground to
act upon, and if you will look at my instructions, I
hope for your approval. I have used really liberal
words to set a limit to ultra-liberalism, and it belongs
to my fortune—to which you have so often contributed—that I can raise my edifice on the soil of Weimar
and ornament it with the example of the worthy Sand,
at the cost of poor Kotzebue. For your comfort let
me tell you that no *Spiegelish* * work has gone to
Frankfurt, that not one *Spiegelish* idea obtains with
me, and that ' *Christ* ' † whom I have found here, thinks
my proposals practical, and highly approves of them.

It is one of the strange facts of my life that here in
Rome I have been called to work for hours together
about the German universities, and from all the Cabinets
of Germany letters have arrived containing the most
urgent requests that I would make an end of the disorder which each German prince provoked and encouraged in his own country, and is now no longer able
to restrain. An example of the kind must really be

---

* Count Spiegel was Hofrath at the Chancellery, and entrusted with
the Report on German affairs.—ED.

† The identity of this person, then in Rome, cannot be ascertained.—ED.

sufficient to excite in every sensible man the greatest contempt for the character of many of these Governments.

My people are so overwhelmed with work that I do not know whether I shall be able to send you a copy of my ostensible and of my secret instructions to Count Buol by the present courier: in any case you shall have them by the next; but, without waiting for them, let nothing hinder you from letting me know your views.

My proposals are confined to the discipline of the universities, and do not at all touch the studies themselves—two questions which are very closely related, but yet in the present discussion necessarily separated. If we meddle with the latter, nothing at all will be done, and a letter from Müller sufficiently points this out to me, in which in speaking of this affair he observes ' that the disorder in the universities proceeds from the Reformation and that it can only be really set right by the recall of the Reformation.' I deny neither the assertion nor its justice. But here on the Quirinal I cannot meddle with Dr. Martin Luther, and I hope that nevertheless some good will come of it without even touching its source—Protestantism. The last very excellent letter of Müller's reminded me involuntarily of Golowkin's proposition for the investigation of ' *Causes primitives de la révolution française.*'

Our stay in Rome is coming to an end. It has been as splendid as safe and useful. The Emperor is greatly pleased with the Pope: not only that no single dangerous points happened to be mentioned by the latter, but the Emperor (whose principles in canonical respects are unquestionable) said to me yesterday, on leaving his Holiness after a visit of two hours, ' that he was sorry the Pope could not be his own first archbishop, for he would certainly never find one better qualified to oppose the exorbitant pretensions of the Roman Curia.' So among other things the Pope assured the Emperor that the fundamental defect of the Institution of the Jesuits was their pretension of independence of the bishops, an assertion contrary to every true idea of ecclesiastical discipline, and which could only lead to disorder without measure! Our clerical Chateaubriands would, if they knew this, certainly be alienated from the poor old excellent Pius : wherefore keep this saying by all means to yourself, for *entre deux* the Chateaubriands are much dearer to me than the Benjamin Constants and Lanjuinais. The sacred *via media* is only reserved for a few, and since on it truth stands, truth is but little known.

My ideas of the splendour of Rome are every day surpassed. One sees here of what man at his highest is capable ; and if I hate the old Romans as thorough Bonapartists, yet I must give them heartfelt thanks for the grandeur which they had strength and sense to leave behind them for posterity.

As a botanist you would find here the greatest delight. What glorious plants! The flowers here bear the same relation to ours that Rome as a city bears to Vienna. I am bringing a great many with me, and I will send you some beautiful seeds.

Gentz to Metternich, Vienna, April 25, 1819.

343. I must on every opportunity come back to the Weimar declaration as among the most important documents of our time. One of the chief authors and protectors of all the mischief in Germany—eight days

after a crime that called on him and his ministers for
vengeance—was pleased to intimate to the German
Bund through his ambassador, that ' Freedom of thought
and teaching must remain at the Universities ; for there,
in the open conflict of opinions shall truth be found
by the students ; there shall the scholar be preserved
from *devotion to authorities*, and there shall he be raised
(not educated) to independence.'   So far have the great
and mighty of this earth gone that they can swallow
such childish stuff !   And not a voice, not a sound,
raised in the assembly !   And we—oh ! that I too must
again renew this *infandum dolorem* !—we must still bear
the ignominious honour that, shortly before these objectionable words (the quintessence of all revolutionary
teaching) from the opening speech at the Bundestag, we
were called to a position, extolled by the criminal principles, not of Freiherr von Hendrich, but of the universities, as a proud memorial of German superiority against
the unrighteous judgment of foreigners.

As none of the ministers at the Bundestag were
inspired or vigorous enough there and then to tell
the Plenipotentiary of the Duke (or, as some one wittily
called him, the Ober-Burschen) of Weimar the horror
which such teaching, at such a moment, must call forth,
I am myself again convinced that the time is not ripe
for great and comprehensive measures.   But for this
reason I fear more than anything formal and public
consultations on these important questions.   When I
consider how far one must go back, how deep one must
cut into the wounded flesh, thoroughly to check the
evil, it seems to me quite madness to believe that in
any court like the Bundestag—indeed, even in a congress
of the first German princes—such harmony, insight,
courage, and determination (and none of these should

be wanting) should be found as will secure, not merely good, but victorious results. Now, in a malady of so evil a character, nothing can be more injurious than unsuccessful or half-successful—that is, half-unsuccessful —attempts. I am quite convinced that in revolutionary times the whole authority may more easily be re-conquered than the half. Half-results are in such crises worse even than none. One often sees, too, that when the truly efficacious, the decisive, is not attainable, wisdom enjoins that the appearance be quietly and patiently maintained, of only commanding what is most pressing and immediately practicable, while keeping the true end of all efforts constantly in view, for by true zeal and untiring perseverance the moment will at last come when a decisive blow may extricate us from all difficulties.

But I understand by half-measures, in the present question, everything which attempts a reform of the discipline of the university without touching the personality of the teacher and the students, and without acting directly on the spirit which animates the whole institution. Such (to my mind) are all attempts to limit or remove the academic jurisdiction; every setting up of a police authority foreign to it, be it high or low; every mixture of authority in the systems and methods of teaching; every regulation prohibiting the young people from associations, unions, &c., even if public and harmless; and, in fact, every alteration in the material organisation of the universities. To pass such measures the Bundestag would certainly be competent; but if at last, after a thousand difficulties and oppositions, we succeeded, what would be gained? Those who had taken an active part would be decried as enemies of academic freedom in Germany, branded, proscribed,

and outlawed. The rebellious principles (the banish-
ment of all authority, the independence of individual
judgment, the free conflict of opinions, and everything
proclaimed by the Weimar declaration) would still continue; they would soon rise in a different form, stronger
than before, and mock at all organised laws; the
spirit which has seized the university, not weakened or
even restrained, but rather encouraged by feeble opposition, would become only more frightful and mischievous.

So long, then, as we are not strong enough to declare
open war against the principles from which the acade-
mical as well as other dangers arose, and to treat the
abuses of the universities as only the necessary companions of greater disorders, every legislative proceeding exclusively directed to the universities will remain
weak and fruitless: and in this state of things it would
be wiser quite to draw away from them and take only
such provisional steps as without any great alteration of
the outward form should act simply on the personality
of the teacher and the students.

Adam Müller, who, to my no small satisfaction (for
his opinion is of weight), without any collusion with me
—indeed, with the fear that I might take it quite otherwise—considers the matter from the same point of
view, even protests against all legislative measures and
proposes two expedients as follows :—

1. The nomination of a curator for each university
in the person of a distinguished (N.B. decorated) man
of the world, if not learned, yet not unacquainted with
literature, of kindly and pleasant manners, who would
be answerable for the whole university, and consequently
must reside in the district. Could not eight or ten
such men be found in Germany who would undertake

such an honourable office, the more honourable at present because of its difficulties ; and if it required sufficient or even handsome salaries, what State expenditure could be more beneficial and honourable than this ?

2. A purification of the professorial chairs without noise or passion, especially by the appointment of objectionable professors to other civil positions where they can do no harm. The ringleaders are known : their number is not large ; if they can be dismissed quietly and their places filled with peaceable, refined men of learning (as for talent, there is not one in any class who could not be replaced by a far better man), an extremely important step towards the reform of the universities will have been taken.

These two measures require no formal negotiations, they can only be quietly arranged between Prussia, Saxony, Hanover, Bavaria, and Baden ; and, in short, they would have the blessing of all well-disposed people. Jena must be set in order when all the others are arranged. The Grand Duke must (as the smallest penalty for his former transgressions) from the first be neither asked nor admitted to the consultations, least of all, as is now the case at Frankfurt, must he take the lead. He must agree to what the other Courts decide ; and at the worst we will set the Emperor of Russia upon him, or put Jena, as a university, under a formal and general interdict.

By these preliminary steps I do not, however, mean to set aside the usefulness, or, indeed, the necessity of a thorough discussion of the great problem between the principal German Governments. But if such a discussion does take place (and it should be as secret as possible), it should above all be considered that questions

concerning the universities should not be handled alone
—that they should not be separated from the questions concerning the freedom of the press or constitution. How far the latter must be decided I cannot
here enter upon, as it would lead me too far, but I reserve to myself to make further remarks on that subject.

My *résumé* would then be :—

1. At first no common legislative negotiation either
in Frankfurt or elsewhere.

2. Confidential discussion of the most urgent preliminary measures with the exception of all those
that touch on the material organisation of the universities.

3. Conferences between delegates of the principal
German Courts, in which everything relating to the
universities, the freedom of the press, and even the
arrangement of the statutes, should be as far as possible
thoroughly discussed. If these conferences had no
other result, they would certainly be a most valuable
means of mutual understanding, explanation, and instruction.

In this plan no part is assigned to the Frankfurt
Gremium. Since I positively know of nothing useful
which these gentlemen could undertake, but much more
probably foresee from their proceedings in Frankfurt incalculable injury, difficulty and danger, I cannot possibly propose anything of the kind.

My proposal *ad* 2 might perhaps be carried out
most easily and quickly this summer in Carlsbad ; and
perhaps simply correspondence, if preferred, might be
sufficient.

No. 3, on the contrary, is of greater importance—requires time, quiet, and much consideration. If such

conferences are decided on, they must of course be at Vienna, and not be opened before next winter.

Postscript of April 27.

I have received your Excellency's letter from . . . .* about an hour ago, just as I was about to send off the above. What you say makes me fear that you will not be quite satisfied with my proposals ; however, as I do not know the communications you have addressed to the Court, it is possible that they may not be altogether incompatible. At any rate, in such an important affair your Excellency shall have my views as clearly as possible : and, grieved as I am in other respects to be away from you at this moment, I am glad to have written down my thoughts before I was acquainted with yours, because it will be easier to me to submit to your better insight and conviction than to surrender my own.

Pilat has received a letter like the one I lately had ; and I hear that the Crown Prince, too, has received an anonymous threatening letter. Pilat was called an infamous wretch, fit for nothing but death, if he did not leave off disseminating his evil principles. The letter to me may have been a bad sort of April-fooling ; but when the same thing is repeated, it wears a more serious aspect.

Metternich to Gentz, Naples, May 7, 1819.

(Answer to No. 343.)

344. From your letters of April 25 and 27, I hope that we shall be agreed about the university affairs.

I have told you long ago that I did not think the Bundestag suitable to conduct this business. There is,

---

* The date is not given : probably an answer to No. 342.—ED.

however, no other central point, and when you know (as 1 do only too well) how feeble the German Governments are, you will certainly see that nothing can come of private consultations, and now every German Prince, even if (like Bavaria) he dislikes the Bund, will find in the Bund the strength which he lacked in himself to favour similar arrangements.

Time there is none to lose, for the Governments are now so terrified that they are willing to act ; soon their fears will be overcome by their weakness. If nothing is done now, the strength of the agitators will be doubled, and their courage will extinguish the last spark of the courage of the Governments. My previous communications will have informed you that I limited the question for Frankfurt to some necessary preliminary propositions.

I have adopted Müller's views and made some additions, which certainly are not less important. Among these are the improvement of university law and the decision that obnoxious professors must not be placed in other universities.

In taking as I do the Weimar proposal for my starting point, I think I do well. With contempt we shall never fight the old fellow there. He is accustomed to it. His mad views, on the contrary, will make a fine exhibition, and it seems to me far better to catch him on his own ground or give him the lie.

I have not forgotten the Emperor of Russia. I have to-day given Stürmer the commission to write a letter to him—and send it to Count Nesselrode by one of his own couriers—which will show you that I can handle the Emperor quite suitably without committing any mistake in respect to German politics.

I shall remain in Carlsbad certainly till the middle

of July. I do not know whether you still think of your journey to Switzerland. The time does not seem to me very well chosen. But I should be very glad if you could join me at Carlsbad. I desire this the more as I appoint a Prussian here, and other Germans may very likely come.

People are asking me from all directions about a conspiracy against the Emperor in Italy. If such a report should come to your ears you may be assured that it is a wicked invention of the party. Italy is quite quiet. Events in France, and the Constitutional farce in Germany excite the hopes of the parties, which, however, in Italy never express themselves except in secret societies. But so long as no great political event takes place in Europe, no movement of any kind is to be expected in Italy. Amongst the Neapolitans, in particular, there is great satisfaction with the course of the Government, and since it is different from its former course, this reacts advantageously upon us, for the public believes that we have something to do with the attitude of the King—and the public is right.

If Russian agents did not go about in Italy and encourage the sects to hopes founded on the liberalism of the Emperor Alexander, there would be hardly any active agitation in the minds of the people. In Italy they have got over their former dissatisfaction. Italians talk loud, but do not act. The history of the last thirty years is an example of this, for during that time, in spite of all intrigues, Italy was never revolutionised, properly speaking. With Italians hatred never expresses itself against a cause, but only against a person. Therefore, in Italy provinces are against provinces, towns against towns, families against families, and—men against men. If a movement broke out in Florence, the Pisan or Pistoian would take the contrary side, because he hates Florence; thus Naples hates Rome, Rome Bologna, Leghorn Ancona, Milan Venice.

I hope, however, soon to make an end of Russian intrigues. I have taken some very peremptory steps in this respect.

Meanwhile, farewell.

Gentz to Metternich, Vienna, May 21, 1819.

(Answer to No. 344.)

345. I received your Excellency's kind letter of the 7th instant yesterday evening, and, heartily as I wish you all pleasure at Naples, I am delighted that when this reaches you your Excellency will already be on the return journey to Germany.

As your Excellency does full justice to my reasons against negotiating the university affairs at the Bundestag, all further lamentations on the course chosen are useless. The argument which you oppose to my reasons is indeed crushing, but also striking and decisive. If the German Courts are so weak that nothing effectual can be done by private consultation with them (and that they are so, unhappily, I can believe without much difficulty), certainly nothing remains but to make an attempt in Frankfurt. . . .

On the point of taking the Weimar proposal as a foundation I cannot satisfy myself, in spite of your Excellency's most acute explanation of the matter.

Count Sedlnitzky has given me the acts relating to the students' affairs. They consist of a sketch of a general Constitution for the students (*Burschenverfassung*), a protocol of the assembled delegates at Jena in

March and April 1818, and an address with reference to this protocol to all the sister universities ; lastly, a copy of the statutes for the general German *Burschenschaft*, corrected from the sketch, October 18, 1818, at Jena. It would not be possible to have these documents printed without commentary, even if it were to be done privately. But I would not undertake so important an affair—in which there is no *periculum in mora*—in your Excellency's absence. Moreover, the whole *Burschenschaft* is in itself—without any regard to the abuses to which it has led, and may still further lead—an institution so thoroughly objectionable, and so dangerous and criminal its aims, that no stone of it should be left upon another, and if the universities are to be retained, it must be forbidden under the severest penalties. This I will demonstrate at the proper time with the greatest clearness.

If I may hope that it will be in any way useful or agreeable to your Excellency I am quite ready to give up my journey into Switzerland for this year, and to take up my quarters in Carlsbad. . . .

Gentz to Metternich, Vienna, June 3, 1819.

346. I send your Excellency a copy of a letter from Müller, and take the liberty of accompanying it with the following remarks :—

1. From what Müller says of many proselytes to the revolutionary sects,* of their uncertain and doubtful position, and of the indifference of the public, and even of the young men, to their writings, it is evident how much can be accomplished if only forty or fifty of the most dangerous men in Germany are carefully watched,

* Adam Müller, in his letter, speaks of Fries, Wieland, Oken, and Froriep.—Ed.

and rendered harmless, either by direct alterations in their positions, or by winning them over by hope, or frightening them by a display of power—by fighting them, in fact, in a dexterous manner. This would be one of the most serviceable diplomatic performances of our time. But to this end we ought to have at a central point like Frankfurt one of the most important men for the cause. And where shall we find such a one? And what ostensible sphere of action shall we give him?

2. Certainly the transition of so many—particularly so many young people—from political fanaticism to religious mysticism is very remarkable.* I do not consider this an advantage. The fact calls for the greatest attention. The malady evidently takes a new form, and the medicine must be different. Here, indeed, we go beyond the last limit of police measures, and if we do not find means to work on the mind, and lay hold of the evil by its deepest roots, we are at the end of our art. A close connection, a true coalition of the noblest and wisest men in Germany, a living *Bund*, an actively deliberative and actively working society of the first statesmen and learned men, can alone solve so great a problem.

3. The papers which have appeared about Kotzebue's assassination cannot possibly make any impression,

---

* Adam Müller mentions, in corroboration of this, that in Halle students were every day leaving the other faculties and going over to the theology lectures, and the good old Knape did not know what to do for the crowd. In Halle the *Mystikers* drew all the applause, and the well-known Schubert, a kindred spirit, established his lecture-room there. The physician Windischmann opened his *Cursus* at Bonn, before all the professors, with a speech, in which, after a series of obscure natural philosophical expositions of the history of the time, he concluded with the declaration that only in the revelation of Jesus Christ could peace be found for the conscience and for knowledge.—ED.

because they deserve little or no respect. Krug is a mere common babbler, without vigour or strength, who is hardly fit to keep a tobacconist's shop. Görres, after the old accustomed manner, with hollow threats and dark prophecies, only gives it to be understood that in every misfortune the Governments alone are guilty, and neither gives the grounds of the accusation nor speaks it out clearly. I consider his writings not merely bad, but in the highest degree objectionable and culpable. Beckedorf's speech to the students is animated by a good spirit; it is, however, too much like a sermon, and for an oratorical attempt not well enough written. La Motte Fouqué cuts antics in doggrel like a rope-dancer: a fool, whose hour has long passed. Steffens alone has risen to the level of the subject. He is known to be a natural philosopher deeply entangled in all the false tendencies of the time. Anything thoroughly correct is not to be expected from him, and Satan, to whom he has sold himself, often peeps out. His judgment on the deed is thoroughly clear, straightforward, and excellent, and contrasts finely with all the indirect apologies, soft infatuations, and underhand sophisms glaring, to the shame of Germany, in all the public papers. Steffens is a man whom the revolutionary party fears, because it confesses his superiority, and Müller is wrong if he thinks that his word will not have much weight.

4. The story of the 3,000 copies of the Grävel book is quite correct, and certainly gains grievous ridicule for our public,* but the connection of the thing must be known in order to see how it looks. This pamphlet, published by Gerold, is patronised most

* Adam Müller wrote on this: ' The great story in the bookselling world, a real scandal for Vienna and Austria, is that 3,000 copies were sold, in Austria only, of the notorious pamphlet " Der Mensch von Grävel." '—ED.

zealously (God knows why) by the different officials of the police-courts, sent into all the provinces, and disseminated as much as possible both openly and secretly. It seems to me that Count Saurau must be at the bottom of it. The favour of it goes so far that a short review of it in the 'Observer,' in which Pilat found fault with some coarse deistical errors of the wretched scribbler, was suppressed by the police officials. For me, however, the history has an important and re-assuring side. It shows what can be accomplished with us by authority, if it takes up a cause earnestly and *con amore*.

The deep silence of the Emperor of Russia on the attempts against Stourdza and Kotzebue has a most peculiar appearance. I cannot say that I grieve over it very much, for he would not have mended matters much if he had taken the right line, and there were a hundred chances to one that he should miss it. But how this silence will be explained excites my curiosity to the highest degree, and if your Excellency knows anything you can communicate to me, I beg of you to have the kindness to remember me.

Metternich to Gentz, Rome, June 6, 1819.

347. The Commission is opened in Frankfurt, and I have letters of thanks from all sides for having taken the initiative.

I beg you to understand the founding of our proposal on the Weimar memorial only in the sense in which I myself put it—namely, not as if the Weimar propositions were the immediate object of the deliberations. This is not so : but the Weimar move served us as the immediate occasion on which a conference might be grounded. Imagine a wood where a captured robber calls for help. I hasten up to him, not to help him to get away, but to hold him as fast as possible.

The Weimar clique is besides in great anxiety. Jena begins to grow empty, and the college funds dull. The *enragés* exclaim against the unanswerable step of the Grand Duke, and call him a counseller to the good cause. Why should we not follow up this theme? We cannot, at least, be accused of Obscurantism if we, instead of speaking from our own grounds, take up the cry of distress of the Liberal Grand Duke. But with these first steps the part of the Grand Duke concludes, for we all renounce his help.

I see, too, with a real feeling of anxiety for my earlier arrival in Carlsbad, that I am here too far from the battle-field. Between July 16 and 20 I shall certainly be on the spot. Take your own measures accordingly.

I hope that you have not for a moment believed in my journey to Paris which all the newspapers have blazoned forth.

The Liberals have raised a great hue and cry over the Archduke Rudolf's dignity of Cardinal. The Italian Independents rejoice over the cause, for they believe the Archduke will become Pope, take a wife, and call himself King of Italy. I see in the affair a red hat and a pair of red stockings, as well as the proof of good political relations between the first Catholic Power and the Church.

You may take my word for it that our Italian tour has in every respect answered the expectations I had formed.

P.S.—Tell Pilat that there is a terrible eruption of Etna, and that Catania is threatened with great danger.

Vesuvius, too, has an enormous stream of lava running in the direction of Pompeii. I am very sorry not to be there. A considerable earthquake has been felt in the neighbourhood of Viterbo. As Pilat is the only reporter of earthquakes, this information will be welcome.

The Emperor has put off his journey till the 11th because the Archduchess Caroline is slightly unwell. I shall follow the Emperor on the 12th.

Gentz to Metternich, Vienna, June 17, 1819.

(Answer to No. 347.)

348. I see with great pleasure, from your kind letter of the 6th inst., that you have not given up the journey to Carlsbad, as some sceptics here wished to make out, and that you even give it a certain importance. Your residence in Carlsbad may certainly do good and will at any rate furnish material for observations and combinations which will not be lost to your fertile intellect. My lodgings are taken from July 15.

I look forward with impatience to the time when I shall draw anew from so rich a source, correcting and confirming my views afresh, and I hope your Excellency will have the kindness to inform me further of your travelling plans.

Metternich to Gentz, Perugia, June 17, 1819.

(Answer to No. 346.)

349. I thank you for your very interesting account of the 3rd inst. I entirely share the views of Adam Müller, and in sharing them I find myself strengthened in the course I have taken. That the students' folly declines or turns to some other side than that of politics does not surprise me. This is in the nature of things.

The student, taken in himself, is a child, and the *Burschenschaft* is an unpractical puppet-show. Then, I have never—and of this you are a witness—spoken of the students, but all my aim has been directed at the professors. Now, the professors, singly or united, are most unsuited to be conspirators. People only conspire profitably against things, not against theories. The last, indeed, may grow to power, but this can never be the case if they leave the sphere of theology. Where they are political, they must be supported by deed, and the deed is the overthrow of existing institutions, and the *ôtez-vous de là que je m'y mette*. This is what learned men and professors cannot manage, and the class of lawyers is better suited to carry it on. I know hardly one learned man who knows the value of property; while, on the contrary, the lawyer class is always rummaging about in the property of others. Besides, the professors are, nearly without exception, given up to theory; while no people are more practical than the lawyers.

Consequently, I have never feared that the revolution would be engendered by the universities; but that at them a whole generation of revolutionaries must be formed, unless the evil is restrained, seems to me certain. I hope that the most mischievous symptoms of the evil at the universities may be met, and that perhaps from its own peculiar sources, for the measures of the Government will contribute to this less than the weariness of the students, the weakness of the professors, and the different direction which the studies may take.· But this feeling will never restrain me from taking steps from above; and, indeed, what seem to me the only possible measures are taken.

If we are together I can give you many satisfactory

explanations of the course of the business, which at a distance I could not communicate to you without an enormous correspondence, and even then must remain futile and imperfect.

The greatest and consequently the most urgent evil now is the press. The measures referring to it which I intend to bring forward at the Carlsbad Congress I will tell you all the more gladly as I wish you to give me your opinion on my ideas without reserve, and put yourself in a position to help me effectually in Carlsbad, where the business must begin without delay.

My proposals are, briefly, the following :—All the German Courts shall unite in measures which seem necessary for the maintenance of the public peace, and from a full sense of the right of mutual support which is the foundation of the German Bund.

They here start from the fundamental idea of the Bund, which consists of Germany and the Sovereign States, that have agreed mutually to support and help each other, and which, while they are separate in administrative respects, form one common power against foreign countries.

The inward peace of the Bund may be endangered and even destroyed by one of the German States attacking the sovereign power of the others. But this can also be done by the moral action of the Government on others, or through the intrigues even of a party. If this party should be supported by a German State—or only find protection in one of them—if with this protection it finds means to rest its lever against neighbouring States on a neighbouring State, then the inner peace of the Bund is threatened, and the Prince who allows this disorder in his country is guilty of felony against the Bund.

All the German Governments have arrived at the conviction that, at the present time, the press serves a party antagonistic to all existing Governments. The nationalities spread over all Germany make it impossible for single States to guard their frontiers from this evil; if this is the fact for single Governments, it will be no less so for all German Governments if but one German State—let it be even the smallest among them—shut itself out from the acceptance of common measures for the maintenance of the general peace.

The Bund has the right of calling upon every single member to fulfill the common duties. In case that member is not found ready of himself, the Bund has the right of compelling him.

From the constitution of the Bund it also arises that everything that is possible to independent sovereigns and European States is not possible to the sovereign States of the German Bund.

For instance, France and England certainly can permit the freedom of the press, and even assert the principle that this freedom is an indispensable condition of the real representative system.

In France and England laws can be made which confine the abuse of the press in relation to the constitution of those two kingdoms.

I doubt, however, whether either of those States would consider it a fundamental idea of the freedom of the press to tolerate all works which are systematically concocted and disseminated in one of the States, even to the generation of rebellion, by a party that is undermining the existing institutions of the other State. In this case the English Government would certainly complain to the French (and *vice versâ*) of the toleration of foreign instigators of rebellion ; and if the Government complained to did not render its assistance, the Government complaining has the undoubted right to declare war, and so obtain help and redress, or at the least to stop all intercourse between the two States.

These remedies, grounded on the rights of peoples, are not practicable in Germany. What can be done among European Powers in this respect by repression, must be accomplished in the German Bund by preventive laws.

In these propositions there is no Obscurantism, and therefore they are not to be assailed as such. Even the instigators of rebellion, indeed, feel this, and will not object to them. They may decry such a state of things as a great evil for Germany, and express a wish for the only alternative known to me—the union of all Germany in one whole, undivided body. This wish has already become the fundamental principle of the fraternisation of practical German revolutionists.

Since, however, this can only be fulfilled by a single German monarchy, or one German free State, it is to be supposed that no German Government will be found, from German feeling, to submit to be chased from Court and home—an inevitable condition to be expected by the victim to the love of carrying out that idea.

The means to this end seem to me to be the following :—

1. There must be a settled difference made between books (real works), and journals and pamphlets.

Scientific matter characterises the former, and, where this is not evident, the number of sheets. Thus, for instance, I take for granted that a Dissertation on Trigonometry consisting of three or four sheets might be reckoned as a *work* ; while a political work, to be reckoned as such, must contain at least five-and-twenty sheets.

Periodicity and the political or moral subject-matter decides their character.

2. It is reserved to every German State to decide whether they will have a censorship of all literary productions which appear within their limits, or whether they will pass repressive laws.

In the second case the law must be for the whole Bund one and the same law: that is, every State which permits the freedom of the press for works must accept the law which the Bund has passed for all States in the same position.

3. All journals, pamphlets, &c., &c., in Germany must be under a censorship.

4. Where freedom of the press for works is permitted, the local Government (*Landesregierung*) must through their public prosecutor carry on the suit which any other German Government may bring in a diplomatic way against either the author or publisher. This suit must be instituted and carried on in the name of the local Government, and the subject of complaint must be considered and treated by it as affecting that Government itself.

In the same way every German Government must be responsible for its own censorship. Every complaint against the latter must be considered as a complaint of Government against Government.

5. The usual regulations as to the printing of the author's name, or at least the place where the work is printed, and the publisher's name, must everywhere be observed.

No publication can be allowed at any bookseller's in Germany except under these conditions. Every anonymous writing in the Bund falls under confiscation.

These are my principal ideas, and I hardly think

that any reasonable objection can be made to them. I deplore, indeed, that the censorship cannot be instituted for all writings without exception. But I am convinced that in many German States great opposition would be made if it were applied to true works. The most pressing evil is, however, certainly met by a firm administration of my proposals, and I doubt not that they will be accepted by the majority of eminent men. The most important German States—as, for instance, Prussia and Bavaria, Saxony and Hanover, even Baden—have to make no backward step in principle, for they all have either a general censorship or at the least a censorship of the journals. In Bavaria the latter is even constitutional: the Government, too, from its incomprehensible toleration, is more culpable than any other.

Postscript.—I beg your indulgence if in my letter you find some undigested expressions. I have much to do, and I hope that in reading, and still more in estimating, my ideas on the laws respecting the licence of the press, you will hold more by the spirit than the words ; but I submit both to your better knowledge and experience.

Gentz to Metternich, *July* 1, 1819.

(Answer to No. 349.)

350. Your Excellency can easily imagine what an impression your letter from Perugia has made on me. My spirits rise and all dark troubles seem to fly, when, at so grave a moment, I see the only man in Germany who can still act freely and firmly treat not only principles and feelings but resolutions from so lofty a level.

I have thought over with great attention your Excellency's resolutions concerning the limitation of the press in Germany. If these proposals are carried out,

certainly much will be gained. I set no great value on
the censorship of the greater works ; 1 shall be extremely
delighted if all the German Governments will consent to
the censorship of the journals, in which, however, I
would propose some different modifications, or rather
supplementary measures, without which the censorship
itself degenerates into mere empty tomfoolery.

But I expect great opposition to the censorship of the
journals from Wurtemberg, Weimar, and other quarters.
The point is whether the dangerous question of the right
of the majority to pass such a measure may not be mooted.
But I reckon confidently on the steps your Excellency
has already taken, and chiefly on the ascendancy which
cannot be denied to your Excellency when once you
declare yourself with decision and energy.

I will, to approach the matter more in detail, endeavour to express and arrange your Excellency's propositions as clearly and methodically as possible. Where
it seems to me that explanatory remarks would be
useful, I will carefully add them. In a word, I will
bring with me to Carlsbad a work on the subject
formed entirely on the groundwork of your proposals,
which perhaps may serve as a guide for verbal conference, and of which you can take or reject what
seems to your Excellency useful or not.

Where this letter will find your Excellency I do not
know, but I believe already in Germany. I think, however, that I shall have a hint from some one or other
before your arrival in Carlsbad. In any case, I shall
start from here on the 15th, for I shall then (in the
usual way) take five or six days for the journey, so that
I shall not arrive there before the 20th. But neither
do I expect your Excellency to arrive before that date.

Postscript.—I perceive with the greatest satisfaction

that your Excellency is enjoying the best health and spirits. A good stock of both was seldom more necessary than now. The present crisis taxes all our powers to the utmost, and it is a question of nothing less than the prevention of the probable disruption of the united German Confederation—therefore, of one of the most dreadful European revolutions. In the last four weeks the symptoms have taken from one day to another so malignant a character that I fear heroic means alone—even amputation in a certain sense—can save the parts not yet attacked.

I knew not whether to laugh or cry when this morning a very worthy tradesman said to me that, till now he had always thought that in Germany too much was made of events, but now he no longer doubted that the danger is great and pressing.

*Durate, et vosmet rebus servate secundis,** is the prayer which I make to Heaven daily for your Excellency.

* Virg. *Æn.* i. 207.

METTERNICH'S MEETING WITH KING FREDERICK WILLIAM III. AT TEPLITZ.

Preliminaries to the Carlsbad Conferences.

351. Metternich to the Emperor Francis, July 30, 1819.
352. Metternich to the Emperor Francis, August 1, 1819.

351. I arrived here the day before yesterday in the evening. Immediatcly after my arrival, the King of Prussia sent word that he would receive me at home the next morning. This circumstance was only remarkable because since his arrival here the King had received no one at home—all, even his own official audiences had been held in the Clary Gardens. Prince von Hardenberg arrived here from Berlin a few hours after me.

Early yesterday I went to the King, who received me in a most friendly manner, enquired particularly after your Majesty's health, and then said: ' You come here to see me at a most important moment. Six years ago we had to fight the enemy in the open field : now he sneaks and hides. You know that I have great confidence in your views ; you have long warned me, and all you have said has come true.'

I answered his Majesty that, knowing your Majesty's feelings, I could assure him (the King) that every truth I had before told him, and especially at Aix-la-Chapelle, was quite as evident to your Majesty as to me. I added that he must be already aware of your Majesty's prompt decision in virtue of which you had without regard to the interests of the Lombardo-Venetian provinces given up that journey. Your Majesty is accustomed always to do that which is most pressing, and the state of things in Germany fixes your whole attention in the double respect of the common weal of the German States and that of your own empire. The Emperor is, said I, convinced that the evil has reached such a height in Germany that the day has arrived for the decision between the principle of preservation or entire submission—consequently, of political death. How the Emperor thinks for Prussia he has shown : that he will grant your Majesty help if you help yourself there is not the least doubt. But the Emperor has, above all, very great and very difficult duties as a ruler : with united strength he may strive to dam up the impetuous stream, but alone he will never risk the danger of shipwreck. In order to help, the Emperor must first see clearly. He must know what Governments there are worth the name to carry out his plan. Prussia, too, is not exempted from taking part in this. But though the King is there, we do not find the kingly power ; if the King leaves a free course to the evil which threatens his throne and—as the examination of the conspirators shows—even his person, the Emperor must withdraw, and for his own benefit take a line very different from the one he is to-day pursuing.

'You know,' answered the King, ' that no one has a better will than I have. But my position is very difficult, for I lack *men*. The possible, however, must be done, and therefore I depend upon you to help me to come to an agreement on a certain definite course.'

I answered the King that it would be no more than my duty by investigation of the evil and by careful consideration to discover the means of safety : that, however, such a difference existed between the determination and the execution of beneficial measures, and that I was so thoroughly acquainted with the internal state of the Prussian Government, that I must freely confess I cherish but small hopes of bringing the affair to success. ' I can speak freely to your Majesty,' I added, ' for you have always taken it in good part. I will do so now, as I did once before when your Majesty invited me to do so. Either the counsel which your Majesty receives is not good or it is badly carried out. The discovered conspiracy is nothing but the action which always follows the teaching. This conspiracy has its origin and its abode in Prussia ; the subordinate conspirators are now known, the superiors are still undiscovered, but they are without doubt to be found in the highest region of your own servants. Your Majesty knows what I think of the State Chancellor. He has rendered your Majesty priceless services, but he is now old and feeble both in mind and body. He desires what is right, and only too frequently supports what is bad.'

' You are aware,' answered the King, ' that I know Prince Hardenberg thoroughly ; his misfortune is the men who are about him, among whom are some very strange characters.'

' Why does your Majesty tolerate these men ? Why have you allowed bad and dangerous institutions so much latitude ? '

' You are quite right,' replied the King, ' but it is always thus when people get old. My desire is that now, whilst you are here, principles should be established which then must be most strictly carried out. I wish that you should settle this absolutely with the State Chancellor.'

' The whole thing is restricted to one point,' I an-

swered. ' If your Majesty is determined not to introduce any representation of the people into your kingdom
(which is less fitted for it than any other) help will be
forthcoming, otherwise there is no possibility of assistance. You can fulfil your promise in meaning, if, indeed,
you had promised the very opposite; the present time
is entirely different from the past. I am ready to impart
my views to the State Chancellor, but I beg your Majesty also to nominate Count Bernstorff and Prince Wittgenstein to this conference.'

' I had intended to do so,' said the King, ' and I beg
you to try and bind these people in writing ; you can
thoroughly rely upon Prince Wittgenstein.'

I have laid before your Majesty the principal points
in a long conversation, in order to give your Majesty
the plainest possible illustration of the ‧position of the
King, and of the administration in its highest sphere.
Where such things can be said there is hardly a Government ; everything is sunk in weakness ; this weakness
is in the men ; the only one who has lately acted with
any vigour is Prince Wittgenstein. . . .

I will extend my stay here till August 2, because
the State Chancellor has much pressed me to do
so. As he stays here with pleasure, he is in a very
good humour. He is, moreover, not in mind but in
feeling close on childhood. The King leaves Teplitz on
August 1.

I will arrange everything here as well as I possibly
can, and as soon as the basis is established I will lay my
views before your Majesty.

In Berlin the well-disposed—and that is the majority
—rejoice over the first strength the Government has
shown for years ; and this gives the Chancellor more
courage. The German newspapers do what they can

to mislead the public as to the exact state of affairs. These must first of all be silenced.

Metternich to the Emperor Francis, Teplitz, Aug. 1, 1819.

352. My Report of yesterday (No. 351) will have thrown as much light as was for the moment possible on the state of my negotiations here.

To-day I am able to lay before your Majesty their definite results.

Having ascertained the wishes of the King of Prussia, I entered into conference with Prince von Hardenberg, Prince von Wittgenstein, and Count von Bernstorff, in order to place as clearly as possible the foundation of our future course before them. To this conference I also invited Count Zichy.

My plan consists in the main of the following propositions :—

1. The almost inconceivable perverseness of the course of most of the German Governments (the Prussian above all) has given such an impetus to the revolutionary spirit that perhaps the last period has arrived when help is still possible.

Formerly the German revolutionists were as much separated as the States in which they lived ; that under such circumstances no effectual blow could be struck by them was soon clear to the conspirators. The military party in Prussia at first thought of aggrandising themselves by the conquest of Prussia ; the civil party in Prussia limited themselves to employing their efforts for the transformation of Prussia. Some men (and it is noticeable that they are nearly all persons engaged in teaching) go much further, and from a revolutionary point of view take the right road. They direct their eyes to the union of all Germans in one Germany.

For this the generation already educated cannot serve them; they therefore turn their attention to those who are to be educated, a plan which commends itself even to the most impatient, for the student generation includes, at the most, a space of four years. Now, the systematic preparation of youth for this infamous object has lasted already more than one of these generations. A whole class of future State officials, professors, and incipient literary men, is here ripened for revolution.

If we now reflect that in the Prussian Government the most numerous and important positions, both in the centre of the Government and in the provinces (especially is this the case in the Rhine provinces), are occupied by pure revolutionists, it is not to be wondered at if Prussia is considered quite ripe for revolution.

Two circumstances have unexpectedly assisted this deep laid plan—the disaffection, almost amounting to madness, of the press in general, and the introduction of demagogic Governments in South Germany. What Prussia's weakness had prepared for years, Bavaria accomplished with one blow, Baden imitated, and Wurtemberg sought to extend still further.

2. To complete this work it now only requires to set up a democratic Government in Prussia. That this measure is not yet full depends on the personal timidity of the King and—I say without hesitation—the systematic efforts with which I have made it my duty to frighten the King from every step which must have resulted in the inevitable overthrow of all the existing institutions. To this end it was necessary that the King, and even the high officers of the State, should be imbued with the most undoubting confidence in the true friendship of your Majesty, and to obtain for myself personally the good opinion of the King. How

thoroughly this has succeeded is shown by the present result.

3. As the first steps were attained by your Majesty's personal course in German affairs as well as in your Majesty's personal attitude towards the King, I made use of the last meeting of the Courts at Aix-la-Chapelle to make myself at home in the internal affairs of Prussia ; and your Majesty will remember the steps which I then took to explain to the King himself his position with regard to his people—or rather with regard to the administration—and to draw his attention to the difference between the principles which must cost him the throne and those which may yet save him.   The salvation of the Prussian monarchy may therefore probably date from Aix-la-Chapelle.

That this evil by its extension produces the means of its own extinction is also seen in Prussia.   Moral, like physical, evil always reaches such a height, if it is not destroyed in its first germ, or at any rate in its very first period, that at last its weakness becomes plainly evident.   The illusion disappears, its imminent and entire dissolution is palpable, and courage often comes in the last hours to the help of the most dejected, and it is fortunate if then the elements of relief are still at their disposal.

This is the present position of the King of Prussia. It is known to your Majesty that, by one of those happy chances which often occur in the life of States as in the lives of men, my journey to Carlsbad happened at the moment of a decision most important for Prussia.   That I consider the present crisis momentous for the whole of Germany I have shown your Majesty by my plan, not only of going to Carlsbad myself, but of there conferring with the ministers of the chief German Courts.   But a good resolution generally leads to manifold benefits, and so it has here turned out.

That the great conspiracy overspreading the whole of Germany would be unmasked just at this moment was so little foreseen by me that it was part of my plan to discover it at Carlsbad. In the same way your Majesty's idea of going straight to Vienna, instead of to Milan, was one of those happy inspirations the object of which can only be known beforehand by Providence.

4. I came here by the pressing invitation of the King, and found him, as I mentioned in my last despatch to your Majesty, in an excellent and, for him, unusually confidential mood. How much this disposition has been increased by my efforts here was yesterday made most evident. The day before yesterday I had begged the King to grant me another audience. Yesterday morning the King came to me himself with Prince Wittgenstein. In a conversation of two hours, and in the presence of that excellent and faithful witness, I unfolded my views, feelings and convictions with the same candour with which I always make it my duty to speak to your Majesty. I thoroughly penetrated the mind of the King, and found the means of exciting in him the most active principle of his character—the repressive—to such a degree that we may hope he will never take the most hazardous of all steps, the introduction of a constitution for his kingdom, without granting me a preliminary examination of what is to be done.

In order to lead the King to right principles, I had prepared a short work which clearly pointed out the true difference between such institutions as the Diets and a so-called representative system. I thought it all the more necessary to place this work in the King's own hands as I saw that he had placed the greatest value

on a far more superficial paper which I had presented
to Prince Wittgenstein, as well as to the State Chancellor
at Aix-la-Chapelle (No. 305).

I take the liberty of sending your Majesty a copy of
the above-named paper.* If your Majesty condescends
to look it over, you will be convinced that only the
utterance of a few sentences—only a few blunders in
the choice of the system to be followed—is needed to
frustrate for ever any possible rescue of the good cause.

5. During my conversations here with the first
Prussian statesmen, I have convinced myself of the following evident facts.

Prince von Hardenberg is morally, as well as physically, in a state of weakness bordering on childhood.
He desires what is right, he knows even what is right, but
there are in him two elements always most dangerous for
a statesman of the highest grade, even if his strength of
mind were greater than ever was the Prince's. The one
is an extraordinary impulse towards liberalism : the other
an unfortunate inclination to get strange people about
him. It may be said without exaggeration that at the
present time there is not a man near him whose opinions
are not either of the purest democracy, or who is not
already an active participator in the conspiracy against
the very throne of Prussia itself.

The King is thoroughly informed of the state of
things. There are in Prussia also two negative powers
in conflict—the weakness of the King with that of the
State Chancellor. The first is the least dangerous, for
the King's weakness is coupled with indolence : that of
the Chancellor, with the greatest activity.

Count Bernstorff is thoroughly right-feeling in prin-

---

* This paper is not to be found, but it was evidently analogous with
No. 305.—ED.

ciple. He is, however, extremely weak, and he has such a deep consciousness of his painful position that he is quite enfeebled by it.

Prince Wittgenstein thinks as I do: he is in the main active, but not nearly so much so as he should be. His influence on the King is far more thorough since the last discoveries so well conducted by him.

The director of the Royal Cabinet, Albrecht, is a quiet and extremely well-meaning man. In Aix-la-Chapelle he already began to draw near to me, and has here laid aside all timidity in this respect. His part is negatively very important, for he makes it his duty to restrain the King from many inconsiderate steps. . . .

I do not wish my presence here to be limited to an empty convention; therefore I have written out the sketch of an agreement, and laid it before our second conference.

This document contains the basis on which alone I seek the safety and prosperity of Germany, and at the same time is a proof that Prussia herself joins with us. The principal features of this basis are as follows. I start from the point of view—

1. That to me purely Austrian must, in the abstract, stand closer than Austro-German affairs.

A good and vigorously managed union of States (*Bundes-Verhältnisse*) is certainly the best and truest weapon of defence for your Majesty's own State: and more, there is no other political combination which can outweigh or replace the advantages arising from this union of States. The more firmly these propositions are established, the more true it is that the same element which if well managed will lead to safety, may through mismanagement or bad and careless execution become highly dangerous.

Therefore from these propositions arises the rule, a real rule of life for Austria—

That we must do everything to regulate and maintain the prosperity of the Bund, or, in case this should prove impossible, we must, relying on our own strength, assume a position very different from that we are taking to-day towards the German Princes outside the Bund.

Faithfully to follow out this principle we must first show most exactly the true position of affairs, and then point out the appropriate ways and means to improve the defects in the Bund.

The course to be followed is clearly laid down in the agreement signed with Prussia.

It is divided into two periods—

(a) The present meeting of the ministers of the most important German Courts at Carlsbad ;

(b) A second meeting at Vienna supplementary to the first.

At the first our principles must be made generally known, and the necessary temporary measures founded on them.

Among these I reckon—

(a) The suspension of the licence of the press ;

(b) The appointment of commissions for the investigation of the German universities, and the removal of notoriously bad professors ;

(c) The formation of a special judicial commission, acting in the name of the whole Bund, to investigate the conspiracy discovered against the Bund.

The second meeting can only be devoted to discussions not of a kind to be accomplished in a few hours or days. Among these I include the correction of the thirteenth article of the Act of Confederation.

All that is most necessary here is provided for by

the engagement of Prussia to grant no representation of the people—that is, not to give themselves up with one stroke to the Revolution.

Your Majesty will have been long convinced (and the present Report will show this truth afresh) how little I reckon on any firmness in the proceedings of Prussia as to their home affairs. This much, however, is certain, that all danger is for the moment averted, and with this state of things comes the possibility that future evil may be avoided by vigorous measures at the present time. My great desire, therefore, in regard to Prussia, is to make use of this present time, and I cling to this firmly.

The means of leading the revolutionised South German States back to a better footing are so critical in their application that they require the most firm and calm examination, and it is only thus that the desired result can be attained. I hope by this hasty but plain representation to convince your Majesty that this matter, which from the harmony of Austrian and Prussian views begins so prosperously, chiefly depends on this—

To save the German Bund by the help of Austria, or to leave Austria the possibility—difficult as it may be—to save herself.

I feel sure that I shall never be called upon to solve more difficult problems than the present. But they do not come of my choice; the evil exists and must be conquered: the causes of the evil lie deep; they must therefore be grasped from the root: this outbreak already overspreads all Germany; the fight must therefore take place in the open field. In these assertions there is no exaggeration : they are the expression of pure truth.

METTERNICH.

On this Report I think it right to make the following remarks :—

1. I think it would be best that every State which has still no representation by Diet should have the bestowal of it deferred, and that at present there should be nothing said on the matter, in order not to put troublesome people in movement, who would with difficulty be satisfied with representative Diets such as are meant in your Report.

2. I hesitate to grant to the Diets a share in the legislation ;

3. Or to grant the proposed assembly of Deputies from the provincial Diets, which it would strengthen against a monarchy formed out of different bodies.

4. I shall never allow my universities to be examined by a commission, for they would thereby be brought into the very disorder and confusion which it is intended to avoid.

5. The formation of a special judicial commission to try the discovered conspiracy against the Bund I think doubtful and unjust. Every subject has the right to be tried according to the laws of his own State, or that in which the offence occurred. Now, the Bund has no peculiar laws against crimes, no tribunal : therefore, who shall judge, and according to what law shall judgment be given ? One must not by unjust measures give occasion to just complaints, which might here be the case. Besides, who will answer for it that the judges shall be properly chosen, and that there will not be long disputes at the Diet as to the manner of trial without bringing matters to a point, thus making them still worse ? . . ..

But it is best, as I have already told you, not to go to work inconsiderately, and perhaps resort to such remedial measures that the evil in question may be made either to take another form or to give place to a new one.

What We can do depends on Us, but we have to do with weak sovereigns and weak Governments, whose fears we must use to induce them to severe but righteous measures, and if this cannot be done, or should the means ordained by the Diet prove insufficient against the inaction or treachery of others, we must isolate ourselves, and then—as I have explained to you—act as the Austrian kingdom, as the welfare of my subjects, requires. This you can threaten to do, if you should see that it is necessary.

FRANCIS.

Schönbrunn, August 7, 1819.

RESULTS OF THE CARLSBAD CONFERENCES.*

Metternich to Count Buol in Frankfurt, Carlsbad,
September 1, 1819.

353. Enclosed I have the honour to send your Excellency a presidential Report on several matters debated here among the assembled plenipotentiaries of the different German Governments.

From the great importance of the deliberations and with the happy conviction that a corresponding result will procure the security of internal peace in the Bund and confirm the federation in its organic formation, I thoroughly confide in your Excellency's sound, wise, and in every respect efficient co-operation. I expect, therefore, as soon as possible, intelligence of the further course of the deliberations, and only remark that in case of any doubt the two ambassadors, Von Plessen and Von Marschall, can give every explanation required, for these two ministers are acquainted with the negotiations so far, and with my views and feelings.

Presidential Proposition.

(Enclosed in No. 353.)

354. The Royal Presidential Embassy has received orders to make the following proposals to the assembly of the Bund.

* There were present at the Carlsbad Conferences—besides Austria—Prussia, Bavaria, Saxony, Hanover, Wurtemberg, Baden, Mecklenburg, Nassau, Hesse, and Saxe Weimar : the two last without full powers.—ED.

His Imperial Majesty believes that the wish of all the members of the Bund corresponds with his own when he calls upon that assembly, before their adjournment, to direct their whole attention to the restless agitation and fermentation of feeling prevailing in the greater part of Germany; to discover the causes of this doubtful appearance, which for some years has day by day been more plainly made known, till at last, it was unmistakably revealed in sermonising writings, in widespread criminal confederations, even in single deeds of horror; and to take into serious consideration the means whereby to secure order and peace, respect for laws and confidence in Governments, general contentment, and the undisturbed enjoyment of all the benefits which, under the protection of a durable, secure peace, would fall to the share of the German nation from the hand of their princes.

The source of the evil—to limit the further progress of which is at present the sacred duty of all the German Governments—lies partly, indeed, in the circumstances and relations of the time, on which no Government can immediately act, but it partly depends on definite needs, errors and abuses, which may certainly be amended by united action and well-considered measures.

Among the subjects which in this latter respect require the closest and most careful consideration the following are most prominent:—

1. The uncertainty with regard to the meaning and misunderstanding of Article XIII. of the Act of Confederation ;

2. Incorrect ideas of the powers of the existing Assembly of the Bund, and inadequate means of improving those powers ;

3. The defects of the school and university systems ;

4. The abuse of the press, and especially the disorders excited by newspapers, journals, and pamphlets.

It is the most earnest wish of his Majesty that the assembly of the Bund should occupy itself immediately with these important matters. And the Presidential Embassy is hence appointed to impart these designs for measures concerning the four points above mentioned, and also to nominate a central commission, whose object and business will be more fully shown in the course of this Report.

His Majesty is convinced that the members of the Bund will see once more in these plans and in the accompanying remarks those principles of justice and moderation which his Imperial Majesty has always taken for his guide, and that the well-disposed in all the German States will misunderstand neither the pure and benevolent views which have exclusively guided his Majesty, nor the straightforward, hearty, and unalterable participation in the general lot of the States called by the Bund to equal advantages, equal duties, and equal efforts.

I. Uncertain Meaning of Article XIII. of the Act of Confederation.

When the illustrious originators of the German Bund determined, at the time of Germany's political regeneration, to give their people a pledge of their love and confidence by the preservation or reconstruction of representative Diets, and to this end signed Article XIII. of the Act of Confederation, they certainly foresaw that this article could not be fully carried out to the same extent and in the same form in all the States of the Bund. The great difference in the position of the States of the

Bund—of which at that time some retained their old provincial representative institutions wholly or in part; others had possessed but entirely lost them; while others again had never had such institutions, or lost them in the earliest ages—must necessarily lead to as great a difference in the management of this important affair. This difference was greatly increased by a new arrangement of territorial boundaries, by the union of States dissimilarly constituted into one common State, and by the fusion of districts to whom representative institutions were more or less foreign with provinces where they had existed for ages.

In this respect, not only the founders of the Bund but also afterwards the Princes of the Bund of that time hesitated to listen to the wish everywhere expressed (and most loudly at the Diet) that for the formation of the above-named representative institutions mentioned in Article XIII. a general standard might be determined upon. If from the non-fulfilment of this wish many evils arose for Germany, yet it would be unjust to mistake the motive which caused this silence of the Bund on this important point—namely, respect for the right of each State of the Bund to regulate their internal affairs according to their own views— and the fear lest by vigorously outspoken general principles, single States of the Bund should be thrown into confusion, and perhaps into indissoluble difficulties.

But the founders of the German Bund could never have supposed that constructions would be placed on Article XIII. in contradiction to its plain words, or that results should be drawn from it which reversed, not only Article XIII., but the whole text of the Act of Confederation in all its chief provisions, and rendered the continuance even of the Bund in the highest degree problematical. Never could they have supposed that the unambiguous principle of representation by Diets (on the confirmation of which they laid so much value) should be changed into pure democratic principles and forms, and claims be grounded on this misunderstanding incompatible with the existence of monarchical States, which (with the unimportant exception of the free towns belonging to this body) are the only constituent parts of the Bund, as will appear immediately or in a very short time must be made plain.

As little ground did there seem to be for the fear that anyone in Germany would ever harbour the idea of curtailing the substantive rights and attributes of the Bund itself by means of the provincial Diets, or that it was really attempted to sever the only band by which one German State is bound to the others, and the whole of Germany united with the European system. Yet all these sad misunderstandings and errors have not only developed during late years, but, by an unfortunate chain of circumstances, have taken such a hold on the public mind that the true meaning of Article XIII. has been quite lost sight of. The daily increasing tendency to fruitless or dangerous theories; the influence of deluded writers, or of those who flatter the popular folly; the foolish cravings; the institutions of foreign countries, whose present political form is as unlike that of Germany as their whole former history is from ours—the desire to plant on German soil these and many other similar and mostly deplorable causes have produced that general political confusion of language which threatens to consume this grand and noble nation, once so gloriously distinguished for solidity and sense. These causes have, even to many members of the Diets, so obscured the standpoint on which they were constitutionally placed, and so destroyed the limits of their true efficiency, that the Government itself is hindered and disturbed in the fulfilment of its most essential duties.

The grounds which had formerly decided the Bund not to interfere directly in the affairs of single States of the Bund must now make place for higher considerations. If the German Bund is not to be destroyed, if Germany is not to abandon its rights and well-being to all the horrors of internal divisions, lawless caprice, and incurable disorder, it must secure a firm and universally recognised foundation for its future institutions. Hence it must be the first and most pressing business of the Bund to enter upon a thorough explanation and interpretation of Article XIII. of the Act of Confederation, in a way applicable to all the States of the Bund in whatever position they may now be, and this derived, not from popular theories or foreign models, but from German ideas, German rights, and German history, and above all by the maintenance of the monarchical principle to which Germany can never be unfaithful, and the maintenance of the Bund, as the only support of her independence and her peace.

In all the States of the Bund where the provincial Diets are not firmly established, the work must be put in hand without further delay, and, indeed, with redoubled activity, so desirable is it to prevent new misunderstandings and to facilitate a final agreement on the carrying out of Article XIII. by the works relating to the provincial Diets already introduced into many of the States of the Bund; and so imperative is it that no resolution should be taken which in any way whatever is in contradiction to the views here expressed, and to the explanation of that Article which may be very shortly expected from the Assembly of the Bund.

II. *The Powers of the Bund and the Means of carrying them out.*

It lies in the very idea and existence of the German Assembly of the Bund that the authority represented by it constitutes the supreme legislative power in Germany in everything relating to the self-preservation and essential aims of the Bund, as is set forth in Article II. of the Act of Confederation. Hence it follows that the resolutions of the Assembly, in so far as they have for their objects the inward security of the whole, the independence and inviolability of single members of the Bund and the maintenance of the legally existing order inseparable from both, must be of universal obligatory force, and that the carrying out of such resolutions must not be opposed by any isolated legislation or any separate resolution. Without a firm and vigorous maintenance of these principles the existence and duration of the Bund is not to be thought of as possible. The further development, as well as the definition of the powers and attributes of the Diet in general, must be reserved for further deliberations on the improvement and maintenance of all the conditions established by the Bund. Meanwhile it will be at once admitted on all sides that (and this the deliberations will prove) the great principle cannot in itself be observed, nor can the laws and resolutions of the Bund have any guarantee for their operation, if the Assembly of the Bund has not entrusted to it the means and strength to carry them out. The composition of an executive law with this object must therefore be one of the chief objects of the deliberations above mentioned; and his Majesty believes he may take for granted the fullest agreement among his allies in the Bund as to the urgent necessity for such a law.

Since, however, the Diet should not be left without the necessary means for the administration and execution of such resolutions and measures as the internal safety of Germany requires, the Imperial and Royal Presidential-Embassy is authorised to submit for immediate examination and deliberation the draft of a provisional executive law drawn up with express regard to Article II. of the Act of Confederation.

III. The Defects of the School and University Systems.

The attention of the Assembly of the Bund, as of individual German Governments, was long ago directed to this object, with the exceeding importance of which all Germany is penetrated. A sound and salutary direction of the educational institutions in general, but especially of the universities which immediately prepare the entrance into practical life, will be considered in every State one of the chief matters for the royal care. But the German Governments lie under peculiar obligations and more than ordinary responsibility in this respect: in the first place, because in Germany the education for the public services and for official life is entirely left to the universities; and then because these universities are a principal member in the whole union of Germans, and as the good which emanates from them is spread over the whole nation, so also their defects are felt more or less at every point in Germany; lastly, because Germany has to thank her universities (famous from of old) for part of the reputation and consequent rank in the European commonwealth which up to this time it has happily maintained, and in the unabridged maintenance of which his Majesty on his side takes the warmest and most active interest.

That the true position of the German universities, with some well-known and honourable exceptions, no longer corresponds with the reputation gained in better times can hardly be doubted. For some time past, sensible and right-thinking men have remarked and deplored that these institutions have lost their original character and deviated from the objects aimed at by their illustrious founders and supporters. Carried away by the stream of agitation, the greater part of the academic professors have mistaken the true ends of the universities, and substituted for them those that are capricious and often injurious. Instead (as was their first duty) of training the youth confided to them for the service of the State to which they were called, and awakening in them a sense of what is expected of them by the fatherland to which they belong, they had followed the phantom of a so-called cosmopolitan cultivation, filled the minds so susceptible alike to both truth and error with empty dreams, and inspired them, if not with bitterness, yet with contempt and opposition to legally established order.

By this perverted course they have gradually, to the great prejudice of the common welfare and injury to the rising generation, engendered the obscuring of the higher wisdom, contempt for all positive teaching, and a pretension to reform social order after a peculiar untried system, till a considerable number of the youth who ought to be learners have transformed themselves into teachers and reformers. This dangerous degeneracy of the universities has not escaped the notice of the German Governments in the past, but partly from their praiseworthy wish not to restrict the freedom of teaching so long as it did not encroach on civil matters, partly from the troubles and pressure of a twenty years' war they were prevented from combating the evil with sound remedies.

But in our days, under the beneficial influence of restored external peace and the hearty and active efforts of so many German sovereigns to prepare a happy future for their people, it may fairly be expected that the universities should return to those limits within which they formerly worked so gloriously for the Fatherland and for mankind. Yet from this very quarter proceed the most determined hostilities to the principles and rules on which repose the present institutions and the internal peace of Germany. Whether by criminal co-operation, or by inexcusable carelessness, the noblest powers and efforts of youth are abused by being made the tools of extravagant political schemes which are not the less mischievous because they are weak. These dangerous courses have, indeed, led to deeds which disgrace the German name, and further indulgence would degenerate into culpable weakness, while indifference to further abuses of such a distorted academic liberty would render the whole German Governments answerable before the world and to posterity.

Certain as it is that, in the present grave position of affairs, every other consideration must give way to the maintenance of public order, the Governments of the States of the Bund will not lose sight of the great question how to remedy the deep-seated abuses of the educational systems in general, and especially to prevent the further estrangement of the universities from their original and only beneficial ends ; and his Majesty therefore holds that the Assembly of the Bund is bound to occupy itself with questions equally important for learning and for public life, for the welfare of families and the strength of Governments, and not to desist until a sound and happy result has been gained by their efforts.

But, in the first place, the evil immediately threatening must be met, and care taken that by efficient measures foolish enthusiasts or declared enemies to existing order may not seek in the present distressing state of many of the German universities further materials for the excitement of men's minds, deluded instruments for the execution of senseless plans, or weapons to turn against the personal safety of citizens. His Majesty has therefore no scruple, in consequence of the provisional authority granted by the Bund in this affair, in offering the annexed sketch of some preliminary measures for the immediate consideration and further deliberation of the Assembly.

IV. Abuses of the Press.

The Press in general, especially that branch of it which supplies the journals, newspapers, and pamphlets, has of late years enjoyed perfect liberty in nearly every part of Germany: for even where the Government has had the right to limit it by preventive measures, the efficiency of such measures has been enfeebled by the power of circumstances, and consequently opened a wide field to all kinds of further extravagance.

The countless evils which the abuse of this liberty has spread over Germany have been seriously increased since the publication in different States of the proceedings of the Diets, including subjects which ought not to leave the sacred keeping of the Senate and appear before the world but in a regular and solemn form, nor serve as the sport of idle curiosity and careless criticism, preparing new food for the rashness of authors, and affording a pretext to newspaper scribblers to raise their voices on subjects which cause doubt and difficulty to the greatest statesmen. How far these injurious pretensions would at last extend, what confusion of ideas, what fermentation of minds, what degradation of authority, what strife of passions, what fanatical errors, what crimes shall proceed from it, need not be further insisted on, and there can hardly be any difference of opinions among the well-disposed and really enlightened portion of the German nation on so notorious an evil.

The peculiarity of the relations in which the States of the Bund stand to one another gives to the dangers connected with the licence of the press a power and extent which they can never have in States where the supreme power is united in one and the same centre, and excludes the employment of the legal means by which in these States an endeavour is made to check the abuse of the press. A confederation of States like that which is formed in Germany with the sanction of all the European Powers is wanting in that mighty counterweight which in close monarchies protects public order from the attacks of presumptuous or evil-disposed authors. In such a confederation peace, harmony and confidence can only be maintained by the greatest mutual care in averting troubles and difficulties. From this high point of view, with which the lawgivers of other lands have nothing in common, must the questions connected with the freedom of the press in Germany be considered. Only in a position of the most perfect peace can Germany, with its federal constitution, endure the unlimited freedom of the press in so far as it is specially united with that constitution. The present moment is less suited for it than any other, for the efforts of so many Governments to secure the present and future welfare of their peoples by good institutions cannot, amid a wild discord of opinions, possibly succeed in the midst of a disorganised contest, which shatters all principles, and throws doubt and suspicion on all truth.

The temporary measures to be taken against the abuse of the press under these pressing circumstances must in no wise hinder the activity of useful and excellent authors, fetter the natural progress of the human mind, or hinder communication or information of any kind, so long as it only keeps within the limits which no legislation has yet permitted itself to overstep. That the supervision of periodical writings shall not degenerate into oppression is guaranteed by the feeling which is openly expressed by all the German Governments on this occasion, and no friend of truth and order need fear the reproach that any tyranny over men's minds is intended. But the necessity for such supervision can no longer remain in doubt, and since his Majesty may expect from all the Governments a harmony of views on this important matter, the Presidential Embassy is commissioned to lay before the Assembly of the Bund the annexed sketch of a provisional resolution for the avoidance of the abuse of the press in regard to newspapers, journals, and pamphlets, for their immediate examination and deliberation.

V. Nomination of a Central Investigation Commission.

Next to the resolutions and deliberations mentioned in the last section of the Report, there may still be necessary a measure both for the protection of public order and the calming of all the well-disposed in Germany, which his Majesty commends to the immediate consideration of the Assembly of the Bund.

The discoveries which have been made in different States of the Bund at the same time have shown traces of a widespread and in several parts of Germany active union, with many ramifications, each more or less matured, whose continued efforts seem to be directed, not merely to the greatest possible spreading abroad of fanatical, dangerous, and revolutionary doctrines, but even to the encouragement and preparation of mischievous schemes. If the extent and connection of these criminal intrigues are not yet thoroughly known, yet the mass of facts, documents, and other evidence already collected is so considerable that the operation of the evil is no longer to be doubted. Opinions will always be divided as to the greatness of the danger ; it is enough that such sad errors should gain so much ground in Germany, that so considerable a number of individuals should actually be led astray, and that, even if the whole may be considered only as a malady of the mind, the neglect of the necessary remedies may bring with it the most dangerous consequences.

A thorough investigation of the matter is therefore of unavoidable necessity. It must in one way or another lead to a beneficial result, for the really guilty will, if the suspicion is confirmed, be disarmed and brought to justice, and the deluded will have their eyes opened to see the abyss near which they stand, and Germany will be placed in a position neither to be deceived as to real dangers and cradled in false security, nor disturbed and misled by exaggerated cares.

But if these investigations are to be successful, they must be made by the Diet as the common centre, and conducted under its immediate supervision. The intrigues and schemes already discovered are directed quite as much against the existence of the German Bund as against individual German Princes and States ; consequently, the Diet is unquestionably both competent and by Article II. of the Act of Confederation strictly bound to take cognisance thereof. Moreover, a central authority so constituted is far more competent than single Governments to arrange the data already prepared and to collect what has still to be ascertained, to examine them with justice and impartiality, and to take a comprehensive view of the whole state of the case. Lastly, by the official publication of the whole proceedings at the close of the investigation by the authorities, the fear will be most effectually averted that the innocent should be suspected, or the guilty escape punishment, and in any case an end will thus be put to many doubts, anxieties, and restless agitations.

These are the grounds on which his Majesty is impelled to propose the appointment of a central commission of investigation with the objects here described, and the Presidential Embassy is directed to lay the annexed sketch of a resolution on these measures before the Assembly of the Bund for their immediate consideration.*

---

* In the 'instructions' sent to Count Buol, at the same time as the above presidential Proposition, Count Metternich shows that ' the Cabinet ' assembled in Carlsbad ' have agreed to give similar instructions to their ambassadors to the Diet, instructing them to agree to the Presidential proposal, and to declare their assent to the resolutions drawn up.' These were, in fact, four sketches or plans for resolutions—namely, (*a*) a provisional executive statute, (*b*) provisional measures regarding the universities, (*c*) a law regulating the press, and (*d*) the appointment of a central commission of investigation in Mayence—and at the sitting of the Diet at Frankfurt on September 20, 1819, were unanimously adopted and officially published for the general information in the different States of the Bund ; which makes it unnecessary to include them in this work, as the substantial contents of this codification is known to the reader without this, by the present document.—Ed.

Letter of Thanks from the Ministers assembled at Carlsbad to Prince Metternich, Carlsbad, August 30, 1819.

355. Most gracious Prince. Your Excellency will not refuse, at the last moment of our present memorable meeting, to give to one and all of us the pleasure of offering you the unanimous expression of our unbounded respect and gratitude.

If we may venture to hope that the difficult and honourable task to which you summoned us has been fulfilled in a manner not displeasing to you, we have to thank your prudent guidance, your ceaseless efforts, and the confidence you have so kindly shown in us and have also so implicitly received.

When you, on the other side of the Alps, heard the audacious, fatally prophetic clamour of licentious writers, and the news of a crime in which superficial or prejudiced observers could see only an isolated action, you discerned with equal clearness the depth of the evil and the means of meeting it, and what we have here achieved and called into life is only the realisation of what you then designed.

The results of our efforts lie mostly beyond our calculation, but you have secured for us a rich harvest in the feeling that we have, by the results of our deliberations, prepared for our august masters the means of fulfilling their most sacred and indispensable duty towards the common fatherland.

Accept, your Excellency, the assurance of our unalterable and devoted respect.

Carlsbad, August 30, 1819.

(Signed) BERNSTORFF, RECHBERG, STAINLEIN, SCHULEN-
BURG, GRAF MÜNSTER, HARDENBERG, WINZINGERODE,
BERSTETT, MÜNCHHAUSEN, MARSCHALL, PLESSEN

Metternich to the Prince Regent of England, Carlsbad,
September 2, 1819.

356.   Sire,—I am too sensible of the favour which
your Royal Highness deigns to bestow on me, to deny
myself the satisfaction of offering my congratulations
on the happy agreement established between the German Cabinets at Carlsbad, and the expression of my
thanks for the support which the ministers of your
Royal Highness have given to all the measures which I
have been able to propose.   A new era is beginning,
and it will be an era of salvation if the German Courts
do not go beyond the limits assigned to them.

Your Royal Highness foresaw the importance of the
subjects which might be submitted to the discussion
which I had arranged to take place on my return from
Italy, and you furnished a signal proof of this by sending
Count Münster to Carlsbad.   Your Royal Highness is
always sure to be met in the path of those principles which would have achieved the great work if
they had not so often been lost sight of in many negotiations of the years 1813 up to the disastrous epoch of
1815.   Therefore it remains to me to make a request to
your Royal Highness, to the fulfilment of which I
attach a very high value.   Questions of as great an
interest for the Germanic Confederation as those we have
just settled have been reserved for the conferences
which will open at Vienna on November 20 of the
present year.   Less urgent in their execution, but not
less useful in their consequences, these questions will
need to be strongly supported by the Courts who wish
to do good, because they are above petty fears, petty
jealousies, and many lower motives which generally
interrupt the development of useful institutions.   You

must not, then, be surprised, sire, if I consider the direct support of Count Münster in the course of the negotiations of Vienna a real benefit. My wish is simple—it is only that the action of Austria may thus be strengthened. I do not believe that our next conferences can extend beyond six weeks, but those will count for much in the future existence of the Confederation.

Permit me, sire, to take the present opportunity of entreating your Royal Highness to continue the gracious favour with which you have long deigned to honour me, and which is due to my devotion for your august person. Deign, &c. &c.

Metternich to Esterhazy in London, Königswart,
September 3, 1819.

357. The assembled ministers at Carlsbad have just terminated their business. I had the honour to inform you, at the time of my arrival in this town, of the object which called me here. It is with very lively satisfaction that I can now assure you that all I wished to submit to the common deliberation of the principal German Cabinets has received their unanimous sanction.

A great affair has, perhaps, never been treated with more harmony and agreement in all its parts than that which we are just bringing to an end. The evils which menace the repose of Germany have been examined with calmness and candour. The German Cabinets have met together there as if they were members of one and the same family. They have placed thorough confidence in the wise and steadfast principles which direct the political and administrative steps of the Emperor. The results of the harmony which is established between the Governments will operate usefully on the present and future measures of the Diet ; and I allow myself to entertain great hopes of the influence which may be brought to bear on the whole of Europe by this first example of the maintenance of monarchical principles by a political body so imposing as the Germanic Confederation.

The labours of the Conference may be divided into two parts, which include all the most essential objects of the Confederation.

The first bears on the measures to oppose to the demagogic spirit, which has made immense progress in Germany within the last two or three years.

The second bears on the organic laws of the Confederation, which are most essential to strengthen and complete the existence of this great political body.

The measures of the greatest interest at the present moment will be proposed at the Diet by the President about the 15th of this month. It was necessary to permit a fortnight to elapse between the definite agreement of the majority of the federal Courts and the proposition at the Diet, in order to allow time to inform those princes who were not represented at Carlsbad of the result of the conferences, and to enable them to give the necessary orders to their ambassadors at Frankfurt, so that they may add their votes to those of the majority.

The organic laws agreed on in principle will be discussed in detail at a second meeting of the Cabinets, which will take place at Vienna after November 15. The Federal Diet will adjourn after having made the first Imperial propositions into laws, and it will be enabled to sanction at the opening of the session of 1820, and in constitutional forms, the resolutions adopted by the majority in the conferences at Vienna during the vacation of the Diet. . . .

I beg you to present the enclosed letter to his Royal Highness (No. 356). I have taken the liberty of addressing him directly, to thank him for the support I received from Counts Münster and Hardenberg at a most decisive time for the salvation of Europe. There ought to be nothing surprising in seeing the ministers of his Royal Highness on all occasions professing the same principles as those of our august master the Emperor—the only ones which may yet be able to arrest the torrent of the revolution. It is nevertheless rare, in the progress of a very complicated affair, considering the essence of the German federation, to meet with Courts so indissolubly united as our own and that of Hanover. If this fact is perhaps connected with the position of the two Courts, the men who are charged with the defence of such great interests are not the less meritorious if they strictly follow the line most favourable to the interest of their prince and their country, and consequently the most consonant with their duty.

I cannot doubt that the Cabinet of St. James's will give its assent to the result of our labours at Carlsbad, as well as to those which have been merely sketched out.

The scenes which many towns in England present show what partisans folly has gained. The easiest trade and the most certain of success during the last few years has been that of rebellion against social order, against the laws existing in all civilised countries, and against reason founded on the experience of all time. A grand example of vigour has just been given in Germany, which must resound in every corner of Europe. It will give an impetus to minds whose principles are most opposite ; the effect which it produces will be different according as more or less strength, calmness, and wisdom is displayed by the Governments. We already begin to see that many men who quite recently hoisted the democratic colours are retiring little by little from the scene ; there are even some who secretly offer their services in favour of the cause which we defend, and a simple meeting of the Cabinets sufficed to accomplish this, without their resolutions being even known ! The gauntlet, besides, was thrown down by the revolutionists ; we have had the courage to pick it up, and I beg you to assure the English ministers that I flatter myself I am personally sufficiently well known to them to allow me to admit that they are not mistaken as to the nature of the principles which we are opposing to the revolutionists, and the energy which we shall display in the conduct of the affair.

Metternich to Freiherr von Hruby, Austrian Ambassador at Munich, Vienna, October 25, 1819.

358. I lost no time in laying before the Emperor your Excellency's Report. His Majesty is deeply agitated by its contents, and thinks it well to write to the King himself. This letter your Excellency will find enclosed in this.

At the audience which you will request you will have a convenient opportunity of imparting to his Majesty clearly and openly the views of the Emperor, as follows :—

Your Excellency cannot describe too vigorously the impression made upon his Imperial Majesty by the strength which has been shown by his Majesty the King in time past, as well as in contrast to the attacks of the revolutionary party against the Carlsbad decrees. The Emperor conjures the King to continue firm, and not to allow himself to be overcome by the intrigues of that party. What that party desires (their words may be as hypocritical as possible) has been made evident to the King by the proceedings of the Chambers.

The Carlsbad decrees are directed against all the evils experienced at present. They are the result of the voluntary agreement of the German Princes ; they were called together by their own feeling of danger; the Emperor had not summoned them to the council for his own needs or his own danger : he had spoken and acted only for the general good. He was placed above the crowd ; he must help it to rise or he must separate from it, and what the common efforts cannot save, he must save for itself.

The King is deluded ; he risks his sovereignty. He will never be endangered by the means used to secure his rights but by the weakness of the Governmental measures. How long has the word of a demagogue or wrong-seeing speculator deserved more attention than his own experience? The King should remember the fine promises which were made to him before the Congress by the Chambers, and their results.

It is said that the King cannot perjure himself. No, never! How thoroughly the Emperor feels this he has shown by the answer he commanded me to give to the question, What would Austria say to the overthrow of the Government? But if it is shown that the Bavarian Government requires some alteration in its different parts to secure to the Crown, and consequently to the people, justice and peace, the King will find means in the sovereign assembly of German Princes itself to bring into harmony all the parts of a work so important for Bavaria.

All the laws after September 20 are nothing but

means for the security of the much-threatened peace in
Germany.   What is wanted here is some remedy, some
repose, some principle.   Help can only come from pro-
portionate remedies, and a State which excludes itself
from the general necessities exposes itself and the
community to inevitable dangers — dangers the immediate consequences of which are incalculable if they
are encouraged by the miscarriage of the measures
already decided on.

Lastly, your Excellency is authorised to draw his
Majesty's attention to the Emperor's position in the affair.
His Imperial Majesty has already bestowed his protection, and only demands to be supported faithfully as far
as lies in the King's power.   He demands this as a friend
of the King, of his throne, and of his peace. . . .

Metternich to Freiherr von Hruby, Vienna,
Oct. 25, 1819.

359. I have no cause to be surprised at anything
we may live to see in Munich.   This Court has for years
gone on in this ever vacillating way, and would still
have followed that course but for the iron hand of Napoleon, who knew how to enchain it by prospects of
advantage.   So soon as the first had lost his strength,
and the second had disappeared, the Bavarian Court
turned round. . . .

If you think it would be at all useful, invite his Excellency Marshal Wrede to come here himself.   I fear
no one to whom I can speak face to face.

Your Excellency can say to Count Rechberg, without reserve, that we have received through couriers
from Warsaw the excellent declarations of the Emperor
of Russia in regard to the course of affairs at Carlsbad ;

that the only objection he made to those beneficial
measures was an expression of fear lest the German
Princes should carry them out partially and feebly, since
most of them had long since lost all power of government. . . .

FROM CARLSBAD TO VIENNA.

Extracts from Metternich's private Letters from September 3 to December 22, 1819.

360. *Königswart, Sept.* 3, 1819.—The peace and quiet reigning here all around me, excite the pleasantest feelings in my heart. I do not belong to those who think that movement is the object of life. There is a very grave tinge about the place where I live. The neighbourhood is rich in picturesque spots. Enormous forests, high mountains, wide valleys, much water, lovely streams surround a well-furnished house pleasant to live in, containing old family pictures, among which there is a portrait of myself as a boy of five years old. I must have been a most ill-favoured child, or the painter not extremely clever.*

The weather is horrible. This high ground is always either cold or rainy ; it would inspire Lord Byron with a truly melancholy poem. Whether the English poet will honour Vienna next winter with a visit, as is

* This portrait is still at Königswart.—ED.

reported, I leave still undecided. Near the good town of Vienna, too, I am always uneasy. I do not love it for its own sake, and still less for my own. But if heaven listens to my secret wishes, I shall end with leaving Vienna very willingly. So it is with all places where people live—they are nothing in themselves, but everything from circumstances. Then, too, there is nothing in Königswart to attach me, not one remembrance, and perhaps, too, no particular thought—unless, perhaps, the thought that one day my ashes will be brought here to repose by those of my father. I do not, however, find anything sad in this idea, for I believe and heartily trust in God. I shall be regretted by many of the great and good—execrated by those who are neither. The standpoint from which I have thought and acted is of such a height that my name remains identified with great events, for the very reason that I had the misfortune to live in a period of revolution.

This period will pass away like all human folly. Happy they who have known how to maintain themselves upright amidst the ruins of generations! I have arrived at the middle of the life of a generation, and fate has laid upon me the task of warning the generation now coming to the front and preserving them from straying on to the steep incline which would surely lead them to their ruin. The Carlsbad epoch is hence one of the most important of my life.

361. *September* 4.—In the last three years I have had a high road, seven miles (German) long, made at my own cost, and I have come to a place where it is very difficult to carry it on, across a deep and muddy valley. I have therefore had a bridge of three arches constructed, which has cost me over 70,000 gulden, and will require some 60,000 gulden more. The bridge will be beautiful,

and very convenient for travellers.   Many people, when
they cross it, would think it had been standing there for
ever ; but I have had a stone placed on it with an inscription saying that I made the bridge.   Of a hundred
travellers ninety-nine will think the builder must have
been either a Crœsus or a fool.

362. *Prague, September* 9.—I never come to
Prague without thinking I hear midnight strike.   Six
years ago, at that hour, I dipped my pen to declare
war with the man of the century—the Man of St.
Helena—to kindle the beacon which was the signal for
100,000 men of the allied troops to cross the frontier.

363. *Vienna, September* 14.—What the return to
his own house of a poor man like me is nobody knows,
because few people are watched with so much envy
and jealousy, few so beset, so celebrated, so decried,
and so praised.   Why has fate brought me what I never
desired, and what (besides its being a womanish fuss)
seems to me the most horrible of human destinies ?

364. *September* 21.—Among the strangers whom
I have met here is Marshal Marmont, an intellectual
man, whom I knew very slightly.   I have talked much
with him, and I see that he finds me different from what
he had expected.   I can speak with him the more
openly, as he is here on family affairs only.   We
meet, therefore, as merely private persons.   After our
last conversation, in which for three hours we talked
over past events, and the present internal condition of
the country, he said :—' Since the last time that I heard
Napoleon speak, before he became mad, this is the first
reasonable conversation I have heard.'

365. *September* 25.—I have just received the news
from Frankfurt that the child which I have carried nine
months will at last see the light !   Its birthday falls on

September 20.* Each party wishes to baptise the child by a different name. Some call it a monster, some a good work, some a piece of stupidity. Truth lies between them. The first legislative word which has been spoken for thirty years, uttered from a sense of reason, justice, and experience, without reserve, as well as without disguise, plain but not dry, with neither mystic nor secret meanings, this word is a great fact, one of the most important of my life. If the world thinks that I am right, I shall rejoice; if it thinks I am wrong, I will excuse it beforehand. Nothing is so free as man's thought, and certain shades in it even contribute to the charm of life and its relations—relations which give to life its greatest value. My part is, moreover, not doubtful. I have never worn a mask, and those who have mistaken me must have very bad eyes. My resolution is taken. Nothing can turn me from it, as nothing can drive me in a direction I do not wish to take. Shall I succeed? By God, I know not!

366. *October* 13.—I fall from one pregnancy into another. Hardly have I returned from Carlsbad than a new labour is prepared for me within three months. My Carlsbad child is ill-tempered : it fights and bites ; it deals heavy blows at many bad people, and more fools. My Vienna child will be gentle and well mannered, but horribly tiresome.† Why must I, of all people among so many millions, be the one to think where others do not think, to act where no one else will act, and write because no one else can? And what will be the end of it to me? I am really a slave, with a heart full of disgust. A function is laid upon me which takes me away from

* See No. 354.
† This refers to the Ministerial Conference at Vienna. See No. 374.—
ED.

everything that is according to my taste, and embitters
the happiness of life. If ever you meet with a really
ambitious man—and they are rare—send him to me. I
will talk with him for a couple of hours, and he will be
cured for some time.

367. *October* 18.—I write to you to-day on the
anniversary of the greatest event of modern history.
This day six years ago the fate of the world was decided.
Napoleon would, however, have been as entirely lost
without the battle of Leipsic as he was after it. But
this day enlightened the world, and will always be
looked upon in the annals of history as the turning-
point of that memorable epoch, showing the beginning
of a new era. The hand of God was armed with twenty
nations to subdue one man, who, to master a people
whom he had placed above all other peoples, had put
himself above all other men. My soul was never more
filled with holy reverence than during the course of that
long day, which I passed between the dead and dying.
Yet peace was in me and around me. Napoleon could
not have had a similar feeling ; on that day he must
have experienced a foretaste of the Last Judgment.

You said lately that you were reading with great
interest Napoleon's correspondence. You are quite
right. This correspondence and the ' *Mémoire de Ste.
Hélène*' * are doubtless, of all the writings which have
lately appeared, the most worthy to engage the attention
of the enlightened. The correspondence gives a picture
of the most marvellous man the world has ever seen ;
it gives his picture at the moment of his ascent, and
every letter of Napoleon's shows that the upward movement was quite a natural one, and arose from the force
of circumstances itself. The manuscript from St. Helena,

* See vol. i. p. 312.

on the contrary, includes everything that explains his decline. It is remarkable that the causes of his necessary and inevitable downfall are the same which bore him to the summit of power and military fame.

I passed the grandest years of his life with Napoleon or near him. I think few men have known him better than I, because I have not confined myself to bare symptoms, but have endeavoured to discover their foundation. When I saw that the whole power for good and evil was embodied in that one man, I could do no otherwise than study him, and only him. Circumstances placed me near this man; they have, so to speak, chained me to him. Hence my study of him was thorough, and every day taught me that it was complete. After my death a very interesting memoir will be found of this man and his influence on the events of his age.* I say his age, because this age really belongs to him. By the writings I leave behind me many circumstances will certainly be explained, many doubts dispelled, and many errors rectified. For many years I have written and laboured at this work. I shall complete it, for I have already made considerable progress, but it will not be published for thirty or forty years, because I will first give time for the death of living persons. This work is one of my favourite employments; it includes the time from the year 1806 till after the Peace of Paris in 1815. Of these nine years I know much. It is hardly possible that anyone should now know all that I knew. I conclude my work with the year 1815, because everything which came after that belongs to ordinary history.† Since that date the age was left to itself; it progresses because it cannot be held back; but led it will never be

---

* See the 'Portrait of Napoleon,' vol. i. p. 269.—ED.
† This may explain the gap which is found in the Memoirs after 1815.

again. It is more agreeable to me, during the rest of my life, to amplify my notes on this period of nine years than to compile a new memoir on the later period, which has become a *simple story*. We have fallen upon a time when a thousand small calculations and small views on the one side, gross mistakes and feeble remedies on the other, form the history of the day. The sea still runs high, but it is only from the storm which has passed over. One may easily upset in such a sea— for the wind is more difficult to reckon on than the storm—but the spectacle is no longer imposing.

I have often told you that in writing I follow the impulse of the moment; and to-day I feel this, for I fancy I hear that noise so strikingly described by the expression ' the roar of the battle,' that sound which was called forth by the clashing together of the strongest forces of modern times. The Austrian army alone had on the 18th shot off 60,000 cannon balls, and since this army represented only a third of the assembled powers, one may venture to assert that on that day more than 300,000 cannon balls must have been fired. Then if we reckon twelve to fifteen million musket-shots, and the whole distributed in the space of ten hours, some idea may be formed of the noise made by the fall of a single man.

368. *November* 25.—I have this day opened the Conferences.* I have spoken more than two hours, and I am sorry not to have had a shorthand writer at my disposal, for if my words were not spoken to the winds, unhappily they nevertheless fly like the wind. . . .

Talleyrand once said, ' Austria is the House of Lords of Europe ; as long as it is not dissolved it will restrain the Commons.' A very true saying.

* See the opening speech, No. 379.—ED.

369. *December* 2.—I have found a moment's quiet. The business of the Conference proceeds very well. I have gone to the root of this matter—a rare thing in moral and political discussions. I told my five-and-twenty friends in an upright and decided manner what we want and what we do not want. On this avowal there was a general declaration of approval, and each one asserted that he had never wanted more or less, or, indeed, hardly anything different. Now I am surrounded by people who are quite enchanted with their own force of will, and yet there is not one among them who a few days ago knew what he wants or will want. This is the universal fate of such an assembly. It has been evident to me for a long time that among a certain number of persons only one is ever found who has clearly made out for himself what is the question in hand. I shall be victorious, here, as in Carlsbad : that is to say, all will wish what I wish, and since I only wish what is just, I believe I shall gain my victory. But what is most remarkable is that these men will go home in the firm persuasion that they have left Vienna with the same views with which they came.

370. *December* 15.—Business always requires a certain time ; this time will be filled up by the beginning of the business and by its more or less tedious course, and it is generally found that its conclusion is only the beginning of a new affair. Of all positions the last is, for a man who represents important interests, the most vexatious. For eleven years I have been what I am, certainly far from the beginning of my task ; but twenty years remain to me, and then I shall be entitled only to ruminate on past affairs, and certainly I shall undertake the conduct of no great business from the day in which I discover in myself irresolution. What have I done during the past eleven years, and what remains for me still to do in the next twenty years? What I have hitherto done has been negative : I have fought against evil more than effected good. If I consider my task from its beginning onwards, I may well be permitted not to love those tyrants and fools who, under the names of philosophers, philanthropists, socialists, democrats, religious fanatics, are nothing, or much worse.

Up to this time I have met with little opposition ; I have sought it in vain, and hitherto have not discovered it. Perhaps for that reason a newspaper has brought the news that a German deputation is coming here to demand my head! The deputation may lose some time about this, but the poor devils would gain very little by beheading me, for the cause has made too great a progress to be now retarded. Shall an earthquake throw down the edifice, or a volcano open beneath our feet? Such catastrophes are beyond our calculation. It will ever be the same! But with my head many others would fall, and probably I should see many others fall before mine.

371. *December* 17.—I have the bad habit of not going to sleep without reading for an hour or half an hour. I generally, however, read nothing which is connected with my business. I busy myself with scientific literature, discoveries, travels, and simple narratives. Novels I never read, unless they have become classics and thus have some literary value. The common novel does not interest me ; I always find them far beneath what I conceive ; impressive situations come before me always too strongly, and I cannot prevent myself from looking at the last page—where people are married or killed—at the same time as the title-page. Then nothing is left for me but to say, Amen, and the romance for me is lost. If the heroes of a romance are to be admired, they are no better than I am myself; if they are not, they are indeed worth but little. I have no need to learn how people express their feelings. I have always been afraid of meeting with empty phrases, where my heart would not find a word. . . . My heart belongs entirely to me : my head does not ; it is concerned in the affairs of the world, which were never so important for me as happiness.

372. *December* 21.—Our affairs here will not extend beyond the end of the month of February. Everything goes on as I had hoped—indeed, as I predicted.

373. *December* 22.—I have passed a very tedious day, which seldom happens. Work often fatigues me, but tedium kills me outright. I cannot stand great dinners, and I have been obliged to be present at one which lasted three hours. This is the unpleasant consequence of a Congress, and one from which, unfortunately, I cannot escape. Happily, I can be alone in a crowd, and the greater the crowd the better I am able to isolate myself.

BEGINNING OF THE VIENNA MINISTERIAL
CONFERENCES.

Metternich to Baron Neumann,[1] in London: five letters, from October 31 to December 17, 1819.

374. *Vienna, October* 31, 1819.— .... The great German business will be completed here in November. All is going on well; rage is in the enemy's camp; it vents itself in lies, not being able to take its revenge. In the meantime we are doing our very best. Nevertheless, the thing is not easy, owing to the petty fears, the small measures, and the real terror of some of the German Governments. But the affair is not in their hands. It rests with Austria and Prussia As long as they do not deviate from the route they have marked out, they will be sure of success, and the Prussian Government, which has not an easy part, will go firmly and well.

375. *November* 16.— .... I beg you to tell Lord Castlereagh that the opening of our important deliberations will take place on the 20th of this month. All the German ministers will be here at that time.

As we only desire what the most ordinary reason and common sense dictates; as, far from any divergence, there exists an absolute conformity of views between us and Prussia; as the conduct of the King of Wurtemberg is not of a kind to attract imitators, I flatter myself that

* Baron Neumann, a man very much in the confidence of the Prince, was at that time head of the Austrian Embassy in London.—ED.

the Bund will come forth from our conferences stronger than it enters them.

The only question is to consolidate the Bund on the same basis and in the same position. The Carlsbad measures will neither be strengthened nor weakened: they exist, they need only to be executed, and they will be.

I enter into these details because it is just possible that the Government of his Britannic Majesty might receive the most contradictory reports from its representatives in Germany. I venture to say there is not one of them who sees clearly the actual state of things. This is the game of the party we are pursuing, who take all possible pains to disguise the truth. It is curious to observe that we have not remarked a single criticism bearing on what was done at Carlsbad; all bear on what was avoided there. It is especially the Commission of Inquiry which torments the factious: they attribute functions to it which it does not possess, for they are fully aware that they would not receive the least support from the public if they raised the real question, which is: If it is good that the Governments should assure themselves of the real existence, the extent, and the means employed by the demagogues, who simply aim at the total overthrow of all society in Germany? This aim is known, proved, followed, and sustained by most criminal means.

This Commission has opened its sittings. The materials on which they work are immense; at present they are principally occupied with the result of judicial inquiries against convicted persons. Unhappily we shall dispose of only too large an amount of material! Europe will receive, when the result of the labour is published, a great lesson on the danger of encouraging

revolutionary ideas, sustained by blind or foolish Governments, and directed by the factious under the mask
of a kindly liberalism!

376. *December* 6.—Our conferences just now take
a very prosperous turn.

Will you reassure Lord Castlereagh from me as to
any alteration of the mind of the Confederation on the
important question of political relations, or on the question of peace and war. There have never been held
any secret committees at Frankfurt on this latter question ; as to the question of the Federal Act, we shall
treat it to the satisfaction even of Lord Castlereagh, and
to the great displeasure of Capo d'Istria, who is waiting
for us there. I beg Lord Castlereagh to believe that I
know all the dangerous sides of the thing, and that I shall
take care to avoid the rocks. The sea upon which I sail
is so well known to me that we shall enter the port when
we are thought to be far from approaching it.

An immense point will be gained by the consolidation of this great social body, founded on a pacific basis
in the very centre of Europe.

377. *December* 9.— . . . . I flatter myself that
Lord Castlereagh will be satisfied with the two first
things I have submitted to the Conference. He will be
convinced by reading them that we are determined to
prove to the allied States what the Emperor understands
by federation, and to convince them as well as foreign
Powers that we do not wish to make any change either
in the bases of the Bund or in the application of those
bases. We recognise but one fundamental law, and
that law is the Federal Act itself. In the first of our
sittings I declared that the Emperor regarded this act
as so sacred that if by chance any fault of expression
should be found in the original copy, his Imperial Ma-

jesty would not allow it to be corrected. This declaration, and the fact of having approached the discussion on the most difficult side—by settling the legal functions of the Confederation—will ensure us the most complete success.

Lord Castlereagh has sometimes reproached me for not pushing things forward on certain occasions; I hope he will now change his opinion of me. I shall always be found very exact on positive questions, for they are the only ones for which I have any inclination.

378. *December* 17.— . . . . The progress of the German conferences could not be more satisfactory than it continues to be. The most complicated question, perhaps—namely, the interpretation of Article XIII. of the Federal Act—is almost terminated. A short but precise paper which I submitted to the Committee charged with the Report has been adopted eagerly and unanimously. All the corollaries which were to be drawn from it, in order to arrive at an agreement, were brought forward, debated, and settled in three sittings of this Committee; the Report was made by the Committee in a general sitting held yesterday, and adopted, except some amendments proposed by the too-zealous friends of the good cause. You see that, although we are here only as the representatives of Cabinets, we have also our *ultras*. I am myself sometimes accused of too great liberalism, when I am simply defending what is right, and above all what is possible and of real utility. But happier than Lord Castlereagh, the adversaries with whom I have to contend are men who wish only for what is good, though not always in a practicable way. It is not in my nature to yield to them.

OBJECT AND IMPORTANCE OF THE VIENNA
MINISTERIAL CONFERENCES.

379. Opening address by Prince Metternich.*

379. The Emperor has commanded me to open the conferences to which we are called, by making known his principles and wishes by a simple and sincere statement, such as becomes his Imperial Majesty at a time of so much importance for the country.

I believe I could not better fulfil the intentions of his Imperial Majesty than by placing before the representatives of the Governments of Germany the idea which has led to our present meeting.

The Confederation of the Bund was formed at the time of the foundation of the European system, for the protection of the internal and external peace of Germany; to offer to the nation as a whole the only possible centre of unity, and to guarantee the independence of each of the Federal States, both in regard to its neighbours forming part of the federation as well as of the federation towards the foreigner.

This Confederation formed by the sovereign princes, with whom were associated the four free towns of Germany, secured to the whole, and to each of its members in particular, whatever their means or their strength, a common and reciprocal pledge of preservation and pro-

* This speech was translated into French for communication to the foreign ambassadors. The German original cannot be found.—ED.

tection, an inestimable advantage, which could only be received with the most lively satisfaction on all hands. The importance of such a union established in the centre of Europe, and the salutary influence which it must exercise in the consolidation of the general peace, cannot be forgotten by those Courts who took part in the transactions of 1813 and 1814, and the Germanic federation was, from its birth, placed under the express and solemn guarantee of all the European Powers.

This federation had received its first fundamental laws by the Act which formed its basis. The Diet may commence its action; but the point is, after further deliberation to fix its functions, the extent of its jurisdiction, the limits of its powers, and even the forms to be followed in the most essential parts of its work. This deliberation, so necessary to complete and consolidate the edifice of which the Federal Act had only traced the chief outlines, should, according to the custom generally adopted, have taken place in the midst of the Diet itself. Obstacles of every kind have caused this important affair to be put off from time to time. This was the first opposition Germany has experienced since the foundation of the federal constitution.

An evil of a different nature, the efforts of which are not less perceptible, has been added to this first cause of stagnation : namely, the injurious influence of a revolutionary party in all the countries of Europe, whose alarming progress makes itself felt in more than one part of the Germanic Confederation ; a scourge destroying the basis of all social order, in the beginning restricting itself to a small number of individuals moved by discontent or by political fanaticism, but soon drawing after it whole generations, exciting the enthusiasm and raising the passions of the multitude by the abuse of a few sacred words, and the deceptive bait of philanthropic theories ; a contagious disease, misunderstood by many of the German Governments, while others have treated it with too much indulgence, and others again have applied useless remedies, which have only brought on new complications.

During the Emperor's last visit to Italy, many of the German Courts addressed confidential overtures to his Imperial Majesty, placing beyond a doubt what at last is beginning to be recognised everywhere—how necessary it is to take measures against a danger which every day becomes more formidable. All the enlightened men in Germany, who are sincerely attached to their country and to the maintenance of order, are filled with the same sentiments and share the same conviction.

Always disposed to devote his attention and his powers to the general good, his Majesty has not hesitated to accept the idea of a confidential agreement between those Courts, where the necessity of combating the evil has been most felt, and others, which by their situation are not so easily reached. His Imperial Majesty has nothing to fear for himself; he hopes that, under the protection of God, the calm and regular action of a well-established government will preserve his States from contagion. But it is not sufficient for the Emperor to see his throne and his people preserved from danger ; he desires to fulfil his duty towards his allies, as much as circumstances will allow. The candour and firmness which his Imperial Majesty has evinced in the first deliberations which have taken place on this subject, the zeal with which he has undertaken the most difficult part in this enterprise, are plainly shown by the proposals which he has caused to be made to the Diet.

Thanks to the glorious unanimity which characterised the conferences of Carlsbad, thanks to the support which the resolutions prepared in those conferences have received from the Diet from the time they were drawn up, a decided step has been taken towards a better state of things ; and, provided the Governments of Germany are all equally determined not to swerve from the path they have chosen, but to follow it, not only in the spirit of justice and wisdom which dictated the presidential proposals of September 20, but with that inflexible perseverance without which nothing great has ever been consummated, the greatest success must crown our efforts.

If the measures adopted by common agreement, and on the scrupulous execution of which his Imperial Majesty thinks he can reckon with entire confidence, justify the hope that the interior tranquillity of Germany will not be disturbed, that none of the pernicious plans which are the object of our just apprehension will be realised, we have still to get over another source of danger—namely, the want of exact definition in many essential points of our federal constitution.

This question was not broached at Carlsbad, except in some general and preliminary observations. But all opinions being agreed as to the necessity of treating it thoroughly, his Imperial Majesty proposed to devote some deliberations to it later on. This proposition was received on all sides with that spirit of concord and patriotism with which the conferences of Carlsbad were constantly animated ; and thus our present meeting was arranged—a decisive moment for the future destinies of the Germanic Confederation.

It seems to me not without use to consider for a few moments the reasons which have induced his Imperial

Majesty to propose this meeting. The Germanic Confederation of the Bund is an integral part of the political
system of Europe. All which at present forms the
public law of Germany is inseparably connected with
the covenant which forms the basis of this Confederation,
for not only the rights which it exercises in common,
but also the separate rights of sovereignty of each of
these States in particular, depend on this covenant. It
is no longer in our power to question the existence of
the Confederation; and it would be as contrary to the
interests as to the dignity of the Princes who have
taken part in it to allow it to languish in a state of
imperfection, condemning it to impotence and inaction.
A common duty, an indispensable duty, requires us, on
the contrary, to raise the federal union to that degree
of strength and perfection which, according to the intentions of i's founders, it should reach. The progress
made during the last three years is far from fulfilling
that intention.

His Majesty is persuaded that a delay so annoying
does not proceed from opposition to the aim of the federation; that the principal cause, if not the only one, is
to be found in the fluctuation of ideas, in the incorrect,
vague, and contradictory notions of the nature of the
federal covenant, and on the relations, rights and duties
connected with it.

To determine these notions, and to apply them in a
safe and precise manner to the different problems which
claim our attention—such is, in the opinion of his Im
perial Majesty, the principal object of the present
deliberations. Experience has shown how difficult it
was to arrive at satisfactory results by the discussions opened on this subject at Frankfurt, and it
is in the nature of things that direct explanations

between the Cabinets should far better advance this work. The Emperor is assuredly as far as any of his great allies from wishing to restrain the activity of the Diet, or from offering the slightest want of respect to an assembly the authority of which, on the contrary, all the members of the Confederation are interested in maintaining and strengthening.

But this assembly is composed of delegates proceeding in legal forms, and according to the instructions of their respective Governments, with the affairs on which they are called to treat. The extent and limits of their jurisdiction must therefore be fixed, and it is not the assembly itself which can or should be charged with fulfilling this condition.

When once the Governments which constitute the Confederation of the Bund shall be agreed on the fundamental principles of their union, and on the sense in which they should be applied to positive questions, the progress of the Diet will become safer and more easy, and this advantage will make itself felt in all branches of its transactions.

The President of the Diet has set forth in a separate proposition—forming one of those of September 20—different subjects of deliberation, about which the ambassadors have requested instructions from their Courts. The same subjects have been indicated in the letters of invitation addressed by the Cabinet of his Imperial Majesty to all the Governments of Germany, as those which are chiefly to occupy us in the present conferences. Many other important questions already submitted to the deliberations of the Diet, but which were left undecided, or only provisionally arranged, are connected with the above-mentioned subjects. All these matters, the discussion of which at the Diet must be prepared and facilitated by agreement between the plenipotentiaries of the federal Governments, are presented in the list annexed to this discourse.

His Imperial Majesty values too highly the preservation and the glory of the great political body of which he himself is one of the principal members not to have the sincerest wishes for the success of the conferences which are about to be opened. His Imperial Majesty has decided to communicate to that illustrious assembly, without reserve, his principles and views on all the points submitted to our deliberations. He indulges the hope that his confederates will see in this step a new proof of zeal for the general good, and for the closest union between all the Governments of Germany, that his example will be generally followed, and that everyone will acknowledge the value of an occasion, perhaps unique, for consulting all opinions, for dissipating all doubts, and for removing all obstacles. Thus we can take credit to ourselves for giving to the Germanic Confederation that perfection, that stability, and—what will be the infallible effect—that external consideration which rightfully attaches to the union of thirty millions of Germans, equal in rank and influence to the first European Powers, and, at the same time, to secure to each particular State that common guarantee against internal and external dangers which, according to the letter and spirit of the Federal Act, was the principal aim of this Confederation.

Prince Metternich's Second Address.

380. In my first discourse I had the honour to inform the Conference that his Majesty the Emperor considered the principal object of our meeting to be that of fixing definitely the meaning (too little understood up to this time) of our federal system, as well as the relations, rights and duties which belong to it, and to apply these notions to the different questions which we are called upon to resolve.

Before we proceed to this business I think it my duty to unfold some general principles, indicating the point of view from which the Emperor has constantly regarded the federation, and the sense in which he has associated himself with a system of which his Imperial Majesty was one of the founders, and to the maintenance of which he will never cease to devote his care.

I. In the pact of union concluded by the sovereign Princes and free cities of Germany, the sovereignty of each of the confederate States is placed under the direct guarantee of the rights of the people, and recognises no other limits than those required by the maintenance of German unity in relation to foreign Powers, and those resulting from common measures for the internal safety and tranquillity of the Confederation. It follows from this first principle that, in settling the prerogatives of the Confederation, there can, in any case, be no question of infringing the sovereign rights of those States which are members of the union—rights expressly guaranteed by the compact upon which this union rests ; his Imperial Majesty having, besides, the inward conviction that, placed in their true light, the engagements towards the federal body impose no real sacrifice on the sovereigns who have contracted them, that, notwithstanding these engagements, their rights of sovereignty remain intact, and that the federal union simply tends to secure to these rights an increase of strength and extent.

II. The Federal Act is the first fundamental law of the Union. No resolution, whether it has for its object the development of the principles of the federation, whether it bears on the interests of the whole, or whether it regards individual affairs, can be opposed to the dispositions of this Act.

Although by this declaration the inviolability of the Federal Act is recognised in the most positive manner, the confederate Governments do not the less preserve the power of interpreting and developing the fundamental law in such a way as seems most convenient to them. This reservation is stated in the text of the Federal Act itself, while Article X., in demanding supplementary laws, has made over to the Diet the drawing up of these laws. Now, experience and careful examination having taught us, as I observed in my first discourse, that it is in all respects better to assign this business to the direct deliberations of the Cabinets, it is evident that our present meeting is fully qualified to discuss the necessary regulations for completing the federal institutions, in order to arrive as soon as possible at satisfactory results on the above-mentioned conditions previous to any subsequent transactions.

III. The assembly which represents the Confederation (the Diet) is responsible to the political body which constituted it, just as the ambassadors at the Diet are responsible to their respective Governments. In a higher sense, each federal State is responsible to the federal body for the faithful accomplishment of obligations immediately connected with the fundamental pact, or which, in virtue of this pact, it has contracted by its consent to common resolutions.

IV. The resolutions of the Diet, given in legal form, being the result of the united wish of the Governments which form the Bund, and consequently obligatory on the whole and on each member of the federation, it follows that, for all the common business of the Bund, the supreme legislative power rests in the Diet.

This principle, incontestable in itself, leads us to the important question of defining those subjects which may be considered as the common business of the Bund. The elements for resolving this question are found either in the text of the Federal Act itself or in a simple and natural interpretation of its dispositions. But, the precise determination of the sphere of legal activity— or, as it was formerly called, of the competence of the Diet—is a task with which the present meeting must and ought to occupy itself; and his Imperial Majesty is of opinion that, both from the importance of the thing and on account of the facilities which will result from it for the whole of our labours, it would be well to give this question the priority in order. The question of competence being directly connected with that of votes in the transactions of the Diet, this question will make a natural transition to Article I. in the table of subjects for deliberation.*

* For the further progress of the Vienna Ministerial Conferences and their results see the documents Nos. 468 to 476.—ED.

EVENTS OF THE DAY, AND FAMILY LIFE.

1820.

Extracts from Metternich's private Correspondence from January 8 to May 15, 1820.

381. *Vienna, January* 8, 1820.—I have worked to-day like a galley slave ; the conferences have lasted quite fifteen hours. I cannot, however, complain of it, because our business goes on so well. Never perhaps have I found more unanimity, a better spirit or a better will. Poor Capo d'Istria has taken quite a wrong standpoint for his last circular.* Surely a man cannot avoid compromising himself when he informs people of the contrary of what they know, what they alone can know, and what cannot be judged of six hundred miles off.

* Apparently an allusion to some circular of Cape d'Istria's, by which Russia endeavoured to excite the smaller German Courts to withstand Metternich's claims.—ED.

. . . . How few are the statesmen who deserve the
name ; each one thinks he can meddle in affairs at a
moment when all ideas are confused, when nothing is
so rash as to form a judgment on the gravest and most
difficult affairs. It is the fate of those men who have
no principle and little knowledge to form a world
of their own and place events in it as they wish.
Theorisers of this kind see what does not exist, believe
the contrary of what is, and will not admit any truth
which conflicts with their hypotheses. But since there
is nothing more positive than fact, and nothing more
true than truth, these hypotheses go off like rockets,
which when once they have burst, do not equal even
the most feeble light which burns on undisturbed. And
truth remains truth in spite of all antagonists.

382. I have passed a strange night. A history of
the war of 1814, by Koch, has just appeared in Paris :
one of the best works which has yet been written on
that subject. Apart from some errors which an author
placed, as he is, outside the affairs can hardly escape, the
book contains much that is true. I took this book to
bed with me yesterday evening, and read it with the
greatest interest. To read the history of an important
epoch in which one has oneself played a prominent part
is a most curious thing. I found myself placed before
posterity, and felt called upon to judge myself. During
this three hours' reading I did not, indeed, feel inclined
to accuse myself; but how much could I have added to
every occurrence, to every page, indeed to every line of
the book. In matters of fact I have really an excellent
memory : I need only to replace myself in the situation
alluded to, and the whole circumstance and everything
connected with it comes clearly before my eyes. I
found the account of the violation of the Swiss frontiers

contained in eight or ten lines—one of the greatest
events at the beginning of that campaign, and one of
the very greatest influence on the result of the war.
The author is, indeed, right enough in attributing to me
alone the full use which was made of this event ; but
where he does not know, he romances. How is it possible to know so much and at the same time not to
know so much as the author !

On this occasion I learned what the will of one
man can do when boldness gives such a one the feeling
to do the right thing, and that a well-considered plan
carried out with vigour is sure of success. In regard
to this affair, I was at that time alone in my opposition
to the Emperor Alexander. I knew everything, both
his obligations and the enormous compromises which
might arise therefrom both to the cause and to myself if
I held fast to my conviction—to a conviction which included both the excellence of the plan and the happy
prospect of success. And see ! I have not deceived myself. The outbursts of anger have passed away, and the
good remains. This last is my reward. My reading
finished, I put out the light, and turned round to sleep.
He does not sleep, however, who wills to do so : I lay
there with 1814 in my head and in my heart—that year
with its blessings, its prodigious consequences, its gross
errors : all this took possession of my mind, and I could
not sleep till five in the morning. If I had had a secretary near me, I would have dictated some notes. This
was another historical night.

383. *January* 27.—To-day I hear everyone fum-
ing about a foolish laudation of me which has appeared
in the ' Moniteur.' What do people want ? From the
moment when a man steps on the stage he belongs to
the public, who have a perfect right to applaud or hiss,

and who make use of the right. If he who treads the stage does but possess a clear character and right feeling he will take both praise and blame as mere reminders that he is placed in the foreground ; his own head and his own heart must tell him whether he is right or wrong. The noise is nothing, the action everything.

To me undoubtedly, I openly allow, stupid blame is pleasanter than stupid praise : the first may amuse, but cannot anger me ; the latter, on the contrary, might make me treat my awkward friend somewhat rudely.

If anyone wishes to write my history, let him leave full freedom to the judgment of posterity, which alone can speak with authority of the men who have contributed to make the history of their time.

384. *February* 16.—I have returned to the world again * ; to-morrow evening I reopen my *salons*. Already I tremble at the prospect of the crowd of tiresome people whom I must receive. Nothing delights such people more than a death or a return to life, *i.e.* the opportunity of condoling or congratulating. If it were only possible that this cursed race would confine themselves to the first of these occasions, at least as far as concerns me ! To die is nothing : but to live for these people—that is worse to me than death !

385. *February* 17.—Here we have snow ankle-deep. The winter seems as if it would never have done, which is dreadful to me, for I have my garden, and therefore need spring and air and sun. Talking of the sun, you have no idea how beautiful my rooms are when the sun shines. They lie to the south, and are therefore pleasant and warm, and I can hardly guard my furniture from its beams. I have a spacious ante-room, a large room where the people who want to see me wait.

---

* The Prince had been ill for twelve days.—ED.

This opens into my library, which is a splendid room. It is filled quite up to the ceiling with books in fine open mahogany shelves. As it is about eighteen feet high, my library must contain nearly 15,000 volumes, though it does not look as if there were so many. In the middle of the room is Canova's beautiful Venus, whose pedestal is surrounded by a circular settee. Then comes my study, a fine large room with three windows; in this are three great writing-tables. I like to change my place, and I do not like to be disturbed at my desk by anyone else writing at the same table. This room is full of works of art, pictures, busts, bronzes, astronomical clocks, and all kinds of instruments. For to science I gladly dedicate my few hours of leisure, and these hours, if lost for business, are a gain for life. The large table in my bedroom is covered with portfolios of engravings, maps, and drawings; besides which I have a considerable collection of works of art arranged under glass. I am often amused at the distraction of strangers, who have to make out their visit amid such a varied collection of things.

In this treasury I pass seven-eighths of my time. Why should I not surround myself with all these objects so dear to me? I live unwillingly in small rooms, and still more unwillingly work in them. In a contracted space the mind contracts, the thoughts hide themselves, and even the heart grows withered.

When my children are good their mother, as a reward, brings them to pay me a short visit. I cannot flatter myself that the children come so gladly from love to me. It seems to them just like a market, for my rooms are very similar to shops. There is no artist in Vienna, nor any artist who comes here, who does not send his works to me. There are always easels standing about with new pictures, new engravings, new drawings, which the worthy artists gladly send to me because I see and receive so many people.

Whenever I have a grand ball my library must be used, and several round tables are placed there, on which covers can be laid altogether for thirty-two. The difficulty then is the Venus, who is in this arrangement somewhat embarrassing. The statue is indeed of the most scrupulous propriety in front, which cannot perhaps so well be said of the back view.

386. *February* 18.—The Emperor is going to send the Prince of Hesse to London with his congratulations to the new King. This is in every respect an excellent choice. His first adjutant is Count Lato Wrbna, one of our most fashionable young men, and a good fellow too, whom for his improvement I lately sent to Brazil, where he went through some remarkable adventures. On board a pirate ship a young and very pretty Spanish lady wanted to have him hanged ; she implored on her knees that they would fasten him upon the great mast, because she had never seen this proceeding, and Count Wrbna seemed to her to be the most splendid model for it. What can the women all have in their heads? Their fancies are unfathomable !

387. *February* 20.—I have just heard of the assassination of the Duc de Berry. Liberalism goes its way ; it rains murders ; there have been already four Sands in nine months.

All is lost in France if the Government does not turn round. Those who are deluded by the ruffians are indeed children, but the criminals are no children. I know the element of intrigue which the Government has now taken up, in the delusion that it would be an element of strength. That is certainly the strength of a wild animal, that will never allow itself to be civilised. It must be admitted that this is not a pleasant moment for a minister.

388. *February* 25.—I really hunger and thirst for my garden on the Rennweg ; for a whole long month I have not been able to pay it a visit. My room is full of the most beautiful flowers from my conservatories, but that is not the one thing which charms me. I long for air and sunshine. I am a child of light, and need brilliant light to be able to live. People who are really bad have no such need.

389. *March* 16.—I have the gravest fears for my poor Clementine. She has now for the third time an attack of fever. She had the first on January 22, the second on February 20, and now she is again attacked with severe fever. She is in such a state of exhaustion that it is impossible to see how she is to get over it. I cannot see a being so dear to me suffer. Clementine is, besides, so good a child, and so attached to me that she will have me constantly near her bed. Since her illness she has grown four inches. In December she was still small : now she is quite tall. Although she is fifteen, she is still quite a child. I have a kind of superstition which experience has unhappily strengthened in me. The extraordinary is always attended with more dangers than the ordinary. Clementine, for instance, is remarkably pretty ; it must really be so, for when she goes out the people gather round her. I would rather she were a child of more common appearance, for such children grow like weeds. I have to-day summoned eight *ma-tadores* of the faculty to a consultation—I myself being present—and all the physicians were of the same opinion. To my heavy heart is added the severe task that is laid upon me. Our great work approaches its end. The complete confidence of my fellow-workers is beneficial, but burdensome. Amid all the confusion Capo d'Istria continually whispers in my ear. He reminds me of a musical amateur who practises on the bugle in the next room. He blows extremely hard without ever getting a tune. His expenditure of breath is enormous, but nothing good comes of it. All is wrong—wrong time, wrong notes, wrong key; *piano* tones where *forte* are necessary; *sostenuto* where it should be *con brio; largo* in the quickest time, with *obbligato* accompaniments. If there is really any sense in it, I have none. With such sense as that, France will come to a 1789 or a February 13. Good heavens, why is it that so many fools are thoroughly good men, as is the case with Capo d'Istria? If they were not, some way would be found of making them harmless; but as it is they must be heard, and they and their nonsense must be admitted to the debates.

390. *March* 22.—My poor Clementine is still very ill. Nothing breaks me down like a sick child; never anxious about myself, I am always so for the children. There are, indeed, no new bad symptoms, but I hold that in itself the long continuance of the fever is very serious.

Meanwhile, whether I like it or not, I must sit for many hours at my writing-table. In painful moments like the present it is more than ever necessary to turn my second nature outside—that nature which makes many people believe that I have no heart. They would deny me a head, too, if I did not occasionally let them know that it remains firm when they knock at it.

My news of the Emperor Alexander shows that people where he is are aware that phrases ruin the world, but save no one.

391. I am still thoroughly miserable. My daughter, indeed, is a little better, but has still so many hills to

climb before level country is reached that a father cannot feel easy. My only hope is in God, who knows better than we poor men what is right and good. I go from my writing-table to the sick bed, and back again. If my heart is restless, so are also my nights, which never happens to me when my head only is in question : a proof what a quite different power the heart has—just that heart which is denied me by the crowd.

392. *March* 30.—My poor Clementine's condition improves very slowly. He who has children himself knows what anxiety is caused by a sick child. It is not enough for me to know that those I love are happy. I want them also to be prosperous. Heaven, if it sees fit, will protect them.

In a position like mine, in which one is smothered with business for twelve hours every day, it is a real happiness to spend some leisure moments in the family circle. If then received by the children with joy, the whole world takes a different colour. In my family circle it is unhappily to-day most gloomy, and I go from the Revolutionists and Demagogues who people my study, to find care and sorrow in the sick room.

393. *April* 2.—The doctors are more cheerful ; they think I should smile, which the father's heart cannot yet succeed in.

I am finishing the building of my garden house ; it only wants the last touches, it will be quite a museum of works of art. The fine arts are indeed good friends ; they are always to be found ; their company always delights, and their *cultus* never leads to disappointment.

Lawrence, whom I expected, unhappily cannot come to Vienna. He is a man full of mind and heart, and I am vain enough to believe that he likes me. I wrote to him yesterday that he is made a member of the Academy here. He may perhaps attribute less value to this nomination than to the circumstance that I have obtained it for him.

394. *April* 8.—My daughter's fate still seems doubtful. For me, alas! it is already decided. If she remains with me, I shall take it as a gift from Heaven. From earthly help I expect nothing more. It is her age which makes me most anxious. For the last eight days she has not grown worse, but neither has she improved. No one can imagine how miserable this state of things makes me. The happiness of my life consists of such simple elements that at least these might be left to me.

395. *April* 10.—Society, like nature and like man, has adopted laws of its own. Old institutions are like old men, they will never be young again; but the moderns must go through their young time of lawlessness and folly. Man cannot make a constitution properly speaking : that is made only by time. Just as little is a Charta a constitution as the marriage contract is the marriage. Let people write as much as they like—and the less will always be the better—and yet you will have nothing in your hand but a sheet of paper. England alone has a Constitution, of which the Magna Charta is but a subordinate element. The English Constitution is the work of centuries, and, moreover, streams of blood and anarchy of every kind supplied the means. Social order ever progresses in this way ; it cannot be otherwise, since it is the law of nature. What is called a constitution to-day is nothing but ' *ôtez-vous de là que je m'y mette.*' What in quiet times disappears like foam, is lashed by the tempest into great waves, and the moral like the material world has its storms. If it be asked whether the revolution will flood the whole of Europe, I cannot wager against it, but of this I am determined, that I will fight against it till my latest breath.

The 'History of Cromwell,' by Villemain, has appeared in Paris : a good book which the author has flung into a world haunted everywhere by Cromwell. Political madness, religious madness, is seen in all classes of society and in the army ; usurpation, democracy, despotism, or weakness in the Government ; a low state of feeling in men ; brilliant surfaces and decaying bodies ; lastly, a general relaxation—these are always the first symptoms at all times and in all places, of the return to order. The dead speak no more, but their sons return ever and anon to their frenzies, the names of which, indeed, are altered. They call them Reason, and give to the new discovery of old errors the name of the Society of Man.

396. *April* 11.—The invalid is in the same condition ; fresh medical consultations only amuse us with hope for the future. Nothing pleases me, for happiness is not without us, but within.

My garden house is gay, but I am sad. Great beds of hyacinths and narcissuses diffuse their fragrance far and wide ; to me they all seem withered. It is best for me to be at my writing-table, because there I am obliged to think of something else. Capo d'Istria still gives me some trouble ; but he does not catch me. I begin to know the world well, and I believe that the flies are only eaten up by the spiders because they die naturally so young that they have no time to gain experience and do not know what is the nature of the spider's web. My axiom is all the more correct, because it is impartial, for the real spiders interest me. I very often watch them, they are the best barometers, and, their ugliness apart, they are quite dear little animals always busy, arranging their dwellings in the neatest manner.

397. *April* 13.—I have this day undertaken to read through the copy of our conferences. This great and important work will be concluded in spite of the joy which all Radicals would have felt if it had been otherwise ; it is a legislative work of the very highest order.*

398. *April* 19.—I still lead a quite wonderful life ; I am everywhere and nowhere. I have estates which I have never seen, and among them some which I hear travellers describe as paradise. Among others a castle on the lake of Constance, which commands the whole lake and gives a panorama of Switzerland. I have only once staid a night at the castle, and then I arrived at eight in the evening and had to leave again at four in the morning ; for a courier who arrived during the night urged me not to lose a moment. If only Heaven had given me for some consolation the smallest portion of that ambition which finds an enjoyment on the most trifling occasion which it never offers to me ! Ambition I have, but it is of so grave a kind that its enjoyments are like those of virtue. My ambition is to do well what I have to do, and to combat evil wherever I find it. It is just this circumstance which gives me so cold a tinge, which comes not simply from patience but rather from perseverance. To me it is really nothing to work ; titles and so-called honours are indifferent to me. I am much more loaded with them than I desire, and if they were taken away, I should hardly remark it. Posterity will judge me—the only judgment which I covet, the only one to which I am not indifferent, and which I shall never know.

399. *April* 20.—Many people would be delighted

* See No. 476.—Ed.

to make their entry in a Roman car of triumph amid the noisy shouts of some thousand bawlers. I do not care for triumphal cars or cries; the shouts of the mob are worth nothing. Rejoicings are only worth anything when the angels smile and evil spirits flee. A man must be like me, born and brought up amid the storm of politics, to know what is the precise meaning of a shout of triumph like those which now burst forth from Burdett and Co. He may have read of it, but I have seen it with my eyes. I have lived at the same time as the Federation of 1789. I was fifteen, and already a man. The most beautiful sun beamed on a hundred thousand enthusiasts who all believed in the dawn of the Golden Age. I was under a tutor who in the year 1793 was an intimate friend of Robespierre, and on August 10 presided over the Committee of Marseillese; this tutor was the best man in the world; he wept for joy, and filled the whole world with his love and his philanthropy. I was his scholar, but, nevertheless, my heart was absorbed in misery.

400. Clementine's condition seems to be something better, but if all goes well her restoration will yet be a work of time. But this long time is dearer to me than the moment when I must give her up entirely. She is a quiet, good child. The day before yesterday she said to me that she had the feeling of coming back to life again, and was greatly delighted, because she would now have all the longer time to show me how much she was attached to me. It seems that the leech which was lately put on her throat gave much relief. An inflammatory complaint which has now lasted three months is indeed severe. Unhappily, she feels very much the return of cold weather; she is quite benumbed with it.

401. *April* 29.—The improvement was, alas! of

short duration. The inflammation returned next day, and in a few hours it took the form of severe inflammation of the lungs. On three successive days she had to be bled. This excessive loss of blood after an illness of three months must weaken her dreadfully, so that we can no longer hope to save her. There are cases where the remedy seems worse than the disease itself.

402. Clementine's condition grows still more serious; it is now evident that this last inflammation has attacked her lungs most severely. To-day she was so ill that the physicians expected her end. In the course of the afternoon she had sat up for some moments. She then went back so that four-and-twenty hours afterwards she lay in a deathlike stupor.

Yesterday the portrait of Clementine, by Lawrence, arrived from Florence. I intended to leave the box for a month unopened. Clementine, during her lethargy, must have heard us speak of it. The first conscious words she said to me were to ask me to unpack the picture and show it to her. I allowed it to be brought. She smiled at the picture, and said : ' Lawrence seems to have painted me in heaven, for he has surrounded me with clouds !' She wished to have the portrait placed upon her bed. This, however, we could not do —life and death cannot be placed so close together.

To-day Clementine performed her devotions. For several days she had imploringly begged to do so. She seems not to have the least fear of death. She is perfectly calm.

Worn as I am with this agitation, I have still to go through long conferences. Yesterday I had one of the plenipotentiaries with me in my room when they brought me word that the physicians had assembled, and were waiting for me in the sick room. When I got up to go, my visitor said to me : ' Pardon me, allow me to draw your attention to some of the Rhine tolls ! ' I assured him that I must go, though the Rhine should flow back to its source ! The man stood there quite confounded, and I left him with astonishment on his face that anyone should do business in that way. But my first business is the preservation of my happiness— a business which, indeed, I do not often follow.

403. Elegies do not belong to my character. I cannot lament. Heaven has doomed me to suffer in silence.

Clementine gets rapidly worse ; her departure may take place any day. She does not suffer—indeed, that follows from the nature of her illness, which is, nevertheless, very severe. Feeling and duty chain me to her bed. I suffer more than she does. She is generally unconscious, and her dreams are sweet but they are all among the fields where in imagination she is wandering. To-day she had herself turned round in bed. To my question why she did so, she replied : ' I do not want always to see the same things ; ' but added immediately, ' Look at that bed [a second bed had been placed in the room, to make a change for her] ; is it not extraordinary that they give me a stone bed ? ' I replied that she was mistaken : that the second bed was hung with muslin. ' Stone or muslin,' said she, ' both are alike to me ; both are white, and that pleases me.' Her presentiments guide her more correctly than her reason. I do not believe that she can last more than three days. Her face is quite disfigured, and Lawrence himself would not know her. Her features are only to be recognised if she smiles ; but this smile comes from a heavenly rather than an earthly being.

404. *May* 11.—Our worst fears were realised on the 6th. At half-past nine on the evening of the 5th my wife called me. Clementine was greatly distressed. I hurried to her, and I had only to look at her and feel her pulse to know that her dissolution was at hand. In spite of every remedy she became worse and worse, so that at one moment I thought she was gone. It was but a swoon, from which she revived and regained her full consciousness. She asked for her confessor, and at midnight breathed her last gently and calmly as she always was in life. I learn from her confessor that she had expected her death for the last fortnight, and only the fear of grieving us gave her strength enough to show the greatest calmness with respect to her state. After her last attack she implored that she might receive the sacrament, under the pretext that it was Eastertide. Her confessor, who had also been her tutor for ten years, gave her some excellent counsel respecting her future; but she answered very quietly, with a smile, ' What you say is beautiful and good, but it is nothing to me: my future is not here below !' Thus died the innocent, who has now no remembrances and no pain. The next morning I took my wife to my daughter Marie, where I stayed two days. Business called me back, and I have despatched it as one might empty a cup of poison.

405. *May* 12.—I am still here alone. My wife and my son are with Marie. I work and think of my misfortune. A most beautiful being has been snatched from the world. There is in society here a lady who is very like my daughter ; when I met her yesterday I was overcome with tears.

I can truly say that I have a certain anxiety about all very lovely girls. The cause of their beauty is mostly the cause of their death. Too great delicacy in the features, a quite transparent skin, a certain blending in the figure, are all proofs of an extremely tender organism. A climate like ours acts on such a one like the north wind on the flowers of spring. I have, happily, the gift of keeping my feelings to myself, even when my heart is half broken. Of this I have given certain proof during the last months. The thirty men with whom I sit daily at the conference table have certainly never guessed what I was going through while I talked for three or four hours, and dictated hundreds of pages.

406. *May* 15.—On this day in the year 1773, precisely at twelve o'clock, I was presented to the world. On the same day, forty-seven years afterwards, I have signed the final act of our conferences. We sat together the whole day yesterday, and we might have come to an end then if my colleagues — or, rather, my children—had not wished to celebrate my birthday by the conclusion of our work.

Seven-and-forty years is a long time, quite too long. I have, in this weary life, thank God, preserved that strong vitality of heart which is a preservative against the passing away of any feeling. At twenty I was the same man I am to-day. I was always what I am, good or bad, strong or weak.

407. *May* 16.—The family circle has assembled again. My wife does not leave the room in which my daughter died. She has collected around her everything which belonged to her. I cannot enter the room without tears, and I soon return to my business, which makes a barrier between me and myself.

EXCURSION INTO BOHEMIA AND COBURG.

Extracts from Metternich's private Correspondence from May 27 to July 9, 1820.

408. *Prague, May* 27, 1820.—I live here at the Palais Fürstenberg, the same Prince who married a Princess of Baden last year. He is having his house put in order, to settle here next August with his young wife. If the Prince comes, and is not beside himself with anger, he must be the most tasteless man that ever existed. His steward received me yesterday, and conducted me through an immense suite of rooms. When I saw the way they were decorated I did not know how to keep my countenance. Wherever the hand of the artist or artisan was busy, sculptures, pictures, furniture, hangings, and other works stare at the spectator like the phantasmagoria of a fever dream. The great chairs in the chief saloon of black polished wood stand on four gilded eagles' claws, and at their backs, in the form of a shield, are different arrangements of cupids

and eagles in gilded wood. The furniture is of blue
damask, ornamented with white muslin in great bunches,
and edged with gold and silver, intermixed with green
and red colours. All the rooms are alike. The two
beds in the principal bedroom are hung with what
represents shell-work and rock-work—on which are
squirrels (as thick as your fist), toads, and bats of gilded
wood—and stand in an alcove, at the entrance of
which hangs a lamp in the shape of a colossal owl,
which draws a globe out of the satin hangings; if the
globe is covered the light shines from the eyes of the
owl. This horrible steward wished to hear my opinion
of all these arrangements. I asked him whether his
master had sent him the designs for everything. He
assured me, with an expression of the greatest self-satis-
faction, that this was not the case—he and the upholsterer
had prepared all these things as surprises for the good
Prince. 'How delighted the Prince will be,' said he,
'when he learns that all these beautiful things have only
cost 80,000 gulden.'

The steward wished me to sleep opposite this owl.
I assured him that I could not be the first to desecrate
their Excellencies' marriage-bed, and betook myself to
a room at the back, in which there were neither owls
nor cupids. Hardly was I left alone in this room when
a clock began to strike which made as much noise as a
church bell. I got up to seek for the clock, but in
vain. At last I found a small picture, representing a village with a church, on the tower of which was
a clock, which struck so loudly that it could be heard
four houses off. As I did not wish to lose my night's
rest, I had the unlucky picture taken down and put
away. I lay down, when just at midnight a flute began
to play quite close to my bed. Looking about, I found

it was my night-table which made this noise. After long search I found a knob, by pressing which the musical box close to my ear was temporarily silenced; but from time to time it repeated its efforts to go off again, sounding something like suppressed groans. This morning, early, I sent for the steward and begged him to take away this piece of furniture, as I did not like to hear music at such unusual hours. ' It is the *somno*,' answered the good man, ' which I had made for the Princess; the Prince's night-table contains a trumpet.' ' Good heavens!' I cried, ' then do not their Excellencies sleep at all?' ' O yes,' answered the steward; ' but young married people are easily tired, and that makes them sleep : besides, the music can be stopped.' ' But why,' asked I,' should there be any music to be stopped?' ' Well now,' answered he, with a self-satisfied air, ' all sorts of pleasant things may happen to the Prince, and then he has always a trumpet ready.' This is all like a dream; but I would not advise any lady to have a *somno* that plays like a flute, or to allow her husband a hidden trumpet. Such amusements would wake up the whole neighbourhood.

I hope to sleep well to-night, for I have had the noisy contrivances one and all removed, to the great anger of the steward. I am certain the poor man despised me heartily for my stupidity and bad taste.

409. *May* 28.—The marriage of the Archduke Rainer with the Princess of Carignan took place to-day. The bride is very lovely. Although she is half a head taller than I am, she has a pretty figure. Her head is particularly fine, her eyes long and tender, her nose small and finely cut, the well-formed mouth conceals the most beautiful teeth I have ever seen; yet, in spite of all these beauties, I cannot think so large a woman charming.

410. *May* 31.—The memorable epochs at which I have visited this town followed quickly upon one another. In the year 1812 I spent two months here with the Empress of the French, and in 1813 gave her husband his death-blow.

Yet, what to me is all that has rushed through my head and flowed from my pen during my public life? My life may be unpleasant for me to experience, but my biography will certainly not be tedious. Especially interesting must be the years which I have passed with Napoleon as if we were playing a game of chess, and during which the object of both was—I to checkmate him, and he to surround me with all his pieces. These fifteen years seem to me to have passed like a moment of time.

411. *June* 1.—This day seven years ago I left Vienna to accompany the Emperor, when he went to place himself at the head of the troops assembled in Bohemia At that very time I found Nesselrode on his travels in a small town; he thought we were quietly in Vienna. I gave him a despatch for the Emperor Alexander, which was so short that I still remember every word of it. It ran thus: 'Your Majesty, we are there; patience and confidence! In three days I will see you, and in six weeks we shall be your allies.'

Confidence did not exist then, but came after a time, and was justified. The patience could not be wanting, because we were quite determined not to move a step more quickly.

412. *Theresienstadt, June* 7.—I have spent half a day at a very beautiful estate. The whole country as far as Weltrus * is adorned by nature. The park is worthy of England.

Often when I have happened to visit a hospitable

* An estate belonging to Count Chotek.—ED.

domain which, far from the world, is removed from all the whirl of diplomacy, I feel like a prisoner who discovers a sunbeam. This light is not for me ; I know that it is only shown to me in order to put me back in my dark cell, and yet my heart is agitated and dreams of a happiness with which I am not permitted to enchain myself. I am certainly one of the men least accessible to ambition, and most accessible to happiness. Wherefore has fate entangled me in a labyrinth which never leads to happiness? We have a saint who attained to heaven because he stood on a column for I know not how many years on one foot. I, though I stand on two feet, may yet compare myself to St. Simon Stylites. His service was an uncomfortable position—mine is not better. He was patient, and I, too, have given many proofs of that virtue. But yet I fear that I shall not attain to heaven, for I have moments of such impatience that in a second I annul the service of many years. The legend asserts that the saint was never impatient, and that made his colleagues despair.

413. *Carlsbad, June* 11.—Here I am again in the Carlsbad so much decried by the Radicals of Germany during the last few years. The night before last I slept at Teplitz, at Prince Clary's ; and last night in Schönhof, a *Schloss* belonging to Count Czernin. According to all accounts, this is a good and honourable man, but notoriously very ugly. Prince Louis Rohan called him for several years ' ambassador from the dead,' a name which has clung to him ever since.

414. *Königswart.*—I came here two years ago to visit the grave of my father. Who could then have thought that I should so soon return to pray by the grave of a child then overflowing with youth, beauty, and happiness ! One of my friends has sent me the follow-

ing verse, freely translated from Ossian :—' Rest softly,
lovely beam. Early didst thou sink behind the mountain, and dreadful was thy departure. Like the moon
on the blue trembling waves. In darkness hast thou
left us, O first of maidens, come back ! '

No one must think that the last line expresses the
feeling of the poor child ; she was simple, like all true
beauty, and had no suspicion that she was more noticeable than any of her friends. How often has she said
to me, when the passers-by stopped to look at her, ' The
people can never have seen a hat like mine : ' or she
looked herself over to see if there was not something
wrong with her toilet. She always thought others more
beautiful than herself; and I saw once that she envied
a little ill-shaped girl her head.

I am certain that Lawrence grieves for her, not on
account of her beauty, for he has painted others still
more beautiful, but because he likes me, and knows
what I feel. Lawrence is a very good man ; he has
plenty of sense, which a man must have to be really
good.

It rains here again, as it always does. As I want to
build, I have sent for my architect, Nobile.

415. *June* 14.—The most necessary article here is
an umbrella. Vegetation thrives with this weather ; the
trees and meadows are wonderfully green.

I had hoped to have eight or ten days here without
being obliged to work, but I found to my horror four
couriers assembled here from all corners of the world.
The enjoyment of retirement is evidently not to be expected by me. I have spent the whole day in writing,
and it is now striking midnight. Of all my dependents,
surely no one is awake longer than I am.

416. *June* 15.—Since my last arrival here I have

established two manufactories of earthenware, which look very modest, but are all the more useful. In one they make jugs for the Marienbad waters ; in the other, earthen pots for the Bohemian cooks. The object of both is to burn up some thousand stacks of wood which would otherwise rot to pieces in the forests. Nothing is more difficult than to promote the interests both of the wood and of my person, and if the former is transformed into pots, I am afraid the same thing may happen to me also.

I do not wish, moreover, anyone to pay me the same compliment which one of her ladies once paid to our Emperor's second wife. The Empress was near her seventh or eighth confinement, and expressed her dread of it ; the lady wished to reassure her. 'But,' said the Empress, 'the pitcher goes to the well till it breaks.' 'But your Majesty forgets,' returned the lady, 'what a very superior kind of pitcher your Majesty is.' There are different kinds of pitchers, it is true, but I know of none which do not break at last ; and I fear that the same lot which I prepare for them will happen to myself.

417. *June* 16.—Queen Caroline has arrived in Dover, and was drawn by the hands of the people from Dover to Canterbury. This does not astonish me ; a virtuous Queen, worthy of the crown, would in all probability be bespattered with mud by the people ; *she* of course must be drawn in triumph.

418. I am making a thorough course of mineral waters, of which I have twenty-two on the estate. I have had public baths built at one place, where there are three excellent but different springs close together.

This is the feast of St. Antonius, which is very ceremoniously solemnised in my private chapel. There is

hardly any place in Bohemia where there is not a full
orchestra and good chorus and solo singers. At the mass
to-day my orchestra surprised me with a *Gloria* which
was sung to the air ' *Ombra adorata*,' in which the first
singer was accompanied with trumpets and kettledrums.
The Latin Paternoster was ornamented with *roulades*,
whereby the words became most absurd, as, for instance,
' *Da nobis papanem papanem, nem pa nem, pa pa.*'
Certainly there could not be a child in the church who
would not be convinced that he understood Latin. The
melody pleased the peasants greatly.

419. *June* 21.—To-day arrived an excellent and
pleasant companion, Prince Schönburg, an enthusiastic
sportsman and gay young fellow—a very agreeable
guest in a lonely house.

My plans for rebuilding the house are ready. My
Schloss consists of a centre and two wings, of which one
is only half-ready. When the whole is finished I shall
be able to house thirty persons comfortably.

420. *June* 29.—I have for some time decided to
build a new vault. The old vault, where my ancestors
and my poor daughter are buried, is badly placed. I
have found a suitable spot for the building itself. I
wrote to you some months ago of the destruction of a
Schloss and a village by fire. Now, instead of rebuilding there a residence for the living, I will make a resting-
place for the departed—for me and mine. A mausoleum
shall be erected to which there shall be no second in
Bohemia, and perhaps not in Europe. I like everything
which defies time. I will therefore make an Egyptian
monument—not, indeed, a pyramid, but a chapel with a
vault in the Egyptian style, the only style which resists
time and age. There is plenty of material lying on the
spot itself; I only need to lay one stone upon another.

There shall not be a bit of wood in the whole monument, which shall be placed in a garden on a mound sixty feet high.*

421. *Rosenau, July 2.*—I left my place on the 3rd, and stayed a night on the way, so as not to reach Coburg too early. The lodging was very bad, which, however, did not signify to me much, for I always take with me my bed and my cook.

Yesterday, at noon, I entered Coburg, and was surprised by all the doubtful pleasures of a strict etiquette. Marshals, chamberlains, pages, &c., awaited me when I alighted from the carriage. I was conducted to my abode like the Holy Father in the procession of Corpus Christi. Visit of the Duke, return visit, visit to the Duchess, to the Dowager Duchess, to the Duchess's sister (Duchess A. von Wurtemberg), then a great dinner, and a greater Court, a great concert and a great supper. My sleeping time only was small enough to enchant me. To-day we shall leave the capital and establish ourselves in the country; etiquette, happily, will remain behind. Rosenheim is a very small *Schloss*; we are only five here: the Duke, the Duchess and a cousin of hers, one of my gentlemen and I. The neighbourhood is charming, the park is six miles round, and is well laid out; I have seldom seen anything prettier or more convenient. In the evening the people had a festival, at which all but I danced with the peasants. I could only escape from dancing with a pretty villager by the story that I had a gun-shot in the calf of my left leg.

422. *July 4.*—The Duke himself shows me about his territory. I find it, not a great, but a very beautiful country.

---

* Schloss Miltigau, burnt in 1820, seems to be alluded to. The family vault was built subsequently (1828).—ED.

The Duke is having his *Schloss* at Coburg rebuilt in the Gothic style. It will be very fine, but very costly, and he will devote to it the third part of his income.

As etiquette is banished, I enjoy my present life very well. Besides I have not touched a pen for three days, which makes me quite happy.

423. *July 5.*—Yesterday the Duke's architect showed me the plans for the new *Schloss*. The man has much talent; his plans are excellent. If the Duke carries them out, it will be an edifice of magnificent dimensions.

The London news makes me quite unhappy. This Queen is really a horrible woman. If people knew what I know about her, they would be surprised at her audacity; and yet there is no cause for surprise when one reflects how many people are taken in by it.

424. *Franzensbad.*—Yesterday, after breakfasting with the Dowager-Duchess, I left Coburg, and was awaited here impatiently by my gentlemen and four couriers. This was the punishment for four days' freedom. The courier from St. Petersburg brings me the news that the Emperor Alexander is somewhat more satisfied with me. I am always pleased when I observe that with time reason ever triumphs over unreason. I have gained a victory over Capo d'Istria, and therefore he does not talk to me any more. The book of the Apocalypse appears for the moment to be closed, and as John preaches no more, he must be in the wilderness. How easily would things go on in this world if everyone would but move in the direction in which their noses lead them. This sometimes apparently useless part of the body seems to have been given to us by the Creator only for the purpose of showing us the way in which we ought to go, as you see sign-posts set up to point out the right road to travellers. These roads are always straight unless there is a pit or a swamp to be avoided.

425. *Carlsbad, July* 9.—The Queen's trial in London a heap of dirt which one cannot touch without defiling oneself. Wellington is quite right, but if I had seen the Prince Regent a year ago, everything would have been prevented. Castlereagh and Co. have not behaved cleverly. Two years ago I could have put them in a position to manage matters differently. Alarm and want of quickness have brought them into a position from which they will not easily emerge.

I gather that this shameful trial makes a shocking impression in England. What would it be if people knew the circumstances more exactly? No English mothers can allow their daughters to read the newspapers for a long time to come.

OUTBREAK OF THE NEAPOLITAN REVOLUTION AND OTHER EVENTS OF THE DAY.

Extracts from Metternich's private Letters from July 17 to October 16, 1820.

426. *Weinzierl, July* 19, 1820.—Since yesterday I have been at the Imperial Schloss. At eleven I left Carlsbad, arrived at Vienna on the 13th, and on the 14th went to my people at Baden, where, however, I could only stay one night. On the 15th, I was summoned back to Vienna by the news of the Neapolitan catastrophe. On the 16th I came here to the Emperor.

In Baden I have much to go through. For three or four months Marie has been unwell : all the symptoms of pregnancy were present. These symptoms disappeared and were replaced by the dreadful certainty of a serious malady. I think her fearfully altered, so worn, so weak, that I have no hope for her. In less than two months I shall have lost two daughters Heaven sends me hard trials ; I submit to its decrees, and I hope they will be imputed to me in a better world.

The Neapolitan event is beyond all calculation ; the consequences will be quickly seen, the remedies must not be long waited for. Are any of these to be depended upon ? I do not yet know, but I shall not be the last to put myself in the breach. Fate has made it easy for me—that is, fate will soon have left me so few ties to bind me to earth that it will be but a small service to put forth all my strength of mind and heart.

This event must make a deep impression on the Emperor Alexander, all the more as the rebels boast of his countenance. Since 1815, Italy has been flooded with Russians, who always were thought to spread the false idea that every so called liberal movement would find a protector in their Emperor. Here is the first movement : two squadrons of cavalry overturn a throne, and throw all the world into inexpressible troubles. It will not go in Naples as it did at Madrid. Blood will flow in streams. A semi-barbarous people, of absolute ignorance and boundless credulity, hot-blooded as the Africans, a people who can neither read nor write, whose last word is the dagger—such a people offers fine material for constitutional principles !

To-morrow I shall remain here, and on the 19th go back to Vienna, where I shall divide my time between the capital and Baden. In Vienna I expect hard work, in Baden severe sorrow.

427. *Vienna, July* 25.—On the 16th I left my daughter : on the 20th she was no more ! I received this dreadful news at the last post before Vienna. I found my wife and children at home, having just returned from Baden. My daughter departed this life at eight in the morning ; her death was like her life,

gentle and calm, as the entrance of a spirit into its true home should be.

My son-in-law remains behind by the body of his wife ; so great was his despair that he was obliged to be watched. In the afternoon he came here and watered my knees with his tears. He was harassed with the thought that I should not forgive him for this misfortune—he who had given up everything to make happy the being whom he loved so supremely. My grief is that of a man on whom great duties are still imposed. I must forget that I am a father—must silence all that nature itself finds it so difficult to overcome. I throw myself into my task like a desperate man on the enemies' batteries. I no longer live to feel, but to act. The burden which Providence lays upon me is very heavy, and would crush many men. As I loved this daughter, she on her side loved me more than as a father. For many years she has been my best friend. I had no need to confide my thoughts to her : she divined them. She knew me better than I knew myself. She had never a thought which did not become mine, never spoke a word which in her place I would not have said. I was constantly impelled to thank her, that she was what she was. I have sustained an irreparable loss. The only blessing is that I feel myself but lightly bound to earth. My daughter would have died at my death ; I do not die at hers. She was therefore better than I am.

In such a mood of mind the world weighs upon my shoulders with all the important matters it has of late heaped up. Even on the day of my daughter's death, I had to sit six hours in a ministerial council and eight at my writing table.

I will do my duty, and from this time forward duty will take the place of life.

428. *July* 26.—Heaven has placed me near a man who seems as if he had been made for me. The Emperor Francis does not lose a word. He knows what he wishes, and his wish is always good. Putting aside secondary considerations, he always goes straight to his object. He never throws down the gauntlet, but is ever ready to pick it up if it is thrown to him. The difficulties are great ; destiny will decide whether we shall conquer. But what strength of mind, what purity of conscience, and calmness of judgment can accomplish, will be accomplished. I also am as if made to continue the fellow-worker of the Emperor on his thorny path.

In this I seek my refuge. The load at my heart oppresses me less ; work rather does me good. Whether I live I know not, and neither do I inquire. I treat myself like a sick man.

429. *July* 28.—It is just eight days to-day since my better half was placed in the grave. Why was it not myself? How much trouble should I have been spared. My poor child rests to-day in foreign soil. Her husband would have her laid in his vault ; my ashes will, therefore, never lie by hers. I comfort myself with the thought that I shall be united with her, and that for ever !

I and my wife, the poor mother, have arrived at a determination which lies very near to her heart as well as to mine. We will make a new sacrifice to duty and reason. Since the three other children have all delicate chests, a continued residence in Vienna would be too dangerous for them. My wife would like to take them for some years to Italy. My son, who must continue his studies, I should gladly send to the University of Padua or Sienna. In my present position and under present circumstances Italy would be impossible for them. Neither could I send my son to Germany ; he might be murdered. For such plans I am too much exposed to the attacks of Radicals of every country. Therefore I will, next September, send the whole family to Paris, where they can remain as long as it is necessary. I shall remain alone in the world, but I shall find comfort in thinking that my family are together, and are removed from the effect of the Vienna climate. During the last twenty years eight persons have died in my house, seven of them from lung disease. Experiences like this cannot be withstood; one must bend before them.

430. *July* 29.—I have no longer any domestic life. Everything is being prepared for the journey. My son-in-law goes with them to Paris, and will remain there, which is a great advantage for my son, as he will serve as father and tutor to him.

The Emperor and I will give the world a great example; we will not leave our posts. If we are destroyed, many will have to smart for their crimes and their folly first. The high character of the Carbonari, the party which has led all the others, is the anxiety.

I have good news from St. Petersburg. Capo d'Istria feels himself thoroughly beaten. Much has to be settled between the Emperor Alexander and me. It is not possible to form an idea of Golowkin's simplicity; it can only be tolerated on account of his good intentions, which are decidedly good. He is one of those men who have no leading thought. Correct and incorrect, ultramontane and liberal, Christian and heathen—such are his changes in one quarter of an hour.

431. *August* 1.—The whole day yesterday I was with the Emperor at Schönbrunn. My life is now like that which I led in the year 1815. I am busy with generals and military affairs of every kind; at first it was only a question of 50,000 men, but with the 38,000

who are already in Italy it will increase to quite a large army. Many people are astonished that we can so quickly set it in motion. No country is so quiet as Austria in time of peace ; none so active as Austria when it is necessary. No great movement is visible, but every thing goes forward quickly. At the battle of Leipsic our allies had only one-third, but Austria brought to the battle-field the other two-thirds of the main force. We are very bad proclaimers of our wares. What will come of it ? God knows. But I know what has to be done to-day, and I shall know what to do to morrow.

432. *August* 6.—I sit at my writing-table like a bankrupt in a tavern. He drinks to forget the loss of his goods : I work to drown the distress of my mind. My head remains clear ; it is with me as if I had two minds, which are like the double bellows that maintain the fire in the great furnaces, making me always blaze up : if one fails, the other increases, which has this result—that I always go forward.

My position has this peculiarity that all eyes, all expectations are directed to the point on which I find myself.

My days and part of my nights are dedicated to my work. I am more strange to myself than all the people who pass by my window. In the evening, at the sight of all I have accomplished, I perceive that life still remains in me, but of the feeling of life I have none.

433. *August* 8.—My head is tired and my heart dried up, and in this state I feel the world resting on my shoulders. If I should deceive myself for a moment I am brought to recollection by the arrival of some courier with the declaration, ' What will you do ? ' They say, ' We have confidence only in you. Our fate is in your hands ; what shall we do ? ' That is the substance of all the despatches which arrive, and two-thirds of the questioners are always ready to perpetrate some folly, because they have neither spirit nor courage.

A little while ago the Emperor Alexander made the following declaration :—' Since the year 1814 I have often been mistaken as to the mind of the public : what I thought true I find now to be false. I have done much evil ; I will make every effort to make it good again.' Indeed, there are many errors which are not known till the evil is to be seen. The man who allows errors to be seen is no statesman ; but if he admits that he has made a mistake, he is at least an honourable man, and that the Emperor Alexander is.

Capo d'Istria appears to have retired to the second rank, out of which he ought never to have advanced.

One of my plagues is the residence of the Emperor at Schönbrunn. True, it is not far off, but the backwards and forwards takes me an hour, and I often have to go twice in the day.

434. *August* 15 (*Napoleonstag*).— This is the day of the great accursed ! if he were still on the throne, and he were alone in the world, I should be happy.

This day twelve years ago, I was at one of Napoleon's *cercles* ; he had the notion of placing himself at the head of the army in Spain, we on our side were making preparations for the war of the year 1809. I was openly and sharply questioned by him with regard to these preparations, and I had the satisfaction of telling him several truths in the presence of the assembled plenipotentiaries of Europe. He expected to do a good stroke of business, and it turned out that it was done by me. In the evening he sent the Minister of Foreign Affairs to me, to assure me of his friendship and perfect satisfaction. Nothing spoils a trick so much as the bold utterance of truth. I would cer-

tainly as soon be cunning as stupid, but I should prefer
to be neither of the two, and if God does not forsake
me, the world will not have to reproach me with either
one or the other.

435. *August* 17.—I am well pleased with all that
I hear from every side. I hear an echo everywhere in
Europe. There is as yet no breath of air from the
North, but it too will soon reach us. If it blows from
the highest summits it will not be warm: if it comes
from the low ground it will smell of mud!

436. *August* 20.—It is said that from uniformity
comes tedium; the uniformity in which I live is not
without change, and the result is that I feel no tedium,
without being any the happier.

I do not always sleep well. If my thoughts get the
mastery over me, I often lie awake; I often remain
lying for an hour without altering my position, and
ruminate; then I feel what is laid upon me, and the
burden seems to me out of proportion to my strength.
Difficulties and dilemmas crowd upon me, till at last I
hear a voice which rises in me notwithstanding every
obstruction. Then I feel myself grow continually
larger, and I end *par me croire immense.* Everything is
in extremes at such a moment when the mind is disturbed by no outward object. Tired out I fall asleep,
and when I wake in the morning I find a plan in my
head quite ready; this plan I have not thought out: it
seems to arise of itself.

Not to misunderstand what is here said, it is necessary to be placed exactly in my position.

437. *September* 1.—My poor Clementine would
have been sixteen to-day. She keeps her birthday in
that place where there is neither sorrow nor pain.
Full of pity, she looks down upon her earthly remains,

which so short a time ago were so full of charm.   She
pities her father and mother, and prepares for them a
sweet and eternal union.   Time is nothing to those who
stand beyond it ; she must feel one with us, but it is
more sad for me because I am so far away from her.

The day before her death Clementine said to her
mother, as I went out of the room : ' Don't you think
it must do anyone good to see Papa ?   He looks so gentle
and calm, that I cannot understand how it is that some
people are afraid of him : as for me, I always think he
makes me well and happy.'   The poor little thing did
not guess that what she thought was calm, was death at
my heart !

438. *September* 3.—It is proposed that the three
monarchs shall meet at Troppau in the latter part of
September.   Lebzeltern has just come.   To-morrow I
shall examine him.

439. *September* 17.—The new Conference will begin on October 20.   I am so accustomed to conferences
that it does not alarm me.   This will be the third conference in less than a year.   If I do not learn the
business it is my own fault.   Nesselrode is coming :
the Emperor Alexander will not meet me alone.

Will anyone come from London ? and who ?   Castlereagh is desired by many, but he will not be able to
come ; for this matter Wellington would be nominated.
Will he come or will they choose to send him ?

After the Troppau Conference is over, a permanent
Conference shall be established in Vienna.   This I had
proposed more than a year ago.   Mean passions have
prevented it, and urgent necessity now brings it forward.

440. *September* 25.—My family has started ; I am
now alone here in my great abode.   As for me, I have
lost one hour in my day, the only one in which I was

quite sure to belong to myself. I always spent the time from 9 to 10 o'clock with my wife and my children. This hour was happiness to them, to me it was a consolation. I have made this sacrifice also. My life consists of sacrifices, and one more privation counts for nothing to one whose life is all privation ; my existence is too much like that of a clock, *Je marche toujours pour marquer les heures.* I serve others while l wear myself out.

441. *October* 1.—The society of the present day has come to its latter end. Nothing remains quiet, either in the moral or physical world, and society has reached its zenith. Under these circumstances so-called moving forwards is moving downwards. The evil, too, attains its highest point, and then falls. Such times appear to contemporaries very long, but what are two or three centuries in the journal of history?

I have not been able to reconcile either my understanding or my judgment to what has happened since the year 1814. That was the possible moment for salvation. I consider myself practical; that I was so then has been made evident.

The world has judged me as it is accustomed to judge itself, and has deceived itself about me as well as about itself. I believe I was not deceived ; I cherish but one passion, that for justice and moderation. They bring me, however, daily perplexities. They urge me to the greatest of all sacrifices—the sacrifice of my private life, and all the enjoyments, great and small, which contribute to make up the life of a man. But if I had to begin over again, I would place myself upon the same ground, because it is the only ground approved by my reason and my conscience.

442. *October* 6.—My life has fallen at a hateful

time. I have come into the world either too early or too late. Now, I do not feel comfortable; earlier, I should have enjoyed the time; later, I should have helped to build it up again; to-day I have to give my life to prop up the mouldering edifice. I should have been born in 1900, and I should have had the twentieth century before me.

The journal 'La Gazette de France' contains some articles signed by a certain Colnet, which are malicious, but well written. The articles always hit hard; they are indeed ultra, which I am not; but as I cannot bear the Radicals, I always rejoice over every well-dealt blow that they receive.

Whoever takes up the 'Journal des Débats' will, without knowing it, read me; there is hardly a week in which I do not send it some papers. But still no one must suppose that all the articles from Vienna in the Paris newspapers are from my pen. The chief correspondent is a ladies' hairdresser; of ten pieces of information which he gives, not one is true. Besides which, he offers his absurdities in a style which could not be more shallow or more stupid.

443. *October 9.*—I have news of my wife. She will be in Paris in two or three days. Her letters breathe of health. She is safely out of the town, and that was the necessity; had she remained in Vienna she would have fallen into marasmus. From great misfortunes comes a peculiar reversed sort of home-sickness directed to foreign countries, and that was the case with her. A place in which one has been happy may, by the loss of that happiness, become unbearable. Every corner, every face, indeed every shadow, recals our pain. The house in which I live is certainly too large: the part which I use is quite separate from that of my wife and children. What in ordinary times is an evil will now be a real benefit to me. The whole of that part is cut off. I cannot without horror go into the room where my poor Clementine died, and I have not been able to prevail on myself to revisit my Marie's house.

444. *Hollitsch, October* 14.—I have instinctively made a circuit to come here. My instinct has often before had to replace the talent Heaven has denied me. Yesterday evening, as I entered Brunn on one side, Lebzeltern came in on the other. I have thus gained an evening and a forenoon, and a few hours in my life are as much as months with other people. What Lebzeltern brings me from Petersburg is both excellent and important—excellent as to the moral feeling of the Emperor ; important as to the confusion of Capo d'Istria's thoughts, as he takes in all my plans. An experienced commander does not allow himself to give way to a feeling of anxiety the evening before the battle ; and I must, under present circumstances, fearlessly bear the thought of joining in the great debates.

445. *Wiczomirciz, October* 16.—I write to-day from one of my estates, the name of which I spare you. It is Ultra-Sclavonian, and, therefore, difficult to pronounce. Since this property lies between Hollitsch and Troppau, I have so arranged that I can remain here two days. In 1817 I came here with Marie, and have not been here since.

Wiczomirciz and Kojetain make a fine estate. The latter, an insignificant market-town, lies in an extremely fruitful pleasant country. Everything here looks pleasant and well-to-do. The meadows in the foreground, the Carpathian mountains in the distance, the beautiful plains, with their fertile fields and well-to-do people, all form the picture of a cheerful rich country.

FROM TROPPAU.

Extracts from Metternich's private Letters from October 19 to December 24, 1820.

446. *Troppau, October* 19, 1820.—Here I am. What I shall accomplish I know not. What I shall do I know. Will anything happen? Yes! Will anything good happen?. Yes! Will the general result correspond with the great sensation? I fear not! This is my catechism till the moment when deeds can take the place of words. The first I love, the latter I hate.

My Emperor is already here; the Russian monarch comes to-morrow.

I am well lodged, and that is something. I shall have no time to be weary, and I hope even that I shall have the opportunity of making my stay here comparatively pleasant.

447. *October* 20.—The Emperor Alexander has arrived. The Emperor Francis was confined to his bed,

and therefore could not go to meet him. I awaited
him on his arrival. He received me like an old comrade
in arms : there are, it is true, arms of various kinds.

I find him grown stronger, but not aged. The
little town contains an extraordinary number of pretty
and convenient houses, and the Conference is very well
accommodated. The Troppau people are quite proud
of the noise they are making in the world ; they are
more astonished than I am, and I am not a little astonished to find myself here.

448. *October* 21.—I have made use of my morning in reading and understanding the Russian Premier.
Judge of my amazement ; he did not make one apoca-
lyptic utterance. This is unnatural, but it is nevertheless true. However, the true is often not probable.
What has happened in Capo d'Istria's seventh heaven?
He has simply fallen to earth—like truth, but not with
his eyes blinded, like hers.

Our conversation began in this way : with both my
feet on the ground I had chosen—the ground of simple
reason—I broke in at once. He stood quite firm. By
way of experiment I left him there. He did not follow
me. I again sprang upon him, and found him taking
even a firmer position ; in fact, a mountain is not firmer.
'*Pour le coup*,' I said to myself, 'this is too strong.
I will put him to the proof. Now I will make an attack
on the apocalypse.' He went with me, even bearing
the torches to light the *auto-da-fé* for the book of the
unreal John. I attacked his past ; he cursed it. I placed
the future firmly before him ; he seemed quite agreeable.
At last I laughed—and he laughed. I believe if I had
wept he would have dissolved in tears. From that
moment I thought to myself, 'Now we can go forward ; and oh, the miracle ! he goes too ! '

So is also the Emperor of Russia. He blames himself—nay, condemns himself. This is too beautiful,
and if I did not touch myself, I should think I was
dreaming. During my three hours' conversation with
the Emperor Alexander yesterday, I found in him the
same pleasant manners which surprised me in 1813:
but he has become much wiser than he was in 1813.
I begged him to explain this change to me. He
answered quite openly : · You do not understand me : I
will tell you. From the year 1813 to 1820 is seven
years, and these seven years are like a century to me.
In the year 1820 I will at no price do what I did in the
year 1813. You are not altered, but I am. You have
nothing to regret, but I have.' ' As is the master, so is
the servant,' I said to myself. Now we will wait ;
Nesselrode is to come.

449. *October* 29.—To prepare myself for my
conference to-day I had an hour's conversation with
Capo d'Istria. I was quite well disposed to hear him.
This encouraged him. He went off and lost himself in
a long investigation of middle-class society ; its strength,
its weakness, its nerves, its sensitiveness, its component
parts, its health or sickness, and its disintegration or
death. The deuce take me if I did not know all this at
twelve years old ! As my attention was directed only
to the outcome of his long discourse, I was at last
thoroughly disappointed. The endless tirade concluded
with the declaration : 'This is the position of the affair !'
This I call political pathology, and nothing strengthens
me more in the supposition that I have some sense than
those occasions when anyone, like him, wishes to be
very clever in order to show off his intellect. In my
opinion, he only really has mind who speaks clearly.
The mind must be a light without smoke. It warms

and vivifies everything that it touches. If it does neither the one nor the other it is of bad quality. A small, mean intellect is nothing but small, mean stupidity. My intellect says to me, ' Capo d'Istria has none.' I wager that he will say the same of me ; and this only a jury can decide.

450. *November* 1.—Evenings on which the storm rages and beats with heavy raindrops on the windows seem to be made for confidential communications. This often repeated experience is newly confirmed by the long conversation I have just had with Nesselrode. He sat just in front of me at the same table at which I write, and left me ten minutes ago. Nesselrode began himself to speak of the impossibility of leaving Golowkin in Vienna ; the Emperor will no longer read his Reports, and Capo d'Istria will not listen to him. This is certainly a very useful man at all times, but especially in the present.

451. *November* 3.—My sister (Duchess of Wurtemberg) came here two days ago. She came to give the Duke a good opportunity to speak to the Emperor Alexander. The latter, who is always glad to find any-one to talk to, has for two days hardly left his aunt. People like much both to see and listen to her, for she has plenty of sense and is also very pleasing.

A comical incident took place between aunt and nephew. He was quartered in a small and bad house. Towards the end of the second evening after she arrived she remarked something move in one corner of the ceiling. On looking closer, she discovered a very small window, which the house-steward during these two evenings had let for so much a head to anyone who was curious to see the Emperor of Russia in friendly society without being remarked. Happily the interview was quite harmless, or we should have had seemingly a new edition of the English trial. If ever Queen Caroline travels through Troppau, care must be taken that she is lodged in this apartment.

452. *November* 4.—People say the kingdom of the Utopians will soon begin. One may rely for that on De Pradt, Benjamin Constant, Wilson, as well as Lady Jersey. . . . The whole Russian policy forms an interesting object of observation. There are people conducting it of whom each one pursues a different end. The Emperor has not only returned to his former views, but takes a standpoint entirely opposed to that which he has occupied for some years. Capo d'Istria must turn with the wind, but against his will, which causes him to make a constant see-saw. Nesselrode is morally dead ; it is just as if he were not there at all.

453. *November* 8.—Horrible weather ! Winter has begun, and will not leave us again for four long months. The most beautiful winter sun is no sun to me, because a warmer cold is not warmth, and light alone is no fire. The Congress has its dark sides : first, the quantity of work ; then, the small town ; lastly, the bad time of year. Such small details are unnoticeable by the Lords of the Creation, but I find that I never accomplish much with a bad setting for my work. Placed on the Tribune of the Capitol, I should speak quite otherwise than I possibly can in Troppau. I require plenty of space, and cannot accommodate myself to the small and contracted.

However, we are coming to great and fitting results.

In my whole life I have only known ten or twelve persons with whom it was pleasant to speak—*i. e.* who keep to the subject, do not repeat themselves, and do not talk of themselves ; men who do not listen to their own voice, who are cultivated enough not to lose themselves in commonplaces; and, lastly, who possess tact and good taste enough not to elevate their own persons above their subject.

454. *November* 10.—The friendliness of the Russian Emperor for me continues. It is a return to the year 1813. If he had been in the year 1815 as he was in the year 1813, there would have been no 1820.

455. *November* 15.—We to-day received the news of the *boutade* of the regiment of Semanoffsky: there is not much in it, and yet it is unpleasant.* There is nothing in the fact itself, but much in the significance which the general public will give to it. Three couriers arrived last night one after the other. Immediately afterwards the Emperor Alexander called for me, and told me of the affair. We looked at it exactly in the same light. The Emperor has so altered altogether that these agreements are now more common.

The Emperor Alexander thinks some ground must have been given to induce the three thousand Russian soldiers to conduct which is so little in keeping with the national character. He thinks, indeed, that the Radicals have made this stroke to intimidate him and bring about his return to St. Petersburg. I do not believe this; it would be indeed too shocking, if the Radicals in Russia could already control whole regiments; but this shows how the Emperor has altered.

456. *November* 20.—If I must sit opposite to Capo d'Istria at the Conference table and read his elaborations, which is worse than to hear him speak, I am so confused,

---

* In the orders of the day left by the Emperor Alexander, dated Troppau, November 14, we find, with regard to this affair, that a company of Semanoffsky's body-guard regiment, renouncing their duty and their obedience, had assembled on their own authority, late in the evening, to make complaints against their officers, and that, when for this violence they were put under control, the other companies refused to submit.—ED.

and my thoughts wander so much that I am always uneasy lest I should perpetrate some stupidity. In all the documents sent forth the thoughts are mine; but the drawing up is by Capo d'Istria, in consequence of which I very often do not recognise my own thoughts. We lose much time in correcting and amending. Thus we yesterday had a discussion of two hours over the choice of the two words *réclamer* and *inviter*. Of what avail was it to point out that the word *réclamer* betokens a right, whilst *inviter* asserts no right? The grammatical difficulty over, no other difficulty arose.

It is really inexplicable how the Emperor Alexander can have patience with Capo d'Istria. I am still not quite clear whether the Emperor knows what he wants; but his language is as plain as mine. I am on the same footing with him as I was in 1813, go to him when I may, and we talk for hours together without ever disagreeing.

457. *November* 27.—I consider the lawsuit against the Queen of England, its beginning, its conduct, and its consequences, as one of the most unfortunate catastrophes of our time. Everything suffers under this scandal—the public morals, the honour of the throne, and the honour of both sexes.

Here, we are gradually attaining results. They are unhappily not successful to the degree I had wished; with Capo d'Istria it is even difficult plainly to carry out a plain benefit. The division of our influence runs, indeed, as follows: I shall gain eighty-five per cent. of the victories, and with the rest he will bring the world to peace, reason to his way of thinking, and sound human sense to do him honour. Capo d'Istria is not a bad man, but, honestly speaking, he is a complete and thorough fool; a perfect miracle of wrong-headedness. He lives in a world to which our minds are often transported by a bad nightmare. Besides, he is a man of such over-powering vanity as passes human comprehension; yet such a man is placed in such a position!

458. *November* 29.—We have just decided that we will await here the answer from Naples : wait, at the least, that is, till the end of December here—still many days to be consumed, therefore, of that shoreless ocean which men call Time. I arrive at the end of one of these days, as I shall once arrive at the end of my existence— *i.e.* without having lived. What remains of me will by that time have been devoured by the paper-worms in the chests, with the exception of that which fifty years after my death will see the light. Then my grand-children, if I have the happiness of having any to leave behind, will learn that they had a grandfather who could see, think and desire.

I conferred this evening for three hours with the Emperor Alexander. Since we have no particular busi-ness to do, our conversation included the whole extent of the horizon. People might think that the Emperor now first came into the world and opened his eyes. He is now at the point where I was thirty years ago. Only from a great elevation can one see well in this world ; but first of all one must stand below in wind, rain, and storm, because from so elevated a position one can only form a true idea of objects when we have already seen them closely. We do not learn to fight in the arsenal, nor to foresee, defy, and master the storm in a harbour.

When I think of things in this way I see how easily it might happen to me, in case I were a Radical or a demagogue, to prostrate the mighty ones of this world.

459. *December* 1.—The soil of Troppau is as greasy and soft as butter. People paddle about in it as if it

were iced chocolate ; so a very good idea has occurred
to the town authorities. As no one can go out of any
door without sinking up to his knees, the magistrate has
had some thousand planks laid down one after the other.
This forms a narrow but very convenient path, which is
trodden daily by the Congress, the Court ladies, their
admirers, and others. This is all very well when people
are going in one and the same direction, but not so when
they meet; the more polite must make way for the less
polite, and put at least one foot off the plank. The
Emperor Alexander walks every day on these planks,
and of course all men who meet him walk into the mud ;
and when any lady comes from an opposite direction
the Emperor himself must go into the mud, unless she
contrives to do so first. Consequently there ensues a
fight in the mire which would give Mr. Cruikshank
opportunity for endless caricatures. Moreover, what
happens to his Imperial Majesty happens also to the
most discreet Minister and clerk. Since the civilisation
of the world, never was such a contest between duty
and disgust, or policy and mud. These walks are the
best test of individual peculiarities. They bring many
virtues to light—*i.e.* neighbourly love, respect for superiors, homage to the fair sex, &c. Unhappily Troppau
affords another and a sad proof of how little this
wretched century knows how to reward virtue. The
most virtuous invariably step into the mud. But enough
on this subject.

460. *December* 5.—It is a pity that Nesselrode
keeps himself so entirely in the background. I do not
comprehend how a man can put himself so completely
in the shade that he should put on another person's cloak
and wear a mask instead of showing his own face. . . .

In writing it very often happens that I leave out

many a verb or noun—a very bad habit. In my private office I have a secretary, whose duty it is to supply these omissions. As he has filled this position for ten years, he knows my thoughts ; but sometimes he does not succeed in guessing, and then he asks me. Generally I take the pen out of his hand and strike out the whole sentence, which is both convenient and useful, for in business one always says rather too much than too little. . . . *A propos* of letters, there is in Paris a very good arrangement, by which a packet or letter can be taken, and a receipt given for it, with a number and device. The packet or letter will then only be given to the person who shows the same number and device. Writer and receiver are by this means for ever unknown.

461. *December* 11.—We have arrived at the end of the first act of the play. As a hundred arrangements have to be made, my study is more than ever like a head-quarters. The King of Naples may come or he may stay away : measures must be taken to suit both cases. If he does not come, action must be taken as quick as lightning, and Jupiter only can thunder by knitting his eyebrows. Ah ! what easy work had Jupiter !

462. *December* 15.—The day before yesterday, in the evening, I had a remarkable conversation with the Emperor Alexander. We remained from seven till eleven o'clock together. One great proof of our mutual friendly feeling lies in Tea. If we drink tea alone together we agree very well.

That reminds me of a story of an acquaintance of mine in Paris who had a mistress. Daily, or rather nightly, he visited her at three o'clock in the morning, talked with her for an hour, then sat down near her

bed and took up his violin, which he played till six
o'clock. Then the fair one had to get up; he lay down
and slept till two o'clock. Now, if his mistress was
pleasant his violin was taken there : if they had a quarrel
no violin was to be seen. Tea is our violin. If we don't
get on well together—there is no tea.

During the above conversation I expressed myself
about Capo d'Istria—tea made it more easy. After I
had read to the Emperor a very interesting document,
I asked him, 'Does your Majesty understand me?'
'Yes, thoroughly.' 'How is it, then, that Capo d'Istria
never understands me?' 'I have often reproached him
with that : it comes to this, that he always thinks you
want something else.' 'And he is not mistaken ; above
all I wish that with his good heart he had also a sound,
manly understanding.'

Thanks to tea, everything was well taken. Ah ! if
that aromatic beverage could only set Capo d'Istria's head
a little right ! Good heavens ! what a cargo of tea would
I have from China !

463. *December* 18.—It freezes sharp. The boards
have become unnecessary ; the whole country is a
board. Everything that comes to us from London is
most miserable, which neither astonishes nor surprises
me. If I can do what I will with Capo d'Istria, all will
go well and quickly. The Emperor Alexander will be,
through his Minister, only an obstruction ; but for the
latter, everything would have been finished to-day.

464. *December* 20.—This evening my cousin (Flora
Wrbna), who does the honours in Troppau, offered
Golowkin a cup of tea. He answered her with a
thoughtful air : 'Do not ask me, for I like it, but it
does not agree with me. I am an unfortunate Tea-
anthropist.'

Golowkin would have less trouble if he studied a greater simplicity of language. It would have been less pretentious of him if he said simply, as the lady said, 'I am very glad not to take spinach, for since I once ate it, I cannot bear the sight of it.'

Here it must be remarked that Golowkin, who considers himself a philanthropist, is especially pleased with the word, although he neither knows the meaning of the thing nor that the Greek Anthropos means man, and the first word means friend. Philo-tea would, therefore, be more correct, and would sound better than Tea-anthrope.

465. *December* 21.—Still no news from Naples—a proof that the scamps there are still quarrelling : to give each other a good beating they have not the courage.

466. *December* 23.—One runs to the other for news : ' Are they going ? ' ' Will they wait ? ' ' Now ? ' ' When ? ' Since the invention of embassies—a very old and honourable invention ; since that of writing—a not less old but often less honourable invention—I have never experienced anything so perfect as the silence of our representative in Naples. But for a little Prussian Jew who is there, because he is everywhere, we should know absolutely nothing. From the little we learn from this Jew, we imagine that the King is coming.

467. *December* 24.—The courier has just arrived. The King is coming, and we are going to Laybach. I start to-morrow morning, my Emperor the next morning, the Emperor Alexander on the 27th.

This is decisive.

FURTHER PROGRESS OF THE VIENNA MINISTERIAL CONFERENCES.*

468. Metternich to Neumann (Letter), Vienna, January 25, 1820.

468. I have no doubt that Lord Castlereagh will be satisfied with the turn which I have been able to give to the political and military question. It is on this question—the most important, without any doubt, for Austria and Prussia—that there have always been the greatest number of opposite ideas and wishes in the German Courts. Some, such as Prussia, wished for what would have been dangerous for the federation and dangerous for Europe to agree to. Others, such as Bavaria and Wurtemberg, have always wished to isolate us in this question of federation. In case of war between Austria, Prussia, and Russia, Bavaria would thus be found at the head of the purely German federation. This attitude would have commenced by a declaration of armed neutrality. The progress of events would have regulated the rest without the possibility of judging of its extent.

The substance of these thoughts is found in many of the instructions brought here by the different plenipotentiaries. It is partly owing to the care which I have taken to adjourn the discussion on this matter that

* In connection with the documents of the year 1819, Nos. 374-380.— ED.

I have gained my cause. It was necessary to establish for the allies such security, and even such advantages, as to blind them to what they consider sacrifices. The acts will be submitted for the ratification of the Courts. It is possible, and perhaps even probable, that on this occasion Bavaria and Wurtemberg will make some resistance, but they will be obliged to give way. One does not pull down a whole building because one corner is inconvenient to live in ; my anxiety is, so to unite the different parts of the federal edifice that even to wish to pull down one is to attack them all.

I have no doubt that the complete result of the Conference will be sent to the Courts from the 12th to the 15th February. An immense work will have been done in a very little time ! Only the experience which I have acquired in the course of the six last years of Congress could have brought about such results as those which we offer to Europe.

Metternich to Rechberg, Bavarian Minister of Foreign Affairs, Vienna, end of January, 1820.

469. . . . . The whole of Germany—her right-thinking men as well as the others—is deceived as to the object of our meeting at Vienna.

Everybody thought we were going to overthrow all that is connected with the forms, which unhappily have been transplanted to the German soil (that soil so historical, so classical, and so great), in the course of the two or three last years. Some have thought we were right to do so, others have raised a great outcry. Now, we are not doing what they expected, and I declare frankly that in my soul and conscience I do not allow myself to regret it, because I cannot regret what is impossible.

This arises, too, from what is now taking place among you, and what will probably present itself still more strikingly in Wurtemberg, as it does everywhere and always, when people only follow the impulse of a party. . . .

I have taken care to hasten the interpretation of Article XIII.,* for I foresaw the necessity of removing, both from you and from Wurtemberg, the only opposition which had any real foundation in justice.

Your Constitution is, without any doubt, the least bad of any in the south of Germany ; whilst that of Wurtemberg seems to me not to work well. I have written lately to St. Petersburg, that I believe the result of our Conferences will be most disastrous for the King of Wurtemberg and for his people, seeing they will be condemned to preserve their Constitution.

This is not exactly the case with you. You can be conservative without positive harm, and by a vigorous regulation you may even gain much. That this regulation should be real, it appears to me urgent—

I. That it should be adopted by all those States which are in a position to do so.

II. That to strengthen it still more, such principles should be expressed in our labours here as may serve for the support of feeble or timorous Governments.

I have spoken on the first of these subjects to Zentner,† and he agrees with me.

As for the second, I shall find some means of bringing it forward, and I have spoken to no one about it.

* Article XIII. of the Federal Act concerning the affairs of the States of the Bund.—Ed.

† Minister and Bavarian Plenipotentiary at the Vienna Ministerial Conferences.—Ed.

If you entertain my idea, try to give some instructions to your plenipotentiaries with reference to it ; for I have no reason for not addressing myself directly to Zentner, if it were not that I desire to do nothing *in bavariis* unless you take the initiative.

I extend this question to one of the gravest complications presented by the form of the new Constitutions : namely, the publicity of the sittings and the shorthand writing of the protocols. I maintain that no monarchy of less than ten or twelve millions of people has the right to resist this form. In the smaller States men are too close to one another ; injuries are too deep, and nothing can compensate for their effects, for the objects of ambition are too mean. I declare that, as an ambitious man, I should prefer to play the part of a Liebenstein to that of a Berstett at Carlsruhe. . . .

Metternich to Neumann, Vienna, February 2, 1820.

470. I am able to tell you that all our business here is concluded. The most important work, the longest and the most directly connected with the whole of the federal system, has already passed once to the *Plenum* and it has been admitted, except for certain grammatical errors which will be corrected here in two days. I will send it to you by the next weekly courier. You will not be able to get a clear idea of all we have done here until you have read it.

You will see from it all the work of this grand Confederation. You will see the rights and the duties of the allies stated, and the sphere of action allotted to the Diet. I hope that even M. de Capo d'Istria will end by understanding them both. He will see that the Confederation is united, and that the Diet is not its sovereign ; that there are several differences between the German's monarchical confederation and the Swiss republican confederation ; that the Canton of Basle has no point of resemblance to Bavaria or Prussia, and even that the part of Director Landamman is not that of the Emperor of Austria.

The States of Baden are about to reassemble. This fact will cause fresh discomposure to Count Capo d'Istria. He will think we are falling into imbecility. Reassemble the States, and make laws against Liberal assassins ! Make the laws of September 20, and talk no more of it at Vienna ? There is something in all that, sufficient to confound all systems. It is, in fact, that here we do not renew, but we build up : we do not return to what has been, but we make good laws against excesses of every kind, and we leave to each State to watch over its own internal safety by guaranteeing a vigorous and general support whenever they may require it.

In a word, we make peace and tranquillity in so far as laws can assure either.

WURTEMBERG'S RESISTANCE TO THE COMPE-
TENCE OF THE CONFERENCES AT VIENNA.

471. Metternich to the Emperor Francis.

471. *Vienna, March* 31, 1820.—Nearly at the end
of the negotiations which had been so happily matured
here, an attempt is made by the Royal Court of Wurtemberg to frustrate all that we have endeavoured to
accomplish during the last four months.

That is, the Wurtemberg Court objects to consider
these deliberations as finally concluded here in Vienna,
but wishes them to be regarded as merely preparatory
works to be concluded at the Diet.

The former would bring peace to men's minds, the
latter disquiet. All the German Governments have
openly shown their wish for the welfare of the Bund.
Your Majesty needed only to speak the word and the
coalition took place, for it was in accordance with the
minds of the German Princes and the enlightened
designs of their plenipotentiaries. The King of Wurtemberg, however, seems to be otherwise inclined. The
King, or—as I still venture to hope—his counsellors,
desire to bring the wants of their country again before
the Diet, although they are already secured by preliminary deliberations, and are inseparable from the general
welfare of all the German Governments. These resolutions of the Conference they wish to produce at the

Diet, with so-called liberal explanations, objections, and phrases whereby an appearance of oppression would be produced as to the community, while the King of Wurtemberg would gain the reputation of patriotic feeling. The thing may, indeed, have to be done, but the King will gain the appearance of only yielding to force.

Carlsbad has greatly enlightened us on this point. The plenipotentiary from Wurtemberg at that place concluded almost every one of his proposals with this addition : ' That, however, it must be drawn up by the other members of the Bund, and imposed on his Royal master.' In the same way this plenipotentiary spoke and wrote about military demonstrations, of the concentration of the Imperial troops in Tyrol, and of Prussian troops on the Lower Rhine. This was the conduct of the King at the deliberations in Frankfurt in the month of September last, and at his visit to Warsaw, as well as since his return to Stuttgart ; and now he behaves in the same way here, and it is beyond doubt that he acts systematically. . . .

The King of Wurtemberg has made an attempt in which he shall not succeed. Your Majesty's firmness and the excellent spirit which animates all the other Governments and their deputies are sufficient to prevent this.

When Count Mandelslohe made this communication to me I thought it my duty to take no step of myself alone.

On the day of battle every combatant must be sure of his next man, and the German Bund can only prosper under the protection and guardianship of a firm and united will. I made this declaration verbally to Count Mandelslohe, and immediately began to consult the other deputies. From the document annexed your Majesty will see the prosperous result of this first step.

Furthermore I venture to lay before your Majesty the sketch of a letter to the King of Wurtemberg. When it has received your Majesty's signature I shall immediately despatch the courier to Stuttgart.

Metternich to Winzingerode, Vienna, March 31, 1820.

472. When handing to me your Excellency's letter of the 21st of this month, Count von Mandelslohe at the same time made the confidential communication which he was charged to present with the protocol of the Conferences at this place.

On this communication being made, my first wish was to discover whether the Royal Wurtemberg Court declared against the substance as well as the form, or only against the latter. This is a point of the greatest importance, and one which I was justified in doubting, although in the protocol delivered mention is only made of the form.

It is not merely whether the results of the Conferences here are binding without further discussion at the Diet, or whether they must be placed before the Diet in the usual manner. The question is of far greater consequence. The Cabinets assembled here have worked out the chief subjects of their negotiations so successfully, they have so happily settled what is most important for the whole of Germany—the question of the competence of the Bund—that the work already accomplished is likely to fulfil our best hopes. Shall this hitherto prosperous work, now so far advanced, be fully accomplished, or shall it be put aside as an unsuccessful, useless attempt ? This is the chief question to-day—a question which I believe (and my opinion is shared by all the plenipotentiaries here present) touches more deeply the future fate of the German confederacy than any difference of opinion about this or that form to be observed with regard to the assembly of the Bund.

As Count von Mandelslohe could not give me much real information on this subject, I had further to inquire whether he was strictly ordered to make this declaration at the first full sitting after our conference, or whether he was authorised to delay this step till an answer is obtained to the present despatch. The Count declared himself bound to execute his commission without delay.

Under these circumstances I could only inform Count von Mandelslohe that I did not feel called upon to enter into the discussion and explanation of the form which had been unanimously liked and agreed upon at the eighteenth session, and that I could take no further step in this matter without a previous conference with all the other plenipotentiaries. I added the necessary reservation that the protesting Court must be responsible for any evil consequences resulting from the retardation of negotiations equally important for the whole of Germany.

This conference I immediately arranged and the result is :—

1. That no interruption must be allowed to take place in the course of the negotiations here.

2. A unanimous determination to hold fast the work which, after four months' application, is so nearly completed, and a general resolution of March 4, in pursuance of which they mutually engage that none of the plenipotentiaries of this conference will condescend to any repetition of the deliberations at the Diet.

Feeling the necessity, for the sake of the German Fatherland and all Europe, of preventing the sad spectacle of a fruitless or inconclusive four months' conference between the German Cabinets, I have taken upon myself to communicate to your Excellency in the enclosure the unanimous opinion of the plenipotentiaries as to the form to be observed on closing the conferences. . . .

In fulfilling this duty I am particularly charged by his Majesty the Emperor to declare solemnly that, in his opinion, there are but two alternatives in the manner of bringing the business here to a conclusion :—

Either to issue the resolutions taken in Vienna (as results definitely accepted) in the form of an Act ratified by the Governments belonging to the Bund, leaving it to the Assembly of the Bund to deposit these Acts in the archives of the Bund, and publish them in the usual constitutional manner ;

Or to make known these resolutions to the Diet in the form of a Presidential Report, all the Governments pledging themselves to direct their deputies at the Diet to give an absolute consent.

All the votes have been given in favour of the former of these modes. It was all the more necessary to reject the latter as his Majesty the Emperor (for reasons shown in the enclosure) feels obliged totally to decline any co-operation in this form.

His Majesty the Emperor does not acknowledge a third mode. He is firmly determined to ground no Presidential Report on a merely preliminary and provisional agreement on the matters negotiated here, and not to allow what is already—by the most careful discussion and deliberation of all German Courts and

Cabinets—on the point of accomplishment, to be again called in question.

Your Excellency will see from this paper and its enclosure, not only the opinion of all the German Cabinets, but also that it thoroughly coincides with that of his Majesty the Emperor.

The desire which animates the Emperor, no less than all the members of the Bund, to secure the welfare and maintenance of the German Bund in the most prompt and judicious way to which their general competence extends—the real existence of which desire is proved by the course hitherto taken by the negotiations here and by the present step—justifies the expectation that the King of Wurtemberg will not refuse his consent and co-operation in a work hitherto carried on uninterruptedly in the glorious harmony so beneficial for Germany.

Metternich to Wintzingerode, Vienna, March 31, 1820.

473. You will receive to-day communications of the greatest importance. The moment is come, Count, when all that is hard of understanding must be understood, and all that is not clear must be made so. It is impossible that all the Courts of Germany should have met together for five months in the same harmonious spirit, with the same feeling of the necessity for consolidating their federal relations, that our conferences should draw near to their close, and that all that has been said and done should only benefit the enemies of general order. And yet this would certainly be the case if what has led to an harmonious agreement should be relinquished at the very moment of this agreement.

I venture to flatter myself that the details into which I entered in my official letter will remove the feeling·

which could only have arisen from some great mistake. You believe that Austria and perhaps Austria and Prussia wish to exercise a pressure on their allies. The fact is not so; the Emperor knows the dangers of the moment and the necessities of all times. . . .

I frankly confess that I do not comprehend the declaration which M. de Mandelslohe has been ordered to insert in the protocol. The case is plain, although I do not allow myself to attach to it the only definite interpretation of which it seems to admit. If it has not this meaning, the letters I send you ought to remove all difficulties : if this is not the case, the cause will not be far to seek. You wish to prevent what has for five years been impracticable at Frankfurt, but is now about to be concluded under the immediate influence of the Cabinets, from coming to anything.

You are very badly served here. Mandelslohe acts the man of honour; Trott does his part—and the part of men behind the scenes never is to arrange affairs. To place two such individuals as you have is the most certain means, not to correct mistakes, but to embroil everything, and render all efforts abortive.

You will see that I am too much occupied with the one affair to be inclined to return to my last letters. Your reply, far from proving that I may be deceived, proves on the contrary that I am right in everything. Yes, I know all that has passed since Carlsbad; I know what you call a momentary support in public opinion, the only advantage that you have obtained. Against whom is this ephemeral support required ? Is it against the enemies of social order or against your allies ? . . . If at Stuttgart they think that Austria's policy is small, very tortuous, and very dangerous to those who allow themselves to be deceived, at least the Minister for Foreign Affairs for Wurtemberg could never reproach the Emperor's minister with perplexing him with a very diplomatic controversy.

There is only one passage to be remarked on in your last confidential letter. You say to me, 'Pray do not forget that we have a Constitution and responsible ministers.'

I do not, in fact, know of Constitution and responsible ministers anything which concerns the question with which we are occupied. The Constitutions are in the Confederation, and neither above nor below it. The responsibility of ministers does not concern the Confederation. You are responsible for the employment of your public money and the acts of your administration. If you admit that the Confederation can suffer in its vital principle from the responsibility, you must at least also grant to this same Confederation the right of naming the ministers. Ask your *soi-disant* friends of the people if they do not find my axiom correct: they will be ready to reply in the affirmative. But what will become of the sovereignty of your King if men like Jahn and Arndt are produced in Germany?

I wait patiently for the new orders your plenipotentiary will receive. . . .*

---

* The result is known. The King of Wurtemberg gave up his opposition and empowered his ambassadors to sign the document. See No. 475.— ED.

METTERNICH'S GERMAN POLICY.

Metternich to Berstett, the Ambassador from Baden at the Austrian Court, Vienna, May 4, 1820.

474. Your Excellency has informed me of the wish of his Royal Highness the Archduke of Baden to be exactly informed of the ideas of the Imperial Cabinet on the political state of Germany. This challenge on the part of a Prince who shows daily the most praiseworthy marks of his strong desire to support the right, and his thorough knowledge of the elements that oppose it, is the more honourable for me, as it imposes on me the duty of apprising your Excellency unreservedly of the point of view from which the present state of things has to be considered.

Time moves on amid storms : the attempt to check their violence would be vain. Firmness, moderation, and a union of well-directed forces—this is all that remains to the defenders and friends of order ; in this alone lies at present the duty of all sovereigns and right-minded statesmen, and he only will have deserved this title in the day of peril who, having satisfied himself of what is possible and just, suffers not himself to be turned aside from the noble aim of his efforts either by impotent wishes or by relaxing his zeal. The object is easy of definition : in our times it is neither more nor less than the maintenance of what already exists. This is the only means of preservation ; and it is perhaps the most likely method of regaining what has been already lost. For this end, therefore, the efforts of everyone must be combined as well as the measures of all those whom one and the same principle, one and the same interest, unite. Combustible matters long in preparation broke forth in the époch between 1817 and 1820. The false step which was taken by the French Ministry during this period ; the toleration which was evinced in Germany to these dangerous doctrines ; the weakness shown in suppressing the abuses of the press ; the precipitation, finally, with which Constitutions were given to the States of Southern Germany—all these causes have excited the parties whom nothing can please to the most miserable abuses.

Nothing shows the impossibility of pleasing these parties more than to remark that the most active intrigues have taken place exactly in that very State where the most indulgence was shown to their supposed wishes.

The evil had reached such a height before the Congress at Carlsbad that only some trifling political combination was needed completely to overthrow social order. The wisdom of the system adopted by the great Courts has protected us from this danger, which might even at this moment be fatal. What course, then, must an enlightened Government take under such circumstances? By putting this question the possibility of salvation is taken for granted, and we believe we are justified in such a hope.

When we now examine the means by which we are to attain so great an end, we find ourselves led back to the point from whence we started. In aiming at a happier future, we must at least make certain of the present ; the preservation of that which is must consequently be the first of all cares. And by this we mean, not only the old order of things as they have been preserved in some countries, but also all the new legally-constructed institutions. The importance of preserving them firm and steady is evident from the attacks which have been directed against them, with a perhaps still greater irritation than against the old institutions. At the present time the change from old to new is attended with as much danger as the return from the new to what no longer exists. Both may equally bring about the outbreak of disturbances which it is important to avoid at any price.

To deviate in no way from the established order, whatever may be its origin, and where alterations are absolutely necessary to make them only with entire freedom and well-considered resolution—this is the first duty of a Government that desires to resist the evils of the age. Such a resolution, however just and natural it may be, will certainly cause obstinate conflicts ; but the advantage of building on a known and recognised basis is evident, because this gives a firm point from which it will be easy to examine and frustrate the necessarily uncertain movements of the enemy in all directions.

We consider as perfectly unfounded the objection which might possibly be raised, ' that amongst the Constitutions hitherto given in Germany there is none which rests on any foundation : that, therefore, none of them offers a point of support.' If this were so, the indefatigable demagogues would not have given up undermining those Constitutions. Every order of things legally introduced bears in itself the principle of a better system ; they must therefore be the work of caprice or of a wild delusion, like the Constitution of the Cortes of 1812. Moreover, a Charter is not a real Constitution; this forms itself with time alone, and it always depends on the judgment and will of Governments to direct the development of the constitutional manner of government, to separate good from evil, to strengthen the public authority, and to protect the peace and happiness of the nation from every hostile attack. Two great means of salvation are at present secure to every Government which, from a feeling of its dignity and duty, is resolved not to ruin itself. One of these means consists of the happy conviction that no misunderstanding prevails among the European Powers, and that also, according to the unalterable principles of monarchy, none is to be anticipated. This fact, which is beyond any doubt, secures and guarantees our position and our strength. The other means is the union formed between the German States during the last nine months, a union which, with God's help, will become indissoluble.

The conferences of Carlsbad and the resolutions prepared there have acted more powerfully and more beneficially than we may perhaps acknowledge to ourselves at a moment when we still feel the embarrassments which constrain us, and when we can only superficially estimate all the advantages which have been gained. Important measures of that kind can only be estimated at their full value when all their results are to be seen. These, however, cannot be seen in the epoch immediately following; but we may already calculate the effects of the resolutions of September 2 by considering the probable advances which the enemies of the public order would have made without them.

The results of the conferences in Vienna, although of the grandest kind, are not so brilliant in their immediate effects, but are all the deeper and more lasting. The consolidation of the German Bund now affords to each of the States of which it consists an effectual guarantee—an inestimable advantage, which could only be certainly secured by the course which has been taken. The uprightness and moderation with which this important work was carried on may have delayed us and prevented bolder and more vigorous measures ; but, even supposing these had been possible, the work would have been wanting in one of its most essential conditions—namely, the free conviction and sincere confidence of all who take part in it. Nothing could compensate for such a want, which would have been especially felt when the resolutions adopted under such auspices had to be carried out. Generally speaking, moral strength is as great a necessity to the Bund as legislative power, and the increased conviction of the necessity for this league and of its beneficial results is in our opinion the most important and fortunate result.

The rules to be observed in future by the German Governments may be pointed out in a few words. They are :—

1. Confidence in the duration of a state of peace in Europe, and in the harmony of the principles guiding the great Powers.

2. Conscientious attention to their own system of administration.

3. Perseverance in maintaining the legal principles of existing Constitutions and a firm determination to defend them against every attack ; but also at the same time—

4. The removal of the principal defects in these Constitutions, carried out by the Government on adequate grounds. Lastly,

5. In case of our own resources being insufficient, the Bund may be appealed to for support, a support which every member has the most sacred right of demanding, and which can less than ever be refused after the present determinations. This is, according to our judgment, the only beneficial, legal, and enduring course. The political system of his Majesty the Emperor rests on the same foundations, and Austria, inwardly calm in the possession of an imposing assemblage of intellectual force and material means, will not use them merely for her own support, but will always apply them for the benefit of her allies whenever duty and prudence require it of her.

I wish that your Excellency may take the opportunity of this candid representation to offer to the Archduke a new proof of our true feelings, and of the lively interest which the Imperial Royal Court takes in gratifying his Royal Highness, as well as in the welfare and security of his States.

RESULTS OF THE MINISTERIAL CONFERENCES
IN VIENNA.

Metternich to the Emperor Francis, Vienna, May 17, 1820.

475. The consent of the Court of Wurtemberg to our Closing Act has arrived this evening. In a full sitting, which I have fixed for to-morrow morning, the protocol about this first part of our business here will be concluded, and the day after to-morrow I shall bring the Acts to be signed.

The second part—the instructions for the assembly of the Bund—has meantime so far advanced that we shall be able to dissolve our conference on the 21st or 22nd of this month.

The work having reached its termination here, all has been done that could be done at present, and I already see the consequences which the propriety of our course will make more and more manifest every day. All the ministers are making preparations for their departure, and there is not one who did not ask from me to-day instructions as to the course to be taken in future by his Court in regard both to policy and administration. One word spoken by Austria will be inviolable law throughout all Germany. Now first will the Carlsbad measures come into their true life, and all those which are requisite for the peace of Germany will be quite naturally added.*

* The document generally known under the name of 'The Concluding Acts of Vienna,' in sixty-five articles, treats of the measures for the security

I intend, if nothing happens to prevent me, to start from here on the 24th, and to be with your Majesty at Prague on the 26th. METTERNICH.

I am glad to know this, and I expect you with real pleasure. FRANCIS.

Prague, May 17, 1820.

Sketch of a Statement to be made by the President.

476. At the session of the Diet on September 20 last year, it was resolved, on the report of the President, to ask for instructions as to various points most important for the improvement of the Bund, so that these points could be discussed immediately after the reopening of the session, and brought at once to a definite conclusion.

Meanwhile his Majesty the Emperor, my most gracious master, guided by the conviction that it is not only the common interest but also the common wish of all your allies in the Bund to develop, improve, and strengthen the indissoluble union by strictly maintaining the original convention with all its aims, has caused Ministerial Conferences to be held in Vienna to which all the Governments of the Bund have sent their plenipotentiaries. These conferences should, according to their original purpose, lead to direct communication and discussion of opinions on both sides, and a common understanding on the subjects on which instructions are to be given.

of the public rights of the members of the Bund by a permanent court, as well as the introduction of a definite order concerning the execution of the sentences pronounced by this tribunal; it refers to various military questions; it gives the authentic interpretation of Article XIII. of the Acts of the Bund, and regulates the relations of the single States to the Bund. By a resolution of the Diet of June 8 the 'Concluding Acts' were raised to a fundamental law of the Bund and published as such.—ED.

At the negotiations opened for that purpose it was soon evident, however, that by a thorough treatment of the proposed subjects many others connected with them would be drawn into the discussion—subjects which had been already discussed at the Diet, but which had remained undecided or been regulated provisionally. At the same time it was acknowledged on all sides that the first condition of successful progress in the legislation of the Bund was an exact definition of the nature of the Bund and the circumstances, duties, and rights resulting from it.

The business resting on these principles presented, during its whole course, a remarkable example of harmony, public spirit, and mutual confidence, the surest pledge of the future strength of the German Bund. Gradually the resolution was formed to bring together the chief results of the conferences into one whole, which, being immediately derived from the *Acts of Confederation*, should have the same force and legality as that fundamental law—thus satisfying the general desire for the completion and development of that law, and facilitating the conduct of affairs at the Diet.

But this work required a peculiar form, because it differed essentially in origin, contents, and aim from common instructions on a particular subject, or only introducing further deliberations. It was, therefore, resolved to include the above-mentioned chief results of the negotiations held in Vienna in an Act drawn up by the assembled plenipotentiaries in the name of their Governments, to have this Act presented to the Diet in the usual constitutional way, and to let it be there declared law in a formal resolution.

Accordingly, I am directed by my Court to lay before this honourable assembly the ' Concluding Acts ' of the Ministerial Conferences on the development and strengthening of the Bund, requesting at the same time that a resolution be drawn up, as agreed upon, and signed by all the ambassadors in the name of their respective Governments.

The Austrian Vote.

The Imperial Royal Embassy is instructed to declare by protocol the consent and approbation of their Court to the elevation of this Act to be a law of the Bund, according to the agreement made, and to deposit the original in the archives of the Bund, adding a copy of it to the protocol.

Sketch of the Resolution.

1. The Concluding Acts of the Ministerial Conferences at Vienna, drawn up by the plenipotentiaries of all the States of the Bund for the development and strengthening of the Bund, is to be raised to be a fundamental law, equal in power and legal force to the Acts of the Bund.

2. The original document in question, duly signed and attested, is to be deposited in the archives of the Bund ; and

3. A copy of it is to be added to the present protocol.

STATE OF POLITICAL AFFAIRS IN MAY 1820.

Metternich to the Emperor Francis, Vienna, May 18, 1820.

477. Nothing of an unexpected nature has happened in the political world since your Majesty's departure.

In France there is a great conflict of parties. The Ministry stands firm ; the election law will pass.

In England the relation between the King and the Ministry is very gloomy. The cause of this is the Queen, who is in Paris, and who either goes to England herself or works as a partisan for the Opposition. The proceedings against the Radicals have come to a favourable termination.

Anarchy is seen in Spain day by day more distinctly. The revolution of March 8 will soon bear its bitter fruits.

A courier has arrived here to-day from Russia. .The Emperor thinks a great deal of the Spanish cause morally, but he will not insist upon taking an active part.

I merely signify to your Majesty the present state of things most respectfully, but in the shortest possible manner.

The collection of Reports I will myself lay before your Majesty, as I need them for the despatches which I must still send out before my departure.

The King of Prussia does not accept your Majesty's invitation, for it just happens to fall at the time of his daughter's marriage with the Archduke of Mecklenburg. The show of politeness has therefore been made, and your Majesty is set free as to your Majesty's travelling plans.

AUSTRIA'S POSITION WITH REGARD TO THE REVOLUTION IN NAPLES, AND BAVARIA'S AGREEMENT WITH METTERNICH'S POLICY.

Metternich to Count Rechberg, Foreign Minister at Munich, Vienna, July 26, 1820.

478. The late events in the kingdom of Naples have shown more evidently and significantly than any former occurrence of this kind that, even in a well-regulated and well-governed State, among a quiet, peaceable nation, contented and satisfied with their Government, the pernicious influence of revolutionary sects can cause the most violent agitation, and quickly lead to an entire revolution. For it has been certainly proved that the movements of the Carbonari alone, without any foreign impulse, without even a show of pretext, have excited those rebellious movements which have induced his Majesty the King of Naples, in a moment of embarrassment, to lay down the government, dissolve all existing authority, and proclaim a Constitution strange to his country, which even where it is found is still new and untried—in other words, he has proclaimed anarchy as law.

His Majesty the Emperor is convinced that this unexpected event will have made the greatest impression on all German Courts. It teaches, by a remarkable example, the danger of looking with scornful indifference on the action of secret unions and stealthy conspiracies, and shows the wisdom of the German Princes in opposing with vigilance and severity the first symptoms of such criminal attempts.

His Majesty the Emperor is particularly interested in these unfortunate incidents by his political and personal ties, by his relationship with several Italian princes, and by the geographical situation of his own countries. The political order of things established in 1815, and guaranteed by all the European Powers, has made Austria the natural warder and protector of public peace in Italy. The Emperor is firmly determined to fulfil this high vocation, to keep away all peace-disturbing movements from his frontiers and those of his nearest neighbours, to allow no infringement of the rights of the Italian Princes, and if legal and administrative precautions should not afford sufficient protection, he will resort to the most vigorous measures.

Fortunately, the present position of the European Powers, and the peaceful spirit which animates them all, are pledges that such measures would not provoke political hostilities or wars. In case force (which his Majesty's well-known love of justice and clemency will only employ in the greatest necessity) should be unavoidable, it would only be used against rebels in arms, and never against a legitimate power.

But even in this case (only alluded to with the greatest reluctance) the Emperor would not claim immediate assistance on the part of his allies in the German Bund. The measures requisite for the maintenance of peace and order in Italy lie entirely beyond the sphere of co-operation of the German Bund as it was originally settled ; and, far from intending to deviate from established principles, his Majesty is ready to make every effort and every sacrifice to prevent such co-operation being required, and to put forth all his strength to avert such danger from the frontiers of the States of the German Bund.

In return, it is certainly desirable and important that Austria, while devoting her care and strength to a matter of public benefit, should be able confidently to rely upon undisturbed peace in the interior of Germany. However much now, or in future, the fate of Italy may occupy the Emperor's attention, his Majesty will always feel the same lively interest in German affairs, and fulfill to the utmost his duties as a member of the Bund. But it is the greatest satisfaction and consolation to know that there need be no fear for our Fatherland as long as the German Courts are guided by the strong feeling of the duty imposed on them by the present critical state of the political world, and by that spirit of harmony, firmness and wisdom which revealed itself so unmistakably during the last negotiations at Vienna (and even since the conclusion of the negotiations) on the part of the chief German Governments. A great honour is reserved for Germany, if she finds in the prudence and resolution of her rulers, in the steadfast support of her existing Constitutions, in the loyal feelings of her people, and in the powerful guarantee of the alliance of the Bund, the means and power she needs in this stormy time to preserve and maintain her inward peace, her lawful order, her independence, her dignity, and her ancient character. His Majesty is convinced that none of your noble allies in the Bund will be insensible to glory of this kind; and you will one day congratulate yourself when called upon to accept your share in it, conscious of having spared no effort, no sacrifice, for so great and glorious an aim.

At a time when the latest events in Italy appeal only too strongly to the attention of the German Courts, his Imperial Majesty considers it fitting to express to his allies in the Bund his own opinions, as well as his firm confidence in his Majesty the King.

With the greatest respect, &c. &c.*

Gentz to Metternich, Salzburg, August 1, 1820.

479. . . . . On Sunday at eleven o'clock I betook myself to Nymphenburg. The King received me with his usual kindness and affability. He had just received the declaration from Count Rechberg (No. 478), and promised to read it with the most serious attention. This gave me the opportunity of speaking of its contents, to which he listened with an unconcealed 'Bravo!' He expressed himself thus:—'That the firmness of his Majesty the Emperor, his calm steadfastness in good and evil days, is well known to him, and that he (the King) can easily imagine what the Emperor must think of such scandals as the revolution in Naples; that all of us must thank God that we have still in Germany a man like the Emperor to take the lead.' He said that he (the King) was as far from being a friend of Constitutions as the Emperor, and that if the . . . Congress of Vienna in 1815 had not spoiled his whole game, he certainly would never have committed himself so far. That, however, he has come off with little injury, and that he will not be led on one step further by the d——. During this tirade some angry, but only passing, blows were struck at former times and occurrences between the Imperial and Bavarian Courts, and the whole ended with a very goodnatured and honourable declaration about the great fame your Highness has lately acquired in Germany.

* Similar declarations were also sent to the other German Courts.—ED.

The King then read me his latest letters from
Naples, which came down to the 15th. His only
anxiety seemed to be lest we might not send troops
enough to Italy. He said he had heard of twenty
thousand men, which did not please him. I said that,
of course, I did not yet know anything definite on this
point, and that his Majesty was well aware that large
armies could not be put in motion in a few days or
weeks. From the point of view taken in Vienna,
however, I felt confident that Austria would not be
wanting in anything requisite for her own safety and
the protection of her nearest neighbours.

The King seemed to fear nothing from Sardinia.
He gave me to understand he had good reason to
believe that the King of Sardinia 'would not bite,'
especially if the Carbonari exercised much influence on
Genoa. He must resolutely join for life and death with
Austria, for no revolution could be tolerated. I perfectly agreed with this very just remark.

According to an idle rumour, which has circulated
in Munich for more than a fortnight, and which the
King also mentioned, the Neapolitan Court was said to
have begged auxiliary troops from Austria before the
outbreak of the insurrection, which could not be
granted, because the Russian ambassador in Rome had
declared he must protest against every Austrian march
of troops. I assured the King, and all those who asked
me about this affair, that the whole story was false from
beginning to end, and probably spread abroad by the
Carbonari from very intelligible motives.

The King—who does not seem to love the Emperor
Alexander very much—expressed his anxiety lest he
might, in our sense perhaps, 'immediately put his
hand to the work' in Italy, which would always be

hazardous. I answered that, of late years, the Emperor Alexander has shown only the best and noblest sentiments, and that, however important, under present circumstances, his moral and political agreement with our Court might be, any obtrusion of substantial help by him was not to be thought of and not needed by Austria.

Amongst others the King put this strange question—whether I did not believe the Crown Prince of Naples had a direct share in the conspiracy. I assured him I had never heard the least hint of his; whereat the King replied very significantly, 'I believe it is quite certain, and for this very reason, that my son—who, as you know, also loves Liberal principles—has told me a great deal too much good of him.'

The King believes that Reggio—a great place of meeting for the Carbonari in Upper Italy—and Modena generally are seriously threatened.

The conversation then returned to Germany. The King did not speak favourably of the King of Wurtemberg, and still less so of his minister; neither did he seem to have a good opinion of the Grand Duke of Baden.

At last I turned the conversation to Baron Zentner, and his honourable conduct in Vienna. What I said seemed to please the King exceedingly; and when I further told him that your Highness had particularly charged me to express to Count Rechberg your deep satisfaction with the whole course so far of the assembly of the Bund, and added that 'I knew from your Highness that the Emperor had several times spoken in the same sense,' it could not escape me with what lively interest the King listened to all I said.

My audience lasted about an hour and a half. His Majesty dismissed me with the words, 'That I might greet your Highness in the most friendly manner from him.'

Afterwards I was invited to dinner at Count Rechberg's, where Baron Zentner, Count Thurheim, Count Arco, Baron Hruby, and others were present.

After dinner I had my last and, if not most impor tant, yet most solemn conversation with Count Rechberg. He led Baron Zentner and myself into an anteroom, and here he made a sort of political confession, from which I mention only the following remarkable words:— 'I begin by passing judgment on myself. For fifteen years I have, prepossessed by old prejudices, opposed Austria as an enemy. I accuse myself, but I excuse myself also. My opinion was the reflection of that which universally obtained in my fatherland, and although I might have corrected many a false opinion in Vienna, the noble principles of his Majesty the Emperor at that time appeared to me only through dim and often distorting glasses. It is one of the ever-enduring services of Prince Metternich to have first shown the true character of the Austrian policy, not only to Bavaria, but also to all Germany. To consider Austria now as anything but a beneficent and protecting power would be to fight against reason and our own interests : with Austria Bavaria must in future stand or fall. We—at least all who think honestly amongst us—heartily acknowledge this ; we wish we could express it with a hundred voices. How far other German Courts participate in these feelings I cannot decide, but they all acknowledge it, and even Wurtemberg cannot but see that she would not long exist without Austria.'

He had tears in his eyes when he spoke these words.

He then begged me to report to your Highness
'that he thought the declaration he received yesterday
in the highest degree just, consolatory, and glorious for
Austria—one which could not fail to produce a very
great impression. If Austria had been uncertain, if
she had hesitated at this important moment, he would,
for his part, have given up Europe as lost. Now he
could still see hope, and if all German Courts would do
their duty, as Bavaria was determined to do, he thought
he might assure your Highness that, in spite of the
restless machinations of the enemy, peace would not be
disturbed in Germany.'

Baron Zentner joined in every word of these declarations. . . .

I have very much regretted that I was not able to
speak to Prince Wrede. He was not in Munich, and
I could not meet him in Mondsee, because he left that
place the very day that I left Munich, and took the
Regensberg road to his distant estates.

I left Munich on the morning of Monday, the 31st,
and arrived yesterday about noon in Salzburg, where I
found very unfavourable accounts concerning my
further journey to Gastein.

Metternich to Gentz, Vienna, August 10, 1820.

480. I received your Report from Salzburg, my
dear Gentz. I immediately laid it before the Emperor,
and he has done it the full justice it deserves. The
picture of Munich is quite true, the elements that rule
there are such as you describe ; and I am rejoiced that
you see that I was under no delusion as to the people
and the situation. . . .

Nothing decided can yet be said from Italy—there,

as everywhere else, the immediate future is uncertain.
The Governments desire what is right: will they be
steadfast in the day of danger? Our position alone
puts a curb on Italy at present. In Naples no one,
not even the first leaders, know where they are going,
where they can go, or even where they want to go.
There the revolution has really dropped from the
clouds; it lies like a spectre on the land. Those who
summoned it have gained their end so quickly that
they are quite astonished to be suddenly obliged to
rule; and turn the thing as you will, there remain
always the same wants and the same means of Government. The State needs money; it requires to be
guarded; justice must be administered. From whence
is the money to come? from whence the protection and
the justice? I believe, if the game were not too dangerous, the best means of quieting the babblers in the
opposition would be to select here and there some, and
lay upon them at once the affairs of government. This
is the situation of the Neapolitan rulers, and the part
they play is very different from that in Spain, for with
them everything was good, and now must become
absolutely bad. Nobody will pay, and nobody will obey.
The return of Prince Cariati must have caused a frightful sensation.

Things look very dangerous in the Roman district.
But when common sense is so shaken and perplexed as
it now is, one can no longer calculate on the future.
I freely confess, therefore, that I know not what can or
will be the end of the affair. However, we are here
quiet, and with our great resources may go calmly forward.

In France the Neapolitan event has caused quite a
sensation. At the first glance the communications

from the Cabinet seem to be good. No one will be turned out of doors by Pepe and his companions.

In St. Petersburg the Neapolitan news has arrived after the King's departure ; in the course of a few days we shall know the impression it has made on him. Meantime, the peasants on the Don have taken up arms on hearing that the Emperor had declared the peasants from Esthonia and Courland free, asserting their desire to be free also. Many troops have marched there to drive out the Liberal devil with the knout.

From Germany I have always quiet, unimportant news. On all sides we are entreated, for God's sake, to send a great many troops to Italy. By September 85,000 men will be on the spot.

I hope soon to see you again. I miss you very much, especially at the present moment.

RESULTS OF THE TROPPAU CONGRESS.*

Metternich to the Emperor Francis, Troppau, November 6, 1820.

481. In order to bring about the fullest understanding, I wrote down the annexed paper (482) during the conversation that took place to-day between the three Cabinets.

The Russian Ministers agreed that it suitably expressed the feeling of their master. I lay it before your Majesty for approval, to know whether I may deliver it as truly representing your Majesty's opinion.

Principles of the Policy of Intervention.

(Enclosed with No. 481.)

482. The allies agree together :—

1. That their aim and object, moral as well as physical, is not limited to giving liberty of thought and action to legitimate power, but is also to enable that power to consolidate and strengthen itself in such a way as to guarantee peace and stability to the kingdom and to Europe.

2. They recognise that to this end the power should,

---

* At the Congress of Troppau, assembled at Metternich's suggestion, there were the Emperor Francis of Austria, the Emperor Alexander and Grand-Duke Nicholas of Russia, King Frederick William III. of Prussia, with the Crown Prince, the diplomatists, Metternich, Zichy, Gentz, Mercy (for Austria), Nesselrode, Capo d'Istria, Golowkin, Alopäus (for Russia), Hardenberg, Bernstorff (for Prussia), Stewart (for England), De la Ferronays (for France).—ED.

in its reconstruction, consult the true interests and needs of the country.

3. That what the King in his wisdom considers satisfactory for the interests of the kingdom, and consequently satisfactory to the sound part of the nation, will be taken as the legal basis of the order to be established in the kingdom of Naples.

Approved and accepted.

FRANCIS.

Circular Despatch of the Courts of Austria, Russia, and Prussia, to their Ambassadors and Agents at the German and Northern Courts, Troppau, December 8, 1820.

484. The events of March 8 in Spain, and July 2 in Naples, and the catastrophe in Portugal, must cause in all those who have to care for the peace of States a deep feeling of grief and anxiety, and, at the same time, a necessity for meeting, in order to consider in common how best to meet the evils which threaten to break out all over Europe.

It was natural that these feelings should be very active in those particular Powers which had lately conquered revolution, and now saw it raising its head again ; and also natural that these Powers, in resisting the revolution for the third time, should resort to the same means which they had used so happily in the memorable combat which delivered Europe from a twenty years' yoke.

Everything justified the hope that this union, formed under the most dangerous circumstances, crowned with the most brilliant success, fostered by the negotiations of 1814, 1815, and 1818, as it had released the European continent from the military despotism of the representative of revolution, and brought peace to the world, would be able to curb a new force not less tyrannical and not less to be despised—the power of rebellion and outrage.

These were the motives, and the purpose, of the meeting in Troppau. The former are so evident that they do not require an explanation: the latter is so honourable and beneficial that doubtless the wishes of all honourable men will follow the allied Courts in their noble career.

The business which is imposed on them by the most sacred obligations is great and difficult; but a happy presentiment bids them hope for the attainment of their aim by a firm maintenance of the spirit of those treaties to which Europe owes peace and unity among her States.

The Powers exercise an indisputable right in contemplating common measures of safety against States in which the Government has been overthrown by rebellion, and which, if only as an example, must consequently be treated as hostile to all lawful constitutions and Governments. The exercise of this right becomes still more urgent when revolutionists endeavour to spread to neighbouring countries the misfortunes which they had brought upon themselves, scattering rebellion and confusion around.

Such a position, such proceedings are an evident violation of contract, which guarantees to all the European Governments, besides the inviolability of their territories, the enjoyment of those peaceful relations which exclude the possibility of encroachment on either side.

The allied Courts took incontestable fact as their starting-point, and those ministers who could be at

Troppau itself supplied with definite instructions from their monarchs, therefore made an agreement as to the principles to be followed as to States whose form of government has been violently disturbed, and as to the peaceful or forcible measures to be adopted to lead such States back into the Bund.

The results of their deliberations they communicated to the Courts of Paris and London, that those Courts might take them into consideration.

Since the Neapolitan revolution takes daily fresh root ; since no other endangers so directly the peace of the neighbouring States ; since no other can be acted upon so immediately, the necessity of proceeding on the above-mentioned principles with regard to the kingdom of Both the Sicilies soon became evident.

To bring about conciliatory measures to that end, the monarchs assembled at Troppau resolved to invite the King of Both Sicilies to meet them at Laybach, a step which would free the will of his Majesty from every outward constraint, and put the King in the position of a mediator between his deluded and erring subjects and the States whose peace was threatened by them. Since the monarchs were determined not to acknowledge Governments created by open rebellion, they could enter into a negotiation with the person of the King only. Their ministers and agents in Naples have received the necessary instructions for that purpose.

France and England have been asked to take part in this step, and it is to be expected that they will not refuse their consent, since the principle on which the invitation rests is in perfect harmony with the agreements formerly concluded by them, and is also a pledge of the most upright and peaceable feelings.*

* England, according to a despatch dated January 17, 1821, declined to

The system established between Austria, Prussia, and Russia is no new one ; it rests on the same maxims which formed the foundation of the agreements by which the union of the European States in the Bund has been effected. The hearty concord existing between the Courts which form the centre of this confederation can only be strengthened by it. The Bund will be maintained on the same footing as that on which it was placed by the Powers to whom it owes its existence, and as it has been gradually accepted by all, from the conviction entertained of its evident and undoubted advantages.

No further proof, however, is required that the Powers have not been guided in their resolutions by the thought of conquest or the desire of interfering with the internal affairs of other Governments. They want nothing but to maintain peace, to free Europe from the scourge of revolution, and to avert, or shorten as much as possible, the mischief arising from the violation of all the principles of order and morality. Under such conditions they think themselves justified in claiming the unanimous approbation of the world as a reward for their cares and their efforts.

Metternich to Count Rechberg, Vienna, December 31, 1820.

485. I take advantage, my dear Count, of the first moment at my disposal, which is the last of my stay here, to give you some account of what has been done and what is going to be done. . . .

Here are the facts in all their simplicity.

Any catastrophe such as that of Naples presents different periods, whether regarded from a domestic or

join in the measure in question. Not so France, whose King wrote to the King of Naples urging him to accept the invitation of the allied monarchs.—Ed.

foreign point of view. The revolt breaks out; it is indubitable and evident; it is the beginning of a conflagration; if they are in good order, take your fire-engines there; ask no questions; do not hesitate; extinguish the fire; success will be certain. Do not take empty fire-engines, but let them be well filled.

Then comes the second period. The revolt takes the appearance of Reform. A feeble sovereign swears to put a knife to his throat. A chorus of Liberals and Radicals join in his hymns; the sovereign is praised to the skies; and the people seem to adore him. Milk and honey are to flow in all the veins of the State abandoned to anarchy; tyrants alone could hinder the development of so fine a work!

This is the history of the months of July to November.

Our fire-engines were not full in July, otherwise we should have set to work immediately.

In the second period, it did not seem to us that our neutral attitude was sufficient; the Naples affair threatened Italy, Austria, Europe equally. It is therefore for the latter to declare itself in principle with us. We take upon ourselves the material part. To go to Naples is nothing at any time, but to remain at Naples and re-establish order in the kingdom of the Two Sicilies is certainly more difficult.

Europe has frankly and well seconded us. We, who were free to hold whatever language we liked, have spoken: those of our allies who could do the same have done so. Those who are more bound by forms have acted according to our principles. The Neapolitan revolt and all its charms have been put in quarantine. You have done more than even the great English and French. You have sent back the agent of the Carbonari who came to boast to you of the happiness of his country ; you have done this, my dear Count, and it was worthy of you.

Agreed in their principles at Troppau, the three Cabinets have carried them into effect. The idea of inviting the King to meet us at Laybach was acceptable. This invitation was made on very simple, but the only correct grounds. You know the autograph letters of the Sovereigns : they are all friendly, for no one is an enemy of the King. The *ostensible* instructions for our plenipotentiaries were more precise. They were ordered to declare—

1st. That the Powers would never recognise anything which is the work of the rebellion.

2nd. That before resorting to extreme measures, they desire to exhaust every means of conciliation, *not between the rebellion and lawful power, but between the real interests of the kingdom and those of Italy and Europe.* That, knowing but one proper instrument for a work so great and salutary, his Majesty the King was invited to meet the three monarchs.

3rd. That at Naples it is asserted that the King is free. That the King, being free, should feel it his duty to take upon himself this great work ; that if the King did not come he would be surrendered.

4th. That as the King's person is not on this occasion to be replaced by any other, the invitation is personal. That our ambassadors would in consequence refuse passports to any other individual, were it even a Prince of the Royal House ; that on the other hand, it would depend upon the King to be accompanied by whomsoever his Majesty should think fit.

5th. That the King, if he were prevented from

leaving the Kingdom, should be placed under the safe-
guard and responsibility of every Neapolitan.

The order has gone, and there is not a folly that our
agents have not committed. Unhappily, there is not a
single head among them. These stormy times, my dear
Count, are weak in heads.

What we had foreseen came to pass among the
parties at Naples. The Radicals and Doctrinaires, or, if
you like it better, the Demagogues and the Liberals,
who at Naples call themselves *Carbonari* and *Muratistes*,
are divided ; they had agreed together before, during,
and after July, with the sole object of overthrowing the
existing order of things, and we were certain that the
Muratists (who must be ruined in any state of the case)
would try to make the King go. But they went further :
they wished to turn the circumstance to advantage to
overthrow Carbonarism and assert themselves. This is
the secret of the declaration of December 7 last. And
to do this the better, they placed our ambassadors in
a false light by making them be present at a Council
where the Duke of Calabria produced that declaration,
while the Neapolitan ministers were met together in
another room close by. Zurlo, who had conceived the
project, sent the declaration in haste into the provinces
in the hope of exciting there a strong feeling in favour
of Liberalism ; but its language was like so much He-
brew to the Neapolitans. The funds rose ; the Parliament, which is merely the *élite* of the sect, attacked
the Ministry, and once more the *Doctrinaires* must be
convinced that in revolutions (which they will adore
none the less) they are, and always will be, crushed by
the extreme parties.

The man who desires the whole is very strong in
comparison with him who only desires the half.

Our ambassadors not only took no part in this action, but they declared themselves incompetent. Why then sit at the round table?

But good often comes out of evil. We should have had to fight the *Muratistes* at Laybach. They died on the road, and of the two I prefer to take in hand Carbonarism rather than Liberalism, and you will be of my opinion. The importance which the King and his Government, including the Prince Royal, attach to the oath of July 8, was proved on December 7.

But, however, there is the King. From this moment everything is simplified, and the positions are made clear. The King's duty is to speak and enlighten his people. He has to pacify his kingdom and organise it so as to procure present and future peace. At the same time he must do nothing which will disturb the repose of his neighbours; and it is for them to guard against that. We have also invited the Princes of Italy to send representatives to Laybach. Austria will furnish the means of pacification, and the Powers, including Austria, will guarantee the results, and these results we are to bring about.

Here then, my dear Count, is a very short statement, and a very heavy budget.

Naples has in the mean time exhausted her treasury. Fifteen millions of ducats have been wasted in four months; there are no soldiers, no arms; no place is provisioned; but the Carbonari, who had not a *sou*, begin to feel their pockets filling, while the proprietors feel theirs empty: undoubted benefits resulting from this beautiful enterprise which the Duke de Campochiaro, at the commencement of his ministry, assured me was quite falsely called a revolution, being nothing but a little family arrangement.

Now see how things stand. The first moments at Laybach will decide the development of affairs. Be quite easy, my dear Count ; we shall not swerve from our principles.

You will be grateful to me for writing such a long letter at the very moment of my departure, though perhaps it shows signs of my haste ; but as I wish you to know how things are, the principles which guide us, and to give you a new proof of my confidence, I do not deserve any credit.

To conclude, this letter is only for the King, yourself, and the Marshal.

Adieu, my dear Count. The King of Naples will be at Laybach on the 5th, the Emperor of Austria on the 6th, and the Emperor of Russia on the 7th of January. I shall be there on the 5th.

Accept my good wishes for the new year, and, in it, may the same friendship and confidence unite us as in that which is passing away.

METTERNICH'S POLITICAL CONFESSION OF FAITH.

486. Metternich to the Emperor Francis (Report), Troppau, December 2, 1820.

486. May it please your Majesty to receive enclosed my 'Confession of Faith' to the Emperor Alexander.

I beseech your Highness to read this short diplomatic composition in the sense in which I have drawn it up, and which is known to your Majesty.

METTERNICH.

The enclosed herewith returned.

FRANCIS.

Troppau, December 2, 1820.

Metternich to the Emperor Alexander, Troppau, December 15, 1820.

487. Sire, I have the honour to send to your Imperial Majesty the enclosed statement. I received your Majesty's commands, and have fulfilled them with an ardour which gives full liberty to my thoughts. Your Imperial Majesty will find it complete on all the questions most worthy of the meditations of every public man, of every man entrusted with grave interests —in short, of every man sufficiently enlightened to feel that to a world of folly he should oppose another full of wisdom, reason, justice, and reformation. I should have despised myself, Sire, long ago, if I did not say what I think. What in a private individual might appear a merit is simply a duty to a man in my position.

What is contained in this statement would excite a disdainful smile from the superficial persons who, full of complacency at their own imperfect knowledge, are impudent criticisers of the first interests of Society—that crowd of bawlers with crude ideas, who are the victims of their own errors, and false prophets, whenever they allow themselves to predict anything but groundless errors. This same smile would appear on the lips of a better class of men—those men who think that the most useless of all enterprises is to say what is self-evident. My conviction, Sire, is that it is always the duty of men who wish to do good to speak, for at all times, and above all at times disturbed by passion, those men who wish to do evil, the vain and the foolish, will speak. It is therefore necessary not to abandon the moral atmosphere to them altogether.

Deign, Sire, while receiving this paper, dictated by my conscience, to accept the homage of my profound respect.

Confession of Faith.

Metternich's Secret Memorandum to the Emperor Alexander.

(Supplement to No. 487.)

488. ' *L'Europe,*' a celebrated writer has recently said, ' *fait aujourd'hui pitié à l'homme d'esprit et horreur à l'homme vertueux.*'

It would be difficult to comprise in a few words a

more exact picture of the situation at the time we are writing these lines !

Kings have to calculate the chances of their very existence in the immediate future ; passions are let loose, and league together to overthrow everything which society respects as the basis of its existence ; religion, public morality, laws, customs, rights, and duties, all are attacked, confounded, overthrown, or called in question. The great mass of the people are tranquil spectators of these attacks and revolutions, and of the absolute want of all means of defence. A few are carried off by the torrent, but the wishes of the immense majority are to maintain a repose which exists no longer, and of which even the first elements seem to be lost.

What is the cause of all these evils ? By what methods has this evil established itself, and how is it that it penetrates into every vein of the social body ?

Do remedies still exist to arrest the progress of this evil, and what are they ?

These are doubtless questions worthy of the solicitude of every good man who is a true friend to order and public peace—two elements inseparable in principle, and which are at once the first needs and the first blessings of humanity.

Has there never been offered to the world an institution really worthy of the name ? Has truth been always confounded with error ever since society has believed itself able to distinguish one from the other ? Have the experiences bought at the price of so many sacrifices, and repeated at intervals, and in so many different places, been all in error ? Will a flood of light be shed upon society at one stroke ? Will knowledge come by inspiration ? If one could believe in such phenomena it would not be the less necessary, first of all, to assure oneself of their reality. Of all things, nothing is so fatal as error ; and it is neither our wish nor our intention ever to give ourselves up to it. Let us examine the matter !

The Source of the Evil.

Man's nature is immutable. The first needs of society are and remain the same, and the differences which they seem to offer find their explanation in the diversity of influences, acting on the different races by natural causes, such as the diversity of climate, barrenness or richness of soil, insular or continental position, &c. &c. These local differences no doubt produce effects which extend far beyond purely physical necessities ; they create and determine particular needs in a more elevated sphere ; finally, they determine the laws, and exercise an influence even on religions.

It is, on the other hand, with institutions as with everything else. Vague in their origin, they pass through periods of development and perfection, to arrive in time at their decadence ; and, conforming to the laws of man's nature, they have, like him, their infancy, their youth, their age of strength and reason, and their age of decay.

Two elements alone remain in all their strength, and never cease to exercise their indestructible influence with equal power. These are the precepts of morality, religious as well as social, and the necessities created by locality. From the time that men attempt to swerve from these bases, to become rebels against these sovereign arbiters of their destinies, society suffers from a *malaise* which sooner or later will lead to a state of

convulsion. The history of every country, in relating
the consequences of such errors, contains many pages
stained with blood ; but we dare to say, without fear of
contradiction, one seeks in vain for an epoch when an
evil of this nature has extended its ravages over such a
vast area as it has done at the present time.   The
causes are natural.

History embraces but a very limited space of time.
It did not begin to deserve the name of history until
long after the fall of great empires.   There, where it
seems to conduct us to the cradle of civilisation, it
really conducts us to ruins.   We see republics arise
and prosper, struggle, and then submit to the rule of
one fortunate soldier.   We see one of these republics
pass through all the phases common to society, and
end in an almost universal monarchy—-that is to say,
subjugating the scattered portions of the then civilised
world.   We see this monarchy suffer the fate of all
political bodies : we see its first springs become enfeebled, and finally decay.

Centuries of darkness followed the irruption of the
barbarians.   The world, however, could not return to
barbarism.   The Christian religion had appeared ; imperishable in its essence, its very existence was sufficient
to disperse the darkness and establish civilisation on
new foundations, applicable to all times and all places,
satisfying all needs, and establishing the most important
of all on the basis of a pure and eternal law !   To the
formation of new Christian States succeeded the Cru-
sades, a curious mixture of good and evil.

A decisive influence was shortly exercised on the
progress of civilisation by three discoveries—the invention of printing, that of gunpowder, and the discovery
of the New World.   Still later came the Reformation—

another event which had incalculable effects, on account of its influence on the moral world. From that time the face of the world was changed.

The facilitation of the communication of thoughts by printing; the total change in the means of attack and defence brought about by the invention of gunpowder; the difference suddenly produced in the value of property by the quantity of metals which the discovery of America put in circulation; the spirit of adventure provoked by the chances of fortune opened in a new hemisphere; the modifications in the relations of society caused by so many and such important changes, all became more developed, and were in some sort crowned by the revolution which the Reformation worked in the moral world.

The progress of the human mind has been extremely rapid in the course of the last three centuries. This progress having been accelerated more rapidly than the growth of wisdom (the only counterpoise to passions and to error); a revolution prepared by the false systems, the fatal errors into which many of the most illustrious sovereigns of the last half of the eighteenth century fell, has at last broken out in a country advanced in knowledge, and enervated by pleasure, in a country inhabited by a people whom one can only regard as frivolous, from the facility with which they comprehend and the difficulty they experience in judging calmly.

Having now thrown a rapid glance over the first causes of the present state of society, it is necessary to point out in a more particular manner the evil which threatens to deprive it, at one blow, of the real blessings, the fruits of genuine civilisation, and to disturb it in the midst of its enjoyments. This evil may be described in one word—presumption ; the natural effect of the rapid progression of the human mind towards the perfecting of so many things. This it is which at the present day leads so many individuals astray, for it has become an almost universal sentiment.

Religion, morality, legislation, economy, politics, administration, all have become common and accessible to everyone. Knowledge seems to come by inspiration ; experience has no value for the presumptuous man ; faith is nothing to him ; he substitutes for it a pretended individual conviction, and to arrive at this conviction dispenses with all inquiry and with all study ; for these means appear too trivial to a mind which believes itself strong enough to embrace at one glance all questions and all facts. Laws have no value for him, because he has not contributed to make them, and it would be beneath a man of his parts to recognise the limits traced by rude and ignorant generations. Power resides in himself ; why should he submit himself to that which was only useful for the man deprived of light and knowledge ? That which, according to him, was required in an age of weakness cannot be suitable in an age of reason and vigour. amounting to universal perfection, which the German innovators designate by the idea, absurd in itself, of the Emancipation of the People ! Morality itself he does not attack openly, for without it he could not be sure for a single instant of his own existence ; but he interprets its essence after his own fashion, and allows every other person to do so likewise, provided that other person neither kills nor robs him.

In thus tracing the character of the presumptuous man, we believe we have traced that of the society of the day, composed of like elements, if the denomination of society is applicable to an order of things which only tends in principle towards individualising all the elements of which society is composed. Presumption makes every man the guide of his own belief, the arbiter of laws according to which he is pleased to govern himself, or to allow some one else to govern him and his neighbours ; it makes him, in short, the sole judge of his own faith, his own actions, and the principles according to which he guides them.

Is it necessary to give a proof of this last fact ? We think we have furnished it in remarking that one of the sentiments most natural to man, that of nationality, is erased from the Liberal catechism, and that where the word is still employed, it is used by the heads of the party as a pretext to enchain Governments, or as a lever to bring about destruction. The real aim of the idealists of the party is religious and political fusion, and this being analysed is nothing else but creating in favour of each individual an existence entirely independent of all authority, or of any other will than his own, an idea absurd and contrary to the nature of man, and incompatible with the needs of human society.

The Course which the Evil has Followed and still Follows.

The causes of the deplorable intensity with which this evil weighs on society appear to us to be of two kinds. The first are so connected with the nature of things that no human foresight could have prevented them. The second should be subdivided into two classes, however similar they may appear in their effects.

Of these causes, the first are negative, the others

positive. We will place among the first the feebleness
and the inertia of Governments.

It is sufficient to cast a glance on the course which
the Governments followed during the eighteenth century, to be convinced that not one among them was
ignorant of the evil or of the crisis towards which the
social body was tending. There were, however, some
men, unhappily endowed with great talents, who felt
their own strength, and were not slow to appraise
the progressive course of their influence, taking into
account the weakness or the inertia of their adversaries ;
and who had the art to prepare and conduct men's
minds to the triumph of their detestable enterprise—
an enterprise all the more odious as it was pursued without regard to results, simply abandoning themselves to
the one feeling of hatred of God and of His immutable
moral laws.

France had the misfortune to produce the greatest
number of these men. It is in her midst that religion
and all that she holds sacred, that morality and authority, and all connected with them, have been attacked
with a steady and systematic animosity, and it is there
that the weapon of ridicule has been used with the most
ease and success.

Drag through the mud the name of God and the
powers instituted by His divine decrees, and the revolution will be prepared ! Speak of a social contract, and
the revolution is accomplished ! The revolution was
already completed in the palaces of Kings, in the
drawing-rooms and boudoirs of certain cities, while
among the great mass of the people it was still only in
a state of preparation.

It would be difficult not to pause here to consider
the influence which the example of England had for a

long time exercised on France. England is herself placed in such a peculiar situation that we believe we may safely say that not one of the forms possible to that State, not one of its customs or institutions, would suit any Continental State, and that where we might wish to take them for models, we should only obtain inconvenience and danger, without securing a single one of the advantages which accompany them.

According to the bent of minds in France, at the time of the convocation of the *notables*, and in consequence of the direction which public opinion had received for more than fifty years—a direction which, latterly, had been strengthened and in some sort adapted to France by the imprudent help which her Government had given to the American revolution—all reform in France touching the very foundations of the monarchy was soon transformed into a revolution. What might have been foreseen, and what had been foretold by everybody, the Government alone excepted, was realised but too soon. The French Revolution broke out, and has gone through a complete revolutionary cycle in a very short period, which could only have appeared long to its victims and to its contemporaries.

The scenes of horror which accompanied the first phases of the French Revolution prevented the rapid propagation of its subversive principles beyond the frontiers of France, and the wars of conquest which succeeded them gave to the public mind a direction little favourable to revolutionary principles. Thus the Jacobin propaganda failed entirely to realise criminal hopes.

Nevertheless the revolutionary seed had penetrated into every country and spread more or less. It was greatly developed under the *régime* of the military despotism of Bonaparte. His conquests displaced a number of laws, institutions, and customs; broke through bonds sacred among all nations, strong enough to resist time itself; which is more than can be said of certain benefits conferred by these innovators. From these perturbations it followed that the revolutionary spirit could in Germany, Italy, and later on in Spain, easily hide itself under the veil of patriotism.

Prussia committed a grave fault in calling to her aid such dangerous weapons as secret associations always will be : a fault which could not be justified even by the deplorable situation in which that Power then found itself. This it was that first gave a strong impulse to the revolutionary spirit in her States, and this spirit made rapid progress, supported as it was in the rest of Germany by the system of foreign despotism which since 1806 has been there developed. Many Princes of the Rhenish Confederation were secretly auxiliaries and accomplices of this system, to which they sacrificed the institutions which in their country from time immemorial had served as a protection against despotism and democracy.

The war of the Allies, by putting bounds to the pre-dominance of France, was vigorously supported in Germany by the same men whose hatred of France was in reality nothing but hatred of the military despotism of Bonaparte, and also of the legitimate power of their own masters. With wisdom in the Governments and firmness in principles, the end of the war in 1814 might nevertheless have insured to the world the most peaceful and happy future. Great experiences had been gained and great lessons, which might have been usefully applied. But fate had decided otherwise.

The return of the usurper to France, and the completely false steps taken by the French Government from 1815 to 1820, accumulated a mass of new dangers and great calamities for the whole civilised world. It is to the first of these misfortunes that is partly due the critical state in which France and the whole social body is placed. Bonaparte destroyed in a hundred days the work of the fourteen years during which he had exercised his authority. He set free the revolution which he came to France to subdue; he brought back men's minds, not to the epoch of the 18th Brumaire, but to the principles which the National Assembly had adopted in its deplorable blindness.

What Bonaparte had thus done to the detriment of France and Europe, the grave errors which the French Government have since committed, and to which other Governments have yielded—all these unhappy influences weigh heavily on the world of to-day; they threaten with total ruin the work of restoration, the fruit of so many glorious efforts, and of a harmony between the greatest monarchs unparalleled in the records of history, and they give rise to fears of indescribable calamities to society.

In this memoir we have not yet touched on one of the most active and at the same time most dangerous instruments used by the revolutionists of all countries, with a success which is no longer doubtful. I refer to the secret societies, a real power, all the more dangerous as it works in the dark, undermining all parts of the social body, and depositing everywhere the seeds of a moral gangrene which is not slow to develop and increase. This plague is one of the worst which those Governments who are lovers of peace and of their people have to watch and fight against.

Do Remedies for this Evil exist, and What are They?

We look upon it as a fundamental truth, that for
every disease there is a remedy, and that the knowledge
of the real nature of the one should lead to the discovery of the other. Few men, however, stop thoroughly to examine a disease which they intend to
combat. There are hardly any who are not subject to
the influence of passion, or held under the yoke of
prejudice; there are a great many who err in a way
more perilous still, on account of its flattering and often
brilliant appearance : we speak of *l'esprit de système*;
that spirit always false, but indefatigable, audacious
and irrepressible, is satisfactory to men imbued with
it (for they live in and govern a world created by
themselves), but it is so much the more dangerous for
the inhabitants of the real world, so different from that
created by *l'esprit de système*.

There is another class of men who, judging of a
disease by its outward appearance, confound the accessory manifestations with the root of the disease, and,
instead of directing their efforts to the source of the
evil, content themselves with subduing some passing
symptoms.

It is our duty to try and avoid both of these dangers.

The evil exists and it is enormous. We do not
think we can better define it and its cause at all times
and in all places than we have already done by the
word 'presumption,' that inseparable companion of the
half-educated, that spring of an unmeasured ambition,
and yet easy to satisfy in times of trouble and confusion.

It is principally the middle classes of society which

this moral gangrene has affected, and it is only among them that the real heads of the party are found.

For the great mass of the people it has no attraction and can have none. The labours to which this class—the real people—are obliged to devote themselves, are too continuous and too positive to allow them to throw themselves into vague abstractions and ambitions. The people know what is the happiest thing for them : namely, to be able to count on the morrow, for it is the morrow which will repay them for the cares and sorrows of to-day. The laws which afford a just protection to individuals, to families, and to property, are quite simple in their essence. The people dread any movement which injures industry and brings new burdens in its train.

Men in the higher classes of society who join the revolution are either falsely ambitious men or, in the widest acceptation of the word, lost spirits. Their career, moreover, is generally short! They are the first victims of political reforms, and the part played by the small number among them who survive is mostly that of courtiers despised by upstarts, their inferiors, promoted to the first dignities of the State ; and of this France, Germany, Italy, and Spain furnish a number of living examples.

We do not believe that fresh disorders with a directly revolutionary end—not even revolutions in the palace and the highest places in the Government—are to be feared at present in France, because of the decided aversion of the people to anything which might disturb the peace they are now enjoying after so many troubles and disasters.

In Germany, as in Spain and Italy, the people ask only for peace and quiet.

In all four countries the agitated classes are principally composed of wealthy men—real cosmopolitans, securing their personal advantage at the expense of any order of things whatever—paid State officials, men of letters, lawyers, and the individuals charged with the public education.

To these classes may be added that of the falsely ambitious, whose number is never considerable among the lower orders, but is larger in the higher ranks of society.

There is besides scarcely any epoch which does not offer a rallying cry to some particular faction. This cry, since 1815, has been *Constitution*. But do not let us deceive ourselves : this word, susceptible of great latitude of interpretation, would be but imperfectly understood if we supposed that the factions attached quite the same meaning to it under the different *régimes*. Such is certainly not the case. In pure monarchies it is qualified by the name of 'national representation.' In countries which have lately been brought under the representative *régime* it is called ' development,' and promises charters and fundamental laws. In the only State which possesses an ancient national representation it takes ' reform' as its object. Everywhere it means change and trouble.

In pure monarchies it may be paraphrased thus :— ' The level of equality shall pass over your heads; your fortunes shall pass into other hands ; your ambitions, which have been satisfied for centuries, shall now give place to our ambitions, which have been hitherto repressed.'

In the States under a new *régime* they say :—' The ambitions satisfied yesterday must give place to those of the morrow, and this is the morrow for us.'

Lastly, in England, the only place in the third class, the rallying cry—that of Reform—combines the two meanings.

Europe thus presents itself to the impartial observer under an aspect at the same time deplorable and peculiar. We find everywhere the people praying for the maintenance of peace and tranquillity, faithful to God and their Princes, remaining proof against the efforts and seductions of the factious who call themselves friends of the people and wish to lead them to an agitation which the people themselves do not desire!

The Governments, having lost their balance, are frightened, intimidated, and thrown into confusion by the cries of the intermediary class of society, which, placed between the Kings and their subjects, breaks the sceptre of the monarch, and usurps the cry of the people—that class so often disowned by the people, and nevertheless too much listened to, caressed and feared by those who could with one word reduce it again to nothingness.

We see this intermediary class abandon itself with a blind fury and animosity which proves much more its own fears than any confidence in the success of its enterprises, to all the means which seem proper to assuage its thirst for power, applying itself to the task of persuading Kings that their rights are confined to sitting upon a throne, while those of the people are to govern, and to attack all that centuries have bequeathed as holy and worthy of man's respect—denying, in fact, the value of the past, and declaring themselves the masters of the future. We see this class take all sorts of disguises, uniting and subdividing as occasion offers, helping each other in the hour of danger, and the next day depriving each other of all their conquests. It

takes possession of the press, and employs it to promote impiety, disobedience to the laws of religion and
the State, and goes so far as to preach murder as a
duty for those who desire what is good.

One of its leaders in Germany defined public opinion
as 'the will of the strong man in the spirit of the
party'—a maxim too often put in practice, and too
seldom understood by those whose right and duty it is
to save society from its own errors, its own weaknesses,
and the crimes which the factious commit while pre-
tending to act in its interests.

The evil is plain ; the means used by the faction
which causes these disorders are so blameable in principle, so criminal in their application, and expose the
faction itself to so many dangers, that what men of
narrow views (whose head and heart are broken by
circumstances stronger than their calculations or their
courage) regard as the end of society may become the
first step towards a better order of things.   These weak
men would be right unless men stronger than they are
come forward to close their ranks and determine the
victory

We are convinced that society can no longer be
saved without strong and vigorous resolutions on the
part of the Governments still free in their opinions and
actions.

We are also convinced that this may yet be, if the
Governments face the truth, if they free themselves
from all illusion, if they join their ranks and take their
stand on a line of correct, unambiguous, and frankly
announced principles.

By this course the monarchs will fulfil the duties
imposed upon them by Him who, by entrusting them
with power, has charged them to watch over the main-

tenance of justice, and the rights of all, to avoid the paths of error, and tread firmly in the way of truth. Placed beyond the passions which agitate society, it is in days of trial chiefly that they are called upon to despoil realities of their false appearances, and to show themselves as they are, fathers invested with the authority belonging by right to the heads of families, to prove that, in days of mourning, they know how to be just, wise, and therefore strong, and that they will not abandon the people whom they ought to govern to be the sport of factions, to error and its consequences, which must involve the loss of society. The moment in which we are putting our thoughts on paper is one of these critical moments. The crisis is great; it will be decisive according to the part we take or do not take.

There is a rule of conduct common to individuals and to States, established by the experience of centuries as by that of everyday life. This rule declares ' that one must not dream of reformation while agitated by passion ; wisdom directs that at such moments we should limit ourselves to maintaining.'

Let the monarchs vigorously adopt this principle ; let all their resolutions bear the impression of it. Let their actions, their measures, and even their words announce and prove to the world this determination— they will find allies everywhere. The Governments, in establishing the principle of *stability*, will in no wise exclude the development of what is good, for stability is not immobility. But it is for those who are burdened with the heavy task of government to augment the well-being of their people ! It is for Governments to regulate it according to necessity and to suit the times. It is not by concessions, which the factious strive to force from legitimate power, and which they have neither the right to claim nor the faculty of keeping within just bounds, that wise reforms can be carried out. That all the good possible should be done is our most ardent wish; but that which is not good must never be confounded with that which is, and even real good should be done only by those who unite to the right of authority the means of enforcing it. Such should be also the sincere wish of the people, who know by sad experience the value of certain phrases and the nature of certain caresses.

Respect for all that is; liberty for every Government to watch over the well-being of its own people; a league between all Governments against factions in all States; contempt for the meaningless words which have become the rallying cry of the factious; respect for the progressive development of institutions in lawful ways; refusal on the part of every monarch to aid or succour partisans under any mask whatever—such are happily the ideas of the great monarchs: the world will be saved if they bring them into action—it is lost if they do not.

Union between the monarchs is the basis of the policy which must now be followed to save society from total ruin.

What is the particular object towards which this policy should be directed? The more important this question is, the more necessary it is to solve it. A principle is something, but it acquires real value only in its application.

The first sources of the evil which is crushing the world have been indicated by us in a paper which has no pretension to be anything more than a mere sketch. Its further causes have also there been pointed out if, with respect to individuals, it may be defined by the word *presumption*, in applying it to society, taken as a whole, we believe we can best describe the existing evil as the *confusion of ideas*, to which too much generalisation constantly leads. This is what now troubles society. Everything which up to this time has been considered as fixed in principle is attacked and overthrown.

In religious matters criticism and inquiry are to take the place of faith, Christian morality is to replace the Law of Christ as it is interpreted by Christian authorities.

In the Catholic Church, the Jansenists and a number of isolated sectarians, who wish for a religion without a Church, have devoted themselves to this enterprise with ardent zeal : among the Protestant sects, the Methodists, sub-divided into almost as many sects as there are individuals ; then the enlightened promoters of the Bible Societies and the Unitarians—the promoters of the fusion of Lutherans and Calvinists in one Evangelical community—all pursue the same end.

The object which these men have in common, to whatever religion they may ostensibly belong, is simply to overthrow all authority. Put on moral grounds, they wish *to enfranchise souls* in the same way as some of the political revolutionists who were not actuated by motives of personal ambition wished to *enfranchise the people*.

If the same elements of destruction which are now throwing society into convulsion have existed in all ages—for every age has seen immoral and ambitious men, hypocrites, men of heated imaginations, wrong motives, and wild projects—yet ours, by the single fact of the liberty of the press, possesses more than any preceding age the means of contact, seduction, and attraction whereby to act on these different classes of men.

We are certainly not alone in questioning if society can exist with the liberty of the press, a scourge unknown to the world before the latter half of the seventeenth century, and restrained until the end of the eighteenth, with scarcely any exceptions but England— a part of Europe separated from the continent by the sea, as well as by her language and by her peculiar manners.

The first principle to be followed by the monarchs, united as they are by the coincidence of their desires and opinions, should be that of maintaining the stability of political institutions against the disorganised excitement which has taken possession of men's minds ; the immutability of principles against the madness of their interpretation ; and respect for laws actually in force against a desire for their destruction.

The hostile faction is divided into two very distinct parties. One is that of the Levellers ; the other, that of the Doctrinaires. United in times of confusion, these men are divided in times of inaction. It is for the Governments to understand and estimate them at their just value.

In the class of Levellers there are found men of strong will and determination. The Doctrinaires can count none such among their ranks. If the first are more to be feared in action, the second are more dangerous in that time of deceitful calm which precedes it ; as with physical storms, so with those of social order. Given up to abstract ideas inapplicable to real wants, and generally in contradiction to those very wants, men of this class unceasingly agitate the people by their imaginary or simulated fears, and disturb Governments in order to make them deviate from the right path. The world desires to be governed by facts and according to justice, not by phrases and theories ; the first need of society is to be maintained by strong authority (no authority without real strength deserves the name) and not to govern itself. In comparing the number of contests between parties in mixed Governments, and that of just complaints caused by aberrations of power in a Christian State, the comparison would not be in favour of the new doctrines. The first and greatest concern for the immense majority of every nation is the stability of the laws, and their uninterrupted action—never their change. Therefore let the Governments govern, let them maintain the groundwork of their institutions, both ancient and modern ; for if it is at all times dangerous to touch them, it certainly would not now, in the general confusion, be wise to do so.

Let them announce this determination to their people, and demonstrate it by facts. Let them reduce the Doctrinaires to silence within their States, and show their contempt for them abroad. Let them not encourage by their attitude or actions the suspicion of being favourable or indifferent to error : let them not allow it to be believed that experience has lost all its rights to make way for experiments which at the least are dangerous. Let them be precise and clear in all their words, and not seek by concessions to gain over those parties who aim at the destruction of all power but their own, whom concessions will never gain over, but only further embolden in their pretensions to power.

Let them in these troublous times be more than usually cautious in attempting real ameliorations, not imperatively claimed by the needs of the moment, to the end that good itself may not turn against them —which is the case whenever a Government measure seems to be inspired by fear.

Let them not confound concessions made to parties with the good they ought to do for their people, in modifying, according to their recognised needs, such branches of the administration as require it.

Let them give minute attention to the financial state of their kingdoms, so that their people may enjoy, by the reduction of public burdens, the real, not imaginary, benefits of a state of peace.

Let them be just, but strong ; beneficent, but strict.

Let them maintain religious principles in all their purity, and not allow the faith to be attacked and morality interpreted according to the *social contract* or the visions of foolish sectarians.

Let them suppress Secret Societies, that gangrene of society.

In short, let the great monarchs strengthen their union, and prove to the world that if it exists, it is beneficent, and ensures the political peace of Europe : that it is powerful only for the maintenance of tranquillity at a time when so many attacks are directed against it ; that the principles which they profess are paternal and protective, menacing only the disturbers of public tranquillity.

The Governments of the second order will see in such a union the anchor of their salvation, and they will be anxious to connect themselves with it. The people will take confidence and courage, and the most profound and salutary peace which the history of any time can show will have been effected. This peace will first act on countries still in a good state, but will not be without a very decided influence on the fate of those threatened with destruction, and even assist the restoration of those which have already passed under the scourge of revolution.

To every great State determined to survive the storm there still remain many chances of salvation, and a strong union between the States on the principles we have announced will overcome the storm itself.

1821.

THE CONGRESS AT LAYBACH.

Extracts from Metternich's private Letters from January 4 to May 21, 1821.

489. *Laybach, January* 4, 1821.—On December 25, in the morning, I left Troppau, and on the morning of the 27th arrived at Vienna, where I remained till New Year's Day. I started from Vienna on January 1, in fifteen degrees of cold. Till the mountain was crossed which separates Carniola from Styria the cold continually increased; but on the opposite side of the mountain I first felt the southern air, and the ice on my carriage windows, which was half an inch thick, melted in less than a quarter of an hour. I breathed new life, as servants often get a pleasant odour when they open the doors of a banquet hall. Laybach is like the anteroom to some comfortable apartments. If Görz were not too small to accommodate a Congress, we would have settled ourselves in that town, because there the Alps are entirely passed. A man can only really live in a country where there is no winter, or not a long winter. I am still the only person here ; the morning will bring an avalanche of statesmen—an avalanche that will cause no joy.

I am very well pleased with my accommodation. I have a good room to write in, a good bedroom, and a suite of reception rooms. The mistress of the house is as ugly as the seven deadly sins, and has seven children who each resemble one of the said sins.

Poor Nesselrode finds himself in a very strange moral position. There are fish which can only live in hard spring water ; others which do better in ponds or stagnant water. The trout belongs to the first class : in soft, stagnant water it becomes flabby ; but if you let a little fresh water flow in, the poor fish soon becomes lively, and gains that appearance of health and strength so peculiar to the trout in water, and its chief merit.

Now, there are men who have not sufficient strength of character to overcome the difficulties which surround them ; others, again, who are more comfortable in the mud. Nesselrode by nature belongs to the class of trout, but unhappily he remains in the mud. Since I have let a little fresh water in upon him he has astonishingly revived. He has become lively, and longs for the harder but healthier medium. He will certainly not remain so, for what is a glass of pure water

in such a swamp? The poor little man has moments
when he thinks he is all right again; if he were a fish
he would be carried away with the current.

Do you know an English novel called "Anastasius"?
In it there is a description of the Greek character (I
think in the fourth, fifth, or sixth chapter) which is very
good and accurate, as indeed is everything in this book
relating to Oriental, and especially Greek, customs. You
will find there Capo d'Istria word for word, exactly as
he is. It is really extraordinary that destiny should
have brought us, who are of so opposite a nature, and
have come into the world seven or eight hundred
miles from one another, to meet upon the same ground.
Nemo propheta in patria, says the proverb. Whether
Capo d'Istria will ever be a prophet beyond his fatherland I doubt.

I should have liked Robespierre better than Abbé
de Pradt, and Attila better than Quiroga. A tyrant
does not alarm me; I should know how to avoid his
attacks, or bear them with honour. But the Radical
maniac, the sentimental Boudoir-Philanthropist, make
me uncomfortable. I like iron and gold, but I hate tin
and copper. This childish feeling is so decided in me
that I never can endure plated things

490. *January* 6.—To-day is the Festival of the
Three Kings; it is very convenient, too, that they now
come together. We are very gallant here, and will
manage it so that the old Ferdinand (King of Naples)
draws the bean.

For the second time the task devolved on me of
picking him up—for he has the unfortunate habit of
always throwing himself down. But many Kings fancy
that the Throne is only an armchair, in which one can
sleep quite comfortably. In the year 1821, however, a

seat of this kind is inconvenient to sleep in, and badly stuffed.

My Emperor came to-day. For some months I have had but one quiet day, and that was yesterday. Such a day is a remarkable one in my life. The Emperor Alexander comes to-morrow, and the next day the King of Naples. My tasks are, unhappily, always of such a kind that it would be very pleasant if the end of one was not the beginning of another. A hard saying of the late Duke of Laval has the fullest application to my business. He said to me once, ' I never lend anyone a farthing; why should I ? At the very best my money will only be given back to me.' There lies in this axiom a truth which is irresistible.

491. *January* 7.— . . . . . Paul Esterhazy was allotted to me for many years. He will be my best biographer, on account of his extraordinary memory Whenever I meet him I am obliged to laugh, for he is always overflowing with old anecdotes which I had long forgotten. He knows my history from the year 1807 till 1815 better than I do myself. He does not know everything, but still he knows much, is shrewd— very shrewd—and perhaps knows more than I suspect. He is to me like a son, and loves me like a father.

492. *January* 10.—To-day, if the earth does not break up or the heavens fall down, or the commonest and vilest ruffians destroy all good people with right and strong wills, we have won the cause. Capo d'Istria twists about like a devil in holy water ; but he is in holy water and can do nothing. The chief cause of our activity to-day arises from my thorough agreement with the Emperor Alexander. Here, again, the tea makes its astonishing power felt.

Is there anything in the world which can to-day

take the place of ink, pens, a conference-table with its green cover, and a few greater or smaller bunglers?

493. *January* 13.—Capo d'Istria has given us the benefit of a new miracle of his genius. Here is a sentence out of an official paper descriptive of the Neapolitan insurrection. Since Isaiah and Cicero, the first as a poet, the other as an orator, nothing more eloquent has ever been uttered than the following words :—' *La sédition, associée aux mystères impies d'une secte antisociale, profitant de l'égarement qu'elle avait provoqué, a adopté une monstruosité politique destructive du Gouvernment auquel elle devait l'obéissance, incapable de lui en substituer un autre, et incompatible avec la paix générale.*' Here we have an insurrection veiled in mystery—an insurrection utilising a confusion, in order to produce a monstrosity, which monstrosity owed obedience to the Government. Further—and, indeed, this is the boldest stroke—this monstrosity, or this sect, or, if you like, the insurrection with its adopted daughter the monstrosity, is incapable of forming a Government, which Government, which cannot be made, is incompatible with the general peace!

These words apparently represent the roll of the thunder; at the proper place they are to strike like lightning. Can the result be doubted? What are battalions and artillery in comparison with such a phrase? May it not be expected that the Neapolitan volunteers will throw themselves in the dust, with ashes on their heads, and will they not with a voice of despair cry *pater, peccavi?*

Never was I more fortunate than in having (under present circumstances) arrived at a discreet age. Now I am safe in presence of such aberrations. At twenty they would have been dangerous: at thirty I might perhaps have become a fool or a maniac, but now I am well armed. I let them pass, listen like a Roman Senator without discomposing my countenance, and *swear*! Capo d'Istria has excused himself, and this is literally true, for the reason given is a mere excuse.

494. *January* 16.—We shall hardly get away from here till the end of March. An army takes thirty days to march from the Po to Naples, and we must await their entry here. At any rate, the present residence here is pleasanter than the former; it is much more agreeable. We have some public amusements, as, for instance, two masked balls in the week, the first of which they say was not very lively; among five-and-forty men there was one lady, who fell asleep in a corner of the room, which did not speak much for the gallantry of the gentlemen. Moreover, there are here some very pretty women, the prettiest being Countess Thurn, who is two-and twenty. They talk also of two other ladies, one of whom is five-and-twenty, the other five-and-thirty; the first limps, which you do not notice if she is sitting; the other has stern manners, but is of a very enthusiastic nature. This lady I will endeavour to install as the poet of our Congress.

495. *January* 24.—Frau von Hittroff is here with her two very pretty daughters. All our Austrians are in love with both. One is to marry a rich young man of good family, who belongs to our embassy at Rome; and the other is to marry our ambassador at Florence, a very clever and agreeable man. He is two or three and forty, while the girl is not yet sixteen. If he is successful and it goes on, I shall be very glad, for I like this worthy man about me, and he is a sort of right hand to me. I am so much occupied with military matters that I hardly myself know whether I do not belong to the military profession.

496. *January 25.*—We are ready ; the diplomatic fight is won ; sound manly sense has conquered. The principle is clear and plainly set forth, and if heaven favours us the execution will be quick and successful. The evening before a battle no general can say if he will win ; but he must count his troops, reconnoitre the ground, think of the retreat, and then let fly at the enemy. Providence only knows how the battle will go, but since providence has bestowed on us the gift of foresight, she at least expects from us that her priceless gifts, reason and conscience, should be taken into council. From the moment when I had the inward conviction of having satisfied this expectation I was calm and content. I am not accessible to fear ; I know no other than the fear lest I should mistake what is good and right. One day a thief, or perhaps a murderer, got in at my window and stood by my bed ; he thought I slept, but I observed him. I allowed him to come nearer without moving, but loosened my sheets so that nothing might be in my way. One jump and I stood up, seized him, threw him out of the window, and lay down again. 'He or I' was my thought. That is logic in business as with robbers. This circumstance took place in the year 1811.

I was yesterday on the Redoubt, which is dreadfully knocked about. It seems that this beautiful country has not always beautiful inhabitants. I saw only one pretty woman's face, and that belonged to a Russian cook, who caused much mischief among the soldiers. As I am not a soldier, I did not prolong my stay more than a quarter of an hour.

497. *February 6.*—To-day sixty thousand men will

cross the Po. In less than thirty days they will sit in the curulian chairs of the Parthenopian lawgiver as a proof that there is no procrastination with me. My enemies must find me very inconvenient. The Austrian proclamation is good, simple, and to the point.*

To-day I have the same feeling as on August 15, 1813, but the feeling of having an army on one's shoulders is somewhat oppressive.

498. *February* 7.—Every hour now brings us news from Italy which, taken altogether, shows that it will not come to a battle. I confess I shall be sorry. If it is necessary to give the insurgents a lesson it ought to be strongly expressed. Nothing is useful which is merely done privately; it ought to be done openly.

At any rate the outcome of it will be a new ex-

---

* This proclamation to the Neapolitan people, which was written in Italian and signed by the Austrian General in Command, Baron Frimont, dated Foligno, February 27, 1821, may be translated as follows:—' Neapolitans! At the moment when by my orders the army has crossed the frontier of the kingdom, I feel bound to make known freely and openly to you the object of my operations. Last July a deplorable revolution destroyed your domestic peace and severed the bonds of friendship which can only subsist between neighbouring States on the basis of mutual confidence. Your king has lifted his voice and spoken to his people in a royal and paternal manner. He has warned you of the horrors of a useless war, which will not be brought upon you by others, but which you will bring upon yourselves. The old and faithful allies of your country have also expressed themselves. They have, indeed, duties to their own people, but your true and lasting happiness is also dear to them, and that you will never find by forsaking the path of duty or by insurrection. Withdraw, therefore, of your own free will from a miserable affair into which you have been led by strangers, and have confidence in your king. Your welfare and his are inseparably united. We are led by no hostile views to cross the frontiers of Naples. The army under my orders will meet as friends all Neapolitans who are faithful and peaceable subjects of their king; it will be always and everywhere under the strictest discipline, and only treat as enemies those who act as enemies. Neapolitans! Listen to the voice of your king and his friends, who are also yours: consider the mischief you would cause by useless opposition; remember that the fallacies to which the enemies of peace and order strive to win you over never can be the source of lasting prosperity.'—ED.

ample. For the first time for thirty years an evil will be publicly combated which has been represented to weak humanity as the highest good. Our children's children will think us very foolish, and this conviction often weighs upon my mind, for I belong to a class of men who live more in the future than in the present. My mind has an historical tinge which helps me over many present difficulties. With me the future is always before my eyes, and I believe I am far less exposed to the danger of error with regard to the future than with regard to the present.

However, I do not carry this feeling so far as to be dangerous to a man in my position. I do not overlook the present; I take it at its real value, but the present is not worth much. This is evident to me, and history has perhaps never displayed such a pitiable crowd of small personages who only busy themselves with follies. Heavens! how we shall all be abused when the day of reckoning comes—and that day will come. Then some worthy man who, among the hundred thousand pamphlets and in the grocers' shops, discovers my name, will find perhaps in the year 2440 that in this far-distant time one being existed who was less wrong-headed than his contemporaries, who carried self-estimation so far as to believe themselves arrived at the culminating point of civilisation.

This evening I spent three hours with the Emperor Alexander. I cannot rightly describe the impression which I appeared to make on him. My words sounded like a voice from the other world. The inward feeling of the Emperor has, moreover, much altered, and to this I believe I have much contributed.

499. *February* 9.—I write in two hours what my copyist can hardly prepare in five; hence it happens

that my writing as well as my style suffers from the
necessary haste. Nine times out of ten I am quite
ashamed when I read it over again. Alfieri asserted
that to write really well a man should copy the manuscript four or five times before it goes to the printer;
then the printed copy should be laid aside for some
months, and then two days devoted to the correction of
each proof sheet. What would become of the world if
this process was imposed on us in the offices? Alfieri
forgot to add that people should only write when they
feel intellectually moved to do so. With us poor people
the contrary is, unhappily, always the case. I generally
write the most when I have the deepest feeling of my
stupidity, because nothing puts me in this flattering
moral position so easily as a long, often senseless, strife
of words.

500. *February* 12.—The Laybach Congress is to-
day like a father who knows a child is about to be born
to him. Will it be a boy or a girl, an angel or a
monster? The poor father cannot know this till the
moment of the arrival.

The star of the Russian Premier begins to decline.
The breach between Capo d'Istria and the Emperor constantly increases; in a team, if one horse pulls to the
right and the other to the left, the carriage will not
reach its destination till the stronger has dragged off
the weaker of the two. The Emperor is the stronger,
and for transparent reasons.

501. *February* 17.—We have to-day received the
first direct news from Naples. The Prince Regent holds
fast to his friends, and these assert that the whole
nation are as one. Now, this will be seen when the
first shot is fired.

Bignon's *brochure* on the Troppau Congress is from

the first to the last page a tissue of erroneous assertions, doctrinaire rubbish, diplomatic pathos, and wilful untruth. I look through nearly all the pamphlets which come out; I read Bignon's in fifteen and Pradt's in five minutes. From the title I gather what it is all about, then I read the conclusion to ascertain the point to be arrived at, and then I dip into five or six places—more I do not need to enable me to have a knowledge of the whole. Just now there are two sexes in politics. The Doctrinaires are neither of the two, and with them I have nothing in common; I hardly ever read them and never listen to them; for such authors I am a good and also a bad public—good, because I buy all the trash with which they weary the world; bad, because I only turn over the leaves of the book without any very deep examination of it. Every malady has its positive symptoms, every writer of the day has a stamp of his own, and the name of the author is sufficient to tell me beforehand the contents of his work.

I lately had a sharp contest with Capo d'Istria, and was obliged to speak to the Emperor Alexander about it. I am certain that at the end of the Neapolitan question his retirement will not be very distant.

. . . I think it natural that Nesselrode should like me; he is an honourable, right-thinking man.

. . . Glorious weather; plenty of sun, which I like. If they give me the name of an *Obscurantist*, at any rate it can never be applied physically. I can always stand at the very focus of the light, that I may absorb and retain it in all my pores.

502. *February* 23.—I have two days of very hard work in store for me. You cannot imagine what stormy days are to be seen in my room. Twenty or thirty persons come in and out; one wants an order, another

some advice, a third an explanation; then the news-mongers, the dissatisfied, &c., &c. No one believes that the Emperor Alexander and I understand one another thoroughly, and yet it is so. The influence of the last four months has been effectual; the stronger has carried off the weaker, according to all the laws of mechanics, physics, and morals. The Russian Premier lies on the ground. Will he ever get up again?

503. *February* 28.—To-day we dissolved the Congress. I made my closing speech. We are to meet in Florence, September 1, 1822. The Emperor Alexander has behaved excellently well. Capo d'Istria has lost the suit and pays the costs. If the Neapolitan affairs go well, he is lost; if they miscarry, certainly he will be saved; but I think they will go well.

504. *March* 3.—There is a stagnation in the news; the army will not take the offensive till the 4th. Laybach begins to empty, and one feels the emptiness more in a small than in a large space. The King of Naples left this morning; the Italians all follow him. I do not lament over the emptiness. It gives me much the same feeling that I have when I step out of a ball-room into my own house. The air is better, the temperature more agreeable, and comfort replaces etiquette. The chorus of Liberals will now strike up in a beautiful manner. I enjoy it beforehand: that is, abuse from people whom I purposely tread under foot pleases me.

505. *March* 7.—To-day the first shot will be fired. The affair may go well or it may go badly. If it goes well, our enemies will exclaim against the absurdity of our putting forth so much military strength; if it goes badly, they will make merry over an enterprise so far beyond our strength. If we had only looked out of the window to see what people in the street were doing, those good people would have jeered at the weaklings who had not passed beyond the A B C of the art of government. A fine time for the *métier* of a minister.

506. *March* 7.—You will have learned the success of our army from the public papers. The whole affair will go off in vapour because it was only vapour.

The populace are like children or nervous women who believe in ghosts; it belongs to my nature to go straight up to every mysterious power. I must see clearly and grasp firmly. When I was a child my playmates thought to frighten me with a ghost. I was then a boy of seven, and going down a dark passage a ghost came to meet me. But, unhappily for the ghost, I had a stick in my hand, and soon beat the masquerader. This story of my seventh year is the story of my public life. I am always flying out at what to others seems unassailable. There now exists an enormous power which is properly nothing but a marvel of phrases; but the latter are false, resting on false foundations, and leading to false results. People wish me to sanction as principles what goes against my nature; if I wished to do it, I could not; rather death a hundred times than accept as truth what to my eyes is openly false.

The Neapolitans will receive us as friends and deliverers. They will load us with caresses and will become our defenders; one after the other they will leave the Rump Parliament with great politeness in the lurch: the people will have nothing of all that their so-called organs say in the press or from the tribune. They wish to live in peace and quiet, and enjoy the blessings of freedom and civilisation, which are nothing but the feeling of certainty for the morrow. If I am wise, seven-eighths of the present world are mad. If I am a fool, how many wise people there are just now!

507. *March* 11.—What a deplorable part Lord Holland is playing! * Do you know what will happen to him? A fortnight will not pass by before he will wish to give half he possesses to be able to recall his shameful words. I know the patriotism of this kind of patriot: when they perceive that their insolence does not succeed, they are awe-struck and repent: such are the heroes of this century of enlightenment.

508. *March* 15.—On the 12th I was awoke very early by the news of the military insurrection in Alessandria and Turin. I said to my informant, ' Well, I have expected it,' got up and went to my Emperor, and then to the Emperor of Russia. We returned together to the first, and by twelve o'clock the following laconic orders were prepared and despatched:—

1. The Neapolitan army is to accelerate all its operations, and not to trouble itself about what goes on in Piedmont.

2. Eighty thousand men are to march from Vienna and the neighbourhood to Italy.

3. Ninety thousand men from Russia must cross our frontiers.

Whereupon we separated and ate our dinner as usual.

509. *March* 22.—If I calculate correctly we shall enter Naples to-morrow: this revolution will be annihilated. A great phantasmagoria is, in fact, broken up; in less than eight days this will be evident to the most unbelieving.

Our army has not lost one drop of blood, and has gained much glory, for no excess, not the slightest

* In the English Parliamentary debates, February 19, 1821.—Ed.

disorder, has taken place. They did not fire, because their fire could not be returned. Scouts were never employed, for the people everywhere came to meet our troops, received them as deliverers, and gave up to them the food they had concealed from the inquiries of their oppressors. Our army climbed over mountains, marched through narrow passes, and arrived in the city with the unanimous cry, ' Long live the King ! Hurrah for Austria ! ' If the peasants are asked where the hostile army actually is, they reply, ' They have fled : they have gone to eat maccaroni.' Behind this nation always stands Polcinello, and before Polcinello we were intended to bow !

This is all very pleasant : still I do not know where I shall find the time for so much hard work. Heaven has endowed me with the qualities of draught oxen. The more I work, the better I am. The last eight nights I have hardly slept more than two hours.

510. *March* 24.—The Piedmontese revolution goes on to meet its entire defeat. Yet a few days and the Reform people of the Directorial Committee in Paris will be unpleasantly surprised. They calculate there on two eventualities : the one, that we shall not venture to touch Neapolitan freedom ; the other, that if we do we shall be beaten. Poor people !

511. *March* 28.—What do Lord Holland and Co. say ? Pepe, Minichini and their friends ? Sixty of these poor devils have gone on board ship, because they no longer knew where to lay their heads in their fatherland !

The first gunshot was fired upon us by the Generalissimo of the insurgents. This Generalissimo with his whole mob has disappeared as entirely as the cedar of Lebanon. The Prince de Carignan, too, has lost the taste for his undertaking. What will become of the poor country? It has a King who would sooner surrender than say Yes: his successor says No, and with that a revolution is destroyed. The example is not bad.

512. *March* 31.—A war of thirteen days, from the first shot to the capitulation of the whole kingdom, is not a very long war. General Foy was right in his wild speech of March 20, when he stated as his conviction that no Austrian would come out of the Abruzzi if ever they succeeded in getting in. The Delphian oracle never prophesied better, and the Sibyls, Madame Lenormant included, have never prophesied anything more positive. Certainly no Austrian will come out of the Abruzzi, because the army, after concluding the Neapolitan expedition, will be divided in order to settle the Piedmontese business for the execution of which it will choose a more convenient road.

513. *April* 3.—I am in the strangest position I have ever been in. I have on hand an extinguished revolution and two revolutions in full blaze: one monarch who will not stir, and another who will go forward with double strides.* The first will not leave Florence unless I go there, and will only follow me; I may write to him ever so much, write to him through the two Emperors, let him be personally entreated by our Ambassadors—he remains deaf and dumb and gives no answer but ' Send Metternich to me.' The other rushes like a madman at death and the devil, listens neither to Emperors nor ambassadors, but writes letter after letter, in which there is nothing but ' Send me Metternich.' But meantime I cannot get away from here. I can neither get the one to go nor the other to stay. The Emperors are wroth and I cross myself. This is certain. Enemies

* The Grand-Duke of Tuscany and Duke of Modena.—ED.

are much the most easy to manage : you run straight at them and make away with them ; but friends !

I write, and write, and I shall soon have used up as many pens as all the geese in Bohemia can furnish, which is certainly no small number.

The history of the Piedmontese Revolution is quite remarkable ; nobody knows it thoroughly. Some do not wish for a Revolution, and yet make it ; others wish for it, but work against it—a Babel of a confusion. This revolution, calculated on the assumed weakness of a man of strong character, and on the strength of will of an inexperienced youth (Prince de Carignan), supported by sects who desire the Spanish Constitution, and opposed by Liberals who do not—is also a horrible confusion. But yet the revolution seems almost superannuated, and this fashion, too, will pass away as well as that of defending the virtue of Queen Caroline of England. I do not say that there will be no more revolutions, but they will be without substance, more like the angling of an old coquette, which among amateurs may perhaps still please, but real love only inspires youth and makes madmen.

514. *April 6.*—We have now three revolutions on hand. The one only needs to have its nose pulled to go down ; the second is very ill ; and the third seems to drag itself along very wearily. Standing behind the scenes as I do, and seeing the operations of this bad machinery, I feel ready to die of weariness. Certainly no one in Europe believes that this feeling of weariness steals quite over me. The only interest is in the worn-out patriots, such as Borelli, Poërio, and many others, who pledge themselves to give up the names of their confederates if a reward is secured to them. Who will have such heroes for ten louis d'or apiece may enquire for them : I am selling off. And I am to bow my head before such patriotism, such citizen-like virtue !

515. *April* 13.—While military operations are going on a minister takes his holidays. The Neapolitan war gave me eight days : the Piedmontese, only four. Every-one must acknowledge that no time has been lost. The Radicals have lied so openly about it that they must now be somewhat ashamed.

The greatest result of the last nine months is the good understanding between the two Emperors. One thing is now certain, nothing will again divide them ; I will answer for that. This result belongs entirely to me, like a child which one man and one woman have on a desert island. To have children there must be two, a woman and a man. I know certainly that in the above case I was the man on the island.

516. *April* 18.—In about three weeks Laybach will be as if extinct. We shall arrive at Vienna a little after the swallows. I am sorry to leave the beautiful country. Beautiful it is, in the truest sense of the word, here where everything is a lovely green and the high snowy peaks of the Alps bound the vast horizon. The sight of this beautiful nature revives the heart which had been stifled at the conference-table. What must my heart be like, that can sit for ever at that eternal con-ference-table——. But I will talk no more of this table : it has done its duty, and may now be put on one side.

517. *April* 20.—Within six weeks two wars and two revolutions have been concluded. We may hope that by sunset the third will be in the same condition.

The Emperor will send Prince Esterhazy as Ambas-sador to England for the Coronation. He will be accompanied by my son-in-law (Count Joseph Ester-hazy), Count Gatterburg (the same who with his trumpeter took the fortress of Alessandria), and Floret. My son will join them in Paris. Victor is a tall and excellent young fellow, the quintessence of a ' fashionable ' new to the world, as people are at eighteen. He does not want for understanding, and if he is in a good mind he makes one laugh, for he has much humour.

518. *May* 1.—The country becomes daily more lovely ; the diplomatists make great excursions. Yesterday, I was able for the first time to go out. Little Nesselrode and I slipped out of the office, and staid out for more than eight hours. Nesselrode is enchanted, like a child who has never seen higher mountains than the banks of the Rhine.

519. *May* 6.—What may happen in the East is beyond all calculation. Perhaps it may not be much ; beyond our eastern frontiers three or four hundred thousand hanged, strangled, or impaled, do not count for much. Ypsilanti, that masked Liberal, that Hellenist, will bring me into a dilemma.

520. *May* 9.—To-day I had a long conversation with the Emperor Alexander. I venture to say there is no one in this world clever and intelligent enough to add anything to what was actually spoken yesterday between me and the Emperor. If ever anyone from black became white, he has. My greatest merit consists in this—by my present influence to prevent him from roaming beyond what is right and good : for the bad begins on the boundary of the good ; and this boundary is so slightly marked that the understanding can hardly discover it without that powerful and wise assistance which is called tact.

521. *May* 13.—We have brought forth a work which may be acknowledged by the most honourable man without blushing. We have made a great epoch

—great because the conduct of it was very difficult. More than great is the result of the concord here established between those who possess the will and the power for action. In three months no one will speak any more of the events of March and April. All will keep silence : the good, because they always are silent ; the bad, because they are not flattered by their discomfiture ; the stupid, because they really do not know what has happened, and others do not tell them.

522. *May* 15.—The spring days here are wonderfully fine : we have eighteen to twenty degrees of heat, and the pleasant influence of the sun acts on me powerfully. My corporeal frame is enamoured of the sun.

I have climbed a mountain from which one can see the loveliest landscape for miles around. When I see such a sight I always wonder how people can settle themselves in an ugly country. The diplomatists have gone off very sorrowfully ; the South has something attractive about it, and that explains several circumstances in the affair. For history is properly only the history of the human mind, which is full of virtues and passions, and really contains very few bad qualities. Perhaps it is the influence of the sun which incites me to so mild a philosophy.

523. *May* 16.—In London, as I foresaw, no one thinks any more of the late events : a proof how wrong one is to flatter popular feeling. If any of their apostles regard this feeling as a religion, they are at this moment, when they get such a slap in the face, bound to show their strength. But such popular feeling is only a piece of buffoonery played by bad performers. It brings inexhaustible treasures to the quacks, but to the wise not a penny. But wise men who use them tenderly are either children or jugglers, and, therefore, not wise. This feeling has with me the value of a real religion, which gives to me what fools call strength, but which, closely analysed, is only reason, and, indeed, only that reason which is mere want of stupidity. That is my secret, but I do not betray it, because it makes people take me for an extraordinary man. I know this is the truth, but I do not wish others to know it.

524. *May* 18.—The town is turned into a village : the streets are empty, everything has passed away, even Laybach's greatness. My only amusement is the Italian opera, which, after many changes, at last became good. 'Eduardo and Cristina,' by Rossini, is what they are performing now, and it is certainly one of his best works. 'Cenerentola,' too, has been very well sung.

525. *May* 21.—I now part from this pleasant and beautiful town that has made so much noise in the world which, like every noise, passes away. But the result is imperishable. We have accomplished good and great things. They will not, indeed, be examined into, because a man is more concerned about an eight-days' fever than busied with eight years' health. My work has much in common with that of a physician : if the patient dies, people say the physician has killed him ; if he gets well, nature has saved him. To-morrow I shall start, and after making a little digression towards the Veldeser lake with the owner of Radmannsdorf, I shall take the road by Wurzen to Vienna.

RETURN TO VIENNA.

526. *Vienna, May* 28, 1821.—I arrived here the
day before yesterday at four o'clock, after a horrible
night, from dreadful weather. Such a journey thoroughly exhausts me. I hate travelling, and in a
carriage I feel so cramped, both physically and morally,
that even in a not very long journey I fall into a sort of
stupor. Certain it is that I cannot endure myself on
a journey.

The public journals announce new honours for me
(the appointment to be *Haus- Hof- und Staatkanzler*).
This is a bomb which has exploded over my head, and
which I could not avoid, because I could not see it
coming. If I had only suspected the mounting of this
battery, I should have endeavoured to make it harmless, which would have been easy. My Imperial master
has managed the business with the greatest possible
kindness—indeed, with a studied care, which is not
habitual to him. But the result is really a finishing

blow for the sufferer. In this new position my sphere of action will be much enlarged. I do not like to take up too much, because I like to master what lies within my province. It is certainly a marvel of fate, that men are often brought into such a position who care the least about it. A part now falls to me which would satisfy twenty inferior ambitions. God knows that I have no other ambition than to do good. If, to attain this object, I had to go back into my hole, I should be happy and content. The thing is, however, done, and cannot be altered. But in my new position neither a wig nor an ermine mantle is necessary. That would indeed have been the worst of all miseries.

I am back again in my own good city. Of course everyone has foreseen and foretold everything. There is no one here who thinks that anything could have been otherwise : the case was so simple and plain. Who here ever thought that Pepe and Ansaldi were heroes ? Carbonarism and intrepidity, liberalism and reason, have, indeed, always been shown to be opposites. Everything has happened so simply : just as all have wished and desired it : like my valet Giroux, who, if anyone asserts exactly the contrary of what he has just said, answers, '*C'est ce que je vous disais.*' To discuss after an event is never possible ; for heroes then spring out of the earth like mushrooms.

527. *May* 30.—How strange it is to return to a place where one feels as if one had never been away ! The same furniture and arrangements remain as we left them. We alone were the sport of agitation, and nothing about us connected itself with it. If I then turn my gaze within and ask what has changed in me, I find no antithesis there. I have already seen some hundred persons ; each thinks he must say something

to me, and among them all there is not one who ventures to repeat to me what he certainly said to others a short time ago : people like my valet are quite innumerable.

528. *June* 2.—With the first sunbeams this morning I visited my villa, which has much improved in appearance. On the front of the villa I have had these words placed : *Parva domus, magna quies.* The first is true enough ; the latter seems to me somewhat false.

The town empties itself just like a blown egg. The good people think that it is summer, because the almanac says so. But I stand out to the contrary, and maintain it is not true. A great quantity of ice must have come down from Newfoundland : that is the only explanation of this cold weather.

529. *June* 7.—No one is more busy than a blockhead, because everything is important in his eyes : no one is more active, because his activity leads to nothing. He soon finds it out, and cannot help himself ; he may do what he will, and make the greatest efforts, still he succeeds in moving nothing but himself. . . .

I will stay two days in Baden, where I will take some baths, and I am now looking for accommodation. I have sold my house in Baden, for I was determined not again to cross the threshold of that unhappy dwelling, which is clouded with the sad recollections of the death of my dear daughter Marie.

530. *July* 13.—At last it is no longer cold, I can spend the day in my garden. I have had the most supremely tiresome people to dinner. Our town is quite empty. It is, indeed, never filled with very loveable people, but there are times when I feel myself loveable in comparison with all who come near me. This comparison happily does not flatter my vanity. My flowers

are beautiful : this is the only impression the day has
left upon me.   I do not remember one single word that
has been spoken.   The newspapers, too, bring me no
new fine thoughts.   The Turks devour the Greeks, and
the Greeks decapitate the Turks : this is the best news
that I hear.

531. *July* 18.—From St. Petersburg, on the whole,
I get very good tidings.   The Emperor Alexander remains just the same as on the day of our separation.
But this alone will bring nothing forward—for that my
shoulder is needed.   As the affair stands, there are three
contingencies : the immediate outbreak of quarrel, an
intervention, or localisation.

In the first two cases, I am fettered on every side :
not so in the last.   Which of them will prevail, Heaven
knows.   The most improbable is that which the world
considers the most probable—namely, my first supposition.   I have despatched five or six couriers, who are
all very quick in their movements.   Nothing less is at
stake than the life or death of sound common sense.
And sound common sense will secure that end which I,
in common with a small minority, hold to be the best,
while a great number of fools and knaves take it to be
the bad cause.

532. *July* 23.—My different despatches are ready.
I feel in the midst of a web, like my friends the spiders,
whom I love, because I have so often wondered at
them.

The Emperor Alexander and I took the same views
of the present affair.   But he has changed his place of
residence, and hence it is uncertain whether he will
remain true to the point of view which is easy for me,
but difficult for him, to take.   The setting in which a
man finds himself has immense influence on him ; it re-

quires great strength of mind to withstand surrounding influence, and still greater to break through it. The Emperor remains firm, but he stands alone. Some wish the contrary of what he wishes, and have pointed it out ; others have not the strength to wish anything at all. To keep him right, the Emperor must be separated from his surrounding. He wills what I will, but those about him will the contrary.

With this feeling, the Emperor Alexander has taken the only resolution that could be taken ; he has withdrawn from all positive action and thrown himself morally upon me. This explains my cobweb. Such webs are pretty to look at, cleverly spun, and will bear a light touch, but not a gale of wind.

I have now made my operations morally complete in every direction ; but this position of things keeps the poor spider at the centre of his fine web. Good for the moment, but as for what concerns the future, the similar views which subsist between the Emperor and myself must have results, or a breath of wind will destroy the web.

533. *Baden, July* 24.—I will take baths here for two days, then stay three days in Vienna, and so on. It has made me very sad to come here, to the place where I lost half my life. Many people, who perhaps are much better than I am, like to be in a place where sad recollections meet them. I, on the contrary, would have such places levelled to the ground : they should not only be uninhabited, but the last trace of them destroyed. I would have them covered with thorns and high grass like a wilderness, the only picture that has any resemblance to my heart. Just for that reason, I love the ashes, and the ancients were quite right to love and reverence them. Death is opposed to

life, the past to the present, what is not to what is. To preserve the remains, while the form and substance are altered, is a beautiful idea, and the only one which suits my way of thinking and feeling. For where there is no longer life, man cannot call it back ; what contains life should perish with him.

My wife has contrary views, and is, therefore, in despair that I have sold the house—the scene of such calamity. She would willingly have kept it, if not have lived in it. I, on my part, have the comfort of knowing that it will shortly be pulled down. In a year or two nothing of it will remain.

534. *Vienna, August* 11.—From St. Petersburg a long letter from the Emperor Alexander to the Emperor Francis, and one to myself, have arrived.* His position is a difficult one. It is no small thing suddenly to turn in a direction entirely opposed to the course of his whole life ! My position is far easier, on account of my antecedents ; meanwhile it is difficult enough. The Prince Regent has decided to come to Vienna in October.

535. *August* 21.—The die is cast. Strangford has left Constantinople. It is not, indeed, war, but I am caught, as I feared, and cannot think of leaving Vienna, because everything rests on my shoulders. It is inadmissible for a soldier to leave his post during the battle. I shall at once cause the meeting of a new Congress.

---

* The Emperor Alexander writes to Metternich, July 17, 1821 :—' The union between the three Courts, whose efforts Providence has so completely blessed, can in future only be founded on mutual and unrestricted confidence. That trust which your august sovereign has placed in my intentions and views will not be deceived, notwithstanding all the difficulties, more particularly inherent to the position of Russia, daily arising from affairs in the East. I have explained myself on this point without reserve to the Emperor Francis. He will, I hope, find in my letter a new proof of the constancy of my principles and the extent of my friendship.'—ED.

536. *August* 28.—-Eight days ago my mother invited me to visit her at her villa, which is a mile and a half from Vienna. I entered my carriage at eight o'clock in the evening. By nine o'clock the report was spread that I had posted off to meet the Emperor Alexander ; hence it was concluded a very grave crisis was to be feared : while the same evening, at eleven o'olock, five-and-twenty of my intimate friends assembled at my house. Another proof that I cannot stir without making a sensation.

537. *August* 29.—I am now reading Madame de Staël's work, ' *Les dix années d'exil ;* ' it is full of thought, very fanciful, but intolerable in style, like all that this remarkable woman writes. All the portraits, with the exception of Bernadotte's, bear the stamp of truth and genius. Fouché's portrait, for instance, is thoroughly given in the following sentence : ' *Fouché est le seul homme qui peut véritablement seconder Bonaparte, en portant, malheureusement pour le monde, une sorte de modération adroite dans un système sans bornes.'*

Of the French she says very justly : ' *Les besoins de l'amour-propre chez les Français l'emportent beaucoup sur ceux du caractère. Une chose bizarre, c'est que les Français, qui saississent le ridicule avec tant d'esprit, ne demandent pas mieux que de se rendre ridicules dès que leur vanité y trouve son compte d'une autre manière. Il est inouï combien il est facile de faire prendre une bêtise pour étendard au peuple le plus spirituel de la terre !* '

How is it that a woman, who says and feels all this so truly, never for a moment doubts whether this same people is really fit for liberty, fraternity, and equality ? Madame de Staël resembles all partisans gifted with imagination : she loves a cause, but not its consequences. As often as she enters the field of politics or **govern-**

ment, or touches on any man's deeds, she is like a person who asserts that there is nothing more wholesome than arsenic, and who yet gives in every page of her book most clever and exact descriptions of the unspeakable suffering which is the consequence of this poison, and depicts the agony before the approaching death. With such a one it is difficult to argue.

Napoleon has often spoken to me of her. She did, indeed, once beg me to obtain for her the permission she so specially desired—namely, to perorate in the *salons* of Paris. My head, however, does not seem to be easily turned, for I was able to withstand her without difficulty.

The story of her journey through Vienna in 1812 is worth mentioning. Herr Rocca, who accompanied her, was cited to appear as a deserter from the French army, and threatened with extradition. Madame de Staël was displeased because they barely promised her that Herr Rocca should not be given up, whereas she wished to introduce him in the Vienna *salons*. The man to whom she uttered her complaints (Police-President Hager) was the best of men, but certainly very dry. When she begged him to produce Herr Rocca, he answered, ' But pray, Madam, are we to go to war about Herr Rocca? ' To which Madame de Staël answered, ' Why not? Herr Rocca is my friend, and will be my husband.' An example this of how little use mere *esprit* is in this world. Talleyrand rightly says, ' *L'esprit sert à tout et ne mène à rien.*' Celebrity was a power to Madame de Staël. The longer I live, the more I mistrust this power.

538. *September* 3.—I daily receive additional proofs that the Emperor Alexander has taken root in my school. I understand him, and that is a great thing. His position is extremely difficult. What will be the consequences? Friend Wellington says, ' *Le diable m'emporte si je le sais.*' I say the same ; meanwhile I go on as if I were certain of being able to control the course of events. The least vain man in the world must in certain positions feign a security which, under ordinary circumstances, would be self-conceit—the most ridiculous of all peculiarities.

Capo d'Istria is in great perplexity. He desires agitation, but the Emperor does not.

539. *September* 15.—Time has so overwhelmed me with burdens that they are more numerous than the hair on my head. My hair, too, has become quite white, at which I am less astonished than at its tenacity in not leaving me altogether.

What pleasant things the Greeks have brought upon themselves! No chapter would be long enough to show what germs of evil this question conceals. The Russian ambassador in Florence is a horrible man ; he kindles the fire with all his might. Happily, his sphere of action is less than the space his own comfortable person occupies. The poor Emperor Alexander does not know what to do with this creature ; but he still retains him. The weather is still execrable. Madame de Staël would not find it difficult to show that the weather is bad because the English Constitution is not introduced everywhere ; Abbé de Pradt would say it was because the colonies are not emancipated ; Sir Robert Wilson, because the Spanish Constitution has not yet made the round of Europe ; and, lastly, Professor Thiersch, because his Teutonic expedition has not yet entered the harbour of Volo.

540: *September* 26.—I returned to-night with the Emperor from an excursion to see the manœuvres, and found whole volumes of letters from St. Petersburg.

Anything good? No! Anything bad? No! Anything sensible! No! Anything unfriendly? No! Clever? No! Reasonable? Still, No! What then—contemptible? Yes!

If I did not know my men, it would be enough to drive one mad.

541. *September* 26.-—There is something peculiar about these miracles of Prince Hohenlohe ; the Pope and the King of Bavaria have put a stop to his miracle-making. When in our days I hear a cause cried up in favour of which public clamour raises its voice, I say to myself there is nothing in it, or some delusion is at the bottom of it. If I hear that a saint makes his appearance with his miracles in the *salons*, I utterly distrust the said saint and all his works : for though princesses are not exactly the best subjects for a miracle, yet they are very good prey for the artist in magic. There is, however, a gulf between Saints Hohenlohe and Cagliostro: the former appears on the boards at Wurzburg, the latter at Paris. Place, however, decides nothing with respect to the number of the credulous and the deluded, for these are everywhere as numberless as the sand on the seashore. Jesus Christ had more labour for thirty years to bring forward truth than Hohenlohe in thirty minutes with his magic. Such is the world. There are hardly any persons in the world stronger in faith than John Paar and Maurice Dietrichstein (the elder). The latter asserts that the blind whom Prince Hohenlohe has not healed, really see, and that it is only out of wilfulness that they stumble over the stones at every corner ; and if he is attacked on this point, he shelters himself with the unanswerable argument, 'But I actually saw it !' Thus everyone has his own manner of believing or of convincing himself. I believe in the

miracles of Jesus Christ, which I have not seen ; Dietrichstein believes in Hohenlohe's miracles, which, he
says, he has seen.

542. *October* 1.—We are here still waiting for the
decision about the King of England's journey to Vienna.
Nothing is more uncertain than everything done by his
British Majesty. He will in any case choose a very bad
time of year. I do not know how he is to be amused.
Preparations will be made for some festivities and they
will succeed thoroughly well, as all such things do in
Vienna; but between enacting festivities and giving
pleasure there is a very wide difference.

VISIT TO THE COURT OF HANOVER.

Extracts from Metternich's private Letters from October 25 to December 31, 1821.

543. From Hanover—friendly reception everywhere. 544. From Johannis-berg—soirée in Cassel—tedium on the journey. 545. From Frankfurt—the Metternichs and Capo d'Istria's. 546. A happy hour—a saying of Napoleon's—feeling of isolation—farewell to the year 1821.

543. *Hanover, October* 25, 1821.—Since my arrival I have led the real Congress life, full of gala days. The hours when I am not sitting at the conference-table I lose at dinners three or four hours long, or at routs, where to be suffocated is the least evil you have to go through. The reception accorded me by the King was that of a dear friend. I do not remember ever to have been embraced with such tenderness, and I never in all my life had so many fine things said to me. After a perfect flood of praises, in which the King was so good as to compare me to all the great men of antiquity, the middle ages and modern times, I came at last to speak of business, and then nothing remained for me to desire. I will do great and good things, without making any pretension to be a Minos, Themis-tocles, Cato, Cæsar, Gustavus Adolphus, Marlborough, Pitt, Wellington, &c., &c.—all which names his Majesty called me as if he were saying a Litany of Saints.

544. *Johannisberg, November* 4.—I left Hanover on the evening of the 31st, and stopped at Cassel on the 1st to see the Elector. There I found in the evening a grand and numerous company, invited by Count Spiegel to introduce me to the notabilities of the town. I left Cassel at two, went through Wilhelmshöhe—one of the finest gardens in Europe—to Marburg, where I staid the the night. On the 3rd, I entered Frankfurt. To-day I could not avoid a great dinner at Viebrich, given in my honour by the Duke of Nassau ; and now I have been here some hours, and am enchanted to find myself here.

Travelling is a terrible affair in my present position. I am bored as monarchs are bored by the attentions of the Courts which entertain me on my journey ; and I am bored as a prophet is, who is constantly asked advice by everyone. Since I was so fortunate as to get rid of the Carbonari, people think I need only show myself to destroy everything that is in anyone's way. Every Government is at this time ill, and all from their own fault : since my German Conferences they look upon me as the chief legislator of Germany, and, since 1821, as the annihilator of the Revolutionists. Each one begs me to destroy *theirs*, or at least to give them my receipts for doing so. On the other hand, the Revolutionists (this is the *petite pièce*), all trumpery people, present themselves to me, as far as possible to assure me of the sincerity of their feelings. It is, for instance, quite amusing to see what is now going on in Frankfurt, one of the most horrible towns in Germany. From the moment people knew that I was coming, they altered their looks and language. The first people who come to meet me at the hotels are the bitterest Radicals, and I do not remember ever to have endured rougher marks of respect. To listen to them one would suppose they had only waited for me to change their religion.

I have with me De Pont and a secretary, Langenau

and Handel. I shall remain here till the 5th or 6th, and be at Frankfurt on the 7th or 8th, and at Vienna on the 14th or 15th.

545. *Frankfurt, November 9.*—. . . Here lie the most mischievous Jacobins at my feet, all full of excuses and protestations. During my journey, I visited no less than five Universities: Leipzig, Halle, Göttingen, Marburg, and Giessen. In Halle I dined on October 18 under the same roof with a hundred and fifty students, who were celebrating the battle of Leipzig, and I everywhere received nothing but marks of respect. When I was getting into the carriage on leaving Halle, all the hundred and fifty students followed me with uncovered heads and loud cheers. The whole day I had a crowd of men under my windows, and wherever I go, joyful cries accompany me. If these people are asked what they are there for, they answer: ' We want to see him.' It is the Italian business which has gained me this kind of notoriety in Germany. Inquisitive people want to see what the man looks like who made up his mind that the Carbonari were simply a number of ragamuffins, and cannot understand how he managed to solve this easy problem. The people hereabouts are good but childish. . . . In Russia, and in the whole Russian diplomacy with foreign countries, there are two parties, which are quite openly designated by the names Metternich and Capo d'Istria. This is not altogether flattering. These two parties detest each other, and are in opposition to one another, like the Right and Left sides in France. As the Emperor Alexander is a Metternich, the party is a respectable one ; the others may be left to their fate.

. . . I shall start to-morrow, arrive at Wurzburg on the 10th, stay the night of the 11th at Nürnberg, on the 12th at Regensburg, the 13th at Schärding, and arrive at Vienna on the 15th.

546. *Vienna, December* 31.—A happy hour is not only good because it is happy (a thing good in and for itself), but also because it strengthens the mind. This reminds me of a saying of Napoleon's. During one of our long conversations we spoke of the time just past; suddenly he cried, ' *Ah! vous ne savez pas quelle puissance est le bonheur! Lui seul donne du courage. Ne pas oser, c'est ne rien faire qui vaille, et on n'ose jamais qu'à la suite du bonheur. Le malheur affaisse et flétrit l'âme, et dès lors on ne fait rien de bon.*' . . .

I now feel as lonely as a dweller in the desert; nothing makes me smile, and nothing occupies me except what wearies me. Follies are intolerable to me ; words without thought are hateful ; mere good nature is like stagnant water : and this is the picture of what people here call society. Words, nothing but words ; of all I hear nothing is to be preserved—the best thing is to forget the sound of them. If then I ask myself when there will be a conclusion of all this, and find that apparently it will continue till the end of all things, I feel a pressure on mind and heart which is difficult to describe. Certain it is that the emptiness of men increases in proportion to the loftiness of their position. If I could lose myself in what makes so many other men happy, perhaps my moral position would be different. . . .

It is striking midnight, and the year 1821 is no more ! Three hundred and sixty-five days are gone in a second of time. We stand at the entrance to a new era like a new-born child. May we hope that fortune will favour us, and that the cutting of the teeth—the first business the child has to go through—will be gone through successfully.

THE EXPENSE OF THE NEAPOLITAN EXPEDITION, AND FUNDAMENTAL PRINCIPLES FOR THE ORGANISATION OF NAPLES AND THE RESTORATION OF ORDER.

547. Metternich to Stadion (Letter), Laybach, March 10, 1821.

547. I now reply to two important subjects contained in your letter ; I ought to have alluded to them some time ago, but I was obliged to allow the storm to pass over before I could write to you.

I. Financial part of the Expedition against Naples.

This question has something of the same character as all that concerns this grave enterprise. It touches at once on the past, the present, and the future.

In the financial question the past cannot be regulated by the present; it is therefore necessary not to be deluded about the future, thus avoiding false calculations, as deplorable in finance as in everything else. We have incurred, and are incurring, great expenses. It may perhaps be necessary still to continue them, but nothing is voluntary in these expenses, and they cannot appear so to any man endowed with good common sense.

The first question of all, which must be at once seen to be so, is this : shall we, or can we, abandon the revolution of Naples to itself, to its own remedies (for every revolution, as well as every evil, carries in itself its own punishment), or must we not rather erect a substantial barrier against it ?

The solution of this alternative cannot be doubtful. We can deplore the revolution in Spain, and abandon it to itself; but it is otherwise with the Spanish revolution transplanted to the soil of Naples. Its triumph in the Italian peninsula would have been much more swift than its repression could have been, or than the punishment which it must bring upon itself.

We were therefore obliged to call to our aid considerable material means. Our finances were heavily strained. None of this expenditure was unnecessary; it was, on the contrary, imposed by the first of necessities—that of existence.

My duty is to impose as few burdens as possible on our finances, and to endeavour at the same time to make these expenses, as far as possible, mere advances. This is what I aim at, while making a calculation which is both financial and political.

As a financial calculation, I prefer the certain to the uncertain, and I never like to flatter myself with the impossible. As a political calculation, I have been able to examine the real state of affairs at Naples, and have endeavoured to avoid any plan for the future founded on inevitable evils.

The Neapolitan revolution has utterly destroyed the finances of the kingdom. It has been brought about in part by the blind fiscal system of M. de' Medici: seeing in the State administration only a treasury, he taxed the provinces far beyond what he ought to have done, and, by overstraining his bow, has broken it.

The King told me he had seen the accounts which were made up to the time of his departure from Naples, and the revolution had not only swallowed up all that remained from former financial operations, but it actually cost during the first six months more than forty millions of ducats.

The financial future of Naples necessarily has two burdens—the maintenance of the army of occupation, and the consolidation of expenses occasioned by the revolution. It remains to be seen if to these two burdens we can add a third—namely, the reimbursement of expenses incurred by Austria for armaments, &c.

My conviction has been that by attempting too much we run the risk of accomplishing nothing. But, this truth demonstrated, I ask if it is not practicable to make a good use of what I can only regard as an impossibility. Our aim must be to repress the revolution, to consolidate peace, and not to risk new disturbances. On finding that the Emperor entirely shared my views, the declaration was made in the protocol which you have for some time possessed. You will have seen from this protocol that we sought to turn the financial impossibility into a political bait. We have declared loudly that we demand nothing, and we have attached a recompense or a punishment for the nation to this same nothing, to this veritable non-value ; thus ensuring to ourselves the chance of perhaps being able to bring in under the name of punishment that which we have declined as a recompense.

I enter into all these details, my dear Count, which your able mind and great knowledge of business and of the political situation would lead you to see at the time, and I beg you not to attach too much importance to a payment which I consider much less connected with battles and other realities of war than with financial possibilities or impossibilities, which must also be strongly influenced by political considerations to be decided by time alone—that is, by the preservation of peace in the kingdom of Naples. You see I have taken care to establish alternatives which will secure to us our incontestable rights. It will be wise and prudent to take care that they are rightly used.

II. Future Organisation of the Kingdom of Naples.

This important question has engrossed my attention from the very day I heard of the overthrow of the existing order of things at Naples. I have thought the matter over with extreme care, and I believe I have arrived at the best terms. My conscience, at least, is easy ; I only hope that events will justify my wishes.

If you now speak to any of the legislators who are to be found at the corner of every street and on every bench at the *cafés*, they reply, without hesitation, that the world can no longer do without the representative system. My conviction is that it will never do with it ; for I do not understand by progress, overturning oneself and everything else, getting up and falling down again.

But we have not taken into consideration for Naples this universal recipe, seeing that we could not do abroad what we constantly refuse to do at home. It would have been hardly prudent, on the other hand, to patch up what has just been destroyed. We have called to our aid the principle of a qualified monarchy, thus excluding both despotism and the representative system.

The King has been very reluctant to acquiesce in our views, but has ended by doing so, and even by perceiving that, with a system of organisation worthy of the name, he will have a better prospect of peace and repose than by a return to a complete despotism, the dangers of which we have already experienced both in Naples and in Sicily.

I send you herewith the protocol, or rather the addition to the protocol, which contains our idea exactly as if it were a spontaneous proposition from the King. By the next courier I will send you a more complete statement of the arrangements I have mentioned. You will see that it describes a constitution which, if quite monarchical, is none the less worthy of the name, for it is not desirable to apply this term to the representative system alone.

How is the thing going on generally? I declare frankly that I do not know. Nothing is so useless as to speculate on happy chances, and nothing is more difficult than to prevent unhappy ones. The King has no credit in his own country, but he is beloved. The revolution has been forced to adopt a mild character, which is to be deplored, but is an unavoidable consequence of our armaments.

The object of the Neapolitan Liberals, who must not be confounded with the Carbonari, has been to arrive at a representative system through the intervention of the latter. From Madrid they would wish to get to Paris. We, who cannot consent to that, have ourselves neither one nor the other.

The whole depends, therefore, upon the blows which are struck. If they are decisive, the thing is done; if they are not, it will drag on; if they fall upon us, the world will be turned upside down. Then will happen what would have happened if we had done nothing, for Italy will go to the devil, and with her France and Germany, just as they would have done if we had remained neutral spectators of the revolution at Naples.

If we are successful, a great example will have been

given to the world, were it only for the one fact that the *inviolability of revolutions* will have been shown to be a thoroughly false claim, although prodigiously convenient to the madmen, fools, blockheads, and weaklings who advance it. What a frightful list I place before you there, my dear Count!

THE NEAPOLITAN, PIEDMONTESE, AND GREEK INSURRECTION.

548. Metternich to Rechberg (Letter), Laybach, March 25, 1821.

548. Events succeed each other with such rapidity in Italy that we may hope this beautiful portion of Europe will not submit to the yoke of the revolutionists, notwithstanding the activity of their criminal efforts. If they will only run their heads against the energy and wisdom of our measures, this last crisis, alarming as it was by its terrible symptoms, will turn against those who have provoked it, and will rally the numerous body of honest men round the legitimate Governments, which are, I hope, convinced that, by following a consistent and determined course, it is still possible to suppress that spirit of faction which threatens society with total subversion.

Thinking that it must be of the greatest importance for your Court to be exactly informed of the real situation of affairs in Italy, of the dispositions of the two Emperors, who are, happily, still together here, and of the result of the first measures which they have adopted, I do not hesitate to despatch the present courier to your Excellency, and send by him a short but exact account of our position.

You will have been informed, sir, of the success of General Frimont's army, of the occupation of the province of the Abruzzi, so important in a military point of view, of the total disorganisation of General Pepe's army, and of the way in which our troops have been everywhere received by the inhabitants. These first results leave us in no doubt as to the success of the enterprise, and the news which have since arrived from the headquarters of the army fully justify our hope. Sora, defended by General De Concilj, the Quiroga of Naples, was carried by our troops after a very feeble resistance. General Frimont passed the Garigliano with his army, and bore towards San Germano, to attack that position, which it was said the Neapolitans had rendered impregnable. A detachment sent by the general-in-chief to reconnoitre found it abandoned. Thus our army marches on without being able to meet the enemy, who is nowhere to be found; but our march is so rapid that the general still hopes to overtake and defeat them if they concentrate their forces.

Whilst the army was marching on San Germano, General Fardella, sent by the Duke of Calabria to the King, his father, bearing messages of respect and submission, passed by the Velletri route on his way to Rome and Florence. We are still ignorant of the details of this mission, which has, however, had no influence on the progress and operations of the army.

These details, which are indubitable, will convince your Excellency that the Naples expedition is on the point of being terminated, and that a fortnight's campaign will have sufficed to throw down this military erection with which they have tried for the last six months to alarm the whole of Europe. This result, and still more the reception given by the people to our army, at least proves that the Neapolitan nation has no sympathy with the revolution, which has precipitated that once happy country into an abyss of misfortune, and that this revolution is entirely the work of certain criminal sects, and of a few ambitious military men.

If the insurrection of Piedmont was at first of a more alarming character, and at the time it broke out made us fear a powerful and dangerous diversion in favour of the revolutionary cause, the progress of events in that country during the last eight days permits us to hope now that the danger will be more readily exorcised than we had dared to flatter ourselves. The plan of the conspirators—which was to induce the King to proclaim a constitution, and to declare himself for the Neapolitan cause against Austria—has been defeated by the abdication of the King. The Prince de Carignan,* who, owing to the circumstance that the Duke de Génevois † was absent, was appointed to the Regency of the kingdom, very soon experienced all the awkwardness of the situation. Forced to promise and swear the Constitution of the Cortes, and to create a provisional revolutionary junta (which had not entered into his plans, nor into those of any of the ambitious officers about him), this Prince wrote to the Duke de Génevois, entreating him to return and take the reins of government, which had devolved upon him by the abdication of the King. The Duke de Génevois, who was then at Modena, not only refused to listen to the entreaties of the Prince de Carignan, but replied to them by an energetic proclamation. He wrote at the same time to the two Emperors to beg their advice and their support. The reply of the two august sovereigns was what it ought to be under the circumstances—cautious, wise, noble, and in every way suited to the principles they profess. They decided at the same time to send a courier to their

* Afterwards King Charles Albert.—ED.
† Ascended the throne under the title of Charles Felix.—ED.

Ministers at Turin, with orders to present himself to the Prince de Carignan, and give him a picture of the woes which would soon overtake the country over which he was one day to reign, and begging him seriously to consider his own situation, appealing to his feelings and his duty as the first Prince of the Blood to induce him to play, on this important occasion, the only becoming part—that of making the soldiers who had been led away by the factious return to their duty, thus restoring tranquillity to his country. These counsels were accompanied by the warning that the two Emperors would never recognise the revolution. We are still ignorant of the result of this step, but we know by the news which we receive daily from Milan that the progress of the revolution is very uncertain, that the perplexities of the Prince de Carignan are increasing, that Alessandria has become the rallying point of the revolutionists in the anarchical sense of the word, that Genoa and Novara still hold out for the King, that many regiments are faithful, that others have dispersed and returned to their homes, that the mass of the people are quiet and passive, that the King is generally regretted, and that there is no national movement in the country. Waiting the issue of this crisis, the Count de Bubna, Commandant-General of Lombardy, is preparing to overawe the factious ; and, besides the garrisons of the strong places, he has an army already more than sufficient to defend our Italian provinces, and which increases daily. Milan enjoys the most perfect tranquillity, and public opinion expresses itself in the most satisfactory manner in favour of the Government.

A new event which must at this time of general commotion powerfully contribute to agitate men's minds is the insurrection of the Greeks in the Ottoman Empire.

The Emperor Alexander received all the particulars by a courier who arrived here on the 19th, and they have been confirmed by our agents.

Prince Ypsilanti, major-general in the Russian service, has put himself at the head of this insurrection, and Prince Soutzo, Hospodar of Moldavia, has declared for it, confessing himself that it is the work of a secret society, which has been preparing the materials for two years. This society is the same as that of the Carbonari, and we have for some time warned the Ottoman Government of it, but they attached no importance to its existence.

In this fresh emergency, the Emperor Alexander has given proof of his noble and loyal character; his views and principles entirely agree with those of the Emperor my august master. In a council which was held in the presence of their Majesties, it was decided ' that the event should be left to itself.' The Emperor Alexander cashiers and removes from his army all the military Greeks who take part in the insurrection; and refuses all support and help to the Greek insurgents.

The two monarchs have simultaneously declared at Constantinople that, faithful to the principles which they have publicly announced, they will never support the enemies of public order; that they will never lend any help to the Greek insurgents; that, on the other hand, they leave to the Porte itself the task of watching over its own safety. As it has remained up to this time estranged from all the affairs of Europe, we do not feel called upon to interfere in its affairs.

These determinations of the sovereigns will immediately be made public. In the meantime I pray your Excellency to lay them, as well as the contents of the present despatch, before the King, hoping his Majesty will see in them good cause for tranquillity. In this hope I send the courier who will have the honour to place it in your hands.

Metternich to Stadion, Laybach, March 26, 1821.

549. The Naples affair is at an end. I hope to be able to send a courier to Vienna in two or three days, to have the *Te Deum* sung and a hundred and one guns fired.

The revolt in Piedmont fares badly for a revolution. I will send to Vienna to-morrow unequivocal proofs that its principal champion, the Prince de Carignan, does nothing but weep. The country does not wish to rise, and all that is required now, in order to put down the small number of the lower orders who are in favour of it, is a decisive stroke on the part of one or other of the general officers, devoted to the King, who have put themselves *en rapport* with the Duke de Génevois. In revolutionary crises, however, one can never found anything on data, often put forth one day and contradicted the next. I therefore confine myself to facts on which positive calculations may be founded.

If order is restored in Piedmont it will be by its own efforts, and that will be an immense gain. If it does not return to duty of itself, it must fall into anarchy, and it is not in a state to dream of a military aggression on our provinces. With the exception of the army, which has remained faithful to the King, and which is at Genoa and Novara, the rest is disbanded, and the revolutionists cannot reassemble eight thousand men capable of marching. They recruit legions, but they are composed of students and bandits. Bubna is in great force. He could at the present moment dispose of ten thousand men of Frimont's army; but he will not concentrate them till we are firmly established at Naples.

There are two contingencies ; either the Russian army is useless, or it is necessary. In the first case, it will turn back immediately, and perhaps will not even cross the frontier, if in a few days we hear that Piedmont has worked its own cure. If the revolution spreads over the whole of Italy, the Russians will do no harm, and the very news of the possibility of their arrival will prevent mere amateurs from rising.

We risk nothing by declaring war on Piedmont, for it declared war upon us by making a revolution. The Junta of Alessandria has formally declared war against Austria, and the revolution at Turin had no other means of doing so than by announcing that it would make a conquest of Milan.

For the rest, this revolution is nothing but a sudden blow on the part of some hot-headed men, supported by the Committee of Paris with the intention of helping Naples. But the inconceivable cowardice of the Neapolitans, and the masterly and prompt operations of our army, have defeated this plan. The only way in which they could keep the party together at Turin was by publicly asserting that all our bulletins were false, and that the Neapolitans were driving us towards the Po.

As for the Greek revolution—let it alone. I answer for it that the Emperor Alexander has as little to do with that now as with the revolution in Piedmont. You may have some difficulty in believing this, but it is none the less true, and I will send you proofs by to-morrow's courier. This affair must be looked upon as placed beyond the pale of civilisation ; it will end, I believe, badly for the Greeks, who depended on a support which failed them the very day they took up arms. It is the same with the Neapolitans, who believed that Russia would be, if not for them, at least against us. You see the advantage of a good reputation in politics.

The question is at present occupying the undivided attention of France. The Government does not support, and never will support, the Piedmontese. The factious may do so ; but they will not be able to accomplish much, unless indeed they overthrow the King and the Charter. If this should take place—that is to say, if France returns to 1793—then we shall certainly do nothing but come home and consider how to save ourselves. Any retrograde movement in Italy in the present position of affairs, would be to make a revolution ourselves in the whole of the Peninsula ; and how long could we keep our Italian provinces in such a con tingency ?

The world is on the eve of salvation or on the brink of ruin. It looks, however, as if the dawn of a better day were beginning to break. The success of the Naples affair may bring a period of repose. It will have cost much, but I have the conviction now, as I have had all along, that if we had acted differently, we should have been smothered in our beds.

What gives me great pleasure is the perfect way in which all our people have behaved in Italy. The armies of Bubna and Strassoldo deserve the fairest pages in our history.

Metternich to Rechberg (Letter), Laybach, March 31, 1821.

550. I send you, my dear Count, the last bulletin from the army at Naples.

A campaign of thirteen days has sufficed to show plainly the baseness of the Neapolitan Revolution. A great work of iniquity was scattered like dust as soon as the first attack was made ; and as for the embellishments of patriotism, where is that national enthusiasm? Where are those patriotic phalanxes? Where the hatred to a return to order? Are the Neapolitans to be the interpreters of their own thoughts, or have the scoundrels in Parliament truly expressed them?

Heaven seems to will that the world should not be lost, and has protected our great enterprise. Wise men have followed it with their good wishes ; enlightened Governments have done the same. We asked no more from them. The particulars in our possession prove to the most blind that, in spite of what is said on the spot, even by the wisest and most sober-minded men, yet the revolution was begun quite independently of the people themselves. It is the same everywhere. It is therefore necessary to protect the people against the attacks of their fanatical enemies — their only enemies, those who deceive the people by directing all their venom against the Governments.

We shall finish the Piedmontese affair as we did the Neapolitan. Another French Revolution only could interpose grave—perhaps insurmountable—obstacles to this second enterprise.

All the venom is at present on the surface. The cure will be so much the more radical; and what we began together in July 1819, can be finished with the help of God and for the salvation of the world in 1821. It is therefore from Carlsbad that the *era of salvation* must be dated.

CO-OPERATION OF THE RUSSIAN ARMY.

551. Metternich to Stadion (Letter), Laybach, April 21 and 22, 1821.

551. Baron Stürmer will have told you, my dear
Count, of the reasons for detaining the Russian army on
the frontiers. The orders are issued, and you will not
see a Russian soldier. If I had not been able to make
them retire even as we made them advance, do you
think we should have had them put in motion?

I received by yesterday's courier your letter of
April 17. I tell you frankly, my dear Count, that it
has given me pain. If you, knowing the principles
which have directed our steps for years, knowing every
shade of our conduct for the last nine months, knowing
the dangers to which all society is exposed in a time of
folly—if you, my dear Count, can reproach me with a
Russian invasion, what means of safety remains to the
world? I confess that if it were in my nature to be
disheartened, I should say to myself: How people seek
to conjure up the perils which threaten us!

Success, doubtless quite unexpected by the knaves,
has crowned our efforts. This success does not astonish
me, for the simple reason that I knew both the means
of attack and the means of defence. The Piedmontese
affair has not cast me down, for the equally simple
reason that it had entered into my calculations as a
thing not only possible, but even probable.

The proof that such was the case is found in the
continual reinforcements which I was the first to beg

the Emperor to send into the Italian provinces, and in the threat of the arrival of the Russian armies, contained in our declaration against Naples. It was not alone to bring this country to reason that we had need of more than a hundred thousand men, and the assured prospect of foreign support. I knew for certain the efforts made by the faction on every side.

Now, from that moment it became necessary either to do nothing and live on from day to day, or to take steps in the right direction; and I do not believe anyone could do that without means proportioned to the difficulties. Among these means I placed first the Austrian forces, which were able alone to complete the certain task, and to avert possibilities; I had also to think of destroying Russian Liberalism, and proving to Europe that henceforth the Radicals will have to deal with the two Powers possessing most freedom of action.

The results now show whether my calculations were false. Facts alone speak in 1821. All the promises, all the speeches of the Emperor of Russia would have been valueless; but his setting in motion some hundred thousand men, their effective march, the expenditure on them of ten millions—these are facts. The command to halt is another fact not less important; and a hundred and twenty thousand men placed in the Russian provinces nearest to our frontiers, with orders to march at the first request of Austria, is certainly a third fact which will prevent these disturbers from counting so readily on the Emperor Alexander in future.

The conduct of Bubna is beyond all praise. In order to be advantageous and useful, it was necessary that he should have troops at his disposal, and above all that he should have unlimited freedom of action. You, who know as well as I do, and perhaps better, the

way things are generally managed, will see that the
Emperor has done a good and graceful thing, by giving
the commander of the province the power of simply
consulting himself and the circumstances of the moment,
so as to act unhesitatingly according to his own convictions and experience.

Immense good ensues from this ; there is now just a
possibility of our surviving. We must not deceive
ourselves ; we are not a single step beyond the possibility. With judgment, with a calm and firm step,
with great rectitude and agreement of thought and
action, good may yet be done in Europe. But the
evil has arrived at a prodigious height. Public opinion
is absolutely diseased, and since a single fact is sufficient
to prove this, I will mention the state of our own
capital. Be sure that at Vienna, as at Paris, Berlin,
London, as in the whole of Germany and Italy, in
Russia as well as America, our triumphs are rated as
so many crimes, our conceptions as so many errors,
and our views as criminal follies.

I possess some courage ; I think I have shown a
great deal in the course of the last nine months, for it
was certainly required in order to take upon myself
what I have done, and that with a full knowledge of
the state of things as well as the responsibility ; but
there is nothing of illusion in me. I know how to
appreciate all the good which has been accomplished ;
the gain is immense, because it has brought to light
a number of truths ; a phantasmagoria such as the
world has perhaps never seen has been destroyed ;
the spell is broken. Yet everything remains to be
done. It is we who will occupy the strongholds of
Novara and Alessandria.

The Emperor Alexander is averse to do this, and

his reasons are weighty. I will tell you the particulars by word of mouth ; our public will charge me anew with folly or stupidity for being annoyed that we have to take upon ourselves this ungrateful task, which in its eyes will be a monument of glory ! The public knows not what it says, for it is ignorant of the true state of the affair. The finances will profit, for the garrisons beyond the Ticino will be at the expense of the Sardinians, although they can reckon on as many forces in Lombardy which must remain to us. No matter ; the thing is a positive evil, and it will require a great deal of skill to prevent its turning into an active evil for the whole of Europe.

I suppose the Emperor will return to Vienna about the middle of May. We are still detained here by the arrangements which have to be made with the two Kings of Sardinia.

The King who has abdicated must be replaced on the throne. This affair must be promptly decided, or Piedmont will once more be ruined ; we gain by the distance more than five days, and five days are much in revolutionary times.

Vincent and Pozzo will arrive here immediately ; we shall send them on to Paris, for that country must not be abandoned to the folly of its Government, which is as feeble as it is badly disposed.

Now I have made a real profession of faith. I do not wish, my dear Count, that you should regard differently from myself a situation which must decide the life or death of the monarchy.

For the rest, I am much fatigued with my labours, and I am at present in the condition of a general who feels the need of repose just when the public are waking up to judge of his operations.

April 22.—The courier was just starting, when **I**
received your letter of April 18. I must reply to you
in a few words, my dear Count, for to go thoroughly
into the subject will require some hours of conversation,
and certainly I could not employ them more usefully.

The result of our conversation, which will simply
be an examination of the present situation, as I know it
and as it can only be known here—for it is a moral
and material impossibility that, away from here, nay,
even beyond a circle of four or five persons, it can
be known or even comprehended—the result I say,
will make you judge of the position quite differently
from what is possible to you at present.

I will content myself with placing before you the
following truths :—

1st. There has never been a question of stationing
a single Russian soldier in the Austrian monarchy.

2nd. Russia does not lead us ; it is we who lead the
Emperor Alexander, for many very evident reasons.
He requires to be advised, now he has lost all his
advisers. He looks upon Capo d'Istria as a leader of the
Carbonari. He mistrusts his army, his ministers, his
nobility, his people.   In such a situation no one can lead.

3rd. France and England, far from being on good
terms, completely distrust each other.   England is
entirely with us. Do not judge of England by what
Lord Stewart told you ; all he said is untrue.   He
would have you indignantly oppose the march of a
Russian army into Piedmont ; well, his Cabinet demands
it with might and main, for it judges rightly, and fore-
sees the incalculable complications which must arise
between Austria and France in the event of an Austrian
occupation.

France is at the head of all the revolutionary movements in Europe, and it would be difficult to say which does most harm and most encourages intrigues, the Government or the Jacobins. They both wish Europe to be revolutionised. The ministry aim at the introduction of the French Charter in all States of the second order, hoping thereby to consolidate themselves. The Liberals wish for the anarchical Constitution of 1791, so as to overthrow the dynasty in France. Thus the Piedmontese revolution has been the result of all kinds of efforts on the part of the Cabinet and the French Liberals.

4th. Piedmont could not exist for three months without a foreign army. The revolution is nowhere more threatening than in the whole of Italy. An important blow has been struck ; some dozens of its chiefs have fled. But the revolution is still there, ready to break out afresh, and, without very firm and prudent conduct, we shall see next autumn a renewal of the scenes we have just come through. We do not believe the whole thing is over, but only that there has been a great defeat ; the difference is immense.

Do you know the true, the only reason why the Emperor Alexander objects to an army, even of ten thousand men, being stationed beyond his frontiers ? Because he is convinced that this body would pass over to the enemy. So much have the liberal efforts of the good people who surround this Prince liberalised the whole army. With such a feeling a man could scarcely be a conqueror.

All that I now tell you is true, thoroughly true. Any calculation otherwise founded is erroneous. I will answer for all the facts, and the future will perhaps but too well justify the exactness of my information and my calculations.

What is the right thing to do when walking in the midst of darkness and confusion? To light a torch and walk steadily and firmly by its light. Do not trust any other lights; they are placed expressly for your destruction, or displayed by incendiaries who try to persuade you that they are only fireworks.

A few hours of conversation would tell you more than twenty pages in writing. The only thing I ask of you in the meantime is to weigh the facts already pointed out: and our material successes are facts. I do not speak at present of moral successes: these have yet to be waited for, and they are much more difficult to attain than material success.

RESULTS OF THE CONGRESS AT LAYBACH.*

552. Metternich to the Emperor Alexander, Laybach, May 6, 1821.

552. Before the separation of the monarchs and their Cabinets, may I be permitted to place in the hands of your Imperial Majesty one word of gratitude and homage? Of gratitude, Sire, for you deserve it, not on my part, nor on that of Austria, but from society at large.

You must do me the justice to admit that I discerned long ago the evil which has been lately unmasked with such awful intensity. You must also remember, Sire, that, although I knew the evil, I did not despair of the remedy, This remedy has begun to take effect; it is the intimate moral union between your Imperial Majesty and your august allies, each being free in his actions. The merit, Sire, belongs to you: for your situation was the most free, and certainly not so near to the danger as that of the other monarchs. Your Imperial Majesty has done an immense good; your conscience must tell you so; and that is the only recompense which a good man earnestly seeks after; it

* The monarchs assembled at Laybach were the Emperors of Austria and Russia and the King of Naples; the diplomatists—for Austria, Metternich, Vincent, and Gentz; for Russia, Nesselrode, Capo d'Istria, Pozzo di Borgo; and for Prussia, Hardenberg and Bernstorff; for France, De la Ferronays, Caraman, and Blacas; and for England, Lords Clanwilliam and Stewart, and Sir Robert Gordon. After the decision of the three northern Powers in favour of armed intervention in Naples, the English and French ambassadors took no further part in the Conferences.—ED.

is the only one which can reach the man placed by providence above other men.

There is but one act of homage which I consider worthy of your Imperial Majesty. Placed as I am between the Emperor, my master, and your Imperial Majesty, grave duties rest upon me. The first is perhaps the most difficult—that of seeking and finding the truth. The day when I lose confidence in my own calculations I shall regard myself as guilty in the eyes of my master and those of your Imperial Majesty. My homage, Sire, must simply be to tell you all my thoughts.

Society would have been irretrievably lost but for the measures which have been taken during the last few months. These measures could not have arrested its fall unless they had rested on the most correct principles. Such being the case, the dawn of a better future begins to appear : the day will succeed if we continue to walk on in the path in which we have placed ourselves. One single false principle, and the night will be upon us, and chaos will succeed that night.

There are two means of enabling us to continue in this path :—Reciprocal and unrestrained confidence, and a frank understanding of the principles on which our conduct must be grounded.

This confidence, Sire, is what the mind has most difficulty in seizing. It has been, and would for ever have been, an insurmountable difficulty, if Providence had not created two sovereigns such as your Imperial Majesty and the Emperor Francis. You know each other perfectly, and this is ever necessary to a good understanding.

To establish for the future that perfect agreement of conduct so decisive for the fate of Europe, it is necessary to lay the foundation as simply as possible on clear, precise principles, and to secure their application by reciprocal engagements no less clear and precise. A great distance separates us, and this inconvenience we must remedy.

I will now state the principles, and point out the engagements to be made.

I. PRINCIPLES.

It is demonstrated that a vast and dangerous conspiracy has since 1814 acquired sufficient strength and means of action to enable it to seize upon a number of places in the public administration. This conspiracy was less evident to the eyes of the world as long as it did not court discovery, and contented itself with the domain of theory. In that domain nothing is surprising : discussions, pretensions, contradictions belong to it by full right. From the day that I saw sound doctrines attacked with impunity, and observed that they ran the risk of being suppressed altogether, I recognised revolution, with its inevitable consequences, disorder, anarchy, and death, where others saw only light fighting with prejudice. Up to that time the conspiracy had only reconnoitred its ground and prepared it. It has grown, and it must grow, thanks to the instruments which a too deplorable folly has allowed it to create for itself.

It has not been slow in descending from the intellectual sphere into that of material facts. One word was sufficient to gain public favour. That word was Constitution, of all words the least precise, the most open to variety of interpretation, and the easiest to make popular, for it acts on the mass of the people through their hopes. Tell men that by means of a single word you will ensure them their rights, a liberty which the mass always confound with licence, a career for their ambition, and success in all their enterprises, and you will have no trouble in making them listen to you. The mass once agitated, they give up everything: they listen, but do not care to comprehend. When the people do really comprehend, they are the first to re-establish order.

This ground taken, as the last resource, authority has been attacked. The factious have had recourse to arms; triumph seemed to them quite certain.

The clear and precise aim of the factious is one and uniform. It is the overthrow of everything legally existing. The ambitious and successful are always impatient and ardent in their demands. Every day in a revolution is equivalent to the career of a man. The day past is nothing, the present day is everything, and that will be nothing to-morrow. Influence, place, fortune, all that human passions most covet, are suspended and attached to the tree of liberty like prizes on the pole at a fair. The people do not want urging to flock to it in crowds. Go to the fair they must, and to get there everything must be overturned.

The principle which the monarchs must oppose to this plan of universal destruction is the preservation of everything legally existing. The only way to arrive at this end is by allowing no innovations.

Your Imperial Majesty knows me well enough to be assured that no person is farther removed than I am from any narrow views of administration. It is simply the attainment of real good that I desire, and on every occasion consider my duty to maintain. But the more positive I am of this the more I am convinced that it is impossible at the same time to preserve and to reform with any justice or reason when the mass of the people is in agitation ; it is then like an individual in a state of irritation, threatened with fever, or already yielding to its ravages.

Let the Governments govern, and authority be something more than a name, for it is nothing without power.

By ruling, it really ameliorates the situation, but let authority remove nothing from the foundations on which it rests ; let it act, but not concede. It should exercise its rights, but not discuss them. It should be just (and to be so it must be strong), and should respect all rights as it would have its own respected.

In one word, Sire, let us be conservative ; let us walk steadily and firmly on well-known paths; let us not deviate from those lines in word or deed : we shall thus be strong, and shall come at last to a time when improvements may be made with as much chance of success as there is now certainty of failure.

II. MEANS.

The monarchs should be furnished with such proofs of mutual confidence, and unity of principle and will, that they may have (to effect the good they desire) nothing to do but to maintain this attitude.

This state of things is less easy of attainment when the Courts are situated at great distances ; therefore, I am most anxious, Sire, to make certain of the means.

With this object, it is necessary that before the separation takes place, your Imperial Majesty should come to an understanding with the Emperor Francis on the following subjects :—

1st. The transactions of Laybach should be regarded by the two Courts as an unchangeable basis until the meeting of the Cabinets in 1822

The ambassadors sent from these two Courts to the other Courts of Europe should receive instructions to regulate their conduct, on every occasion, with the greatest care, according to the principle I have just laid down. The factious and feeble, encouraged by the false policy of many of the Cabinets, will combine to disturb this union between the two monarchs. What they cannot succeed in destroying, they will try to injure in public opinion. The strongest and most persistent efforts of the abettors of the existing evil will be naturally directed against the most powerful barrier which could be opposed to it. All this is simple and natural, and consequently certain. Energetic and precise instructions should be given to the representatives of the two Courts, requiring them to support each other on every occasion in all explanations respecting the transactions at Laybach and their consequences.

2nd. In a time of continual agitation cases may present themselves which it is impossible to define beforehand.

The two monarchs must agree among themselves :—

To judge any fortuitous case according to the principles which were applied at Laybach in similar cases ;

Not to hesitate to place themselves in an attitude agreeable to these principles ;

Finally, to put off any explanation with other Courts until after an exchange of communications, which the two monarchs must immediately open, rather than run the risk of differing in their explanations or their conduct.

The geographical position of Austria should make your Imperial Majesty attach a particular value to this engagement on our part.

3rd. An affair of very grave importance, the **revolt**

of the Greeks, requires the most perfect understanding between the two monarchs. Your Imperial Majesty's opinion on the matter I know, and I have taken the liberty of devoting to that subject a short separate paper. I shall have the honour of sending it to your Majesty, but it will contain your Imperial Majesty's own ideas.

4th. The most absolute uniformity of judgment on the dangers and exigences of the moment, exists between your Imperial Majesty and your august ally, and, allow me to add, myself.

This addition, Sire, is not pretension. I would not allow myself to make it if I did not believe it to be really useful. It is proved that the factious of all countries and of all shades have established a centre of information and action. Chance, too, has its limits; therefore it was not chance that we have been so successful in the commotions and catastrophes of the last twelve months.

To this centre of information another must be opposed. Not so with action. Conspiracies alone depend on a single centre of action: the cause which we defend, Sire, the cause of God and man, must be assisted at every possible point. Our measures are all matured, and to be put in motion it is only necessary to follow a line of principles agreed upon. Legitimate power does not run the same chances of defeat as revolutionary action.

My wishes, therefore, are confined to the establishment of a centre of information, and for this Vienna offers every advantage. It is central, and our means of observation in Germany and Italy are numerous.

Your Imperial Majesty deigns to give me a certain amount of confidence. Assist me to justify that confidence by the triumph of a cause which is yours as much as ours, and in which the whole civilised world will one day proclaim its interest.

If, Sire, you can find a thoroughly trustworthy man, place him at Vienna, and accredit him to me. Give him all the data which your Imperial Majesty can collect concerning the movements of the factious in the various countries of Europe. That man would know all that we know. The consequence will be a focus of light such as does not exist at present. We shall obtain results which perhaps we do not expect. We shall know the truth and not be led away by appearances, and in the end we shall baffle our opponents.

Such, Sire, are the moral and material measures which I propose to you. They are drawn up with the conviction that, without steady observation and continued action, we shall never do the good which is our duty; any divergence from our path will have an influence for evil, like a false movement in the day of battle: it is only by learning all we can that we can hope to beat the enemy; and, in short, to attain this end, the most glorious the mind of man can conceive, it is absolutely necessary to unite our efforts and make common cause.

Metternich's Circular Despatch to the Austrian Ambassadors at Foreign Courts, Laybach, May 12, 1821.

553. The meeting of the allied monarchs and their Cabinets at Troppau was held to determine the point of view from which they would regard the unhappy events which had overthrown the legitimate Government at Naples; to arrange a common line of conduct; and in a spirit of justice and moderation to contrive measures calculated to secure Italy from a general overthrow, and the neighbouring States from most imminent dangers. Thanks to the happy agreement of views and feelings which reigned among the three august sovereigns, this first task was soon accomplished.

Principles clearly announced and embraced on both sides with all the sincerity of conviction could not fail to lead to analogous resolutions ; and the bases established at the time of the first conferences have been invariably followed during the whole course of a meeting signalised by the most remarkable results.

Transferred to Laybach, this meeting took a more decided character, owing to the presence and concurrence of the King of the Two Sicilies, and the unanimity with which the princes of Italy acceded to the system adopted by the allied Cabinets. The monarchs were convinced that the Governments most immediately interested in the destinies of the Peninsula would do justice to the purity of their intentions, and that a sovereign placed in a most painful situation by acts of perfidy and violence associated with his name would resign himself with perfect confidence to measures which would both put an end to that state of moral captivity and restore to his faithful subjects the repose and well-being of which criminal factions had deprived them.

The effect of these measures was not long in manifesting itself. The edifice raised by revolt, as fragile in its construction as corrupt in its foundations, resting only on the cunning of some and the sudden blindness of others, disowned by the great majority of the nation, odious even to the army formed to defend it, has given way at the first contact with the regular forces. Legitimate power is re-established ; the factions are dispersed ; the Neapolitan people are delivered from the tyranny of those audacious impostors who, flattering their dreams of false liberty, practised upon them the most cruel vexations, imposed enormous sacrifices solely for the satisfaction of their own ambition and greed, and went far to irretrievably ruin a country of which they never ceased calling themselves the regenerators.

This important restoration is consummated by the counsels and efforts of the allied Powers. Now that the King of the Two Sicilies is again invested with his full rights, the monarchs content themselves with seconding by their most ardent wishes the measures adopted by this sovereign for the reconstruction of his Government, and the securing, by good laws and wise institutions, the real interests of his subjects and the constant prosperity of his kingdom.

During the course of these great transactions, we have seen burst forth here and there the effects of the vast conspiracy, so long directed against the Powers which have enjoyed happiness and glory for hundreds of years. The existence of this conspiracy was not unknown to the monarchs; but in the midst of the agitations which Italy has endured since the catastrophes of the year 1820, and the attendant confusion, it has developed with increasing rapidity, and its true character has come to light. It is not, as one might have believed at a less advanced period, against such and such form of government particularly exposed to their abuse that the dark enterprises of the authors of these plots and the foolish wishes of their blind partisans are directed. The States which have admitted changes in their political *régime* are not more protected from their attacks than those whose ancient institutions have withstood the storms of time. Pure monarchies, limited monarchies, federative constitutions, republics, all are confounded and proscribed by a sect which treats oligarchy as something raised above the level of a chimerical equality. The chiefs of this impious league, indifferent to every kind of stable and permanent organisation, aim solely at the fundamental bases of society. To overthrow what exists, and substitute whatever chance suggests to their disordered imaginations or their sinister passions—this is the essence of their doctrine, and the secret of all their machinations!

The allied sovereigns cannot forget that they have but one barrier to oppose to this devastating torrent—namely, the preservation of all that is legally established. This has been the invariable principle of their policy, the starting-point and the end of all their resolutions. They have been stopped by the vain clamours of ignorance or malice, accusing them of condemning humanity to a state of stagnation and torpor incompatible with the natural and progressive course of civilisation, and with the improvement of social institutions. These monarchs have never manifested the least disposition to oppose genuine ameliorations, or the reform of abuses which creep into the best Governments. Very different views have animated them ; and if the repose which the Governments and people had the right to believe had been secured to them by the pacification of Europe has not brought about all the good which should have followed, it is because the Governments have been obliged to concentrate their thoughts on the means of effectually stemming the progress of a faction which, spreading error, discontent, and the fanaticism of innovation, would soon have endangered the existence of all public order. Useful or necessary changes in the legislation and administration of States should emanate from the freewill, the thoughtful and enlightened conviction of those to whom God has given the responsibility of power. Any departure from this line of conduct necessarily leads to disorder, confusion and evils much more insupportable than those which it pretends to cure. Convinced of this eternal truth, the sovereigns have had no hesitation in proclaiming it with frankness and vigour ; they have declared that, while respecting the rights and independence of all legitimate power, they regard as legally void and unauthorised according to the principles which constitute the public law of Europe all pretended reforms effected by revolt and open force. They have acted in accordance with this declaration at Naples and in Piedmont, and in those events even which—in very different circumstances, but by equally criminal combinations— had given up the eastern part of Europe to disorder. The monarchs are all the more determined not to depart from this system, that they consider the firmness with which they maintained it, in an epoch so critical, to be the real cause of the success with which their efforts for the re-establishment of order in Italy have been crowned. The Governments of the Peninsula have proclaimed that they had nothing to fear for their political independence, the integrity of their territories, or the preservation of their rights, in begging for help, which was given to them on the sole condition that they should use it to defend their own existence. It is this reciprocal confidence which has saved Italy, and in the space of two months has arrested a conflagration which, without the intervention of the allied Powers, would have ravaged and ruined the whole of that beautiful country, and threatened for a long time the rest of Europe.

Nothing has more effectually shown the force of the moral power which connects the salvation of Italy with the determinations of the monarchs than the prompt and happy *dénouement* of the revolt which had broken out in Piedmont. Conspirators, partly composed of foreigners, had prepared this new crime, and to ensure its success had put in motion the most detestable of all revolutionary measures, that of inciting against authority the armed force whose function it is to obey it and to maintain public order. Victim of an inexplicable treason (if anything is to be called inexplicable while political crimes find voices to defend them in Europe), a sovereign justly enjoying the respect and affection of his subjects is obliged to abdicate a throne which he had adorned with his virtues ; a considerable portion of his troops is dragged into the abyss by the example and intrigues of a small number of ambitious men ; and the vulgar cry of the anti-social faction, echoing through the capital, reverberated in the provinces. The monarchs assembled at Laybach were not long in replying to this. Their union was strengthened and increased by danger, and their protecting voice was soon heard. When the faithful servants of the King saw that they were not abandoned, they employed all that remained to them of their resources to combat the enemies of their country and the national glory. Legitimate power, though hampered and paralysed in its action, was not the less mindful to maintain its dignity and its rights, and, help arriving at the decisive moment of the crisis, the triumph of the good cause was soon complete. Piedmont was delivered in a few days, and nothing remained of a revolution which had reckoned on the fall of more than one Government but the shameful recollections carried away by its guilty authors.

Thus, in following without deviation the principles established, and the line of conduct agreed upon in the first days of their meeting, the allied monarchs have

accomplished the pacification of Italy.   Their principal
object is attained.   None of the proceedings concluded
there have belied the declarations which truth and
good faith had inspired.   They have remained faithful
under every trial that Providence had in reserve for
them.   Called more than all the other legitimate
sovereigns to watch over the peace of Europe, to protect it, not only against the errors and passions which
might compromise the relations of one Power to
another, but also against those fatal attempts which
would deliver up the whole civilised world to the
horrors of universal anarchy—they would feel that
they profaned their august vocation by the narrow
calculations of a vulgar policy.   As everything is
simple, plain, and open in the system which they
have embraced, they submit it with confidence to the
judgment of all enlightened Governments.

The Congress which has just concluded is to reassemble in the course of next year.   It will then take
into consideration the duration of the measures which,
by consent of all the Courts of Italy, and particularly
those of Naples and Turin, have been judged necessary to secure the tranquillity of the Peninsula.   The
monarchs and their Cabinets will approach the examination of that question in the same spirit which has
hitherto guided them.   Motives of undoubted weight,
and fully justified by results, determined the sovereigns
to interfere in the affairs of Italy.   They are far from
wishing to prolong this intervention beyond the limits
of strict necessity, sincerely hoping that the circumstances which imposed this painful duty upon them
may never again occur.

We have thought it useful, when the sovereigns
are about to separate, to recapitulate in the preceding

paper the principles which have guided them in their late transactions.

You are consequently charged to communicate this despatch to the Minister of Foreign Affairs at the Court to which you are accredited.

You will receive at the same time a declaration (No. 554) conceived in the same spirit, which the Cabinets have had drawn up and printed in order to make known to the European public the sentiments and principles with which the august sovereigns are animated, and which will always serve as guides to their policy.

Declaration.

(Supplement to No. 553.)

554. Europe knows the motives which induced the allied sovereigns to combine to suppress conspiracies and put an end to the troubles which threatened the general peace, the re-establishment of which has cost so many efforts and so many sacrifices.

At the very moment when their generous determination was accomplished in the kingdom of Naples, a rebellion of a still more odious kind (if that were possible) broke out in Piedmont.

Neither the ties which for so many centuries had united the House of Savoy to its people, nor the benefits of an enlightened administration under a wise prince and paternal laws, nor the sad prospect of the evils to which the country would be exposed, could restrain the designs of these instigators of rebellion.

The plan for a general subversion was drawn up. In this vast combination against the repose of nations the conspirators of Piedmont had their *rôle* assigned to them. They have hastened to fulfil it.

The throne and the State have been betrayed, oaths violated, military honour despised, and neglect of every duty has speedily brought the scourge of all disorders.

Everywhere the evil has presented the same character; everywhere the same spirit has directed these unhappy revolutions.

Unable to find a plausible reason to justify them, or national support to sustain them, it is in false doctrines that the authors of these revolutions seek an apology; it is on criminal associations that they found a still more criminal hope. To them the salutary control of law is a yoke which must be broken. They renounce the sentiments which inspire true patriotism, and substituting for well-known duties arbitrary and indefinite pretences of universal change in the constituent principles of society, they prepare endless calamities for the world.

The allied sovereigns recognised all the dangers of this conspiracy to their full extent, but at the same time they saw the real weakness of the conspirators behind the veil of appearances and declamations. Experience has confirmed their presentiments. The resistance which legitimate authority has met with has had no strength, and crime has disappeared before the sword of justice.

It is not to accidental causes, nor even to the feeble resistance made in the day of battle, that the speedy success must be attributed. This rests upon a principle more consoling and more worthy of consideration.

Providence struck terror into consciences so guilty, and the disapproval of the people, whose fate was compromised by these authors of mischief, made them drop their arms.

Destined simply to combat and suppress rebellion, the allied forces, far from maintaining any separate interest, came to the assistance of the subjugated people, and the people regarded their aid as a support in favour of their liberty, not as an attack on their independence. From that time the war ceased ; from that time the States which rebellion had reached have been friendly to Powers which desired nothing but their tranquillity and well-being.

In the midst of these grave conjunctures and in a position so delicate the allied sovereigns, together with their Majesties the King of the Two Sicilies and the

King of Sardinia, have thought it indispensable to take measures of temporary precaution, such as were dictated by prudence and regard for the general safety. The allied troops, whose presence was necessary for the re-establishment of order, have been stationed at convenient points, with the sole view of protecting the free exercise of legitimate authority, and assisting it to efface the traces of these grave misfortunes.

The justice and disinterestedness which have presided at the deliberations of the allied monarchs will always regulate their policy. In the future, as in the past, its aim will ever be the preservation of the independence and the rights of each State as they are recognised and defined by existing treaties. The result of so dangerous a movement will yet be, under Providence, the strengthening of the peace which the enemies of the people endeavoured to destroy, and the consolidation of an order of things which will secure peace and prosperity to the nations.

Moved by these feelings, the allied sovereigns, in fixing a limit to the conferences at Laybach, wished to announce to the world the principles which guided them. They are determined never to depart from them, and all lovers of peace will see in their union an assured guarantee against the attempts of the ill-disposed.

With this object their Imperial and Royal Majesties have commanded their plenipotentiaries to sign and publish the present declaration.

Laybach, May 12, 1821.

Austria : METTERNICH, BARON DE VINCENT ;
Prussia : KRUSEMARCK ;
Russia : NESSELRODE, CAPO D'ISTRIA, POZZO DI BORGO.

METTERNICH'S MISSION TO KING GEORGE IV. OF ENGLAND IN HANOVER.

Metternich to the Emperor Francis.

555. *Hanover*, *Oct.* 24, 1821.—True to my plan for the journey, I arrived here in good time on the 20th. I heard, when at Brunswick, that the King was confined to his bed with the gout. On my arrival I was told that this is only a slight attack, the consequence of a cold taken by his Majesty at the review of the troops.

I found everything ready for my reception on the part of the King. I have also spoken to Lord Castlereagh, and convinced myself that it is the King's wish, as well as his own, to bring about a thorough understanding between the two Courts in the present crisis. The first conversation was sufficient to show that this agreement would be accomplished without difficulty.

On the following day the King summoned me. He is residing at a country house which lies about the same distance from Hanover as Schönbrunn from Vienna.

I found the King looking much better than I expected. A well-known English *arcanum* called 'Wilson's Remedy' had already moderated the attack of gout. The King was lying in a *chaiselongue* in a rather fantastic Austrian hussar's coat. He wore the small crosses of the Austrian order.

He received me with all the marks of pleasure, and at once began the conversation by assuring me that your Majesty had done him two great favours in life. The first—and he pointed to the *toison* I always wear—the other that your Majesty had sent me to him.

He now began a long speech, which certainly lasted half an hour, and was meant to impress me with the feeling of his attachment to your Majesty, whom he never mentioned without saying ' Our Emperor.' My personal praises followed in a way that only embarrassed the man who was their object ; between which he did not fail to make the most violent personal attacks against the Emperor Alexander and still worse against Count Capo d'Istria.

After these alternate attacks and laudations he came to the motives for my coming here. He began with a long recapitulation of the events of late years, in which he conceded the principal part to Austria, and ended with a frightful explosion against his own ministry, especially against Lord Liverpool, but entirely excepting Lord Castlereagh, whom he described as a faithful, vigorous man, quite devoted to the good cause, as proof of which he concluded by saying, ' He understands you ; he is your friend : that says everything.'

When the King had finished (and I guarded myself from interrupting him), I took care to return to everything he had said. I passed over his fierce attacks, and endeavoured to make him see the real position of affairs.

The result was that we arrived at the same point of view ; the King became more calm, and expressed himself with the greatest justice and propriety.

After a conversation of more than three hours, he left me with the invitation to come to him when and how I should think well. He expressly reserved to himself the further unfolding of his views on the position of affairs, foreign and domestic.

I now first commenced a regular official negotiation

with Lord Londonderry (Castlereagh).   My courier from
Vienna had arrived with copies of my last despatches
to Constantinople and St. Petersburg, and I took these
as the groundwork of our agreement.   I have the satisfaction of assuring your Majesty that Lord Londonderry, when I had explained this basis, pronounced it
so clear that he has adopted it unconditionally as the
most reasonable and fitting.

My business here may be divided into two parts.
The course taken here with regard to the Turkish
complication is so firm and consistent that we shall
certainly be able to prepare a very difficult solution for
their evil game.   Lord Londonderry and I have sent a
courier to Count Bernstorff, to summon him from Mecklenburg, where he is just now.   If he cannot come, I
hope I shall meet him on my journey home.

Count Lieven has not arrived, for what reason is
quite unknown. We know that he left St. Petersburg on
September 25, but at the first halt he would find an
invitation from the Emperor to go to him at Witepsk
for the review, and as that may have detained him ten
or twelve days, we expect him every hour, and I am
very anxious for his arrival.

My second object here is the home affairs.   It is
necessary to keep the ministry in their places, or if this
is not practicable, at any rate to reconstruct a ministry
under Lord Castlereagh's leadership devoted to the
cause, or to us, which is the same thing.

In this critical question I quite agree with Lord
Castlereagh's thoroughly right and judicious views.   I
hope to be able to support him with the King.   That I,
however, must keep within very precise limits, is a necessity of the case, for it can never be the true interest
of one State to meddle in the home affairs of another.

My part here, therefore, can go no further than to
show myself an unselfish and calmly reflective friend of
the good cause. My personal knowledge—which is, unhappily, only too great—of the obstructive character
(combined as it is, however, with many talents) of Lord
Liverpool, leads me to consider as a real benefit his
leaving the ministry with a view to its recomposition
under Lord Londonderry as Premier. Our political
standpoint would certainly gain by England's taking a
more vigorous grasp in the world's affairs.

I confine myself to this preliminary statement of my
attitude with regard to the business of the hour the
more willingly as the result will be seen in but a
few days. . . .

Attachment to your Majesty's person and the whole
Austrian system pervades every idea of the King. It is
his great desire to visit Vienna in the course of the next
year, and Lord Londonderry encourages the idea. If
nothing unforeseen occurs, he will certainly come in
June, and in July go to Carlsbad, then home by Berlin,
Hanover, and Paris. From this short sketch your Majesty will be satisfied that my relations here, political
and otherwise, leave nothing to be desired.

My journey through the whole of Upper and Lower
Saxony has afforded me every kind of evidence that the
preservation of peace lies entirely in the hands of the
Governments. The student affair has been so turned
to ridicule that its political tendency would have quite
disappeared if the least vigour had been shown in the
matter of some notorious professors. But even these
are only like the few branded logs in a huge pile. If
the Greek affair succeeds, so much is for the moment
gained that a very little help will put all right.

The eyes of the well-disposed are everywhere turned

on Austria ; every word of ours tells, and if, when the present political crisis reaches a moment of repose, we only vigorously bring forward our system in Germany, much good will ensue. I am able to make this assertion with the more confidence as princes and ministers pour in upon me from all sides, and beg from me orders rather than mere advice.

I cannot yet point out the route by which I shall go back. At any rate I will return in the early part of November to Vienna.

Metternich to the Emperor Francis, Hanover, Oct. 29, 1821.

556. The King of England has set out on his journey. He goes by Cassel, Marburg, Wetzlar, Coblenz, and Brussels. His health is quite re-established.

I believe I have thoroughly attained the object of my journey. My agreement with Lord Londonderry is concluded. England takes the same ground as we do, and this in the following sense :—

1. The two Cabinets consider the maintenance of peace between Russia and the Porte as the most important object of their common efforts. To facilitate these they will leave nothing undone to enlighten Russia as to the danger of a breach, at the same time calling upon the Porte for an exact fulfilment of the treaty and moderation in its demands.

2. Since the unanimity of the declarations of the two Courts that exercise the most direct influence on the Porte will have a most salutary effect, the two Cabinets have drawn up one despatch to St. Petersburg and another to Constantinople, in which the above views are strongly and vigorously developed. These decrees are included in the despatch, and are drawn up with the care proper to remove from the Russian Court the

delusion that a conference (on their part) between the ministers is necessary for an agreement in fundamental views. Lord Londonderry's instructions, therefore, are grounded mostly on English, mine on Austrian, arguments. On both sides the conclusion arrived at is, the necessity that Russia should maintain peace ; for, under present circumstances, the evils consequent on any political war would be incalculable.

That the two Powers will exert their whole influence on the Porte to attain this all-important object ; but that it does not come within the province of the Powers to interfere with actual force in case of opposition being made ; that, lastly, the views which may be entertained by Russia of the greatest possible strengthening of the friendly relations between that Power and the Porte must be put forth by Russia herself, and can in no way proceed from the allies. In these sentences your Majesty will find the pure basis on which we take our stand thoroughly shared by England. My conversations with Lord Londonderry had the good result of very much strengthening his language. Your Majesty knows the English ministry too well to doubt that the instructions to Bagot and Strangford would not have been nearly so precise as they are but for my co-operation. I have now the pleasure of pointing out to Russia how much can always be done with England if one knows how to speak her language.

With regard to the great question of the moment, I consider the result of my journey as all the more decisive as Count Lieven, who arrived here yesterday, has just left the Emperor Alexander, and, according to the first conversation which Londonderry and I had with him, is quite convinced that that monarch will certainly maintain peace. Everything that I have heard from Count Lieven shows me that the Emperor Alexander still remains in the same mind that he was at Laybach.

My presence here has been of great advantage in another way : I hope, and believe, namely, that Lord Londonderry will be present at the Italian Congress next year.

As to the home affairs of England, I believe I have put an end to much mischief. I have spoken out to the King with much freedom and loyally supported the ministry. I do not think that Lord Liverpool can maintain his position : if this is not possible (and his resignation in a good manner would be a happiness for England and Europe), the King at least remains. If this happens, Lord Londonderry concedes to me the whole merit of a result which can only act beneficially on our future standpoint. . . .

The presence of the King will have a very good effect here, although it does not amount to quite so much as it ought to have done. He would make a much better appearance if he could put aside certain peculiarities in his temper and manner.

As to his attachment to your Majesty and to Austria's system, nothing more can be desired. He not only allows no opportunity to pass of making this feeling public, but he perhaps does too much in that way. At all his dinners the first toast which the Duke of Cambridge gives, is, of course, the King ; the second, proposed by the King, is your Majesty. With the first the band plays ' God save the King ; ' with the second, ' God preserve the Emperor.' At state dinners, when the people were assembled beneath the windows, they accompanied these toasts with loud hurrahs, which were not more noisy for the King than for your

Majesty.   During the first toast the King remains quiet, and during the second his voice is louder even than that of his people.

Count Bernstorff cannot come here.   As I cannot meet him on my road, and as I have no object of any kind to induce me to travel by North Germany, I will take the route by Frankfurt, which is better for travelling, and will only make a difference of a few hours.   I can thus stop at Cassel and see the Elector, visit the Duke of Nassau, and confer with the ministers there and at Darmstadt, and put many things in order for the next sitting of the Diet.   Once at Biebrich, I can go for four-and-twenty hours to Johannisberg, and reach Vienna by November 12.   By the other route I should reach Vienna on the 9th, but in this short delay I see no disadvantage worth consideration.

METTERNICH.

Noticed and approved.

FRANCIS.

Vienna, December 27, 1821.

*THE PRINCE DE CARIGNAN'S SHARE IN THE RE-
VOLUTIONARY INTRIGUES IN PIEDMONT.*

*Metternich to Zichy, in Berlin, and to Lebzeltern, in
St. Petersburg, Vienna, December 6, 1821.*

557. His Majesty's ministers should be informed
that the Provisional Government in Piedmont have been
occupied in carefully collecting exact *data* concerning
the part which the Prince de Carignan is supposed to
have taken in the revolution in that country ; that the
result of this inquiry is very unfavourable to the Prince,
who is seriously compromised by the depositions of
several rebel officers ; but that, nevertheless, there is
not sufficient positive evidence against him to bring him
within the power of the law. These *data* have been
corroborated to me on my return from Hanover, by
Baron de Binder, who is here on leave. The conversations which I have had with that ambassador, while
leaving me no doubt on this head, have at the same
time enabled me to see clearly enough that King
Carlo Felice, who seems convinced of the guilt of the
Prince de Carignan, has not given up the idea of
removing him from the succession to the throne, which
he wishes to secure for his own son by a pragmatic
sanction. I am even afraid, from the manner in which
Baron de Binder expressed himself in telling me of the
project which they attribute to his Sardinian Majesty,
that this ambassador, when he was confidentially consulted at Turin, did not pronounce against the project

as decidedly as he ought to have done. This hesitation may have been caused by the general persuasion at Turin, even among individuals who are most devoted to the King and the monarchical cause, that the Prince de Carignan has not held himself aloof from the revolution in his country ; that he was led away by some young ambitious military men, who wished to play a part under the sanction of his name ; that, lacking entirely both temper and energy, he knew neither how to restrain or direct them, and has ended by displeasing all parties.

It is certain that when the heir presumptive to the throne is so weak as to allow himself to be dragged into playing a part so derogatory to his person and his country, the friends of the monarchy must dread the moment when he will be called by Providence to reign ; we can imagine the general fear at the thought that the Prince de Carignan, when he ascends the throne, will most probably become the sport of factions and parties, and that his reign may be the era of new internal troubles. There is, in fact, no doubt that the accession of the Prince de Carignan to the throne, after the part he played in the last revolution, may give just cause for anxiety. But, without deceiving ourselves on this point, we cannot discover in the fear of possible or even probable evil, any good reason for departing from those principles which the allied sovereigns have constantly professed ; or permitting ourselves to prejudge a question so delicate as that of depriving Prince de Carignan of his right of succession to the throne, especially when there is no substantial proof of his guilt, so that he cannot legally be tried. It seems to me that the allied sovereigns have neither the right nor the power to do so, and that in arrogating either to themselves they would give an example as dangerous as it is contrary to their principles.   Such is, at least, our opinion on this important question, and as we think it well that it should be known to his Majesty's ministers, your Excellency is requested to allow this dispatch to be read by the Minister of Foreign Affairs.*

* See Nos. 548–550.   We know that the Prince de Carignan made use of his enforced absence from Italy to reinstate himself, for he took military service under the Duke d'Angoulême (1823), and so distinguished himself by personal bravery at the taking of Trocadero—the most brilliant exploit of the whole campaign—that a reconciliation took place between the Prince and King Carlo Felice.—ED.

1822.

COMPLICATIONS WITH CAPO D'ISTRIA AND OTHER EVENTS.

Extracts from Metternich's private Letters from January 5 to August 25, 1822.

558. *Vienna, January* 15, 1822.—The force of habit is so strong a power that one may come to take pleasure even in privations. I can quite comprehend that a prisoner to whom freedom is given after twenty years of confinement will feel quite strange in the outer world when he no longer hears the rattle of his chains.

It is remarkable how little is needed in order to act. The power comes of itself; will and memory are all that is necessary; but just for this reason so few know how to act. That the public thinks everything grand and difficult arises from the way in which the great mass of the people looks at things. Some really think it so, others encourage the delusion in order to make themselves safe in case success does not follow; both these classes are active, and set great machines in motion; but great machines are inconvenient and cumbrous things. There is always one essential point, and one only; everything else is extraneous. Hence, if we go straight up to it, attack it, destroy it, or use it according to our needs, the enormous structure will disappear like smoke. This is, however, what most people do not do; rather, they become alarmed, or they begin to depreciate the importance of the matter, or they attempt too much at once, and thus sink in the mud, and are stifled in it. What, then, shall I say of Capo d'Istria?

I remember, when I was a boy of seven years old, saying to one of my professors, 'Do you know what I think about the world? The laws which govern it go exactly contrary to optical laws; the closer you approach objects in the world the smaller they become.' My professor did not allow me to pursue this theme, and broke out in anger. 'My friend,' said he, 'you speak like an inexperienced youth; with such principles you will never accomplish anything, and will always go wrong.'

559. *January* 11.—The Court ball, which took place two days ago, gave me the opportunity of making some truly philosophical if not amusing reflections on the Vienna carnival. There 200 persons of both sexes, locked in each other's arms, turn constantly round from Twelfth Day to Ash Wednesday; so that a sprightly pair may in this time make a distance of 400 miles, while another pair less nimble will perhaps accomplish only 200. When at last Ash Wednesday arrives, and the dancers separate, they are greatly astonished to find themselves in the same place from which they started. With us in Vienna, only our bodies turn, our heads not so easily, and only too frequently it happens that the mothers sadly discover in Lent that the vigorous waltzers on whom her motherly eyes lingered with especial hope had clasped her little daughters so tightly only to make the more sure of duly accomplishing the 400 or the 200 miles. As I have nothing to do with this pirouetting, and watch all the bustle very calmly, Lent brings me no disappointment. But yet I find the carnival very tiresome, although I only use my legs to get over the ground, for nothing is so insupportable to me as a ball where not a corner is to be found to enjoy a quiet chat. And this is my destiny at the *fêtes* at which I must be present. I grow weary and fly. It is really not worth while to set a whole orchestra in motion to produce such an effect. There is nothing so frightful as movement without object, and noise without interest. Vienna is now full of such movement and noise. For some time after the ball I always speak in cadences, and divide my sentences into eight periods, just like the waltzes with their eight-time.

560. *January* 21.—The Russian Premier still keeps us waiting for his decisions. What a confusion of ideas! How mischievous is his example! How it agitates men's minds, pours oil on the fire, and spoils the position! Since the world began was there ever such a man? And yet he will end just like all the others who have gone before him, but who have not gone so far as he has by a long way. But this end, the surest remedy for deep-seated evils, will it not come too late ? And before the dreamer is got rid of many things will have gone to rack and ruin.   That the barrier is not yet demolished can only be explained by the equanimity of the Emperor Alexander ; but is this equanimity sufficient ?   Will it never be broken through ?

Nine-and-twenty years ago to-day Louis XVI. was executed.   When I call to mind the share I then took in the world's affairs, I feel as if I must be a hundred years old.

561. *January* 23.—To-day I have received very interesting accounts from St. Petersburg, which may explain the relations between the Emperor Alexander and myself.   Reading alone, however, will not suffice ; one must also know.   Health and disease can neither be written nor read.   To judge of them one must see and examine.   The Emperor Alexander wishes very much that I should come to him—an absolute impossibility.   He desires only a few moments, but I am not master of a single one.   Alexander is dying to be rid of the whole concern—an astonishingly easy matter, and I really think a *tête-à-tête* of a few days would be sufficient to attain this end.   But even that short space of time is now an impossibility.   Alexander inquires how then was it possible for me to go to see the King of England.   This question a child might answer, but the Emperor Alexander is of all children the most childish.

Poor little Nesselrode wishes to send Strogonow to Vienna in place of Golowkin.   He thinks I require an amiable man.   How little he knows me.   To get this fancy out of his head I wrote as follows : ' I have liked you for sixteen years ; I respect you ; you possess my confidence.   If we meet we confide in each other.   I believe in you and understand you. Now, are you amiable? Not in the least, and you never make any pretension to be so. Therefore I beg you not to make me contradict myself.' I do not know that this language is amiable. I quite fear that it is not so, but it is to the point.

562. *February* 9.—There cannot well be anything more scandalous than the debates in the French Chambers. What questions have been raised there! How extraordinary was the dispute between General Foy and Count Castelbajac on fidelity. It has been left to the French to show that there can be two kinds of it. The revolutionists attach the idea of place to that of fidelity, while the Royalists connect it with the person. The latter are right, for I may assert that General Foy would not pledge his fidelity to the bed, but to the person, for otherwise any trifler would be faithful if he only always lay in the same bed.

How can people enter into such absurd discussions? And if anyone is so fortunate as to find an opponent stupid enough to start such a question, why is he not crushed with some sharp saying? What a capital answer Castelbajac, the ex-Bonapartist general, might have given if he had only repeated the compliment which Napoleon paid to Ségur when he met him in the Tuileries on his return from Elba. When Ségur assured him of his unalterable fidelity, ' There are two kinds of fidelity,' answered Napoleon : ' the fidelity of the dog and the fidelity of the cat. You, gentlemen, have the fidelity of the cat, which never forsakes the house.' In Castelbajac's place I would have asked General Foy whether he considers General Bertrand possessed fidelity or not?

One of the most wretched *coryphæi* of the *doctrinaire* party, Royer-Collard, informs the world that public

liberties are ' *des résistances.*' I, for my part, believe
that public liberties are health. Health is a much more
positive thing than mere resistance of death, which is a
negative force ; a kind of resistance which is only
disease, and is therefore neither health nor death.
According to Royer-Collard, an organised State might
have arrived at the summit of perfection when disease
was the basis of its existence ; up to this time I have
thought that health was the best regimen, but it seems
that I am only an Obscurantist or a fool. All this nonsense talked in a place which is thought an Areopagus
brings me to anger and despair. My mind is disturbed
by nothing so much as by pretension to intellectual
power and its consequences—impudence, vanity, osten-
tation, senselessness, and all the absurdities so boldly
brought forward. Capo d'Istria takes Royer-Collard for
a very deep thinker. I am so convinced that he considers me a blockhead that the conviction is the greatest
consolation—the only one, too, which he can give me.
If ever the day comes that he thinks me right, I shall be
inconsolable.

I have had my portrait taken very successfully. I
have given the original to my mother, and am now
having it copied. The workmen here are very slow,
and there is no way of pushing them on, because they
then punish one by working badly.

563. *February* 10.—I have just received a group
in marble by Canova, and had it put in my pavilion. It
is a charming work of art, which only troubles me in
one way—I do not know, that is, what the innocent and
the prudish will say to them. The first probably
nothing ; the second a great deal. This group was executed by Canova for Malmaison, and I believe the Emperor of Russia has bought it. I got Canova to make

a copy of it himself. It is one of the most tender and at the same time one of the most voluptuous creations of the artist. He has modelled the marble with love and grace. The group represents the first kiss that Amor gave to Psyche, and the two children kiss as if they had never done anything else. But whenever the very pure and innocent visit me I must hang a dressing-gown round Amor and throw a sheet over Psyche ; except on such occasions, however, I will leave them in their simple god-like forms. If these charming creatures did not weigh three-and twenty hundred-weight I would have them set on rollers ; but they are immoveable, and consequently faithful, like the cats and General Foy. I am delighted to think, therefore, that, in spite of his wings, Amor can never leave my house. These wings are a true work of art. In Rome there is an artist who only makes wings ; the first sculptors employ him, and it is quite extraordinary how delicately he handles the marble.

564. *February* 22.—The famous courier from St. Petersburg has arrived, and he does not fall short of his predecessors, for he brings me only senseless double-meaning phrases, injurious to those who wrote them, having no relation to facts, and in thorough contradiction to all that lies before one's eyes : full of ' nonsense ' and badly written ; the outcome of all this rigmarole is—nothing. So, as I always said, this ' nothing ' is not war, for war is something. It is not necessary to trouble one's head much to understand that, and, as I am in the right after all, there is in this feeling a great compensation for many annoyances.

My answer will be, that I will not answer ; and of all answers that is the most decided. On this occasion as on so many others, facts must speak for themselves,

and they have mostly quite another power than mere
words. The misuse of words is a misfortune of our
age. The perfection of man's wit will not succeed in
building even a hut with mere words, and the most
eloquent phrases will never shelter anyone from the
rain though he may take refuge under a whole thesis.
Capo d'Istria, too, will be wet to the skin—that I will
answer for. The struggle between Capo d'Istria and me
is like the conflict between a positive and a negative
force. Forces of like nature would neutralise each
other; and thus neither of them can prevail as long as
one of them is not used up by friction. Now, I do not
feel myself to have lost either weight or size; but for
such a contest what patience is needed!

565. *March* 3.—Among the amusing incidents of
the time is what has happened to the Emperor Francis.
He has received a letter with the signature ' from a
friend,' inviting him to propose Capo d'Istria as King of
Greece. That Capo d'Istria himself has no share in this
I am convinced, for he thinks only of a republic. But
this absurd step is significant of his friends. I at any
rate would give my vote for his being placed on the
throne, for he would be certainly much better placed
there than where he is.

A remarkable request has been made to me, which
I should have mentioned before. Ali Pasha, of Janina,
sent to me—when he found his possessions limited to
that town, and was in daily fear of his rebellion against
the Porte coming to an end—a confidential messenger
with a letter in which, with many pompous commen-
dations, he requested that I would send him a ' Constitution-maker.' Exclusively occupied with the welfare
of his subjects, he had discovered that the best security
for the happiness of his people lay in the bestowal of a

Constitution ; that he was convinced of this, but did not know what a Constitution really is, and therefore begged me to tell him of a person experienced in the matter. I gave the confidential messenger, a quite uncultivated Albanian merchant, my answer to the Pasha ; it contained, in a very few words, the assurance that I had no ' Constitution-maker ' at my disposal, but that, since Ali Pasha did not himself know what a Constitution is, I begged to advise him, in gratitude for the confidence reposed in me, that the best Constitution for the Pashalic would be subjection to the Porte.

Janina had fallen before the Pasha's messenger returned to him.*

566. *March 5.*—The bomb has burst ; it was filled with cotton-wool. I have this day received a courier from Lebzeltern informing me of Tatistscheff's arrival.

Since no one knows what is to be done when the magazine of follies is exhausted, it is now desired to explain them. The man was chosen who came first to hand, for the simple reason that in Russia nothing is so rare as a man. The expressions of the Emperor Alexander to myself personally leave nothing to be desired. My despatch of January 28 to Lebzeltern † has caused the bursting of the gun. It was certainly composed for that purpose, and the moment evidently was not badly chosen.

Now the affair will go off! It is time too. In what a position is the Emperor Alexander ! Since the world began nothing can be compared to the incredible character of his proceedings, and one will never be old enough not to live to see things which the boldest imagination could with difficulty conceive.

---

* It is well known that Ali Pasha had been executed February 5, 1822, by Kurschid Pasha, and his head sent to Constantinople, which caused **great** rejoicing there.—ED. † See No. 615.—ED.

567. *March* 6.—Tatistscheff has arrived. I saw him, and I hope that Capo d'Istria will be considered wrong. He is wrong before God, but he must also be so before man.*

568. *March* 8.—I am now fighting with Tatistscheff. The good man is just like an eel. Happily, I am an old fisherman !

Since the fall of Carthage no affair has been conducted like this one. It is extraordinary that we must always be asking if people are misleading one, if they will fail one or act serviceably, what they will do, or what they will not do. Hence an Areopagus of the most loyal, upright, and far-seeing men of all times have to lose themselves in useless hypotheses. In the midst of all this, I have the feeling of not being mistaken myself, and of being able to point out what seems undefinable.

At any rate, I shall do nothing to embarrass the matter still further ; I feel, indeed, that I shall clear up many things. . . . Whether anything happens or not will be decided by the small words Yes or No. I do not know a prettier word than the French *oui*, and much prefer it to the German *ja*, which stretches the mouth so terribly.

569. *March* 11.—I am working at some despatches and endeavouring to make my standpoint clear to the gentlemen. I think it is a good one, and unless I am much deceived, I shall bring the affair to a conclusion.

If anyone could have overheard my conversation with Tatistscheff, he must think one of two things— either there was a wish to deceive me, or in his country it is not known what is desirable or feasible. The

* See Nos. 616-621.—ED.

former would be too absurd to take into consideration; the latter is so in harmony with my knowledge of the country that without hesitation I adopt it as correct.

Tatistscheff must think that I am accessible to flattery, for he stuffs the censer right under my nose. But when one has lived so long as I have, one's nose is not very sensitive.

570. *March* 22.—I have been two days fighting with the storm. In Greece they begin to be furious. Between Greece and Russia there is just now a relation like that expressed by a certain Gascon nobleman: 'If you go forward, I will go back; but take care! for if you go back, I shall step forward.' This is the state of the affair, thanks to the Russian Premier. Although the thing will blow away like so much dust, yet it annoys me. Bad things occupy me day and night, while the good take but moments. Capo d'Istria and a moment! That does not rhyme. If I had to read through all that I have written during the last ten years, I should certainly need four years and more for the work.

571. *March* 27.—Capo d'Istria wastes his life in trying to shove me to one side. After some months lost for the peace of the world, the Emperor Alexander in despair clapped both hands to his head, and came to me with the request that I would put its contents to rights for him. And this is the case again to-day. Capo d'Istria knows better than any man in the world how to complicate an affair, and the present one is so complicated that the Emperor Alexander can neither move backwards nor forwards. Since the month of June I have foreseen the thing, and even the very day when the head would again be brought for me to put in order. To-day, too, I must again begin the same labour which falls to me in every great affair. The whole thing only commences to-day. Capo d'Istria has the fault of certain authors, who write an interminable preface before they touch the real subject of their work. The reader then expects something which he does not find in it : and inquires, at the conclusion of the work, for what purpose the preface was intended.

The Emperor Alexander is certainly self-willed, but one must not forget that this self-will of his is of a grand style.

572. *April* 3.—The affair is to-day as it was nine months ago. I can now see thoroughly through Tatistscheff. I know all there is in the man. Unhappily, I find there many empty spaces—which the good man imagines to be full. If people think to play the cunning with me, they are mistaken. This, however, has not been the case. The Emperor Alexander wants to find his way in a labyrinth, and begs the clue from his old Ariadne.

573. *April* 8.—What a good episode in my life is the establishment of the Italian opera here ; it has at last succeeded, and I have gained a real and great victory.

I have been present at a rehearsal of ' Zelmira.' Everything in it is good : the music and the singers, and David is the first singer of his kind. He unites everything : a beautiful tenor voice with a depth and a compass that gives on the one hand the very idea and essence of manhood, and on the other has nothing of it. He takes, without effort, the upper C with the natural voice, and goes down with ease. His method is unrivalled, and his execution perfect ; in a word, he leaves nothing to be desired ; and there are few things in this world on which I could venture to pronounce such a judgment.

In the months of April, May, June, and July, we shall have ' Zelmira,' ' Corradino,' ' Moses,' ' Elisabetta,' by Rossini ; a little *opera buffa* by Generali ; and ' Gabriella di Vergy,' by Carafa. The troupe consists, besides Colbrand (now Madame Rossini), of a charming singer, Ekerlin, who bears a German name ; beside Mombelli, David, Nazzari, Botticelli, Ambrogio, who are all one better than another—with the exception of David, who surpasses them all. At the head of all is Rossini himself, with an orchestra and chorus which astonish everyone. It may be supposed what delight this gives to a *melomaniac* like me. There are moments when the sunbeams penetrate the darkness of my prison, and so I feel most thoroughly.

574. *April 9.*—My workroom is always like a headquarters. Every moment brings a new interrupter, and if work wearies me, still more do these perpetual interruptions. Habit does much for most things, and I possess that of not losing the thread which is every moment broken, but my head suffers very much in consequence. There are times when my poor head is so tired that I long to lay it down anywhere alone and sleep.

575. *April 11.*— . . . I suffer, too, from some follies, one of which is the sea. I love it as I love few things ; it seems to me always so beautiful, and it is a real misfortune for me to be obliged to live so far from the sea. And I cannot look from a bridge into the water without longing to jump in, but certainly not from despair, for that is a feeling I do not know ; I never despair, probably because my hopes are not too elevated. My folly is the water, which I love immensely. One of our principal German Radical professors has lately published a work in which he attempts to show that men proceed from water—*i.e.* that we were fish, and in time became men.*

576. Tatistscheff is going back to St. Petersburg. I do not know what more I can say to him ; if he has not understood me, it is not my fault : but I feel as if he had understood me. I have persuaded Tatistscheff to have his portrait taken—not because I want to have it particularly, but to let the painter (Daffinger) make fifty ducats by it. It is a very good likeness.

577. *April* 19.—I have obtained an order for Neumann ; it will please him, because it will show that I do not forget him. The order cannot give him a larger *footing* in the world.† Tatistscheff has just entered his travelling carriage. To me his departure is a weight off my heart. I have gladly laid aside business. Tatistscheff, too, has gone off very well pleased with me, which is, at any rate, better than the contrary. Capo d'Istria will not agree, but how can one content the man ?

578. *April* 21.—If I have to send off one courier I must always send five. To all I say the same thing, it is true, but to be understood I must speak to each one in his own tongue. Only Capo d'Istria is, in this respect, quite peculiar : since he speaks in order not to be understood, he has no occasion for refinements of meaning ; and never saying what he does mean, he also never says what he does not mean. That is the whole secret of these famous apocalypses. Two months ago an excellent work appeared in Paris, ' *Des Séductions Politiques*,' by Lourdoueix, a friend of mine—according to my ideas, the best history of the time that has yet been written. There is not in it one assertion to which I would not have subscribed.

---

* *Urschleim,* by Oken (?).—ED.   † Neumann had very large feet.—ED.

579. *April* 20.—I have news of Tatistscheff. He has met a courier (Russian) destined for London, where people will be frightened to death when they hear a European army spoken of! The concern hangs together by means of a conspiracy formed by Capo d'Istria, Strogonow, and Pozzo di Borgo. About this conspiracy I care nothing; I will break it up. The triumvirate may divide the world between them : one shall undertake Eastern, another Western Europe, and the third shall, according to the plan, hover equally over the whole. And in the midst is the Emperor Alexander !

To prevent the shrieks of Jupiter being heard by Saturn, care was taken that his cradle should be surrounded by drums. Here the opposite has been done ; the joke is, however, too bad.

580. *May* 4.—Yesterday and the greater part of to-day I have been in Eisenstadt. Its glass-houses are some of the finest in Europe. Yesterday evening we had a concert there. In that enormous mansion the company consisted of only six persons. I do not understand why I hear nothing from Paul Esterhazy. Londonderry will not know what to do, nor Wellington ; they both wait till they know what I have done, or will not do. Thus do people endeavour to gain time ; and this is no great evil, for it is better to make no use of the passing day if it is not clear what ought to be done in it. Certain it is that out of Vienna no one knows how the affair really stands. Does anyone think Capo d'Istria knows? Not in the least—no more than the Grand Vizier ! Does anyone think the Emperor Alexander is better informed? God forbid ! All wish something, without knowing how the thing is to be got hold of; and the peculiar charm of the position is that no one knows exactly how what he

wants is to be attained. I know what I want, and
what the others are able to perform. I am thoroughly
armed; my sword is drawn and my pen mended;
my thoughts are bright and clear as a crystal
spring, while many people are now wading in turbid
waters.

581. *May* 8.—A courier with despatches from
Esterhazy has arrived to-day. It has happened in
London just as I expected. The good people have
fallen into a panic of fear. The difference between
Londonderry and me is that he does not know, as I do,
what the Emperor Alexander wants, and what Capo
d'Istria does not want. What the Emperor Alexander
may do is something different, because Capo d'Istria
cannot be prevented from entangling him in a net, and
setting him up to his neck in the mud. Londonderry
does not know all this, because he has not been much
in contact with the Emperor Alexander. Many things
in this world must be seen to be believed, and then, too,
one must have good eyes to see that which really does
exist. Our last views on the Spanish question of intervention must be well received in London.* But Londonderry will never understand the gist of the
matter rightly, which is this, that the Emperor
Alexander will have nothing to do with the Turkish
question, and Capo d'Istria is horrified at the Spanish
question. Capo d'Istria takes up the latter as a means
of forcing the Emperor Alexander into the former. He

* The following may serve to elucidate the matter. The King of Naples,
to please his nephew, the King of Spain, had applied to the allied Courts in
order that these Powers might be induced to unite to protect the throne and
people of Spain from the threatened catastrophe. Russia was prepared for
intervention, but only under the condition that this should be carried out
by a European army, to which the five Powers should furnish contingents.
Prince Metternich declared this condition inadmissible and impracticable.—
ED.

now writes all his Reports in the following extraordinary form: ' You see that the Emperor Alexander
is going wrong; he is going to meet ruin, and you will
go with him. You have only to choose between two
evils; I beg of you, therefore, to choose the less.'

Again, another case in which Londonderry and I
go quite different ways. He breathes fire and flames;
but I say, ' Very well; come now, we will talk the
matter over.' Londonderry will have a memorandum
written to point out that what is absurd cannot be
reasonable. I, on the contrary, think it sufficient to
send quite a little card of invitation, in which certainly
' an answer will oblige ' is not left out. Under these
circumstances Capo d'Istria may say to his master: ' See
what people you have to do with! Propose what you
may, you will never get hold of them; while you (the
Emperor) will always be caught. Give up your friendship for their system, which is only an absurdity. Let
every man bake his own cake, and do you bake yours.
Let us go forward : fame and glory await us in
Constantinople.'

Now, if anything can save the Emperor Alexander
and the cause of sound manly sense, it will be the card
of invitation, and not the memorandum.

I do not know whether I am a fool, but certainly I
am surrounded by them. It would be only polite of
me to become a fool too—if I am not one already.

582. *May* 13.—Whether the King of England
will really come here I do not know. Stewart writes
to me that he does not quite believe it, and he may be
right.

The decision is close at hand. On April 30 Tatistscheff arrived at St. Petersburg. My last news are
down to the 29th. The next will bring the disclosure.

I send this, however, without waiting, by a fresh courier, with some rather interesting accounts from Greece. Capo d'Istria is wroth with me, which I think very natural. He complains that in my thoughts I separate him from the Emperor, although they are always one. As proof of this, Capo d'Istria assured Nesselrode that the Emperor desires something quite different from what he desires; and this they call logic.

583. *May* 15.—Against this day (my birthday), without which I should not have been, I have only one charge to bring—that it already has taken with it a great number of years.

According to my latest news from Lebzeltern, affairs go on strangely in St. Petersburg, but not badly. I say not badly, because the Emperor Alexander deserves something different from his minister. How can these two people hang together so long? All the world is astonished at it but me.

584. *May* 20.—I have prepared a long and difficult work for Turkey, where they begin to go on quite tolerably. If the Gordian knot is disentangled, I may flatter myself with having accomplished a very great work quite alone.

585. *May* 22.—I am now in a most extraordinary position. I have nothing to do. I await results on all sides, and hence I have not to talk or write to anyone. However, I am not dull; I am like old Kaunitz, who, when the beautiful Madame de Witt said to him that she did not know what dulness was, answered, 'I have this in common with you, Madame, that I am not dull myself, but I suffer much from the dulness of others.' Not to be dull and to enjoy are two very different things. Separated from my family,

I have no family life, to which the greatest pleasures of life belong. I have indeed my two gardens, the sun, and the Italian Opera, which is certainly something, but yet not happiness.

I often make parties to the country, which always consist of fourteen or eighteen persons. The neighbourhood of Vienna offers many occasions for such excursions; it is only necessary to drive a mile [German] in any direction to find oneself in a beautiful country. It is a good side of society here that all feel in the same family circle. If a stranger joins the party, he feels like a child of the house; he has no need to think what he will do — others do that for him. Politics are always kept at a distance and nothing reminds one of them, unless it be the occurrence of some great event. To-day I go to bed without being sleepy, and I will read two or three chapters of Livy, which I have already gone through five or six times. I thus take rest from the scribbling of Abbé de Pradt and Company.

586. *May 26.*—I have news of the Turks; these people are not so stupid as the world believes or might believe, and as many wish to make one believe. I have reports from St. Peterburg which shew me that I am not mistaken. On the contrary, I see that I have judged my people well, and more cannot be required of me. Capo d'Istria is quite calm again, and, moreover, will ruin himself. I accept no miracles now, but if I must do so, I would admit that Capo d'Istria is stronger than nature.

My accounts from St. Petersburg come down to the 11th. In the Cabinet the contest has begun, which was sure to happen, because I knew what I was doing. I am certain that the Emperor Alexander has never heard the language of his country spoken with such sincerity as I have caused him to hear it through Tatistscheff. Since Capo d'Istria does not speak this language, since, on the contrary, he uses a language foreign to the country and to its interests, a conflict must take place—a conflict which will end only with the one or the other party. The pure language of reason must at last prevail. If ever there be a liquidation in Russia, we shall see a moral bankruptcy, such as History has never seen ; that bankruptcy will bring with it the most natural and truest interests of Russia. If this failure of the leading ideas of the day occurs—and it must occur—I shall have proved to the world what the will of one man can do, a will which rests on the simplest basis of common sense.

587. *May* 31.—A courier from Lebzeltern has arrived during the last week. The suit is won, and that so thoroughly that perhaps no one else knows that it has taken place.*

Tatistscheff returns in a few days. The Emperor Alexander has received all my Reports ; Capo d'Istria is ready ; Russia plays a wretched part. Therefore I will show that I can be a prudent, wise, and firm friend. I will do for the .Emperor Alexander what the fools and rogues have not been able to do. I do not to-day think of Austria : that is not necessary ; one must help those who need it, and therefore come to the help of the Emperor Alexander. But what people they are in St. Petersburg ! Mere masks that must be known to know what they hide. The following maxim, taught me by experience, has to-day been again verified : **Not romance, but history ; not belief, but knowledge.**

* See ' Victory of the Austrian Cabinet,' Nos. 622–625.

I can imagine the face that Londonderry makes at it. He must feel as happy as a man who is going down under an avalanche. He is a fool if he does not consent to what I have proposed, which, moreover, everyone must do who has honourable feeling and honest views. Equilibrium would otherwise be destroyed, which would enormously increase the evils. Capo d'Istria does now what he did during the Neapolitan question : he is silent. There are times when confused ideas and wiredrawn phrases only cause delay, but bring no consequences ; other times, again, when they bring ruin and disgrace —and such a time is the present.

588. *June* 11.—Tatistscheff has just arrived. I will meet him, because I want to know how the weather-cock stands ; then I will return to my moral repose.

589. *June* 14.—I have despatches from St. Petersburg and London ; the first are very plain, for they put the whole affair in my hands.

The Emperor Alexander will be with us in the beginning of September. I hope Londonderry has courage enough to come, but I foresee that he will hesitate ; the reasons for his coming are, however, so weighty that his non-appearance would be a folly : a sad but true word. He will receive from Russia and Berlin the same invitation as from us.

In St. Petersburg they are astonished that Tatistscheff should for once have taken the straight road : he follows the direction of his own interests, and follows it well, because he is a cunning fellow. What few people understand is the advantage which can be taken of cunning people ; I, for my part, have never feared them even if they are clever. As an opponent, only a thoroughly honourable man is difficult to conquer.

There is an enormous difference between rowing and steering. How many statesmen have mistaken their business—so many take the oar whose business is with the rudder! Everything in this world is but a 'simple story,' * and one may be sure that the more intricate a matter looks the simpler it really is. I am a man not at all stiff-necked, but very persevering; nothing will make me deviate from my principles, and therefore I am an extremely inconvenient minister to my opponents.

590. *Baden, June* 17.—I came here yesterday evening. Tatistscheff followed me to-day. We go backwards and forwards between Vienna and Baden without making a trouble of it on either side. Our aim is to save time, and to do well what must be done. My position again is very remarkable : I am at the centre as the chief motive power in an affair which is quite simple, but has been for months embarrassed by unreason and unjustifiable measures. How different would everything have been if my Report had been accepted at first instead of at last; that, however, was not Capo d'Istria's purpose.

591. *Vienna, June* 19.—Tatistscheff is like my shadow. I work, too, a great deal. The Emperor Alexander wants to know what I think, and I consider it my duty to conceal nothing from him.

Capo d'Istria plays sometimes the part of a mouse in a hole, sometimes that of the watching cat. If the affair is going contrary to his wishes, he squeaks in his hole; if there are any difficulties, the cat shows her claws. To behave so is not worthy of a great man who has fifty millions of men behind him.

* Refers no doubt to Mrs. Inchbald's *Simple Story,* published 1791.
—Tr.

592. *July* 1.—Capo d'Istria is quite out of the affair, but still there. He counts on time, like me. So far he has been mistaken, but I have not: he will still go wrong, but I pray God to keep me from that.

Tatistscheff feels the necessity of going right so strongly that he does so. My talent has consisted in bringing him to a position from which he cannot deviate without breaking his neck—and the good man loves his neck.

593. *Baden, July* 2.—The Emperor Francis arrived here yesterday, which is very agreeable to me, because it will save me ten or twelve hours in the week. Like me, he expects his fate here. We shall know, in ten days or a fortnight, what are the intentions of the Emperor Alexander. What he intends we know, but we must learn the time he proposes. I take the middle of September for the date: I wish Londonderry may be here by the end of August. I hourly expect news from London. Expectation is always irritating to the nerves. Certainty is better, even if it is not good. I know many people who are contented to know nothing, but who also are never in expectation.

594. *Vienna, July* 15.—All I hear from St. Petersburg is good.

I have completed my water-cure at Baden. I had to stay for the eighteen days; but I could spare no more time for going into the water. Besides, the heat is very great, never below 22 degrees, often as much as 30. The temperature exceeds the average temperature of Naples, so that the vegetation has taken its departure for the year 1822. My meadows are turned to hay, and my trees to broomsticks. Happily, my pavilion is still quite habitable, cool and comfortable.

Since Vienna has lost her society I live quite in

my business. Every two or three days I work with
Tatistscheff. Fortunately, it is easy to work with
him.

595. *July* 25.—From hour to hour I expect news
from St. Petersburg. They will give me the only information I want. That is, they will tell me the day on
which I shall see the Emperor Alexander. One other
question will also have a certain interest—shall I meet
Capo d'Istria? I trouble myself little about it. The
man is dead, and I fear neither the dead nor ghosts.
A dead man is nothing, and a returning ghost never
represents anything but a very miserable living person.
Man only lives once; to rise again, one must cross to
another world. Being born again into the same world
is only a shadow of the first life. Capo d'Istria's rule is
over. I have fought with him for a long time, and yet
I have always gone on my own way forwards. Capo
d'Istria is an unskilful general; cunning, learned in
pretexts, he lacks judgment of the situation, the
strength and weakness of which he does not appreciate. He supports castles in the air by aphorisms
which are not worth the trouble of attacking. If one is
right and goes steadily forward, the adversary must be
vanquished.

596. *July* 27.—This evening I was for the first
time at the German opera. But a German voice is quite
pitiable in comparison with an Italian. People don't
open their mouths, and seem to think the nose is also an
organ of the human voice.

It is remarkable that a wrong spirit and bad taste
always go together; thus we see that all malcontents
have a horror of Italian music. In Germany people are
always quarrelling about whether German or Italian
music is to be preferred. Our country joins in the fray.

A dispute across the frontiers does not prevent the spread of the epidemic, just as it does not prevent the spread of knowledge and thought. Now, there is here a minority who wish to pass themselves off as the majority, and is Liberal, Radical, and Doctrinaire, hating, therefore, Italian singing. It was to be expected that this minority would be present at the German opera, which, however, was not the case. It recommends what it laughs down, and the house remains empty. These devil's advocates are always either the dupes of their own system (these are the most sincere), or they try to deceive others (these are the most numerous).

597. *August* 1.—To-day's news tells us that the Emperor Alexander will arrive on September 7. The same news informs us of something which does not astonish me—Capo d'Istria is not coming.

The Emperor Alexander praises me beyond measure, and asserts that he has confidence only in me. Does anyone wish to know what sort of impression that makes on me? It raises a smile, and nothing else. I know, too, that the same Emperor desires Londonderry's presence, and that is good. Here we shall remain for at least three weeks, and that is absolutely necessary.

Capo d'Istria has written to Golowkin a singular farewell letter.

598. *August* 15.—I have just begun to read O'Meara's work. There is occasionally some truth in it, in the same way as there is with a valet speaking of his master. In what Napoleon has said to his wretched biographer (O'Meara) there is a blending of great and little, true and false mingled together, but always with a background in which the relater's motives are evident. There are no such conversations as Napoleon held when he meant to treat a question thoroughly. The characteristics, however, of this celebrated man are well seen in these, especially for those who knew him. O'Meara, however, did not know him: O'Meara believed in him, and a man like Napoleon is only rightly judged of when we do not believe in him. In turning over the leaves of this book I often meet my own name. The more evil I find said of me the better I like it. According to my own conviction, Napoleon never knew me, and, still more, never divined me. The cause is very simple. Napoleon was the man in all the world who most despised the human race. He had a strange aptitude for discovering the weak sides of men, and all passions are weak sides or produce them. He loved only men with strong passions and great weaknesses; he judged the most opposite qualities in men by these defects. In me he encountered a calmness which must cause despair to one who founded his calculations on passions. Hence he denied the existence in me of every quality bearing on pure reason or which is reason itself. I have often involuntarily laughed in Napoleon's presence, when I remarked that he judged me falsely. Therefore I knew Napoleon much better than he knew me. Seven years of resolute study suffice to know a man, especially a man whose nature and actions are all external—that is, for a calm observer who is not led astray by any feeling of fear and awe.

599. *August* 18.—I am still reading O'Meara's book. God in heaven! how the poor devil has been imposed upon. The account of the agreement between Napoleon and the Emperor Francis about the flight from Elba is good. It is to me as if I, too, were listening to Napoleon; he has often tried to make me believe the same. I let him talk till he had done, and then

I only said to him 'That is false.' Then he looked at me, smiled, and said as he turned away, ' *Sono bugie per i Parigini.*' What a book I could write after O'Meara's method, if I had every evening written down all the nonsense I had heard in the day. I see, too, that Napoleon was much grieved to lose his *Signor Dottore.* What good stuff for a romance-writer!

All may be said in two words : Napoleon was a very small man of imposing character. He was ignorant, as a sub-lieutenant generally is ; a remarkable instinct supplied the place of knowledge. From his mean opinion of men, he never had any anxiety lest he should go wrong. He ventured everything, and gained thereby an immense step towards success. Throwing himself upon a prodigious arena, he amazed the world and made himself master of it, while others cannot even get so far as being masters of their own hearth. Then he went on and on, until he broke his neck. He ended as he must have ended, and was judged as all those are judged who find means to subdue the common herd. As a legitimate ruler of a small State he would never have been heard of except as an arbitrary monarch. As a military commander in any country whatever, as an administrator wherever the storm of revolution raged, he would always have come out strongly. In the situation in which he was, he must have played the part he did play, and which no man of better principles could have ventured to undertake.

600. *August* 20.—What dreadful news ! * I have only a telegraphic despatch from Paris, but what a blow ! I am armed against all contingencies ; my cause will only be lost if I fall myself.

601. *August* 22.—I now know all, and that all is

* Londonderry's (Castlereagh's) madness and suicide.

very sad. What poor weak creatures we are! It was madness! simple madness! Londonderry had had one attack some years ago. The Government and his family knew the secret, and everything possible was done to conceal the circumstance from the public.

His affair with the King and all his fears were but symptoms of the impending paroxysm. It is a great misfortune. The man is not to be replaced, especially not for me. He may be replaced by a man of higher intellect, but not with his experience. Londonderry was the only man in his country who had gained any experience in foreign affairs; he had learned to understand me. Now it will take years before another reaches the same stage of confidence.

Through Stewart, who has arrived here to-day, I shall learn many particulars. There is something so horrible in the affair that the mind can hardly take it in. Londonderry was supposed to be very calm, but he was not so. The stupid world always judges the inner man by the outside, and nothing is so deceitful.

602. *August* 25.—Stewart has learned all the incidents which preceded the catastrophe. It is now known that Londonderry was seized with madness ten days before his end. He gave so many proofs of approaching insanity that it is incomprehensible to me that it was not obvious to the people about him, and that greater precautions were not taken. The catastrophe is one of the most shocking that I have ever known. He was devoted to me in heart and spirit, not only from personal inclination, but also from conviction. Much which would have been easy with him will with his successor, whoever he is, bring fresh labour. I awaited him here as my second self. My work would have been reduced by half, because I should have had him to share it with me; now I am left to my own strength. I am not alarmed at that, but I feel myself overburdened. I have just requested the presence of the Duke of Wellington, the only man who can in a measure replace him.

ON THE JOURNEY TO VERONA AND BACK

Extracts from Metternich's private Letters from September 17 to
December 29, 1822.

603. Rendezvous with Prince Victor. 604. From Innsbruck. 605. From
Verona.—importance of the Congress. 606. Salon Lieven. 607. Satis-
faction with Prince Victor. 608. From Venice. 609. Gentz's arrival in
Venice. 610. Farewell from Emperor Alexander. 611. His departure.
612. Alone in Venice. 613. From Innsbruck. 614. Parting of the two
Emperors—departure of the Emperor Francis.

603. *Vienna, September* 17, 1822.—The route
which I have suggested that my son should take, in
order to meet us at Innsbruck, will bring him through
the most beautiful part of Switzerland.*   At Lake
Constance he will stop at Hersberg † long enough only
to enjoy the most glorious prospect in the world.   The
castle—or rather, house—consists of nothing but four
walls, and I hardly think it contains anything more than
a couple of chairs.

604. *Innsbruck, October* 9.—We arrived here at
six o'clock on the evening of the 7th.   Victor had been
here already three hours.   He received me on the
steps of the hotel, is very well, and has become tall,
strong, and handsome.   How delighted I was to see
him again I need not say, and how delighted I should
be if I could pass some time with him.   In a few hours
we shall leave this place, pass the night at Brixen, in the
morning travel to Trent, the next day to Lago di

---

* The Prince's family was then at Johannisberg.—ED.

† Castle belonging to Prince Metternich.—ED.

Garda, and stay the night at Roveredo. Early on the 12th we shall arrive at Verona. The whole journey will be made in company with Nesselrode, Pozzo di Borgo, and Lebzeltern. I take Victor in my carriage, and leave Lebzeltern to go with Floret. We are in good company, and our journey, which will take twelve days from Vienna to Verona, is a time of rest for us, and of the greatest enjoyment to me. I am so unaccustomed to the use of these two expressions, that I am quite astonished to see them come from my pen, but still more astonished to see the realisation of these unwonted ideas. We travel through the loveliest country, in the most glorious weather, and as there is no hurry we can make excursions to the right and left. We are a small but happy company, and I shall number this journey among the pleasantest recollections of my life. Victor seems very glad to see me again. All he has said to me gives me great pleasure. I shall have the opportunity of talking much with him, and I will not lose it.

605. *Verona, October 22.*—I have just begun the greatest work ! Confidence is placed in me, as I place confidence in the others, for the Congress consists of honest men. The evil element of perpetual dissension (Capo d'Istria) has ended his career, and with him disappear a thousand perplexities and difficulties. My personal relations with the Emperor of Russia are the most intimate possible, as for the peace of the world they ought to be. He believes in me just as my Emperor does, and the business gains thereby as it would by no other combination.

The Congress of Verona is the most important since the year 1814, and will bear, I hope, golden fruit. Good fortune has so often stood by my side that I now always invoke it to the victory of the good cause, and if I once have it I will not let it go.

606. *November* 12.—Count Lieven is here my only social resource. I pass most of my evenings with him, and many of the members of the Congress follow my example. The heart of the society is formed by the Duke of Wellington, Ruffo (Neapolitan ambassador), Caraman (French ambassador), Bernstorff (Prussian ambassador), &c. &c.—in other words, the *salon* of the Princess Lieven in Verona is like ours in Vienna.

607. *November* 27.—I am extremely satisfied with Victor; he will be a good and useful man. His conduct here is faultless, his heart is pure, and his understanding very sound. In the last few days I have allowed him to undertake a real work of art. In order to show me how he understands the English and French languages, I have given him a very important English despatch to translate. He throws himself thoroughly into his work, and gets through his task in a comparatively short time. His translation has astonished all my officials, and, indeed, the whole conference. There was not a word to alter, not an expression to change. It will be placed with the other documents as a work of the first rank. Moreover, Victor loves his work as much as his Vienna friends and comrades love the *Prater*.

608. *Venice, December* 16.—I left Verona this morning at five o'clock, and crossed over the Lagunes in a gondola at three in the afternoon. It was a beautiful day; the Emperor of Russia had made his entry into Venice two hours before. I saw only the remains of the splendour of his entry. The roads from Fusine to Padua were full of carriages, and the Lagunes were crowded with gondolas. I know the Emperor was ravished with the beauty of the scene. The sun did good service to the entry.

I have good accommodation, plenty of sun and even stoves; also a splendid state-bed, which seems more suited for a Danaë than for me, so I have my little camp-bed put in its place. In the evening I went to the Fenice, where they gave ' *Il Matrimonio Segreto*,' the history of a marriage so secret that I will be hanged if I could understand anything about it. What was wanting on the part of the singers was made up by the appearance of the house; the Fenice was in grand *gala* and looking wonderfully beautiful. I expected every moment to see Nesselrode climbing over the boxes: he is in the greatest enthusiasm about Venice.

But the old Venice is also most astonishing, when we think that in a very great city we are dwelling in the midst of the sea. Looking at the long circuit of embankments running for miles into the sea, which form a calm mirror of water out of the ocean itself, we cannot but be amazed at the creative power of man.

The first person to visit me was friend Rossini. Concerning his bad singers, I felt myself obliged to call out in an unpleasant manner, ' *Vi siete ingannato.*' He comforted me about his wife's throat, and complained very much of his first tenor, an Irishman who had been three months learning Italian. When Rossini said to me, ' *Canta come compone certo ambasciatore d'Inghilterra che si crede Maestro di capella,*' he thought he had said everything.

It is striking midnight on the Campanile, and I must go to sleep.

609. *December* 17.—Gentz has arrived. I have in regard to him a new proof of my knowledge of men. When I asked him how Venice pleased him, he answered in his pedantic manner, ' Since my arrival I have been convinced that Italy really has charms, but I have not found anything of all that has been said about this country; do not tell me of Verona and her antiquities, or of Vicenza or Padua, where I can see nothing: but Venice! Do not, however, suppose that I am enchanted with the position of the city in the midst of the water: I hate the water; neither do the palaces or the churches, nor the Piazza San Marco, charm me, for a Piazza is always a Piazza, and the larger the palaces are the more difficult they are to heat. All this does not make Venice answer to its reputation; it is the wonderfully pretty little streets! What genius it required to venture to build them so narrow, and with what taste were they ornamented by the shops!'

When I was yesterday walking about with Tatistscheff and Nesselrode in the city, I laid a bet that just these streets would please Gentz and gain his heart. Such are men! Everyone measures things according to his own standard, and taste is as different as everything else. Gentz likes everything small, and is afraid of everything that is not small.

In the evening the Piazza was illuminated and the Church of St. Mark. Tatistscheff and Nesselrode then came to me and played whist.

610. *December* 21.—Our stay at Venice is coming to an end. The Emperor Alexander leaves in the morning. I have to-day taken a preliminary farewell; the last leave I shall take at Innsbruck on the 28th. He has been much pleased with his stay here; has seen and admired everything: the apartment which he occupied in the palace has a wonderful view of the Giudecca, the Piazza San Marco, and the Riva degli Schiavoni. He thinks the Giudecca like the Neva, and the Palace of

the Doge like some of the palaces in Moscow. I am on the best footing with him, and there is but little danger now of its being otherwise. My work is no small one!

Yesterday we had a concert at the Court, at which Rossini was conductor. His wife begins to get her voice again, but I fear that it will never thoroughly return.

611. *December* 22.—The Emperor Alexander started to-day. Tatistscheff gets no title at present.

Before his departure the Emperor took a hearty leave of Nesselrode, and thanked him for the extraordinary service he had done him at Verona; and that was a comfort for Nesselrode, on which I heartily congratulate him.

The day after to-morrow I shall leave Italy, to return again in nine or ten months.

612. *December* 23.—I am to-day the only stranger remaining in Venice; I have not left my room, for it is so cold outside, and the loveliest objects in the world cannot please me in such weather.

The Londonderrys (formerly Stewarts), man and wife, left this place to-day. On leaving they both cried like children; I do not know what sort of a face I made, for my nature is not given to weeping. They do not know what to do with themselves, and I should not be astonished if they soon come back again to us. Certain it is that they left Vienna very unwillingly.

613. *Innsbruck, December* 23.—I left Venice on the 25th, and arrived here the following night, crossing the Brenner Pass between ten and eleven in the evening, with a temperature of fifteen degrees of cold.

The Emperor Alexander has to-day returned from his excursion with his family, and I this evening spent three hours with him. He had talked a great deal to his son-in-law (King of Wurtemberg), and all that he said was good: what the son-in-law will do may not, however, be quite so much so, but it does not much matter to me. The great car is in motion, and since the small ones see fit to exclude themselves from the movement they run the danger of getting under the wheels and being run over. Very little special mechanical knowledge is required to see this, but unhappily there are men who do not possess even that.

I expect to remain here till the 31st. I may leave on the 30th, but may not; and my road runs through Munich, taking me into the midst of the New Year festivities; I shall not get to Munich till the evening of the great day, and shall remain there two or three days, and on the 6th enter Vienna.

614. *December* 29.—The separation took place to-day. Our two friends parted from one another in the fullest and happiest harmony. May Heaven protect them!

For the sake of propriety I had to go to the theatre this evening, but the cold drove me back in ten minutes. Certainly it was never before heard of to have the theatre placed over the ice-cellar of the town! Just near the entrance, I observed a quite peculiar sharpness of the air, of so cutting a cold that my curiosity about physical matters led me to try to discover the cause, and I was not a little astonished to find the fact I have mentioned, after which discovery I quickly hurried away. They gave a piece that has succeeded well in Germany, ' The Little Alpine Rose.' The first act represents a churchyard in Switzerland; the last, a masked ball at Moscow. The whole is taken from a pretty anecdote which appeared some years ago, in what collection I know not.

From the ice-cellar I went to the Lady-ruler of the land, where I found the remaining members of the Congress assembled, the number being reduced to eight persons.

AUSTRIA'S ATTITUDE IN THE EASTERN QUESTION.

615. Metternich to Lebzeltern, in St. Petersburg (Despatch), Vienna, January 28, 1822.

615. I believe the moment has come when it will be useful to explain to the Russian Cabinet all the steps we have taken in the Eastern question.

I intend to make the following observations with a freedom worthy of the greatness of the subject, and in agreement with the purity of intention of the Emperor, our august master. While the immediate future is still veiled is perhaps the most favourable moment to make known the truth without appearing to be influenced by calculations to which it is a stranger.

Here is a very brief sketch of our conduct relative to that question and the difficulties we have encountered.

The revolt of the Greeks, however different might be its long-standing and permanent causes from the revolutions which the Grand Alliance was called upon to combat, nevertheless directly originated in the plots of the disorganised faction which menaces all thrones and all institutions. This truth was immediately recognised by the monarchs assembled at Laybach; it was announced by them in the face of Europe, and the character of the abettors of this revolt would have warranted the first judgment of the two Emperors, even if this judgment had not been founded on incontestable data.

Nevertheless, I was persuaded from the time of the first news of the great explosion that neither the evidence of facts, nor the wise and enlightened views of his Majesty the Emperor of All the Russias, would suffice to eliminate from the new complication many difficulties and embarrassments. Neither did I hesitate to submit my conviction to his Imperial Majesty, that the affair, whatever might be the firmness of the monarchs and the uniformity of their principles, could not fail to prove a heavy trial to the sovereign of Russia in particular—the most difficult perhaps that he has yet had to surmount. His Majesty the Emperor Alexander understood and agreed with me. My opinion was founded on considerations which facts have but too well confirmed.

I have taken into account—

1st. The peculiar position of the Russian monarch with regard to the Porte, both in a political and religious point of view;

2nd. The impression that must be made on the Ottoman Government by the simultaneous insurrection of its Greek subjects in Europe, and the tone taken by that insurrection from the beginning;

3rd. The untiring efforts of the Greek religionists to make up by the popularity of their cause for what it lacked in solidity, and the support lent to them by zealots in religion like the Radicals in politics, atheists as well as visionaries;

4th. The stupor of the Turkish Government, its weakness, its jealousy, its fanaticism, supported by the fanaticism and barbarism of the Mussulman people.

The embarrassments resulting from this position of

things could not but exercise a painful influence on the measures to be taken by the allied sovereigns. They had, to a certain extent, all the chances against them, while their opponents hoped to turn everything to profit.

If the Alliance remains intact, if peace is to be maintained in Europe, the Courts must expect to be overwhelmed with the reproaches of an ignorant multitude, easily deceived by words seeming to breathe only sentiments of humanity and religion. In case of a rupture of the peace, the malcontents would see new hopes and more flattering prospects opening before them than any they have been vainly expecting for the last eight years. The first and most certain effect of the war would be a general attack on the Alliance, the existence of which would become doubtful if one of the allied Courts should take upon itself the burden of the war, and which would cease to be formidable in the eyes of the revolutionists when the forces of several of the Powers were employed in the East.

In such a combination our course would not be doubtful. Forced to choose between two evils, we should feel bound to choose the less. We would rather abandon ourselves to the confidence with which the character and the intelligence of His Majesty of All the Russias inspires us than to the vain hope of repressing (with enfeebled resources) the enemy within any limits whatever. We have traced for ourselves an unvarying rule of conduct, and no consideration would make us deviate from it. To try to serve the cause of peace by all the means in our power; to maintain at the same time, with all the zeal and perseverance our position allows, the just demands of his Majesty the Emperor of Russia; to push as far as possible, in terms which would

certainly not be warlike, our declarations concerning the
Porte ; never to lose sight of the origin of the revolt of
the Greeks, nor the consequences which may result from
it for the future preservation of the internal peace of
the Ottoman empire—such should be, and such have in
reality been, the bases of our calculations and the principles which have guided us in our communications with
the Courts, as in our explanations with the Porte.

However simple these principles may appear, they
present great perplexities in their application. The steps
we have taken may be taxed with a want of energy by
a public frightened and excited by the faction ; they
may be exposed to false interpretations at St. Petersburg,
and to entirely opposite ones at Constantinople. It was,
however, better to run all these risks than to depart
from a path which conviction and consideration point
out as the only path practicable.

I do not fear from those who know how to judge of
great affairs the reproach of not having uttered threatening words to the Porte. Such words, pronounced by
a Power of the first rank should be supported by material demonstrations. If anyone accuses us of not having
made use of the latter, cast a glance over Europe, Sir,
and you will have the key to our reserve. The day
that Russia and Austria allow it to be supposed that
the employment of their united forces is indispensable
in the Levant, Italy, Germany, and France will be lost.
This is what the party has waited for with so much
impatience during the last few months—a triumph which
we most certainly must take care not to afford it. Do
you believe that the military powers of Austria and
Prussia, the only ones we can take into account on the
Continent—the former weakened by the absence of some
of their best troops in a remote country, which has just

escaped total destruction; the latter less dreaded by the faction, because in its perfidious calculations it reckons on paralysing them to a great extent—do you believe that these two forces united are not more than sufficient to overcome conspirators who count on the weakness of some Governments and on the blind ambition of others; on the defection, in short, of the greater part of the armies in Europe?

This reasoning appears to us so conclusive that in order to overthrow it one must deny all the facts which have taken place before our eyes during the last two years, of which each day increases the number and weight.

But one might perhaps say, If this is the state of things, how have the decisions been so long protracted? I will tell you without hesitation.

The difficulties inherent to the individual position of each of the two Powers of which the insurrection of the Greeks has disturbed the pacific relations, have come forward in the course of the affair; this is the danger we have always feared more than any other, and which I regard as the principal source of our present perplexities.

The Porte, in removing the question from its primitive basis, and appealing to religion, has committed a grave error, which, however, does not surprise us much on the part of a theocratic Government, which can find no extraordinary resources except in the first cause of its political existence.

The position of Russia has been in this respect still more difficult than that of the Porte. At Constantinople they have only had to defend themselves on one ground; while at St. Petersburg they have had two questions before them, not only different, but absolutely opposite in their application. The Greeks, as rebels, had no title to the favour of the Emperor of Russia ; these same Greeks, as persecuted Christians, placed in certain relations with Russia by virtue of existing treaties, were in some sort justified in invoking the support of that monarch. To get out of the difficulty it was necessary carefully to separate these two questions. If amongst the men who are firm enough in their principles to desire the preservation of peace before everything—and it is only they whom my calculations concern—there are still found at St. Petersburg some who have confounded these questions, they have certainly to reproach themselves with a mistake. That this mistake has not been shared by those who have considered the affair in its grand and true point of view is a fact demonstrated by the circumstance that the rupture has not yet taken place. It being nevertheless certain that it will take place, the problem, instead of being solved, is still more complicated.

We have at last arrived at the term of the decision, and I consider as such the first despatches we receive from you after the arrival of our courier of December 31.

The resolution to begin the war may have been taken at St. Petersburg—for it will not be taken at Constantinople—or perhaps the Cabinet of Russia may have preferred an amicable arrangement.

In the first case, while deploring the fact, we shall not cease to make the strongest remonstrances to the Divan, until the first Russian troops have crossed the frontier. Our conscience imposes this duty upon us ; for the more we are convinced that a new era (which I certainly cannot regard as regenerative) is commencing for Europe, the less do we wish to have to reproach ourselves for not exhausting every means to prevent it. Tranquil concerning the intentions of his Majesty the Emperor Alexander, but keenly sensible of the dangers and catastrophes which menace society, we turn our eyes towards the West, and will defend the last barriers still arresting the torrent of general destruction, and if necessary we will perish in the breach.

In the second case, we see but one way of arriving at a satisfactory arrangement, which is to separate as clearly and explicitly as possible the questions which must be treated of with the Porte.

I understand by this separation the distinction between the rights which belong to Russia and the Porte by virtue of the chief existing treaties between the two Powers, and the very just and natural wishes which his Imperial Majesty the Emperor of All the Russias may form for the security of the Greek nation, returned to duty and allegiance to the Ottoman Porte.

The first of these questions concerns the two Powers directly. As it bears only on known antecedents, it should be less difficult to treat and to decide. An enormous advantage which would result for Europe would be the ridding men's minds of the dangerous notions that have seized them, and bringing back the people to the hope of maintaining general peace.

The second question—essentially distinct from the first, with which it could not be amalgamated without both suffering equally—should be treated according to the principles of a clear and elevated policy. The insurrection which has just taken place in the Ottoman Empire has brought two nations together. These people are destined to live under one sceptre; it is their interest, as well as that of the sovereign, that scenes such as those which have just taken place should not be renewed. It is not less the interest of the whole of

Europe that the internal peace of the Levant should not, ever and anon, be in danger of being disturbed, and the interest of Europe is greatly influenced by the general disposition of men's minds in that part of the world. Thus considered, this question seems to us to concern all the great Powers.

TATISTSCHEFF'S MISSION TO VIENNA AND ITS RESULTS.*

Tatistscheff to Metternich, Vienna, March 8, 1822.

616. The Porte will declare officially and directly to the Russian Imperial Ministry :—

' That it accepts all the conditions contained in the letter from the Imperial Ministry to the Grand Vizier, and in the note from Baron de Strogonow dated July 6 (18).

' That Russia is authorised by her treaties, and by the rights of protection which they secure to her in favour of the Greeks, to demand the inviolability of the religion which she professes, the reconstruction of the churches, and a just distinction between the innocent and the guilty.

' That Russia shall be fully satisfied on these three points.

' But that, for the present, considering the circumstances of the Mussulman nation, the Porte is unwillingly obliged to confine itself—

' 1. To evacuating entirely and without the least delay the Principalities of Wallachia and Moldavia ;

' 2. To entrusting provisionally the administration of these countries to the respective divans, under the presidency of Greeks, chosen by the Porte, according to the rules established for the nomination of hospodars :

' 3. To sending one or more Turkish plenipoten-

* See Prokesch, *Geschichte des Abfalls der Griechen.*

tiaries to the spot, at the same time asking that the
Emperor on his side should send there one or more
Russian plenipotentiaries.

' 4. To furnishing the Turkish plenipotentiaries with
the necessary powers to enable them to settle with the
Russian plenipotentiaries not only all that concerns the
execution of the treaties in the Principalities and their
provisional administration, but also to concert with them
the measures by which the Porte should be associated
with Russia, so as to secure a happy and peaceable
existence to those Christian provinces of the Ottoman
Empire which the treaties have placed under the protection of his Imperial Majesty, and which these deplorable
events have drawn into the gulf of revolution.'

Tatistscheff to Metternich, Vienna, March 14, 1822.

617. The insurrection which has just taken place
in the Ottoman Empire has brought two races face to
face. These people are destined to live under one
sceptre, and it is their interest, as well as that of the
sovereign, that scenes such as those which have just
passed should not be renewed. It is not less the interest of the whole of Europe that the internal peace
of the Levant should not be ever and anon in danger
of being disturbed, and the interest of Europe is
strongly augmented by the general disposition of men's
minds in that part of the world.

The measures which will be established in common
in a negotiation between the allied Powers and the Ottoman Porte will have for their object :

1. To put an end to the war in those provinces
which are still in a state of insurrection ;

2. To secure their tranquil possession to the Ottoman Porte ;

3. To make an arrangement, by means of which all the peaceable inhabitants of the insurgent countries and all those who lay down their arms will enjoy the free exercise of their religion, possess their lands in quietness, and see their goods, their persons, and their lives placed under constant and real protection.

Let the Porte preserve the *suzeraineté* over the Greek nation in the Morea and other countries where they have risen and demanded their absolute freedom; let these countries be included in the Ottoman Empire; and let not the repose of Europe be disturbed in the future by intestine war in any of these States; a complication which will be continually recurring unless new relations are established between the contending parties.

Metternich's Memorandum for the Emperor Alexander, Vienna, April 19, 1822.

GENERAL OBSERVATIONS.

618. The present complication between Russia and the Porte presents two branches of different questions, which, in our consideration of the state of things, must not be confounded, and which, to ensure order and clearness, must still be separated, even if it is found possible to include them in the same negotiation.

The first concern what we may call *strict rights*; the second concern the *general interest.*

Questions concerning strict rights are all, or should be all, decided according to the existing treaties and conventions subsisting between the Empire of Russia and the Porte.

Questions of general interest should find their solution in the need common to the Porte and to all

Christian Powers of consolidating the relations between the Ottoman Empire and its Christian subjects in such a manner that the internal tranquillity of the Ottoman Provinces, instead of being constantly threatened by troubles and disturbances, should be secured by just and wise dispositions, suitable to the rights and dignity of the Porte, the well-being of its Christian subjects, the tranquillity of neighbouring empires, and the maintenance of the grand pacific system of Europe.

Actual Position of the Negotiation.

1. Russia has the undoubted right of requiring the strict fulfilment of all the stipulations contained in her different treaties and conventions with the Porte. Many of these stipulations having been infringed by the measures which the Porte has taken since the disastrous insurrection of the Greeks, Russia has demanded of the Porte, as the first condition of the re-establishment of pacific relations, the full and entire execution of these said stipulations. The Powers allied to Russia have supported this just demand with all the influence which their position enables them to use with the Porte. The Divan has invariably recognised the duty of executing existing treaties and conventions, and has openly declared its wish to conform to them; but it has added to these declarations restrictions founded on pretended difficulties either temporary or local—restrictions which have up to this time made all reconciliation impossible between Russia and the Porte.

2. On the other hand, his Imperial Majesty of All the Russias, from the commencement of the present crisis, has seen that, in order to arrive at a definite arrangement, it would be impossible not to bring forward those questions which we call here of general

interest. His Imperial Majesty's enlightened conscience, his religious principles, the particular interest which he takes in the happiness of his co-religionists, and in fact all those feelings of humanity for which he is so re-markable, have induced the Emperor, in his direct com-munications with the Turkish Minister, to declare that, while condemning the Greek rebellion, he cannot remain indifferent to measures which are to decide the future fate of that interesting portion of the subjects of the Porte in Europe. Nevertheless this question, never having been distinctly treated of between the Cabinet of Russia and the other allied Cabinets, the latter have not mentioned it at Constantinople, and no proposition with regard to it has been or could be addressed by them to the Divan.

Such is at present the exact state of the negotiations with the Porte.

Subjects which these Negotiations will embrace in the Future.

His Imperial Majesty of All the Russias, applying those principles of justice, moderation, and benevolence of which the Cabinet of Austria is so deeply sensible, to an affair which offers such grave considerations for the personal dignity of the Sovereign of Russia and for the interests of his Empire, has invariably announced his resolution of not separating these considerations, how-ever grave they may be, from those which concern the preserving intact the political system which is at pre-sent the only foundation and condition of the tranquillity of Europe and the preservation of social order. This generous resolution imposes on the allied Cabinets the duty of uniting all their efforts to bring the affair to an issue equally calculated to satisfy the just and magnani-

mous views of his Majesty the Emperor Alexander, and
to preserve Europe from the dangers which the troubles
of the Levant may create for it, either in the present, or
in the immediate future.

With the object of forming a clear idea of the steps
to be taken to arrive at this twofold object, let us
still regard the question in these two great divisions.

1. The support and execution of existing treaties
ought not to give rise to any difficulty. The respect
due to treaties is the basis of public right in Europe,
and the Porte, unless it wishes to renounce the position
it has hitherto occupied among the European Powers,
cannot hesitate for a moment to recognise this principle.

2. Questions of general interest should be founded
on desires in themselves just, and as acceptable to the
tribunal of good policy as to that of humanity. These
desires should consequently combine the advantage of
those to whom they are addressed with the real interests
of those in whose favour they are formed ; it is only
thus that the object can be attained.

As there can be no question of infringing the rights
of the Grand Seigneur, it is clear that any ideas which
the Cabinets may bring forward concerning the future
condition of the Greeks, must be restricted to subjects
of legislation and administration, and not touch on the
fundamental relations between the Turkish Government
and its Christian subjects.

Austria is certainly as far from claiming for herself
as from recognising in any other Power the right of
intermeddling in the internal affairs of a foreign State,
so long as changes introduced in its *régime* do not
jeopardise the safety of neighbouring States. But in
the present position of the Ottoman Empire there are

circumstances which warn the European Powers, and should convince the Ministers of the Porte themselves, of the necessity of some efficacious remedy to obtain, not a momentary lull bought with bloodshed, but a solid and permanent peace, without which the existence of that Empire, and the peace of Europe, cannot be secured. It is in this necessity that is found, not only the sole principle of right which would justify and direct the steps taken by the Powers in approaching the Porte with questions of general interest, but also the only means at their disposal to induce that Power not to repel their advances.

To work on this foundation it is above all indispensable that the Ottoman Government should proceed to an act of real amnesty, and that it should cause it to be observed and executed in its full extent. It is equally indispensable that the insurgents should submit to this act.

The Ottoman provinces on the left bank of the Danube are placed under certain regulations. The pacification of the two Principalities will not be difficult; for this their evacuation, the re-establishment of the old order of things, and the maintenance of the rights guaranteed by treaties, will suffice.

The difficulties of the question are therefore reduced, properly speaking, to the affairs of the Morea and the Isles. But these portions of the Porte's European domain again are under a great variety of regulations : and the difference of their position in this respect proceeds from their contact more or less close with the Mussulman population and the local authortiies.

It seems that the reasonable desires—desires compatible with the sovereign rights of the Porte—which may be formed by the Christian population of these countries in general, would be very conveniently classed under the three following heads :—

1. Free exercise of their religion ;

2. Legislative arrangements for the safety of their persons and their goods ;

3. Regular administration of justice.

It is not for the Austrian Cabinet to enter into a detailed analysis of these subjects, nor to examine how the general principles may be applied to different circumstances and localities. Many of the data required for such an examination seem to us to be wanting. But we do not hesitate to admit that there are wants and grievances, and that the common interest of the Government and the people should lead them to seek means of satisfying the one and remedying the other. We know, besides, that there are many laws and administrative regulations which time, ill-will, or negligence have caused to fall into neglect, but which might be made use of to facilitate the establishment of a more perfect *régime*, and better adapted to the present circumstances. In short, whatever the difficulties of the task, it appears to us that, the general principle once established, they need not be considered insurmountable.

SUMMARY AND CONCLUSION.

If, as we believe, the questions are clearly presented and defined in the preceding exposition, it would be on the following points that the Powers would henceforth direct their communications with the Porte.

1. The Divan having admitted the principle of the full and entire execution of the treaties, and there being nothing to discuss but the time and mode of application, it will be necessary to insist without delay on the immediate evacuation of the Principalities, the

re-establishment of their old *régime* and all appertaining to it. The last overtures from the Russian Cabinet contain opinions and statements with regard to this which it will be certainly useful to bring forward.

2. Representations must be made to the Ottoman Government showing the necessity of publishing a new act of amnesty for the insurgent provinces, and stipulating for the return to order within a certain time, but adding to that representation the assurance that the allied Powers, if the Porte wishes to profit by their good offices, will unite their efforts to induce the insurgents to submit to this act.

3. The Porte must be required to nominate plenipotentiaries to meet at some given place and time those who will be appointed by his Imperial Majesty of All the Russias, also by the Courts of Austria, France, Great Britain, and Prussia, to negotiate and agree upon measures considered necessary by the five allied Powers to secure to the Ottoman Empire a prompt, solid, and durable peace, and to restore the diplomatic and friendly relations at present suspended between Russia and the Porte.

In the first place we must discover whether the allied Powers are agreed on the point of view established and the plan traced out in the present despatch ; and then whether they agree on the best means of making known at the Porte what it is as much for its own interest as for that of the Powers to comprehend and accept.

Taking into consideration the real position of things, the distances, and the exigencies of the case, nothing seems either premature or unduly protracted in the scheme of the present Memorandum.

Metternich to Tatistscheff, Vienna, April 19, 1822.

619. In sending your Excellency the several de-spatches intended for his Imperial Majesty of All the Russias, it only remains for me to mention an idea, favoured by reason and experience, but which neverthe-less I can only touch upon to your Excellency in the most confidential manner, as it is impossible for me to judge beforehand of the means of execution.

In my Memorandum (No. 618) of this day, I have said that if his Imperial Majesty of All the Russias approves the ideas in this despatch, it will be well to establish and confirm the identity of views and opinions between the five Cabinets, and to arrange with each other the best means of making known to the Porte what its own interest, not less than regard to the wishes of the Powers, should lead it to comprehend and accept.

Nothing will facilitate this agreement so much as a meeting of the monarchs and Cabinets. Next Septem-ber is fixed for the meeting of their Imperial Majesties. But in regard to the object I have just pointed out, that period may appear remote. Can the time of the meet-ing be made earlier? It is not for us to decide, and the Emperor my master does not allow himself even to express an opinion on a question connected with so many special considerations, which must be left to his august friend and ally to determine. His Imperial Majesty contents himself with declaring that for his part he will be ready to assist in bringing about an agreement between the monarchs by means of an earlier meeting. Still he cannot but acknowledge that, by fixing an earlier period, there would be a gain of pre-cious time, and a better opportunity for negotiation, **as** no demonstration would make more impression on the Porte than the bare announcement of such a meeting.

As, nevertheless, from the moment that his Majesty the Emperor Alexander consents to the measure proposed in the Memorandum, it will be necessary to consult together as to the time and mode of putting it into execution ; and as it will be very important to gain all that it is possible in the time, it seems to us that it will be no less desirable than easy to bring together at Vienna persons furnished with instructions from the five Courts, and authorised to exchange the opinions of the monarchs as to the best method of coming to an agreement as to their intentions, and the steps to be taken by the Powers.

In the very probable supposition that the meeting of the monarchs cannot take place sooner, the conferences between the Ministers will still have the great advantage of having prepared the work and accelerated the decisions which are so desirable.

I submit these ideas to your Excellency with entire confidence. Make them known to his Imperial Majesty of All the Russias, if you find them worthy to be received ; in any case it appears to me superfluous to assure him that they are dictated as much by the feelings of friendship which animate the Emperor my master for the Emperor Alexander as by the solicitude which his Imperial Majesty feels in the interests common to both of them.

Metternich to Nesselrode (Letter), Vienna, April 19, 1822.

620. I have made your negotiator my courier, my dear Count. M. de Tatistscheff felt what I feel—namely, that speaking is better than writing when one desires to be really understood. He will therefore speak to

you, and he will speak truly when he assures you that
we desire to come to a perfect understanding with you.
But there is at all times and in all circumstances a condition *sine quâ non* in understandings : it is to speak
clearly, to say what one wishes, how far one would go,
and to what extent assistance can be given. As for
possibilities, we need not waste time in talking of them.
Believe me I do not deceive myself in any respect, I see
the necessities, the difficulties, the bad as well as the
good side of the position. If M. de Tatistscheff does
not carry away the conviction that for the moment
there remains nothing for me to say to enable him to
understand the Emperor's mind, it is because he has not
comprehended my words ; but I have a feeling that
such is not the case.

The affair which occupies us is in itself very simple ;
it is only complicated by incidental causes, and they
often suffice to make a really simple affair very complicated. I will tell you in a very few words my opinion
of the situation.

Your Emperor desires what my Emperor desires—
what in reality their allies desire no less.

Your Emperor sees as mine sees, that the faction is
there, its mouth open to swallow social order at the
first shaking of the great pillars on which that order
reposes.

Your Emperor has to weigh many considerations, all
of which we are ready to admit.

But the evil exists, and it is necessary either to conquer it or to run the risk of falling beneath it. Our
sovereigns are strongly tempted to choose the first of
these alternatives, and quite determined to avoid the
second. It is therefore very necessary that they should
understand each other. To the end that their agree-

ment may be effectual, it must be extended to the
Allies, and in order to this there must be a wise and
scrupulous choice of terms, and great exactitude in the
announcement of principles.

That granted, how are they to arrive at understanding each other? For this, my dear Count, allow me to
refer to the explanations which your Ambassador will
give you.

It only remains for me to beg you to believe yourself, and to convince his Imperial Majesty, that I have
this desire; that I discussed the matter with M. de
Tatistscheff frankly and unreservedly; that, in short,
you are mistaken if you give to any of my words a
meaning contrary to reason, and inapplicable, not only
to Austrian but to European questions, those questions
of life and death which absorb all our thoughts. If I
were proposing an Austrian policy I should be very
wrong to treat it as I do this, which occupies me from
morning to night. But I cannot see that this is Austrian
policy, unless that name is given to our extreme desire
not to be eaten up by our brothers and friends. In
that case my policy is Austrian policy, and I shall do
my utmost to carry it out, and certainly shall succeed
better than those good friends desire.

Adieu, my dear Count! For the love of God, no
prejudices. Let them say all they can say: we despise
words. Let us go on and understand each other. Will
that be the end of the work? I hope not; then we can
begin to act, and to do all the good things we have
been hindered from doing since the events of 1821.
Much evil to avoid and much good to accomplish—this
is a grand and noble task.

Metternich to Lebzeltern, at St. Petersburg, Vienna,
April 22, 1822.

621. I send off the present courier after the departure of M. de Tatistscheff. He left us on the 19th, in
consequence of an understanding between him and me
on that decision.

Your Excellency will find in the enclosure the last
results of our transactions. They will prove to you
that we have not ceded a single inch of ground ; we
have remained firm to the principle which has served as
foundation to all our explanations since last May, and
if we hope to gain opportunities for conciliation, we are
still but following out our own plans.

I must make your Excellency aware of the attitude
which M. de Tatistscheff and myself have taken and
maintained during the whole time of our conferences.

My last despatches will have convinced you that
your presentiments with regard to the real motives of
M. de Tatistscheff's journey were realised from the
opening of his mission. My anxiety was to make myself
thoroughly acquainted with all that his mission concerned, which might include complications even with
St. Petersburg itself.

I was not long in discovering a restraint on certain
points which enabled me to perceive that he was the
bearer of double instructions. My efforts have not been
unavailing. As we advanced in our conferences the
attitude of M. de Tatistscheff was more decided. It
was very soon clear to me that although he was the
bearer of the Emperor's words, it was impossible for him
to forget entirely that he had instructions from the
Cabinet. From that time in my conversations with him
I laid the most stress on the first of his functions, and

I showed him that with regard to the second he would find in me a safe ally, in order by removing difficulties of various kinds to arrive at the good end towards which the thoughts of our two monarchs uniformly tend. I must do justice to M. de Tatistscheff, whose whole conduct was agreeable to my wishes. If his explanations were somewhat confused, this was merely the necessary consequence of double instructions not only different, but actually in complete opposition to one another.

One circumstance contributed to show this. M. de Golowkin had received from the Cabinet authority equal to that of M. de Tatistscheff. Your Excellency also saw these gentlemen presented together at our second interview. M. de Tatistscheff soon saw that in that manner we should never arrive at a conclusion, and that consequently the most important part of his mission would have failed.

I thought it best to seem indifferent to the embarrassment of M. de Tatistscheff, and I left him to manage his own affairs. The third time he came alone, and begged me for the future not to mention our transactions to his colleague, till we could show him a result arranged beforehand between ourselves. This was the cause of the division which your Excellency remarked in my despatches.

The only official part is the note which I signed on the 19th. M. de Golowkin knows nothing more of our work.

The Russian Ambassadors sent me on April 12 the proposal for the Protocol enclosed. I saw M. de Tatistscheff the same evening, and I told him I would not sign it. He said he had been obliged to send me the proposal to justify himself to his Cabinet, but that I was at liberty to do as I wished. I then told him that I would address a common note to him and his colleague, in the drawing up of which I should take care to avoid making use of any of the expressions in the Protocol, and there-fore would not compromise our secret conferences.

All the confidential and secret despatches are there-fore absolutely unknown to M. de Golowkin. M. de Tatistscheff has said that he wishes them to go to his Imperial Majesty direct. He has even prevailed upon me to introduce in a secret letter the idea of hastening the time for the meeting of the Sovereigns. I had inserted this proposal in the first Minute of my Memo-randum, and M. de Tatistscheff struck it out. 'It is possible, it is even probable,' said he to me, ' that the Emperor after having read this principal despatch, will communicate it to the Cabinet. If it is mentioned there, it is possible that the Cabinet, who dread such a meeting above everything, will make this a pretext to attack all the rest.'

By the present and preceding despatches I flatter myself I have made your Excellency aware of the whole of the negotiation between M. de Tatistscheff and my-self. It is for you now to serve the cause by great reticence and by continuing in the course you have hitherto followed, weighing carefully what is to be said, and perhaps even communicating with the Secretaries of State.

I have nothing more to tell you except that on April 19, the very day of M. de Tatistscheff's departure, I received the Russian ambassadors and made over the official note to them. It was just as I had expected ; M. de Golowkin thought the text too brief. I replied to this just criticism by remarking that M. de Tatist-scheff having been sent to us simply as a bearer of words, I must for my part refer to my words. I added that in this respect I was in a far worse position than the ambassadors, seeing that I could not, like them, boast of having a witness to call in my favour.

As M. de Tatistscheff declared himself perfectly satisfied with this explanation, M. de Golowkin was fain to be so also.

I know, however, for certain, that there have been grave discussions between these gentlemen in the course of our conferences. Whilst M. de Tatistscheff and my-self were making good progress, M. de Golowkin thought that nothing was being done; he therefore reproached his colleague, who told him that the responsibility rested on him, and on him alone. This circumstance is not without interest for your Excellency, for it will explain what may seem contradictory in the Reports of the two Ministers, and in the effects which they may produce, or have already produced, at St. Petersburg.

VICTORY OF THE AUSTRIAN OVER THE RUSSIAN CABINET.

Metternich to the Emperor Francis, Vienna, May 31, 1822.

622. By the courier who arrived an hour ago from St. Petersburg, I have a despatch from Lebzeltern o the 22nd inst., giving the details of perhaps the greatest victory that one Cabinet has ever gained over another.

The Emperor has adopted all our Reports. Tatist-scheff will return here in ten or twelve days, in order to place the rest of the negotiations in our hands. The Emperor goes further. The news of the evacuation of the Principalities has made such an impression on him that Bagot and Lebzeltern are commissioned to make known to the Porte, through the two ambassadors at Constantinople, that his Majesty is ready to re-establish diplomatic relations with the Divan immediately. Count Capo d'Istria is quite beaten, and is for the present silent.

I feel myself very fortunate that I may venture to believe that the whole position of things in Europe can now take a definite and decided turn. We have here a power difficult to calculate, and that I, so far as the thing depends on me, will neglect nothing to demolish the party, of this your Majesty will not doubt. . . . The Emperor will not come before the beginning of September. As the matter stands we shall not want his Majesty sooner.

METTERNICH.

The victory of which you here speak is perhaps the finest and the most difficult of your Ministry—one for which I cannot sufficiently thank you. But the world shall know also what a benefit you have brought about: hence you are to take pains to make this plain. I know too that I may depend on your making use of this victory with your accustomed zeal for the good cause and for my welfare, and I wait with impatience for Lebzeltern's despatches.

FRANCIS.

Laxenburg, June 1, 1822.

Metternich to the Emperor Francis, Vienna, June 3, 1822.

623. I have the honour to enclose for your Majesty's inspection Freiherr von Lebzeltern's extremely interesting despatches from the 16th to the 22nd May.

In reading these, your Majesty will share the feeling which they have excited in me. Since politics have been carried on in an enlightened manner, never has a Cabinet compromised itself like the Russian Cabinet.

All the remarks which your Majesty will find used by Count Nesselrode himself on the loss of Russian influence on the Turkish kingdom are correct. The present Russian Cabinet has with one blow destroyed the grand work of Peter the Great and all his successors. Everything is here on a new basis, and what Russia loses in moral strength the Porte gains. We have done them here a service which they can never sufficiently reward, and it will maintain ours as well as the English influence.

I have already prepared my despatch for Constantinople (No. 624). In a few hours I shall send it off.

In the morning I shall send a courier to the allied Courts.

I shall have the honour of laying these despatches before your Majesty on Wednesday.

METTERNICH.

The enclosures are herewith returned, and I await the arrival of the despatches to be sent for my inspection.

FRANCIS.

Vienna, June 3, 1822.

Metternich to Count Lützow, in Constantinople, Vienna, June 3, 1822.

624. A courier sent by M. de Lebzeltern on May 22 (N.S.) has brought news so important that I will not delay an hour in sending the present despatches to your Excellency.

The good genius seems to be triumphing over the evil one: our efforts have not been vain, and the faction which up to this time had restrained the generous disposition of the Emperor of Russia has been obliged to give way to reason. The despatches which your Excellency and Lord Strangford should have received directly from Lebzeltern and Bagot, before the arrival of the present courier, will have told you so much.

The courier sent by Baron de Lebzeltern informs me :—

That the Emperor Alexander has received the communications which we made through M. de Tatistscheff;

That the news of April 25, which Lord Strangford had wisely sent without loss of time to St. Petersburg, produced such an effect on his Imperial Majesty as to induce him to attempt a direct step at Constantinople by means of the representatives of the Courts of Austria and England ; in short

That M. de Tatistscheff had received orders to return

to Vienna as quickly as possible to carry out his previous conferences.

Such is the information on which I ground the present despatch to your Excellency.

Thus the affairs can be proceeded with, both at Constantinople and Vienna.

That I may have some idea of the direction affairs
may take in the first of these places, it is indispensable
that I should know the contents of the despatch which
you and Lord Strangford received direct from St. Petersburg. That communication cannot be long in reaching
me. I know exactly the business which awaits me after
the arrival of M. de Tatistscheff; it is quite enough for
me to know that the Emperor Alexander has approved
of my secret despatch.

If I did not consider the present moment of immense value, I should have preferred to delay the
despatch of these directions until the arrival of the first
accounts from M. de Lebzeltern: they would then be
more complete. But I am so anxious not to prolong for
your Excellency and Lord Strangford a period of sus-
pense (however short), that I send immediately without
loss of time.

The information I am able to give you to-day, Sir,
will much strengthen your position, and as I wish that
Lord Strangford may be able to take a similar position,
I beg him, as well as your Excellency, to consider the
following overtures as addressed to you in common.

You will find in the enclosed* the details which I
have sent to London concerning the whole of M. de
Tatistscheff's first visit.

Consider this despatch well, and I beg the Eng-

---

* These enclosures were Metternich's notes of the conversations with
Tatistscheff. (See No. 616.)—ED.

lish Ambassador to do the same. You will both be convinced of the following facts :—

1. That I felt from the first that the Russian negotiator must be charged with a double commission, and I was not long in convincing myself of the fact.

2. That from that time all my anxiety was to follow the line of the Emperor of Russia, and not that which his minister has followed for ten months.

3. That I founded the success of the enterprise on the following bases :—

Removing the chance of immediate war ;

Reserving to the Russian monarch the possibility of justifying himself in his own eyes and those of his nation with respect to the disastrous position of the Greeks which must ensue from the renunciation of the war, after the hopes of this people having been so long directed to the material support of Russia ;

Keeping this within proper limits, admissible therefore by all the Powers.

4. That, in short, in the interest of the cause, I have sent M. de Tatistscheff to St. Petersburg with a double despatch similar to the instructions which he brought to Vienna.

The communication which I have made at London, Paris, and Berlin of the results of my negotiation with M. de Tatistscheff has furnished me with the most satisfactory proofs of the entire and uniform approbation of the three Cabinets. The only thing wanting to complete the work was the assent of his Imperial Majesty of All the Russias. This arrived by the last despatch from St. Petersburg, in which are enclosed M. de Tatistscheff's letters.

The explanations which it seemed to me necessary

to make, especially to Lord Strangford, as to the true spirit which guided us in the choice of means proposed to his Imperial Majesty of all the Russias, by my Memorandum of April 19 (No. 618), are so fully given in my despatches to Prince Esterhazy, that I do not consider it necessary to recur to them here. It must be evident to Lord Strangford, that though I allowed myself to touch on the amelioration of the fate of the Greeks, I have not sacrificed the practical sense which has guided the allied Cabinets up to this time. The present complication has been brought about by a criminal faction, and, considering the end which at present awaits it, must not only injure the cause of the Greeks, but lessen that influence which the policy of Peter the Great and his successors had constantly exercised on the Porte until the end of the year 1820, and to which the Russian Cabinet knew how to give as much force as extension.

Several grave mistakes and the lapse of but a few months have been sufficient to destroy this influence and prepare a new era for the Ottoman Empire. If the Porte owes this benefit to the mistakes of the Russian Minister, it owes it no less to the rectitude of the conceptions and conduct of the allied Cabinets : it is to complete the work now commenced, that our labours must henceforth be directed, and it is in the hope of seeing them crowned with success that I address another appeal direct to the enlightened zeal, energy, and talents of Lord Strangford.

This is my opinion, and my whole opinion, on the necessities of the moment. I do not forget those of to-morrow ; but before approaching them it is absolutely necessary that I should be informed on many essential points, upon which the next courier from our ambassador in Russia and the arrival of M. de Tatistscheff can alone throw the light required.

The examination of my transactions with M. de Tatistscheff will prove to you, Sir, as well as to Lord Strangford, that the basis of the pacific measures we have proposed may be divided into two periods:

The first must be occupied by the agreement between the allied Cabinets ;

The second by the overtures which the allies, in consequence of an arrangement among themselves, will make to the Porte.

The Russian Cabinet has just made, through your Excellency and the English ambassador, a direct appeal to Constantinople. There is in this an inversion of the steps we proposed, and nevertheless a clear gain. I understand by gain—

1. The gain of precious time in the supposition that the Porte hastens the reconciliation ;

2. The advantages we derive from the very fact that the precipitation of the Russian Cabinet, if it should lead to results contrary to the present apparently pacific intentions of that Power, could only fall on Russia herself.

Your Excellency is consequently authorised to proceed, together with the English ambassador, in the path which the correspondence of Messieurs Lebzeltern and Bagot may have indicated to you. Your Excellency sees that I do not admit that the English ambassador has found any difficulty whatever in accepting the invitation which Sir Charles Bagot must have addressed to him.

Russia has forestalled the agreement proposed in my Memorandum of April 19 by a direct appeal to Constantinople. It is necessary to separate the periods, and to understand that the more we gain now towards an agreement between Russia and the Porte, the less there will be to accomplish in the second period. It is impossible not to see in this fact an immense victory for the cause of real and definite peace, and great facilities for subsequent negotiation between the allied Cabinets.

We therefore desire most ardently that you will succeed in effecting at Constantinople as much as possible with the least possible delay. If the Divan knows its own interests, it will share our wishes. It is Lord Strangford's part to make it feel this.

If the Porte should insist on diplomatic relations being re-established as soon as possible, it will be for you, too, to make the most at St. Petersburg of the advantages which would ensue to the Ottoman Empire from the condescension of his Imperial Majesty of All the Russias in this respect.

Whenever it is shown that Russia will not maintain the exaggerated pretensions of the Greeks by force of arms, it concerns that Power to diminish as much as possible the number of victims caused by the continuance of the revolt. The Cabinet of Russia is convinced that freedom of speech is one of its most powerful weapons for promoting the submission of its co-religionists. It is therefore reasonable that it should seek to place itself in an attitude which would enable it to make use of this weapon. We could not give this advice, but on the part of the representatives of the two Courts at Constantinople it is simple and natural. You are thus equally with Lord Strangford at liberty to explain yourself to the Russian Cabinet according to the impressions you receive in the different places to which you have been sent by Russia herself, to make the most of the means of conciliation, whilst our attitude should lean to many other aspects of the question.

I will cause this courier to be followed by another as soon as I am in receipt of the next communications from St. Petersburg. In the meantime I believe I have given your Excellency all the latitude necessary to enable you to advance in the new direction affairs have just taken.

One thing I cannot too strongly recommend to you, and that is to take all your steps, in conjunction with Lord Strangford, in such a manner that the parts shall be distributed between you with the same success as before. I am equally desirous that you should both take care to keep on good terms with the representatives of France and Prussia, so that not only the Porte, but the Cabinets of these two countries, can have no doubt that, if there is any difference more or less of activity in the parts played by the ambassadors and envoys at Constantinople, there is none either in the principles which the allied Courts profess nor in the determinations and wishes of the monarchs. It is by the demonstration of this grand concord that we shall find a powerful means of action on the Divan, and a means no less powerful to enable the Emperor to give full play to the principles which serve as a foundation and guide to his personal resolves. . . .

I request your Excellency to communicate the present despatch and its contents, without any reserve, to the English ambassador.

Metternich to the Emperor Francis, Vienna, June 13, 1822.

625. Herr von Tatistscheff has to present to your Majesty an autograph letter from the Emperor Alexander. I have promised him to inform your Majesty

of it immediately on your Majesty's arrival, not doubting but that your Majesty will appoint the morning for
its reception.   At the same time I told him that one
o'clock was likely to be the hour to suit your Majesty.

He awaits the commands which I beg your Majesty
to make known to him through the Lord Chamberlain.

I have seen a copy of the Emperor's letter.   Nothing
more is to be desired either in that or in the whole
despatch, of which your Majesty will receive an account
to-morrow.

I pray your Majesty to say to Herr von Tatistscheff
that you have been shortly informed by me of the state
of things, and that your Majesty has appointed to-
morrow morning to receive the fuller details.

Let your Majesty deign to add that you know the
share that he (Tatistscheff) has himself had in bringing
about this good position ; that your Majesty doubts not
that the Emperor Alexander desires only what is best in
everything, but that his position was difficult, and that
by the part he has taken he will cover himself with
lasting honour ; that he may reckon on your Majesty
as his best and surest friend, which your Majesty desires
to be on this as on every occasion.

Tatistscheff hopes that you will at the same time say
that your Majesty counts on the arrival of the Emperor
Alexander in September, considering this meeting as a
means of present and future safety, and looking on the
meeting of the monarchs as crowning the work.

I have spoken to him of the alteration in the choice
of the place of meeting, and he agrees with me. The reason
why he desires that your Majesty should personally speak
to him of the meeting is because the Emperor Alexander
would feel himself strengthened by your Majesty's words,

and would give his decision at once, which might otherwise be thwarted by Capo d'Istria.

METTERNICH.

I will see Tatistscheff at noon to-day, and speak to
him as you desire.

FRANCIS.

Vienna, June 13, 1822.

OUTBREAK OF THE SPANISH REVOLUTION.

Metternich to the Emperor Francis, Vienna, July 21, 1822.

626. The accompanying newspaper contains the latest accounts of the state of things in Madrid.

From this it seems that the fate of that country either must be decided very soon or is already decided. It is evident that Spain must shake off the Revolution. Everything depends on one single step of the King— will the King take that step? According to my feeling he has already hesitated too long. Not on deliberation, but on action now depends the fate of the King and his whole people

METTERNICH.

The enclosures are herewith returned. If, for want of courage and determination, the King of Spain does not conquer, that will happen of which I have once spoken with several of our Princes.

FRANCIS.

Vienna, July 22, 1822.

Metternich to the Emperor Francis, Vienna, July 23, 1822.

627. The house of Rothschild has received to-day by a courier from Paris the enclosed newspaper. This will inform your Majesty that the affair in Madrid has taken the turn which from the timid character of the King was only too much to be feared.

The King would have saved himself personally, and he would have saved his kingdom, if he had but for one minute shown personal moral courage.   Instead of this, he seems to have been dissolved in tears.

The result must now inevitably be evil instead of good, which it might have been.

All faithful servants of the King will be sacrificed by the party.

What will happen to the King God knows ! The insurrection in the provinces will not be put down the sooner from this state of things, and Spain will lose the certainty of salvation in a civil war the consequences of which cannot be calculated.

If I had been in the Palace I would have taken the King and the Royal Family, and, with a strong guard, without delay I would have broken through the insurgents, and thus in a few hours saved the King, his family, and the kingdom.   It appears that Morillo, who had the power to do this, must himself be bad.   The Duke of Infantado, who apparently has contrived the whole thing, is known to me as a loyal but very weak-minded man.   The reaction of this event will act very injuriously on the whole of Europe.

METTERNICH.

This outcome of the disturbances in Madrid is certainly very bad, and is a disgrace to the King.

FRANCIS.

Vienna, July 24, 1822.

AUSTRIA'S UNDERSTANDING WITH ENGLAND ON THE EASTERN QUESTION.

628. Metternich to Lord Strangford, English Ambassador at Constantinople (Letter), Vienna, July 31, 1822.

628. My Lord,—The letter which you addressed to me on June 25 [1] arrived so shortly before the departure of the ordinary post for Constantinople that it was not possible for me to reply to it by that medium. This letter contains much that is interesting; it embraces questions so important, and treated in such a luminous manner, that I have had no difficulty in making myself master of the contents before writing to your Excellency. Even this delay will show you the value I attach to your communications.

That we may understand each other, my Lord, it seems to me necessary to go back to the time when you wrote that letter.

The invitation of Bagot and De Lebzeltern reached your Excellency at the same time as that of Count de Lützow. The mere fact of this invitation must have convinced you not only that the pacific disposition of his Imperial Majesty the Emperor of Russia corresponds in its course with the grand character of that sovereign, but that the desire of advancing the arrangement of a difficult and painful affair determined the Emperor to declare the evacuation of the Princi-

* Published by Prokesch in his *Abfall der Griechen* (1853), tom. iii. page 368.—ED.

palities a sufficient reason for beginning a negotiation with the Porte as soon as possible, so as to further the re-establishment of its relations with Russia.

On the other hand, the Internuncio has communicated to your Excellency my despatches of June 3. They contain the Memorandum of April 19 (No. 618), and will have informed your Excellency that M. de Tatistscheff had taken that despatch to St. Petersburg to submit it to his august sovereign.

At the time of the drawing up of these despatches I had already made sure that his Imperial majesty agreed to them, and that he would send the same negotiator to us again to meet in conference with the ministers of the allied Courts at Vienna, to concert means of action on the principles settled between M. de Tatistscheff and myself during the first visit of that minister. Since then your Excellency will have heard of the arrival of M. de Tatistscheff at Vienna, and of the confidential conferences established here between the ministers of the five Courts.

To these conferences I owe the advantage of being able to extract from the explanations which have already taken place the substance of the reply which I have to make to you, my Lord. While placing the principal subjects in the same order which you have followed in your letter, I shall try to explain with as much precision as possible my feeling on the questions you have treated.

The first is the evacuation of the Principalities. Your remarks on that important subject are as judicious as they are true; they are open to no objection: I adopt them in their entirety. Nothing can excuse the Porte if it does not proceed to that evacuation in good faith, without tergiversation and without delay. I admit all you say, my Lord, as to the numerous embarrassments which, in the critical situation of the Turkish Government, may impede the execution of this measure; but everything should give way to the necessity of fulfilling a formal engagement such as the Porte has made to the mnisters of the allied Courts in the clearest and most positive terms. This engagement, more than once renewed and confirmed in consequence of your different representations, has placed you, my Lord, in so strong a position, it gives you so much right and latitude of action, that you will be perfectly justified in constantly pressing forward the accomplishment of a measure which must precede all our other operations.

The direct communications from St. Petersburg will have informed you that it is not to the immediate and complete execution of the four points of the Russian ultimatum—points admitted in principle by the Grand Seigneur—but to the simple fact of the evacuation of the Principalities, that his Imperial Majesty has connected the offer of sending a plenipotentiary. It seems to me that the grandest proof of moderation which the Emperor Alexander could give to the Porte and to his allies was his insisting only on that clause with the view of smoothing over the difficulties to which the events of the last year have given rise between the two Powers. The Porte is consequently more than ever bound to agree to a measure which moreover imposes no real sacrifice upon it, but, on the contrary, if it were not required by the Powers in conformity with the stipulations of treaties, would be dictated by its own interest and that of its subjects.

I also agree with your Excellency as to the incon venience of insisting on the Porte sending plenipotentiaries before having positive assurances on the article of evacuation. The nomination even of Hospodars, supposing it definitely decreed, would not compensate for the non-execution or imperfect execution of that article. You will have seen, my Lord, by many of the recent explanations of the Russian Cabinet, that his Imperial Majesty, while admitting that there may be difficulties in the choice of men for the government of a country, does not recognise in these difficulties a valid excuse, either for continuing to inflict on that country the sufferings and ravages which weigh on the Principalities, or for postponing the execution of the treaties.

I flatter myself, however, my Lord, that thanks to your cares and perseverance, supported by the activity of your colleagues, the evacuation will have made real progress in the interval which has elapsed since the departure of your letter, and that it will soon be concluded. If in this case you have thought fit to approach the question to which I have alluded, your next communications will probably inform us of the first results of your labours.

Following the Memorandum of April 19 you have, my Lord, in your letter separated the subject of the amnesty from that of sending plenipotentiaries.

It is true that these two subjects were placed thus in the above-mentioned work, where they simply served to indicate the bases of agreement between the Powers. But in fact they cannot be treated separately, and this I will endeavour to show.

The great affair which occupies us offers two points of view, distinct in themselves, but both tending towards the same end. One regards the execution of the treaties between Russia and the Porte, and in the Memorandum of April 19 bears the designation of ' questions of right.'

The other is what in the same paper we have placed under the head of 'subjects of general interest.'

The allied Courts have up to this time in their communications with the Porte insisted only on the articles comprehended under the first of these heads; but what is at present the direct object of our efforts? It is to re-establish as soon as possible the former relations between Russia and the Ottoman Empire till late events disturbed and suspended them. We all know and recognise that it is impossible to put an end to the state of uncertainty in which the Porte is, and the troubles of every kind which desolate almost all parts of the Empire, unless it arrives at a full and entire reconciliation with its powerful neighbour. Now, to bring about that reconciliation it is not enough that what we call questions of right should be properly regulated. The Emperor of Russia will not re-establish his ordinary diplomatic relations with the Porte on the one ground of the return of that Power to the strict observation of treaties.

His Imperial Majesty did not recall his embassy to Constantinople simply for the violation of these treaties. He did not wish his representative to be the spectator of scenes such as those which daily took place under his eyes in May 1821. His Imperial Majesty does not wish to appoint another representative to be the spectator of similar scenes and to be recalled in his turn. And what in truth would the Emperor gain, what would the Porte and Europe gain, by seeing a Russian embassy present itself at Constantinople, establish itself there, only to be removed again? Would this second recall be accompanied by the same arrangements as the first? And, independently of that great obstacle, could the Emperor Alexander after all proceed to the re-establishment of a

permanent embassy at Constantinople without having
shown by patent acts that, while condemning the revolt,
he has neglected no legitimate and pacific means to put
an end to these cruel reactions and to re-establish tranquillity in a neighbouring State, now a prey to the most
frightful revolutions?

Such is, my Lord, the position in which the question
is now placed. The Emperor of Russia has decided not to
re-establish the embassy at Constantinople until he has
satisfied himself on what he regards as a sacred duty,
and assured himself at the same time that its continuance will be probably secure from any fresh interruption.
The negotiation which his Imperial Majesty proposes to
the Porte must first of all furnish him with this guarantee.

I well know that this determination will at first open
up a vast field for the Turkish Government to take
umbrage, and that it will object strongly to the prospect
of a transaction in which it sees only danger to its power
and humiliation to its pride. But your Excellency, in
consulting the second part of the Memorandum of April
19, will have perceived that the concessions to be obtained from the Porte will be circumscribed within precise and moderate limits; and if at the time of the first
explanations on this subject, we could make the Porte
comprehend that there is to be no attack on its sovereignty; that we only demand from it, for the re-establishment and consolidation of the internal peace of its
empire, things just, practicable, compatible with its
dignity, agreeable to its true interests, and manifestly
required by circumstances and the local situations of
the moment, I should be far from renouncing the hope
of conquering a repugnance which is perhaps in a great
measure owing to the false and exaggerated ideas which

that Government has formed on the intentions and projects of the Powers. I believe, my Lord, that without engaging you in a discussion on these delicate points more than is necessary to reply to the questions which the Porte will address to you on these subjects, you will find in the general situation and in the urgent needs of the Ottoman Empire irresistible reasons to place before the Divan to induce it not to reject this negotiation.

If the Sultan wishes to re-establish his authority over the insurgent provinces otherwise than by force of arms—and it is doubtful if he could still reckon on the efficacy of that force—he must make an amnesty and conditions acceptable to the Greeks. The observations of your Excellency on the uselessness of a mere act of amnesty, such as the Porte has several times tried, are perfectly just; it is therefore necessary that the act which must lead to a real pacification should be of an essentially different character. We have seen more than once that a measure which in one form would have been without effect may under another form bring about satisfactory results.

It seems clear to us that the Ottoman Government, in the state of exasperation and unbounded distrust which at present reigns among the Greeks, cannot obtain by its proclamations, however they are drawn up, the faintest resemblance to a submission, as long as the allied monarchs, and especially the Emperor of Russia, do not raise their voices in support of the Sultan. But they can only make these voices heard when they have fixed and well understood bases to offer as conditions of the submission. It is then only that they can address themselves to the insurgents with the dignity suited to their high station or with any reasonable hope of success. If their voices are heard the end is gained : if not, those who refuse to hear will have to depend upon themselves ; they will be abandoned by the Powers, and left to be treated as the Turks always treat rebellious subjects.

By following out this idea, you will be convinced, my Lord, that if in the Memorandum of April 19, the amnesty and the negotiation are found separately mentioned, these two points are not the less inseparable. You will also see that this negotiation, on which Russia and her allies insist, is neither a gratuitous pretension nor a project conceived with any other views or interests whatever than those of the pacification of the Ottoman Empire. This is the first and indispensable condition of the termination of these unfortunate complications. Everything is included in the propositions which the Powers address to the Porte. The re-establishment of direct relations with Russia is impossible until an end is put to those horrors which are ravaging the Ottoman provinces. There is no way of arriving at this end except a complete and solid amnesty. This amnesty, in order to be something more than a mere string of words, absolutely requires the concurrence of the European Powers. On the other hand, such a concurrence can only take place when there is a complete understanding on the fundamental bases of the amnesty and on the necessary clauses in order to make it acceptable to the insurgents. In short, that these clauses may be determined, they must be discussed and considered in a previous negotiation. This reasoning seems to me so unanswerable that the Porte itself, in spite of all its objections against the intervention of Christian Powers in questions of which it believes they are ignorant, must in the end see the force of it, unless it declares frankly that it attaches no value to the re-establishment of its relations with Russia, nor to the pacification of its provinces, nor to the future fate of its own subjects.

You observe, my Lord, that the Porte would perhaps lend itself more willingly to a general negotiation, if it could hope to obtain by it some real and positive advantages. You quote the wish of several members of the Divan, that the Powers allied to Russia would undertake a mediation between her and the Porte, in order to smooth the difficulties relative to the Asiatic frontiers, adding, however, that you are decidedly averse to such an idea. In this I see the extreme wisdom of your Excellency, and all who may be informed of the fact will no doubt applaud with me. I need no great consideration to rate such a project at its just value. It would alter the character of the negotiation to which we invite the Porte, and mix subjects together which have nothing in common with the object at which we aim. The present case is not one for the calculation of gain and loss, or an arrangement of claims and concessions. It is a grand plan of pacification conceived by the allied Powers with the most disinterested and enlightened views, and in which the Porte (however indifferent it may be as to the maintenance of peace in Europe) is called more directly than any other Power to join for the preservation of its people, its power, and its future existence. Any advantage which the allied Powers may derive from this negotiation to consolidate the general tranquillity, however great it may appear to us, will nevertheless be far less than what must result to the Porte. How could it pretend to compensations in an affair where it is as much a question of working out its own salvation as of avoiding the most terrible catastrophes? Nothing could be imagined worse for the success of the negotiation, than gratuitously to add one difficulty more to those it already has. If such a proposition could have issued from the Russian Cabinet, would not the Porte have accused Russia of complicating questions to render them interminable, or of serving her own private interests? For the rest, I leave this point, my Lord, to the ascendency which you have acquired over the minds of the Turkish ministers, and of which you have given more than once a striking proof. You will, I have no doubt, be able to make them comprehend what a mistake it would be to bring forward a claim which would certainly be rejected by the Powers.

I come at last to the different plans suggested by your Excellency to induce the Porte to make some conciliatory and honourable advance towards Russia, in consequence of the evacuation of the Principalities and the nomination of Hospodars. I accept as perfectly sound, wise, and useful, all that your Excellency proposes on this head. A notification, drawn up in terms chosen or at least fully approved by your Excellency and your colleagues, and addressed directly to his Imperial Majesty of All the Russias, or to his Cabinet, could not but produce a favourable effect; and, indeed, any act of the Porte which stated its sincere desire to resume its former relations with Russia, and proclaimed a just and reasonable confidence in the intentions of the Emperor Alexander and his august allies, would be a great step towards the accomplishment of our wishes. Nevertheless, my Lord, I am far from admitting that the success of such a step would dispense with the necessity of insisting on the sending of the plenipotentiaries; and after all that I have had the honour to explain to you in this letter on the object and aim of a negotiation which we consider the only means of arriving at the pacification of the Ottoman Empire, you cannot have any doubt on the subject.

I will end with a short *résumé* of the observations contained in the present letter.

1. The evacuation of the Principalities, a measure to which the nomination of the Hospodars is only regarded as an accessory, must be effectually accomplished.

2. To enable us to make a definite arrangement, the Porte must acknowledge to the Ministers of the allied Courts, as a fact no longer to be hidden, the necessity of offering the insurgents an amnesty drawn up in terms likely to bring them to submit to its authority.

3. As soon as the Porte has acknowledged this fact, it must be convinced that under present circumstances any amnesty which is not strengthened by the concurrence and support of the allied Powers, and particularly of Russia, would be ineffectual and useless.

4. As this concurrence and support can only be obtained by means of a preliminary negotiation, the Porte cannot refuse to appoint plenipotentiaries for this negotiation, which is moreover the condition *sine quâ non* of the re-establishment of its relations with Russia.

5. Any step, any act of the Porte tending to facilitate its reconciliation with Russia will be highly approved by the allied Powers, provided it is not a pretext for eluding the negotiation proposed by the Powers with the wisest and most salutary intentions.

Your Excellency now knows my whole mind on those points which in the present state of the question I regard as most essential. Being approved and shared by the ministers with whom I have the honour to confer on this important affair, and in every way according to the intentions of your Government as far they are known to me, I believe, my Lord, that my sketch may serve you as a guide in any steps you may take with the ministers of the Porte. As to the time for making use of it; as to the choice of modes of conquering the difficulties, of which no one can judge better than yourself; as to the modifications which may be caused by chances and incidents impossible to foresee; we leave all that to your prudence, your zeal, and your talents. These qualities will enable you to fulfil the difficult task with which you are charged. I have only to add, &c.

RESULTS OF THE CONGRESS OF VERONA.

Protocol signed by the Plenipotentiaries of Austria, France, Prussia, and Russia, at Verona, November 19, 1822.

629. The plenipotentiaries of Austria, France, Prussia, and Russia, thinking it necessary to determine the cases in which the engagements made with the Court of France by the Courts of Austria, Prussia, and Russia—in the supposition of a war declared or provoked by the present Government of Spain—would be binding for the Powers who have taken part in them, have agreed to determine precisely the said engagements in the following terms :—

ARTICLE I.

The three cases in which the eventual engagements between the four Powers who have signed the present *procès-verbal* would become immediately obligatory are :—

1. That of an armed attack on the part of Spain against the French territory, or of an official act of the Spanish Government provoking directly to rebellion the subjects of one or other of the Powers.

2. That of his Majesty the King of Spain being declared to have forfeited his throne ; or an action being brought against his august person, or an attempt of the same kind being made against the members of his family.

3. That of a formal act of the Spanish Government infringing the rights of the legitimate succession of the Royal family.

ARTICLE II.

Considering that independently of the cases above specified and defined, there may arise at one or other of the Courts what might be regarded as of the same value and producing the same effects as those designated in Article I., it is decided that should such non-specified case or any other analogous case be realised, the ministers of the allied Courts accredited to his Most Christian Majesty should unite with the Cabinet of France to examine and determine if the case in question should be considered as belonging to the class of the *casus fœderis* foreseen and defined, and as such demanding the direct application of the engagements taken by the Powers.

METTERNICH, LEBZELTERN, MONTMORENCY, CARAMAN, COUNT DE LA FERRONNAYS, CHATEAUBRIAND, BERNSTORFF, HATZFELD, NESSELRODE, LIEVEN, TATISTSCHEFF, POZZO DI BORGO.

Conference Protocol.

630. The ministers of the Cabinets of Austria, France, Prussia, and Russia are met to-day with the Duke of Wellington to confer with his Excellency on the *procès-verbal* signed yesterday (No. 629), and on the instructions that each of these Courts proposes to address to its minister at Madrid.

The Duke of Wellington has explained the different points of view from which, as plenipotentiary of the British Government, he regards both these steps; and in consequence of the discussion produced by these explanations, the Duke has undertaken to communicate to the ministers of the four Cabinets the substance of his observations in writing, in the form of a confidential note.

The question of the Protocol was treated afterwards;

and after many forms having been examined, each of which presented difficulties or inconveniences, it was arranged :

That there shall be no general Protocol on the negotiations and conferences relative to the Spanish affair.

That the despatches exchanged between the ministers or presented to the Conferences shall be regarded as simple communications from Cabinet to Cabinet.

That it shall be the same with the confidential note announced by the Duke of Wellington.

Metternich to the Emperor Francis, Verona, December 11, 1822.

631. Sire,—I have the honour to send without delay to your Imperial Majesty the enclosed Reports, which I have received from Paris by a courier sent by the Government to the French Ambassadors. Your Imperial Majesty will also find enclosed a letter from the Viscount de Montmorency. My mind is made up after perusing a private letter which the Marquis de Caraman received from M. de Montmorency, and which he gave me to read. From all these things put together it appears to me—

1. That the French minister reckons on connecting himself directly with the three Continental Courts.

2. That he wishes the sending of instructions from the Cabinets met at Verona to the representatives at Madrid to be considered as a question of prudence.

Now, in this there is some confusion of ideas.

We foresaw the possibility that the French Government would not be able to decide on connecting its diplomatic course with our own. It was determined that in this case the instructions to the embassies of the three Courts should be sent without delay.

The French minister, by deciding to place himself on the same moral ground with the allies, seems to desire that the course arranged should undergo some modification. He shows this by his proposal to declare that the time of sending the instructions to Madrid must depend on questions of prudence to be considered by the Conference at Paris. In that the French minister deceives himself. There exists, relative to the sending of these instructions, a stronger power, and one which must decide it quite independently of every other calculation—the end of the Congress. Our despatches should consequently be expedited; the discretional question exists for France alone, and is confined to the simple fact of deciding if that Power wishes to recall its own embassy at the same time as the allies; it cannot be extended to the consideration whether the recall of the ministers, either of the allies or the representative of France, can be suspended even momentarily. I do not doubt that your Majesty will regard the alternative from the same point of view in which it appears to me.

I pray your Majesty not to notice the remark made by M. de Montmorency relative to the despatch from the Austrian Cabinet to Count Brunetti. This remark arises from a mistake on M. de Montmorency's part.

Deign to accept, Sire, the testimony of my profoundest respect.

Circular Despatch sent by the three Allied Courts—Austria, Russia, and Prussia—to their Ambassadors at the other Courts. Verona, December, 1822.*

632. The Monarchs of Austria, Russia, and Prussia, at the conclusion of the Conference at Verona, sent the following circular despatch to their ambassadors at the other Courts. The original documents were signed by the three Cabinet ministers—Prince Metternich, Count Nesselrode, and Count Bernstorff.

Verona, December 14, 1822.

You were informed on the conclusion of the Laybach Conferences in May 1821, that the allied Monarchs and their Cabinets would meet in the course of 1822 on the proposal of the Courts of Naples and Turin, and with the concurrence of the other Italian Courts, to arrange as to the continuance of the measures which had been adopted for the maintenance of peace in the Peninsula after the sad events of 1820 and 1821.

This meeting has now taken place, and it is our present purpose to make known to you its results.

By the Convention, signed July 24, 1821, at Novara, the provisional formation of a military line in Piedmont

* This circular despatch was sent by Prince Metternich to the Munich political paper for publication, as is shown by a letter from Metternich dated Munich, January 3, 1823 :—

'. . . I had a long conference this morning with Messieurs de Rechberg, Wrede, and Zentner, where I obtained as good terms as I possibly could for my great affair. My presence here will do much good, but it naturally excites the attention of the Liberals. This attention has been brought to a height by the insertion which I have managed to-day of the circular despatch of the three Courts, and of the despatch of M. de Villeta to M. de La Garde in the Munich *Gazette.* I shall hear this evening the kind of sensation which these two pieces will have produced on the public.'

In the Frankfort *Journal* of January 5, 1823, this despatch is translated into French.—Ed.

by a corps of auxiliaries for one year was arranged, with the reservation to decide at the meeting in the year 1822 whether the condition of the country required the longer continuance of this measure, or whether it might be repealed.

The plenipotentiaries of those Courts which had signed the Convention of Novara, together with the plenipotentiaries of his Majesty the King of Sardinia, entered upon this investigation, and it was decided that the presence of an auxiliary force was no longer necessary to preserve peace in Piedmont. The King of Sardinia himself pointed out the mode in which the gradual retreat of the auxiliaries should be effected ; and it de-- termined by a new convention that the departure of the troops from Piedmont should begin on December 31 and conclude on September 30, 1823, with the evacuation of the fortress of Alessandria.

His Majesty the King of the Two Sicilies, who had taken part in the Convention at Naples on October 18, also declared to the three Courts that the present condition of his country permitted him to propose a reduction in the number of the auxiliaries stationed at different places. The allied sovereigns have had no hesitation in acting on this proposal, and the auxiliary forces stationed in the Two Sicilies will be as quickly as possible reduced to seventeen thousand men.

Everything therefore goes on according to the wishes of the monarchs as expressed by them at the conclusion of the Congress of Laybach, when they declared ' that, far from desiring to extend their intervention in the affairs of Italy beyond the limits of stern necessity, they cherished the desire that the state of things which imposed this painful duty upon them would soon pass away never to return.' Thus disappeared the false alarms, hostile constructions, and gloomy prophecies which have been disseminated over Europe by ignorance or perfidy, to mislead the people as to the pure and noble intentions of the monarchs. No secret scheme, no ambition, no calculation of their own advantage united them in the determination which an imperious necessity alone had dictated to them in 1821. To make a stand against revolution, to overcome the disorders, troubles, and crimes which had overspread Italy, and restore this country to peace and order; to afford to legitimate Governments the protection to which they had a right—these were the objects to which the thoughts and the efforts of the monarchs were solely directed. In proportion as those objects are attained they have withdrawn and will continue to withdraw the assistance which necessity alone called for and justifies. They think themselves happy to be able to leave the security and peace of the people to the care of the Princes whom Providence has entrusted with it, thus taking away the last pretext for the calumny which cast a doubt on the independence of the Italian sovereigns.

The object of the Congress of Verona, assigned to it by a definite Convention, was fulfilled by the resolutions passed for the relief of Italy. But the allied sovereigns and their Cabinets cannot but glance at two great difficulties with the progress of which they have been much occupied since the Congress at Laybach.

An event of great importance took place before the conclusion of the Congress. What the spirit of revolution began in the Western Peninsula, what was attempted in taly, has succeeded in the East of Europe. At the very moment when the rebels in Naples and Turin were retiring at the approach of legitimate power, a rebellious firebrand was cast into the Ottoman Empire.

The coincidence of the events leaves no doubt as to the similarity of their origin. The outbreak of the evil at so many different points, everywhere conducted in the same manner and using the same language, unmistakably betrays the common focus from whence they all issue. The instigators of this movement flattered themselves that the counsels of the Powers would be embarrassed by dissensions and their forces neutralised by the cry of new dangers in different parts of Europe. The hope was vain. The monarchs, determined to refute the maxims of rebellion in whatever place and under whatever form they might appear, at once declared their unanimous decision. They will pursue the objects of their common care with unremitting attention, withstanding every consideration which might turn them from their path; they will follow the voice of conscience and duty, and uphold the cause of humanity in behalf of the victims of an enterprise as rash as it is criminal.

During this period—one of the most remarkable in the history of their alliance—numerous confidential communications took place between the five Courts, which had established such a satisfactory understanding in regard to the Eastern question that when they met at Verona the results only of that understanding had to be set forth, and the Powers friendly with Russia hope by common effort to put aside every obstacle to the entire fulfilment of her wishes.

Other events have called the attention of the monarchs to the pitiable condition of the Western Peninsula.

Spain is now undergoing the fate which awaits all States unfortunate enough to seek what is good in a way in which it can never be found. It is passing through the fateful circle of its revolution, a revolution which deluded or evil-disposed men represent as a benefit, or indeed a triumph, of the enlightened century. All Governments are witnesses of the zeal with which these men seek to persuade their comrades that this revolution is the necessary and wholesome fruit of advanced civilisation, and the means by which it acts and is supported the noblest flight of enthusiastic love for the fatherland. If civilisation can have for its aim the destruction of human society, and if it were possible to admit that the armed force which is only meant for the preservation of peace in the kingdom can seize the Government of that kingdom unpunished, certainly the Spanish revolution may claim the admiration of the age, and the military rising of the island of Leon may serve as a pattern for reformers. But truth has soon asserted her rights, and Spain only presents another sad example (at the cost of her happiness and her fame) of the inevitable consequences of such transgressions of the eternal laws of the moral order of the world.

Legitimate power fettered and turned into an instrument for the overthrow of all rights and all lawful liberty; all classes of the people drawn into the stream of revolutionary agitation; caprice and oppression exercised under the guise of laws; a whole kingdom given up to disorders and convulsions of every kind; rich colonies preparing to set themselves free by the same maxims with which the mother country has built up its public rights, and which it vainly condemns in another hemisphere; the last resources of the country destroyed by civil war— this is the picture which Spain now presents, these are the vexations with which a noble people worthy of a better fate is afflicted; lastly, these are the grounds of the just anxiety which such a concurrence of the elements of discontent and confusion must awake in the countries contiguous to the Peninsula. If ever a Power was raised in the very heart of civilisation hostile to the principles of conservation, to the principles on which the European confederation rests, that Power is Spain in its present state of decomposition.

Can the monarchs look with equanimity on the evils heaped on one country which are accompanied with so many dangers for others? Dependent only on their own judgment and their own conscience in this grave juncture of affairs, they must ask themselves whether it can be longer permitted to remain quiet spectators of calamities which daily threaten to become more dangerous and more horrible, or even by the presence of their representatives give the false appearance of a silent consent to the measures of a faction ready to do anything to maintain and support their pernicious power. The decision of the monarchs cannot be doubtful. Their ambassadors have received orders to leave the Peninsula.

Whatever may be the result of this step, the monarchs declare before Europe that nothing can move them to waver in a resolution approved by their most heartfelt convictions. The greater the friendship they entertain for the King of Spain, the livelier their interest in the well-being of a nation which has ever been distinguished for its virtues and its grandeur, the more strongly do they feel the necessity of taking the measure on which they have decided, and which they will know how to maintain.

The above statements will convince you that the monarchs in their last negotiations have remained unalterably true to those principles which have given them so great an influence in all the chief questions of our day relating to order and conservation. Their alliance, essentially supported and maintained on those principles, far from losing its earlier character, from time to time gains in strength and solidity. It would be superfluous further to vindicate their just and benignant sentiments from the unworthy calumnies which are every day refuted by notorious facts. All Europe must at last acknowledge that the system followed in the most perfect harmony by the monarchs equally conduces to the strength and independence of Governments and the true interests of the people. They know no enemies but those who, conspiring against the rightful power of the one and the good feeling of the other, draw both into one abyss. The wishes of the monarchs are directed towards peace alone, but this peace, although thoroughly established between the Powers, cannot spread the fullness of its beneficence over the whole of society so long as the fermentation at work in some countries is fostered by the false persuasions and criminal efforts of a faction which conceives nothing but revolution and rebellion—so long as the heads and instruments of this faction, whether by taking the field openly against thrones and Governments, or brooding in secrecy, prepare their hostile plots or poison the public.mind, terrifying the people with subversive and lying representations of the present and gloomy anxieties for the future. The wisest measures of the Governments cannot succeed, the best-intentioned plans of reform have no result, confidence cannot return to men, till this fosterer of the most hateful machinations is reduced to complete impotence ; and the monarchs will not feel that they have concluded their great work till they have torn from this faction the weapons with which it threatens the peace of the world.

While imparting to the Court to which you are accredited the facts and explanations set forth in this document, you will at the same time call to remembrance what the monarchs consider to be the inevitable condition of the fulfilment of their benevolent desires. In order to guarantee to Europe, not merely the peace which it enjoys by the protection of treaties, but that feeling of internal repose and lasting security without which in nations no true happiness can exist, they must be able to rely on the loyal and persistent co-operation of all the Governments. In the name of their own best interests, in the name of the public order whose preservation is concerned, in the name of the future races of mankind, we invite you to this co-operation. May the Governments all be imbued with the great truth that power is given into their hands as a sacred deposit of which they must give an account to their people and their successors, and that they expose themselves to the gravest responsibility if they fall into errors or listen to counsels which sooner or later will deprive them of the possibility of defending their subjects from the ruin which they themselves have prepared. The monarchs are confident that they will find in those who are in supreme authority (in whatever form it may be) true friends and allies—allies who adhere, not merely to the letter and to the positive declarations of the negotiations, but also to the spirit and the principles on which the present European system is founded, and they flatter themselves that this declaration will be taken as a fresh proof of their unalterable intention to devote all the resources entrusted to them by Providence to the welfare of Europe.

Metternich to Ottenfels, in Constantinople, Venice,
December 21, 1822.

633. It would be difficult to add anything in the
way of instructions to the preceding despatch. The
Protocols of our Conferences at Verona tell everything,
and the final conditions of any possible arrangement are
there given. The results of these conditions are as
follows :—

1. That the Porte should as an act of courtesy to
Russia announce the determinations already taken and
carried out with regard to the Principalities.

2. That the Porte shall arrange amicably with the
Courts who demand the navigation of the Black Sea,
unless she prefers to continue the abuses to which the
Russian flag, granted to so many foreign vessels, has
offered facilities. Of the two the Porte must prefer the
first of these alternatives, which is by far the most advantageous.

3. Finally, that the Porte shall herself pacify Greece.

Everything is included in these three points, for
the resumption of the ordinary diplomatic relations do
not deserve to occupy our attention seriously ; the
advantage of this resumption is so much on the side of
Russia that interest, and interest only, will here do all
that the Powers may be excused from attempting.

I advise the most entire agreement with Lord
Strangford. This ambassador must have learned to
know the truth of the situation, for he has seen it on
the spot. He arrived at Vienna under the most unfavourable auspices for himself; he quitted Verona
in possession of the undoubted confidence of the
Emperor of Russia. I, for my part, have contributed
to this fact as much as possible. Lord Strangford

knows it, and ought to be pleased. He ought to be convinced of two great truths, which he can never keep too much before him—namely, that the Emperor Alexander sincerely desires to see the end of the trouble in the East, although he has a very just feeling of the numberless difficulties which any grave error committed by the Divan may throw in the way of the realisation of his peaceful intentions.

As to the point of view of our Cabinet, Lord Strangford must be satisfied that nothing can be clearer or more disinterested than our fears and our desires. The course you personally take will be extremely helpful to us. Unite openly in pursuing the same aims as the British ambassador, and take care to give me every possible proof of zeal in supporting the conditions which Russia has presented as decisive.

The Emperor Francis to King Max Josef of Bavaria, Innsbruck, December 30, 1822.

634. *Monsieur mon Frère et Beau-Père !*—I think it may be agreeable to your Majesty to be informed of the particulars of the business which has just been concluded at Verona. I have therefore ordered Prince Metternich to pass through Munich in returning to Vienna. He will give your Majesty an account of the results at which the Congress has arrived, and of my view as to the good which will result for the federation from the application of the same principles in Germany. The views and sentiments of your Majesty agreeing with mine, I do not doubt your satisfaction with all that you learn from my Chancellor.

I myself sincerely regret that it was not possible to see your Majesty on my return to Austria. The severity of the season and the necessity for my return to my capital prevent a pleasure which I only put off to the first convenient opportunity.

Receive, etc., etc.

FRANCIS.

King Max Josef of Bavaria to the Emperor Francis, Munich, January 3, 1823.

635. *Monsieur mon Frère et Beau-Fils!*—Prince Metternich has brought me your Majesty's letter from Innsbruck, and has lost no time in informing me of all the important affairs which were discussed under your Majesty's happy auspices at Verona.

I have had great pleasure in conversing with your Majesty's Chancellor, who has so materially assisted in bringing about the grand results of the Congress, and to whose care Europe owes the tranquillity she has enjoyed during the last few years. He will inform your Majesty of my sentiments, and of the agreement of my views concerning Germany with the principles professed by the allied Powers.

Your Imperial Majesty will believe how much I regretted the impossibility of seeing your Majesty when passing through my country: the extreme severity of the season alone prevented me from coming to meet your Majesty.

Receive, etc., etc.

MAX JOSEPH

Metternich to the Emperor Alexander, a private Memorandum on the Formation of a Central Commission of the Northern Powers in Vienna. Verona (no date).

636. Of all the evils that now afflict the social body, that which ought especially to arrest the attention of the Governments is the criminal part played by the different sects.

One of the weakest sides of the human mind is the inclination which in all ages has attracted it towards the vague domain of mysticism. There are a number of uneasy spirits who are tormented by the necessity of creating some occupation for themselves, whose activity, unable to fix on objects of definite utility, urges them towards the most sterile abstractions. Dupes of their disordered imagination, dupes of whoever will serve their mania for irregular schemes, these men have constantly been like plants in a nursery for the secret societies.

The societies have always been influenced by the varying character of the age. If there are among them some who have remained faithful to certain principles of their primitive institution, the greater number are always ready to depart from them and yield to the powerful impulses of the moment. Thus it is that in a time of religious exaltation, secret associations are armed for the maintenance of this or that dogma. Now that the spirit of the age is directed towards reforms in the modes of government, these same associations exercise all their troublesome activity in the field of politics.

Where the secret societies do not go to meet factions, these factions, knowing the advantage to be gained from the sects, are not slow to find them out.

It is necessary to point out three principal epochs from which may be dated the extraordinary extension acquired by the sects of late.

The French Revolution, at its commencement, caused the suspension of the work of the sects. The arena was open to all the aberrations of the human mind as to all its ambitions; what would the *adepts* have gained by secret conventicles? They had plunged themselves into a career which, while flattering the dreams of their imagination, offered the prospect of a brilliant fortune. Thus the revolutionary administrations in France were recruited from the sects, and the Masonic lodges found themselves empty; in the same way we have seen the revolutionary army of Naples fill up its ranks with *malcontenti*. It was under the Empire, and as a consequence of the expurgations made by Bonaparte in the administrations, that the secret societies began to be reconstituted. Strong of will, Bonaparte calculated that, instead of employing useless efforts to hinder their reorganisation, it would be easier to him to restrain them by subjecting them to a severe control, and even making them subserve his designs. Hence, while covering them with ridicule, he managed to establish an active police in the associations which seemed to him susceptible of being guided; towards all the others, on the contrary, he displayed an inflexible severity.

The fall of Bonaparte delivered the world from an immense weight, but this weight having pressed on both good and bad, good and bad both alike felt released from the shackles which had bound them. Unhappily the elements of the good were distorted or paralysed, while those of the evil did not remain inactive, and the revolutionary spirit was soon seen to take a new flight.

But the factions themselves were not long in discovering that the people, wearied by so many violent shocks, were no longer disposed to serve their designs actively or *en masse*. It was reserved to the country the most withdrawn from civilisation, and unhappily the most internally excited, to create a new mode of bringing about disorders.

A general uneasiness reigned in Spain; no people, however, were further from rising than the Spanish people. Thus the revolution of 1820 was the direct work of a conspiracy hatched in secret, prepared and arranged by means of a secret association. If there could be a doubt of the truth of this fact it would be removed by the indiscreet avowals made public by one of the most active and shameless of the instruments of military rebellion in the Isle de Léon.

A Government which was a perfect cipher was unable to destroy what crime had brought forth. The success of the conspiracy of the Isle de Léon marked the second epoch in the progress made by the secret societies.

The revolutions in Italy in 1820, and above all in 1821, seem to show the third.

If the military revolt in Naples may be regarded as merely a servile imitation of that of the Isle de Léon, this cannot be the case with the Piedmontese revolution. This was evidently directed by the dissidents of France, and if enlightened observers had long suspected the existence of a vast revolutionary association in Paris connected with those in foreign countries, the open revolution at Turin tore away the veil that had up to that time concealed its character.

There seems to us a real interest in studying the characteristic differences which exist in the two Italian revolutions. One was more local than the other. The genius of the Neapolitans and that of the Piedmontese, even the geographical position of the two States, was bound to make, and actually did make, a notable difference in the two revolutions. We believe we do not go too far in considering the Neapolitan revolution as the work of pure Carbonarism, owing its origin to no other but national sources, although it may have been fomented and supported by Spanish influence. The revolution in the Sardinian States on the contrary was placed under the combined direction of the Piedmontese revolutionists and the French dissidents. If this assertion were not otherwise supported we should find undoubted proof in the moral situation of the two kingdoms.

That of Naples seems to us much further from a revolution such as that of 1820 than Piedmont is or will be for a long time.

The organisation of secret societies in France, such as exist now, does not seem to go further back than 1820. The proceedings commenced in Germany in 1819–1820, and the labours of the Central Commission of Inquiry at Mayence furnish more than one proof that the German revolutionists at that time entertained but very indirect relations with the revolutionary centre in Paris. It was only after the measures taken at Carlsbad had forced the principal heads of the secret associations in Germany to seek a refuge in France, that many of them betook themselves to Paris, where they found little opportunity of coming to an understanding with the French Liberals. Hatred against Bonaparte gave the first impulse to the secret associations in Germany, and this fact caused a difficulty in approaching the French leaders. The philanthropic nonsense of Teutonic professors and students made them despised by those of the factions who were too practical to be caught by such follies. It was only after the year 1821 that direct relations could be established between the German and French revolutionists, and at the head

of the former were the German Bonapartists.   The
places in Germany most remarkable as showing the
combination of French and German revolutionary
material are the kingdom of Wurtemberg, the town of
Frankfurt, and some Swiss towns.   Those who in these
places played the first parts were the brothers Murhard,
some other literary men at Frankfort, and the editors of
the *Gazette du Neckar*.   This paper is under the immediate influence of the director of the committee in
Paris, and his chief editor, Dr. Lindner, has acted for
several years as agent for Bonaparte in Germany.   The
second editor was a commissary of police under Bonaparte.

Up to this time the French Radicals have followed
in the tracks of their own revolution.   Many attempts
made in France to excite the masses to rise must have
proved to these men that there was not now the same
chance of such efforts succeeding as in 1789 ; on the
other hand, their attention could not but be fixed
on the new means by which success was obtained by
the military revolt in Spain, and as the same means
afterwards was able to overturn the legitimate Government at Naples in three days, the French revolutionists
must adopt it as the most efficacious and expeditious.
We feel the less hesitation in placing the introduction
of Carbonarism into France no further back than the
year 1820—or perhaps even the commencement of the
following year—because we see in the revolutionary
outbreak in Piedmont traces of two distinct influences,
which doubtless had the same object, but proceeded in
a different manner.   The revolt in Turin was evidently
directed and prepared by the joint efforts of the Piedmontese and French revolutionists, whilst that in Alessandria, of which all the machinery was put in motion

by pure Carbonarism seemed to be quite separate from that in the capital.

The very secrecy of associations of this kind assists their rapid progress. Thus, in all the attempts that have been made during the last ten months to organise military revolts in France, we see the tools of French Carbonarism playing a part everywhere.

Having shown in this rapid sketch the pernicious influence exercised by the sects on the great political concussions of late years, we do not hesitate to assert that these societies are a malady which consumes the noblest parts of the social body and that the roots of this evil are already deep and widespread. If the Governments do not take vigorous measures not only to prevent its ultimate progress, but to restrain it within manageable limits, Europe runs the risk of falling under the ever-renewed attacks of these associations. But that the remedy may be efficacious the danger must be faced, and since the evil conceals itself in darkness, it must be sought for and attacked with a force equal to its own.

The factions at present employ two means. One is the formation of secret societies and all kinds of sects ; of these the most practical is that of Carbonarism. This institution, which arose among a people little civilised but excitable and enthusiastic, bears the impress of their character. Quick in conceiving projects, the Southern Italian executes them with equal facility. One end in view, and that clearly set forth in the higher grades of the association ; simple means and plans, free from the metaphysical rubbish of Masonry ; a government really reserved for its leaders ; a certain number of grades to classify individuals ; disobedience and indiscretion punished by the poignard as well as enemies—

such is Carbonarism, which of all the political sects seems to have approached the most nearly to perfection in its practical organisation.

The factions have found a second means in the fusion of their interests and the establishment of a central point of direction. Nationality, political limits, everything disappears with the sect. The committee which leads the Radicals throughout Europe is, no doubt, at Paris, and every day will show this more and more.

What means have the Governments to oppose to this evil?

We know but two :—

In the first place they must make common cause and unite in one the interest of each in his own preservation; in the second place they must establish a central focus for information and direction.

The faction aims equally at all the States; pure monarchies, constitutional monarchies, republics, all are threatened by the levellers.

Never has the world shown examples of union and solidity in great political bodies like those given by Russia, Austria, and Prussia in the course of the last few years. By separating carefully the concerns of self-preservation from ordinary politics, and by subordinating all individual interests to the common and general interest, the monarchs have found the true means of maintaining their holy union and accomplishing the enormous good which they have accomplished. France is now paying dearly for the illusions to which her last administrations were given up. The present ministry seems to take a course tending towards the principle of alliance. England must always be placed in a class by herself with regard to the present question.

However enlightened and honest may be the intentions of her Government, her policy on any of the points touched on in this memoir can never be identified entirely with that of the Continental Powers.

As this *solidarité* exists between the three Northern Courts, it is necessary to bring the French Government to join in it as much as possible. This will be done more easily by one step actually taken than by explanations and reasonings on the necessity of this *solidarité*. The step to be taken should, we think, be the creation of a centre of information to be obtained from every direction.

To this end we propose the following measure. The Emperor of Russia and the King of Prussia shall depute an individual worthy of all confidence at Vienna. The Emperor of Austria on his part will select an *employé* of his Government. These three persons shall form a secret committee. This committee is intended to form a central point of information. To this end each Government will take measures to bring to the knowledge of the committee all the traces of conspiracy which they may discover.

The Central Commission of Inquiry, established at Mayence, will continue its functions agreeably to the almost unanimous desire of the Confederation. The labours of this commission will come under the inspection of the committee.

The resources that the Governments will have at their disposal will be very different from those of the association which is to be abolished. The Governments, strong in all the forces of a vigilant administration, will have less to fear from the machinations of the sect; every discovered plot loses its dangerous character, and furnishes an offensive weapon to legal power. By watching over the lives and the peace of their people the Governments will maintain their power on the ground of justice and right, which can never be the case with sects, whatever may be the mask with which they are covered.

END OF THE THIRD VOLUME.

WESTMAR COLLEGE LIBRARY,